THE DREAMS OF ADA

ROBERT

THE DREAMS OF ADA

MAYER

BROADWAY BOOKS

NEW YORK

PUBLISHED BY BROADWAY BOOKS

Published in the United States by Broadway Books, an imprint of
The Doubleday Broadway Publishing Group, a division
of Random House, Inc., New York.
www.broadwaybooks.com

BROADWAY BOOKS and its logo, a letter B bisected on the diagonal,
are trademarks of Random House, Inc.

A previous edition of this book was originally published in 1987 by
Viking Penguin Inc.

Portions of this book first appeared, in different form, in *Vanity Fair* as
"The Murder Dreams."

Book design by Michael Collica

Library of Congress Cataloging-in-Publication Data
Mayer, Robert, 1939–
The dreams of Ada / Robert Mayer.
p.   cm.
1. Ward, Tommy—Trials, litigation, etc.   2. Fontenot, Karl—Trials,
litigation, etc.   3. Trials (Murder)—Oklahoma—Ada   I. Title.

KF224.W3M39 2006
345.766'02523—dc22

2006048445

ISBN-13: 978-0-7679-2689-8
ISBN-10: 0-7679-2689-7

PRINTED IN THE UNITED STATES OF AMERICA

3   5   7   9   10   8   6   4

To Philip Spitzer

CONTENTS

This story is true. Nothing has been invented. The dialogue was spoken in the presence of the author, or is the best recollection of the participants. The names are real, except for a few near the end of the book that have been changed for legal reasons; such changes are noted.

Up ahead they's a thousan' lives
we might live, but when it comes, it'll
on'y be one.

—*The Grapes of Wrath*

THE DREAMS OF ADA

DISAPPEARANCE

Half a block from Main Street in Ada, Oklahoma, less than fifty yards from the railroad tracks, stands a small white building that looks like a garage. Beside it on a metal pole is a black-and-white wooden sign, the letters faded, that says: PECAN CRACKER. Ada is, among other things, pecan country; on the outskirts are commercial pecan orchards; in the grassy yards of many houses are one or more pecan trees. In the fall, when the pecans are ripe, the adults knock them off the trees with long poles. The children gather the fallen ones from the ground. The nuts not intended for commercial use are taken to the pecan cracker. There, in the small white building, the pecans are dumped into the funnel-like tops of machines.

One by one the hard pecans fall into moving gears. The top set of gears cracks open the largest pecans. Smaller pecans fall through, untouched, to another set of gears. These mesh closer and crack apart the smaller pecans. Still some escape and fall again: to another set of gears. These gears mesh tighter still; like steel claws they crack apart even the smallest pecans. Few pecans are too small, few shells too hard, to be cracked and broken, and to tumble in pieces into unmarked paper sacks.

Ada (pronounced *Aid-a*) is a city of about 17,000 people, the county seat of Pontotoc County, ninety miles southeast of Oklahoma City. Well-known to crossword-puzzle addicts ("city in Oklahoma, three letters"), it was named after a dark-haired girl, Ada Reed, daughter of the town's founder, back when Oklahoma was Indian Territory. In a rural area of farms, rolling hills, thick woodlands, it is a small industrial hub.

This is quarter-horse country, where horses bred for quick bursts of speed are sold at periodic auctions. It is oil country, with scores of pumps grazing like metal horses in every direction. Oil money built most of the magnificent mansions on upper-crust Kings Road. It is also a factory town. The gray turrets of the Evergreen feed mill tower only a block from Main Street like the superstructure of a battleship. The Brockway factory, a few blocks away, forges 1.3 million bottles and jars a day for Coke, Pepsi, and Gerber Baby Foods, among others. Blue Bell jeans employs 175 local women to sew 45,000 pairs of Wranglers and Rustlers a week. Ideal cement is produced in the town, as are Solo plastic cups. The Burlington Northern Railroad track slices diagonally across Main Street, several freights a day shrieking to a halt in the innards of the feed mill.

Main Street dead-ends into East Central University, which makes Ada the modest cultural hub of the area. But Ada is perhaps most of all a religious town, mainly Baptist, where you can't buy a mixed drink without an annual "club" membership. There are fifty churches in the town (forty-nine Protestant, one Catholic) and four movie screens.

On Saturday night, April 28, 1984, a few minutes after 8:30, just a few hours before the town would spring its clocks forward to daylight saving time, a car and a pickup truck pulled into the parking lot of McAnally's, a convenience store that stands almost alone out on the highway at the eastern end of town. The car was being driven by Lenny Timmons, twenty-five years old, an X-ray technician. Beside him was his brother David, seventeen, a high school student. Both lived in Moore, Oklahoma, ninety miles away. Driving the pickup truck that pulled in with them was their uncle, Gene Whelchel, who lived just east of Ada, in a village called Love Lady. They were planning to play poker that evening, and they needed some change.

Lenny Timmons cut the engine and the lights of his car. Gene Whelchel did the same in his pickup. The night was dark already; the area around the two gas pumps in front of the store was illuminated by fluorescent lights. So, too, was the inside of the store, which they could see through the glass double doors, and through a plate-glass window. An old-model pickup truck was parked crosswise in front of the store, near an ice machine.

Lenny Timmons, tall and slim, with a neatly trimmed dark beard, got out of the car and walked toward the store. His brother remained in the car. Gene Whelchel, in his truck, puffed on a cigarette. As Timmons entered the store, he passed in the double doorway a young couple, who were leaving. The woman came out first, the man right behind her.

David Timmons, waiting in the car, saw the couple emerge from the store and walk toward the pickup. He noticed the man's arm around the woman's waist. Gene Whelchel also glanced their way. They seemed to him like a pair of young lovers. The couple walked to the passenger side of the truck. The young man opened the door. The woman climbed in, and then the man beside her. After a few seconds the engine started, and the pickup drove off. Gene Whelchel puffed on his cigarette. David Timmons waited.

The inside of the store was bright to his eyes as Lenny Timmons entered. The shelves, lined up parallel to the entrance, were stacked with candy bars, paper products, cold remedies, tampons. In the glass-enclosed refrigerators were milk, soda pop, juice. Timmons, needing only change, saw the cash register and the checkout counter to his left. He approached the counter and waited for the clerk. There was none in sight. As he waited, he noticed, idly, an open beer can on the counter, a cigarette burning in an ashtray. Behind the counter he could see an open school book, a brown handbag.

A minute passed, perhaps two. The clerk did not appear. Timmons glanced impatiently among the rows of shelves. Perhaps the clerk was in the beer cooler, he thought, or in the rest room. He waited.

Growing more impatient, he went to the front door and opened and closed it several times. Each time he opened it a buzzer went off, a signal to the clerk on duty that someone had entered the store. There was no response.

He looked behind the counter. The drawer of the cash register was open. The money slots were empty, except for some coins.

Gene Whelchel looked at his watch. It was 8:40. He wondered what was taking Lenny so long. Then Timmons hurried out of the store, approached the pickup. He told his uncle, then his brother, that something was wrong. The three of them entered the store. They looked around, checked the walk-in cooler, the bathrooms. They could find no clerk. They were careful not to touch anything. There was a telephone on a wall of the store. They called the police.

Ada police headquarters is in the City Hall, a modern one-story brick building with basement offices, on Townsend Street. A young officer, Kyle Gibbs, was manning the dispatch unit that night. He took the call about a robbery at McAnally's, jotted down the information. One of the officers on patrol duty was Sergeant Harvey Phillips, a tall, dark-haired, rugged-looking cop, fifteen years on the force. Gibbs dispatched Sergeant Phillips to what he assumed was the scene of the reported robbery—the McAnally's convenience store out on North Broadway, at the sparsely populated northern edge of town. Sergeant Phillips folded his long frame into a squad car, pistol secure in the holster on his hip, and headed out that way, crossing Main, passing the looming gray feed mill with a red warning light at its highest point, bumping over the railroad tracks as he did, passing the stores on Broadway, closed for the evening, crossing Fourth Street, speeding north toward where Broadway becomes one of the highways into town. Toward McAnally's.

Moments after Sergeant Phillips sped away, Kyle Gibbs had second thoughts. McAnally's is a small chain of convenience stores in the region. There are three in Ada: one out on North Broadway, one out on East Arlington, one close to downtown at Fourteenth and Mississippi. The caller hadn't said which one he was calling from. Gibbs telephoned the store on North Broadway, to make sure he had sent the patrol car to the right place.

No, the clerk at North Broadway said. There had been no robbery there. No trouble at all.

The dispatcher hung up. The robbery wouldn't have been downtown. The caller had said something about a highway. Gibbs radioed new instructions to Sergeant Phillips, who was just reaching Richardson Loop and North Broadway. Phillips swung the squad car around, headed east instead of north. He reached the scene of the robbery—the McAnally's out on East Arlington Boulevard—about ten minutes after leaving headquarters, about twice the time a direct route would have taken.

In a suburban-style house seven miles south of town, surrounded by two acres of lawn and a swimming pool, Detective Captain Dennis Smith of the Ada police force was at home with his wife, Sandi. They were planning to go to bed early, because they had to get up early the next morning. Though a veteran of eighteen years on the police force, the detective supplemented his income with a paper route. Every morning, seven days a week, he and Sandi, who worked as a building inspector for the city, started their day by driving around town delivering 650 copies of the *Daily Oklahoman*, out of Oklahoma City, the largest newspaper in the state. Sandi would drive the family car while the detective, a stocky, sturdily built man, bald almost in the manner of television's Kojak, hurled the rolled-up newspapers onto the lawns of subscribers. Getting up early wasn't fun; tonight, because the clocks would be moved forward, they would get even less sleep than usual.

Tricia Wolf was at home that night, with her husband, Bud, and their three young children, in a graying frame house at 804 West Ninth Street, in a working-class section of town. After supper they watched television in the small, veneer-paneled living room dominated by a four-foot-high oil painting of Jesus; the painting had been done by Bud's father, C. L. Wolf, an electrician and amateur artist; it was one of their proudest possessions. The children—Rhonda, nine; Buddy, six; and Laura Sue, five—took turns taking their Saturday-night baths, getting help from Bud or Tricia with their hair. It was a weekly ritual, so they would be fresh-scrubbed for church in the morning.

In one of the town's better restaurants, District Attorney Bill Peterson and his wife, Dean, were enjoying a meal out. This was somewhat unusual; they generally preferred to spend their evenings at home. It was not for lack of money. Bill Peterson's grandfather, P. A. Norris, had been one of the wealthiest men in the region, had owned the First National Bank on Main Street, had donated the land for the football stadium at the college, which bears his name: Norris Field. Some of this wealth had been passed along to his grandson, William Norris Peterson. But this night was special: April 28 was Mrs. Peterson's birthday.

Don Wyatt, in his large, comfortable house on Mayfair Way, had much on his mind that night. He was one of the town's leading attorneys, was getting wealthy by winning a lot of accident and personal-injury cases for the people of the area against insurance companies, and had been planning to expand his staff. But on February 9, his offices in a building he owned on Main Street had burned. Thousands of files had been scorched or destroyed. For weeks the staff had been trying to reconstruct them, working in small rented offices on Twelfth Street, while Wyatt bought a plot of land out on Arlington Boulevard, and personally designed a lavish new office building, and watched impatiently, hauling away the trash himself on weekends, as the spacious new building began to take shape. It was both a frustrating and a forward-looking time.

In a small apartment downtown at Fourteenth and Rennie, above his father's dental practice, Steve Haraway was looking ahead, too. Though in his mid-twenties, he was a senior at the local college, having taken a couple of years off to work. He was due to graduate in less than a month. His pretty bride of eight months, Denice, was also a senior, would finish up in August. Both were working their way through school. Denice had been student teaching; they'd talked about possibly moving to Tulsa or Oklahoma City after graduation.

Steve had gone to work at 10:30 that morning at the We-Pak-Um convenience store on Arlington. When he got off work around seven, he went home to the apartment to study for final exams. He expected Denice, a clerk at McAnally's, home from her job around eleven.

The red, white, and blue lights atop his navy blue squad car were revolving as Sergeant Phillips swung to his right off the highway, at the very spot where four-lane Arlington Boulevard narrowed to a two-lane road out into the countryside, and pulled up in front of the store. The light flickered across his face as he unbent from the car and strode, long-legged, toward the door. The Timmons brothers and Gene Whelchel were waiting. They showed him the open and nearly empty cash drawer, described the light-colored, old-model pickup they had seen. They told him that on leaving it had headed east, away from town. Phillips returned to the squad car, radioed a description of the pickup to Kyle Gibbs at headquarters. It went out over the police frequency. In Ada, the police, the sheriff's department, the highway patrol, and the Oklahoma State Bureau of Investigation all use the same frequency, which is changed periodically. Any law enforcement officer in the area who had his radio on would hear the description, could give chase if he happened to see the pickup. The people in it would be wanted for questioning in the apparent robbery of McAnally's.

Other people could hear it, too. Many Ada residents have scanners in their homes. They can be useful in times of emergency—to keep track of tornado warnings in the area. They can also be cheap entertainment on a quiet evening if there is nothing good on television.

When he'd sent out the description, Sergeant Phillips went to look for the clerk. He saw a car, a 1969 Pontiac Sunbird, parked beside the building. There was no one in it. He checked the bathrooms and the cooler. There was no one in them. In the store he talked again with Whelchel, who told him of the couple they'd seen. Phillips picked up the brown purse behind the counter, looked inside it. He pulled out a driver's license. It had a picture on it, of an attractive young woman with dark blond hair. At first, sitting in his pickup truck watching the couple leave, Gene Whelchel had not made a connection. Now, knowing the clerk was missing, he did. He lived out this way; he used to stop in the store fairly often, would chat sometimes with the clerk while making his purchases. The woman they'd seen leaving, he told Phillips, was the clerk.

The name on the driver's license was Donna Denice Haraway.

Sergeant Phillips returned to the squad car. He sent out her name and description. The store manager, Monroe Atkeson, who lived nearby, was called. He arrived in a few minutes. He was told what had transpired by Phillips and by Whelchel, whom he knew slightly; they had gone to school together.

Atkeson locked the front door, closing the store for the evening, though closing time on Saturdays was eleven. He checked the tape on the cash register, and counted up the money on hand. There was $500 in a locked safe. There was $400 under the counter, ready to be put in the safe. There was $150 under the cash drawer. He estimated from the tape that the amount of money missing from the bill slots in the drawer was $167. The last item rung up on the tape was for 75 cents. His best guess was that that was for the can of beer now sitting open on the counter.

As the men waited for a detective to arrive, the manager put the money away, closed the cash register. He tossed the beer can into the trash. He emptied the ashtray with a single butt in it, so the store would be clean and ready for business when it opened the following morning.

Nobody stopped him. Nobody gave a thought to fingerprints.

Marie Titsworth is a small, dark, gentle Indian woman, who makes her living cleaning houses for people in Ada. Once a part of Indian Territory, the Ada area is home to a large number of Indians. The Chickasaw Nation headquarters is in town, as is the Carl Albert Indian Hospital.

Two nights earlier, on April 26, Marie Titsworth had called the police to her home. Her son Odell had gotten drunk, was arguing with his girlfriend, and things were getting violent. She wanted both of them out of the house. Several uniformed officers responded. Odell refused to leave the house. He fought with the police when they tried to subdue him. This was not an unusual scene. Odell had four felony convictions, for burglary and assault. There was no love between Odell Titsworth and the Ada police department.

The officers wrestled him to the ground, handcuffed his wrists behind his back. Odell, on the ground, was still kicking, and an officer kicked back. Titsworth's arm was broken. Finally subdued, he was taken in a squad car to the emergency room at Valley View Hospital, where his arm was set in a cast and put in a sling. It was a spiral fracture of the upper arm, very painful. The doctor told him he might have to sleep sitting up for a while.

Under the regulations of the Ada police department, a full written report must be filed on any incident in which someone is injured during a police action. This is to help with any charges the police might want to bring, and to defend the police against any possible lawsuits. On Friday night, Detective Mike Baskin, one of the four detectives on the thirty-three-man force, went to Valley View to interview the emergency room staffers who had treated Titsworth. But, having worked all night the night before, they were off duty; they would be back on Saturday night. So it was that Baskin, normally off on Saturdays, was working the evening of April 28. He drove to police headquarters, exchanged his own car for a squad car, and went to Valley View. When he got there, about 9 P.M., he waited for a while. Then he was told that the staff was having a busy night, and was asked if he could come back later. He said he could. He was on his way back to headquarters when the news of the robbery at McAnally's, and of Donna Denice Haraway's possible abduction, crackled over the police radio. Mike Baskin drove to the scene.

The Timmons brothers had already left when he got there. He was filled in by Gene Whelchel, Harvey Phillips, Monroe Atkeson. Baskin, too, gave no thought to fingerprints, to possible evidence. The clerk apparently had been abducted. His first priority was to find that light-colored pickup, to find the girl.

He called the highway patrol, arranged to meet several officers at a nearby intersection. Just as the officers arrived, an orange pickup ran a stop sign. Baskin and the others went after it when the truck sped away. It wasn't the right color, but it was fleeing.

The truck finally stopped on a dead-end street. Baskin and the patrolmen approached, warily. Inside were two young men and a girl. They were scared. He had fled, the driver said, because he did not want to get a traffic ticket for running the stop sign. Neither the truck nor the girl matched the descriptions from McAnally's. The officers didn't bother to write a ticket. They had more important things to do just then.

They divided the town into areas to search. Baskin, twenty-eight years old, round-faced, stocky, a policeman for eight years, a detective for one, drove out east along the highway for two miles beyond McAnally's. He turned right onto a narrow blacktop that led to a development called Deer Creek Estates. Here, he knew, there were houses scattered acres apart, on rolling hills, far from the highway. If you wanted to assault someone in a quiet place, where her cries would not be heard, and leave her with a long walk back to the road, so you had time to get away, this might be the place. Baskin cruised the dividing and redividing narrow blacktops, looking for the grayish pickup. He found nothing but dark trees silhouetted against the sky.

He headed back toward town, cruised the narrow streets. Nothing. He went out to Kerr Lab, a federal environmental research facility at the southern end of town; it is set far back from the main road, behind a large parking area, surrounded on three sides by thick woodlands—another likely spot for rape and abandonment. He did not find the truck or the girl.

He drove back to McAnally's, where the others were milling around. He decided he'd better let his boss know about this one. He telephoned Detective Captain Smith at home.

The captain and his wife were already asleep. They had to deliver newspapers in the morning. Smith listened groggily to Mike Baskin's tale.

"Treat it as a crime scene," he said.

He hung up the phone and soon went back to sleep.

Months later, Dennis Smith would think ruefully that, had he known all that was to follow, he would have gone to the scene himself that night. But there was no way of knowing, even then, if that would have made a difference.

In the small apartment above the dental offices of Dr. Jack B. Haraway, one of several apartments in the two-story brick building, Steve Haraway's studying was interrupted by the ringing of the phone. Was this Steve Haraway?—yes—whose wife works as a clerk at McAnally's?—yes—is she at home?—no, she's working tonight—well, you'd better get over to McAnally's, your wife is missing.

Missing?

He hurried down the flight of stairs, tall, thin, dark-haired, light-complexioned. He had talked to Denice on the phone less than two hours ago, about 7:30. When he got home from work. They talked around that time every night on the four days she worked: Thursday through Sunday. Missing? Nothing had been wrong; things had been slow at the store; she'd been able to get some studying done.

He drove out on Mississippi, curled right at the four-way stop sign. They'd met nearly two years before, when Denice—Donna Denice

Lyon, then—moved into an apartment in the building owned by his father. He was living in a smaller apartment then. She moved in along with her younger sister, Janet. He and Gary May had stood there and watched them move in. Very pretty, Donna Denice was, though shy. She'd be going to East Central.

He sped out Arlington, going east, past the blinking yellow caution light at the entrance to Valley View Hospital. Directly across from it was We-Pak-Um, where he himself had worked all day. It was still open.

They'd been married in August, at the First Christian Church, in which his parents were active. An imposing edifice, across the street diagonally from the courthouse square, from the county courthouse. He sped out Arlington. Invisible in the darkness on the right was the foundation of a new building, a future law office: Wyatt & Addicott.

And then, a quarter mile farther, McAnally's.

Yes, that was her driver's license. Yes, that was her purse, her car keys. Yes, that was her car parked beside the building. Her schoolbooks. Yes. Yes.

No, he wasn't sure what she'd been wearing; he'd been gone when she left for work. But he could be pretty sure. Blue jeans. She always wore blue jeans to work. And tennis shoes. They were comfortable. Some kind of blouse—he didn't know which one today—and a hooded sweatshirt that zipped up the front. She usually took the sweatshirt; it was cold in the walk-in cooler. Yes.

There was nothing more he could do here. If she called, she would call him at home. He'd better get home and wait by the phone. Yes. If they learned any more, they could call him there.

He went home to the apartment. When he and Denice got married, they'd moved into hers; hers was bigger. The telephone still was listed in her name, Donna Haraway, though she much preferred Denice. Her things were all about, intermingled with his. Nothing was out of place in the apartment; no clothes, no suitcases were missing.

Only she.

He stood, sat, stood. Waited for Denice to call. The word only eight months old on his tongue: his *wife*.

In Ada, as in many rural areas, convenience stores are a part of everyday life that scarcely exists in major metropolitan centers: Al's Qwik

Stop, Beep & Buy, Butler's Mini Mart, Circle K, E-Z Mart, Love's, McAnally's, Sweeney's, We-Pak-Um, others. Main Street is still a busy shopping area, but except for the movie theater it is pretty much locked up and deserted by 6 P.M. For those who need gas and don't mind serving themselves—most people in Ada don't mind—or who want a pack of cigarettes or a six-pack of beer, a container of milk, a fast-reading magazine to help pass the evening, the convenience stores are the places to drive to. In some, such as Butler's or J.P.'s Pak-to-Go, you can shoot a game of pool on a single table in a partitioned-off game room, if you don't mind the noise from the electronic games against the walls. In others, such as Love's Country Stores on Main Street or Mississippi, you can sit in a pastel curved plastic booth and sip coffee from a paper cup or eat a prefab Saran-wrapped ham-and-cheese sandwich. The convenience stores provide a welcome source of jobs for college students and for women with no job skills, whose children are grown. The risk in being the lone clerk in one of these stores late in the evening comes with the $3.75 an hour. Some store owners lessened this risk by keeping two clerks on duty at all times. Others, such as O. E. McAnally, didn't. McAnally's did not have a game room or food tables, both of which, incidentally, reduce the risk of robbery by keeping customers in the place. Nor did it have an alarm system.

The fact that Denice Haraway worked in a convenience store was of little concern to her family. Such stores and fast-food restaurants were their way of life. When Denice was growing up in Purcell, a small town thirty miles to the west, her mother managed the local Dairy Queen; from the time she was thirteen, Denice worked there after school. When she graduated from Purcell High School and the family moved to Ada, her mother got a job managing the Love's Country Store on Mississippi; Denice went to work there. Even as she was working in McAnally's that night, her younger sister, Janet Weldon, was working in a convenience store near her own home in Shawnee, forty-five miles to the north. The two sisters often called each other, store to store, to chat during slow times.

Between 6:30 and 7 on April 28, Janet called Denice at McAnally's. They chatted for a time, sister stuff; Janet was hoping to come down to Ada soon, to go on a shopping spree. Then Denice said she had to hang up, there were customers in the store. She would call back later.

Several hours passed. Denice did not call back. Janet, in Shawnee, dialed McAnally's again. A man answered. Janet asked to speak to Denice. She couldn't do that, she was told. Denice was missing.

Frightened, Janet hung up, called their mother, who lived once again near Purcell. Something was wrong. Denice was missing, the police had said.

Janet hurried to her car, drove through the darkness toward Ada. In Purcell, the girls' mother, Pat Virgin, divorced from their father and remarried, was frantic. She got into the family car with her husband. He drove her through the night to Ada.

O. E. McAnally, a slim, white-haired gentleman who owned the store, was at his home in another town, 110 miles away, when he was called by Gene Whelchel; his number was posted on the wall in case of emergency. He told his wife what had happened. They liked Denice Haraway; she had worked for them for almost a year; she was solid, reliable; she had passed each lie-detector test that O. E. McAnally made his employees take periodically, to make sure they weren't stealing from him. Together, McAnally and his wife made the two-hour drive to Ada.

Another young woman working in a convenience store that night was Karen Wise. In her twenties, slim, wearing glasses, a lot of dark hair framing her face, Miss Wise was working at J.P.'s Pak-to-Go, three-tenths of a mile east of McAnally's—the very last store out on the highway. She had been working there only a few weeks. As sheriff's deputies and highway patrolmen fanned out to look for the gray pickup, one of them stopped at J.P.'s. He told Karen Wise that the clerk at McAnally's was missing, and he asked her if anything unusual had happened at J.P.'s that night. Miss Wise said that, as a matter of fact, yes. Two men had been in the store, shooting pool in the game room, she said, and they had given her the creeps, especially the way one of them kept looking at her; they'd been acting weird, she said; then they'd left and driven off in an old-model pickup. That had been about 8:30, she told the officer—which was a few minutes before

Lenny and David Timmons and Gene Whelchel drove up to McAnally's.

It was Saturday night, late. McAnally's was dark, but not deserted. Monroe Atkeson, the manager, having turned off the outside lights, sat alone, hoping the phone would ring, hoping Denice would call. In the apartment at Fourteenth and Rennie, her clothes were in the closet, her makeup in the bathroom; all her personal possessions were there. Steve Haraway sat among them, waiting for her to call. At police headquarters her mother was near collapse. She could hardly walk, had to be supported by her husband. Janet Weldon was there. They talked about Denice, about how when Janet spoke to her earlier in the evening nothing had been wrong. They recalled the last time they had seen her, two weeks before, at a family gathering at Ron's house. Ron Lyon was Denice and Janet's brother, was married, had three kids; they talked tearfully about how much Denice loved the kids; about how she was not planning to have her own right away, but how down the road a bit she would.

Detective Baskin watched discreetly. There was nothing he could say to comfort them. He saw their tears, their terror; he pitied them. But he felt he had to be honest in response to their questions. The more time that goes by without hearing from Denice, he told them, the less hope there will be.

He gave them a form to fill out, for missing persons: name, age, height, weight, eye color, hair color; places for any birthmarks, any scars; a place for her dental records.

At the Ada *Evening News*, on Broadway at Tenth Street, the presses rolled, shuddered, printing the Sunday edition. There was no story in the paper about the disappearance of Denice Haraway. It had happened too late; the news would have to wait till Monday. On Interstate 40 a delivery truck sped toward Ada from Oklahoma City, carrying the early edition of the *Sunday Oklahoman*, which Detective Smith and his wife would hurl onto lawns in the morning; it, too, had gone to press too early for a story about a missing clerk in Ada. At police headquarters, Mike Baskin suggested that everyone go home; there was nothing more they could do tonight. The dispatcher would remain on duty, in case there was any news. The family, reluctant to leave, finally went out into the dark night air.

Baskin went home to get some sleep. He was awakened about 2:30, again about 4, again about 6, by calls from the dispatcher, patching through calls from the family. No, there wasn't any news, he told them. He would let them know of any news.

He tossed in his bed, slept fitfully. Till at last dawn broke, an hour later, by man-made clocks, than it had the day before.

The religion that pervades much of life in Ada is most visible on the streets on Sunday mornings: people walking to church, people driving to church, orange buses with the names of churches printed in black letters on the side carrying children to Sunday school. There are sections of Ada where there is a church on every corner. They are often used to give directions; to get to Tricia and Bud Wolf's house, you go to the Nazarene Church and turn left. Downtown, the First Baptist Church and the First United Methodist Church are imposing edifices which, back to back, cover an entire city block. The First Christian Church, almost as large, to which Dr. and Mrs. Haraway belonged, is only a block away. Scattered through the town are scores of others: Faith Assembly of God, First Apostolic Church, First Assembly of God, Free Will Baptist, Fellowship Baptist, Unity Missionary Baptist, Philemon Baptist, Morris Memorial Baptist, Oak Avenue Baptist, Trinity Baptist, Church of Christ, Church of God, Church of God in Christ, St. Luke's Episcopal, St. Peter's Episcopal, the Evangelistic Temple, First Lutheran Church, Church of the Nazarene, Calvary Pentecostal Holiness Church, First Pentecostal Holiness, Pentecostal Holiness, First Presbyterian (out on Kings Road), others. The lone Catholic church is on East Beverly. (Some Ada natives recall being brought up to believe that Catholic nuns ate children.) For many in the town, religion was the genuine cornerstone of their lives, enabling them to endure whatever fate had to offer; in restaurants and coffeeshops, as well as in private, these people often talked about Jesus reverently but familiarly, as if He lived next door. For others, as for some churchgoers everywhere, the religion was hypocritical. "The thing I can't stand is how they hide behind the Bible around here," said one rancher, who found it more useful to feed his horses that morning than to go to church. "They go to church on Sunday, but they'll cut your throat for a two-dollar bill on Monday."

For Bud and Tricia Wolf, churchgoing was as life-sustaining as eating. Sunday mornings and Sunday evenings and Wednesday evenings as well they went to the Unity Missionary Baptist Church, a pale frame building on Seventh Street; during Bible Study Week they helped to teach the classes; every summer they spent a week in Arkansas at Vacation Bible Camp. On this particular Sunday they got the kids dressed in their best church outfits, took their Bibles, climbed into the family car, a dark green 1972 Pontiac with a faded bumper sticker that said, "Life Is Fragile, Handle With Prayer," and they drove to church. They were surprised to see how many cars were already in the parking lot. They were even more surprised when they stepped inside and found the service already in progress, Sunday school already over. As dozens of pairs of eyes turned to look at them, Tricia flushed a deep red, understood what had happened, knew that everyone who was looking at them knew what had happened. She slunk into a pew with embarrassment. They had forgotten to turn their clocks ahead; they were an hour late.

On the other side of town, Detective Captain Dennis Smith did not go to church that morning. He rarely went anymore, rarely felt guilty about it. He and Sandi made their rounds delivering the *Oklahoman*. Then he went to headquarters, to see about the missing girl.

Donna Denice Haraway was born Donna Denice Lyon on August 19, 1959, in Holdenville, Oklahoma, about twenty miles east of Ada. Her parents were Jimmy Charles Lyon, a truck driver, and Patricia Lyon. She had an older brother, Ron, and a younger sister, Janet. In her early years the family moved to Purcell, where she attended school. At Purcell High she was in the Pep Club and the National Honor Society. She wore her hair long and straight in those days, and had a serious demeanor. She was not a student leader; working after school at the Dairy Queen managed by her mother, she did not have much time for extracurricular activities; she was also on the shy side.

She graduated from Purcell High on May 17, 1977. In the school yearbook, *Dragon*, where the pictures of the most popular girls appeared six or seven times, hers appears only twice—once with the Pep Club, once with the senior class. Her name is spelled Denice in one caption—which is correct—and Denise in the other.

Upon graduation she was accepted at Oklahoma State University in Stillwater. She attended for one semester, working after classes to pay her way. But the expense was too much. She moved back home and went to work to save up money for college. She attended Seminole Junior College for a time. When Janet graduated from high school in 1979, the family moved to Ada, where their mother became manager of Love's Country Store on Mississippi. Denice went to work for her mother, and began taking classes at East Central. When her mother moved back to the Purcell area, Denice got a job at Wall's Bargain Center on Main Street, a discount clothing store. She and Janet shared an apartment. When her job at Wall's began to conflict with her class schedule, she quit and got a job at McAnally's, where her schedule could be more flexible.

When she worked at Love's, she dated for a time a man from Texas. She seemed to be in love with him, but it didn't work out. When she and Janet moved into a new apartment at Fourteenth and Rennie, she met Steve Haraway, who lived in the same building. They began to date. They were married on August 6, 1983. Though Steve's father, Dr. Jack Haraway, was a prominent member of Ada society, a member of the Rotary Club, with a nice house east of the city, the young couple moved into Denice's apartment, and continued to work after school to pay their expenses.

Steve was the outgoing half of the couple. He was in the ruling clique of Pi Kappa Alpha, the largest fraternity at East Central. He was gregarious, talkative. Denice was the shy one, sweet but quiet. Steve's friends liked her, but felt they didn't know her well. Steve maintained contact with his single friends at Friday night "boys' nights." Every Friday the Holiday Inn had a seafood buffet. While Denice worked at McAnally's, Steve and his friends from school ate seafood there, laughed, joked. Then he'd go home to Denice.

At the college, Denice was a good student, though not exceptional. In February she began student teaching at Hayes Elementary School, which was halfway between her home and the college, as part of the requirements for a teaching certificate. She taught second-graders, the class of an experienced teacher named Donna Howard. Denice would stand or sit at Mrs. Howard's desk in the front of the class, running the lessons, while Mrs. Howard sat and observed in the back. Denice had a good rapport with the kids, showed every sign of becoming an effective teacher. Each Friday she would take home teachers' guides, to prepare lessons for the following week. On Friday, April 27, she took home the teachers' guides as usual.

In the early hours of Sunday morning, the news of Denice Haraway's disappearance traveled over the telephone wires. Steve Haraway's best friend, Monty Moyer, who'd been called by Steve, in turn called Steve's second-best friend, Gary May, who spread the word to another friend: volunteers would be needed to search the county. Most of Steve's Pi Kappa Alpha fraternity brothers offered to help; so did the Ada Amateur Radio Club, some of whose members undoubtedly had heard the news crackle over the scanners the night before; so did the Ada Rifle and Pistol Club. The entire police force was called in to work, and the sheriff's department, and the highway patrol. Normally all but deserted on Sundays, Ada police headquarters was as crowded, and as solemn, as any church in town that morning. The two men to whom those congregated there turned for guidance were Gary Rogers and Dennis Smith.

Gary Rogers was the resident agent for the Oklahoma State Bureau of Investigation (OSBI). He lived in Ada and had an office at Ada police headquarters. He was quickly assigned by his superiors to head the investigation into the disappearance of Denice Haraway. A slim, neat man, Rogers was almost dandyish in appearance at first glance, with carefully slicked brown hair, a neatly trimmed moustache. In the gray business suits he wore on most workdays, he gave the appearance of being manicured rather than tough. But below the business suits he wore western boots; below his left armpit was a holster containing a loaded revolver. On other days, more relaxed, he might wear complete western garb, looking almost like a cowboy, except for the slick hair, the neatness of the moustache.

The man directing the investigation for the Ada police department was Dennis Smith, the detective captain. In appearance and personality he was much the opposite of Gary Rogers. Smith was barrel-chested whereas Rogers was slim. The top of his head was as bald as a melon; the only hair remaining was a fringe on the sides and around the back. He preferred to go tieless, wearing short-sleeved Ban-Lon shirts on days when the job's demands did not require a suit. Whereas Rogers had the businesslike manner expected of OSBI agents, Smith was a stormier presence, closer to the movie image of a bulky small-town sheriff. Whereas Rogers was under orders, like all OSBI agents, not to talk to the press—a publicity office in Oklahoma City would take any inquiries—Smith could make his own rules. Tough-looking, he had a gentle voice which, without warning, could suddenly turn gruff. His sense of humor was sometimes sadistic; he seemed to enjoy putting people on the spot for a moment and watching them squirm. But he could also show compassion. To some, his pale blue eyes seemed to twinkle in his large head; to others, this was a threatening glint. "He's got them hard eyes," one acquaintance would say.

On a large map, Rogers and Smith divided Pontotoc County into sections. The volunteers at headquarters, as well as the officers, were assigned different sections to search. Two to a vehicle, they moved out into the city, then into the areas around the city, and then farther away into the countryside. They drove up and down state roads, county roads, the narrow blacktops or dirt roads of oil leases. Mostly they were looking for an abandoned gray pickup, a late sixties or early seventies model gray-primered Chevrolet. That was the description given by Gene Whelchel and the Timmons brothers. Descriptions of the two men Karen Wise said had been "acting weird" at J.P.'s Pak-to-Go also were sent out. One of the men was described as being from twenty-two to twenty-four years old, five-feet-eight to five-feet-ten, with blond hair below his ears, and a light complexion. He was said to be wearing faded jeans, a white T-shirt, and tennis shoes. The other suspect was also described as twenty-two to twenty-four years old, with shoulder-length light brown hair and a slim build. He was wearing faded jeans, a blue T-shirt, and tennis shoes. The three witnesses at McAnally's had seen only one man leaving with the woman. He roughly fit the first description. None of them had noticed anyone else waiting in the truck. But police believed there must have been someone else behind the wheel, since both the woman and the man had entered on the passenger side.

When they came to bridges over creeks, or to dumping areas strewn with refuse, the searchers got out of the cars and pickups and threaded through the underbrush, looking for bits of clothing, looking for a body. Steve Haraway himself went, paired up with his friend Monty Moyer. Gary May was paired with another friend. Fraternity members had come from Oklahoma City to help.

The search began shortly after lunch—more commonly called "dinner" in Ada—and gradually widened to the farthest reaches of the county, which encompasses 714 square miles. When the sun set and darkness settled over Pontotoc, some of the searchers went home. Others continued the search, shining flashlights out the car windows as they drove slowly on the narrow roads. It was two o'clock in the morning before the last of them—Steve Haraway's closest friends—gave up and went home. None of the searchers had found anything of interest—no gray pickup, no trace of Denice Haraway.

The news of the disappearance, and of the search, was reported to the town by the local radio and television stations.

After a long day of fruitless searching, spirits were low at police headquarters. Then came a report from McAlester, sixty miles to the east, site of the state penitentiary. A trooper there had stopped a pickup that matched the description. There were two men inside who also roughly matched the descriptions, but they were wearing cowboy hats and cowboy boots; there was no young woman with them. The men detained in McAlester while their pictures were taken and they were fingerprinted. For a time, Dennis Smith and Gary Rogers had hopes for a quick solution to the case. But within a few hours, the men were cleared of any involvement.

As hour after hour passed with no trace of Denice Haraway turning up, the specter of another young woman loomed large in the minds of the police. Her name was Patty Hamilton.

Patty Hamilton was an eighteen-year-old girl who had lived in Seminole, in the adjoining county, thirty miles north of Ada. She used to work as a clerk in the U-Totem convenience store, at 401 West Strother. Shortly after 4:30 in the morning of April 9, 1983—one year and nineteen days earlier—Patty Hamilton had disappeared while working. Her disappearance was reported by a customer who entered the store and found no clerk. About $110 was reported missing from the cash register. Patty's locked car was found parked outside the store, with her purse in it. Her keys were in the store. On the counter were two cans of soda pop. There was no sign of a struggle. Less than an hour earlier, Patty had been talking on the phone with her mother, who worked all night as a dispatcher for a Seminole cab company. She told her mother she was going outside to sweep the driveway. She had not been heard from since; had not been seen, dead or alive. Police believed that Patty Hamilton probably had been abducted and killed. But there was no evidence, no suspects. Leads checked out in the early days had proved fruitless. With more than a year gone by, there weren't any leads anymore. The disappearance remained a mystery.

The OSBI case agent in the disappearance of Patty Hamilton was Gary Rogers. The last thing he needed in Ada was another Patty Hamilton case.

Dennis Smith was exhausted. Nearly a thousand man-hours had gone into the search that day. They had turned up not a single clue. But his eighteen years of experience told him there was only one logical explanation for the disappearance of Denice Haraway: she had been taken from the store to be raped. And rape victims, when their attackers are through with them, usually find their way to a road, or a phone, within a few hours.

Donna Denice Haraway had not.

They had found no body, no clothing, no weapon, no blood. But as he sagged into his bed, the detective captain was already convinced: Donna Denice Haraway was dead.

2

OF DEER AND CALVES

Dennis Smith's grandfather had been a farmer in Arkansas. He moved to the Ada area around the turn of the century, when it was still called Ada, I.T.—Indian Territory. The first white settlers, two brothers named Daggs, had ridden their horses up from Red River County, Texas, early in 1890, and had built log homes near what would later become a cement plant. A fellow named Jeff Reed came up with them to help drive their cattle. It is Reed who is considered the founder of Ada. Impressed by the site, he returned to Red River County, sold his interests there, and came back to Ada to live.

At first the place was called Daggs Prairie, after the first two families to settle. Jeff Reed dealt in cattle for about a year, then opened up a small store. The store became a trading center for the Indians and the few white settlers in the area; it gave the settlement its first commercial importance. Indians raised small crops for subsistence; the Daggs brothers began farming to sell the produce. The only transportation in the area was on horseback. Virgin, untilled lands stretched for miles in every direction.

The settlement soon became known as Reed's Store. As the place grew in population, one of the Daggs brothers opened a second store. Local residents began to want a post office, and J. B. Reed set out to get them one. He prepared a petition, spent months traveling through the countryside to get the required number of signatures; sometimes he rode fifteen miles to get one more. The first name he proposed to the Post Office Department was "Sulphur Springs," after two such springs nearby. It was rejected, because there was already a town by that name in the Territory. The second name he suggested was "Reed's Store." It, too, was rejected. The third name he submitted, "Ada," was accepted in 1903. It was the name of his eldest daughter.

Slowly the new town grew. More settlers arrived to farm the land. More stores opened. All over the west railroad lines were being built, and several local men formed a company to start a railroad. They routed it through Ada. A bridge was built over Sandy Creek, the first bridge in the county. A man from Shawnee bought a corner lot at Main Street and Broadway and opened the First National Bank. A man named George N. McKnight was elected mayor, a fellow called "Uncle Dick" Couch became the town marshall. By 1903 there were several dozen stores in Ada, selling all manner of merchandise— hardware, meat, feed, lumber. Seven doctors had opened offices, two dentists, a dozen lawyers. The Ada *Weekly News* had begun publication. The Oklahoma-Indian Territory Anti-Horse Thief Association held its convention in Ada that year. More banks opened. A baseball field was built. More than 20,000 bales of cotton were marketed in Ada that fall.

Into this new town bustling with horse-drawn wagons. Dennis Smith's grandfather arrived from Arkansas to try his luck at farming. He watched as Ada, Indian Territory, became, in 1907, part of the new state of Oklahoma. He saw stone masons arrive, churches rise on many street corners, small factories open. He watched the early livery shops give way to the first automobile dealers, saw prospectors arrive, hunting for oil and natural gas, and finding both. In the 1920s and 1930s the town prospered from an oil boom; the Kings Road mansions began to go up.

Dennis Smith's father did not participate in the boom, did not get rich; as always, the rich were the minority, even in boom times. Smith's father went to work as a janitor at the First National Bank on Main Street. He would remain there until he retired in 1972 and moved to Odessa, Texas.

Ada is a place where people tend to stay, generation after generation. While some of the children who grow up there move off to big cities in search of larger opportunities, most do not. It is a place of roots, not rootlessness; of extended families, not nuclear ones. Most people own modest frame houses in which they raise their children, who in turn raise their own children in the same or similar houses. There are plenty of jobs to go around—at the feed mill, the glass factory, the cement plant, for the men; at Solo Cup, Blue Bell jeans, the convenience stores, for the women. It is a place of simple living: work, children, television, hunting, fishing, church. When the photo portrait-maker died, his son took over the business, to continue immortalizing the next generation of Adans, in life, in full color; the son of the monument maker went into *his* father's business, to continue immortalizing Adans in death, in gray granite.

If there was fear in Ada, it usually was the fear inspired by tornadoes, or the fear people find deep in their own souls or in their personal relationships, never simple, even in simple towns. Or the fear of God. But there had rarely been fear in the streets.

Dennis Smith was born in 1943, romped as a toddler on Ada's quiet lawns while the nation was at war. When he was in the third grade, he was sent to a charity camp called Sheep Creek, about fifteen miles out in the country. The camp was owned by the wealthy Norris family. He spent a month there, splashing about in a lake, learning to swim. The boys had no life preservers but would strap large gallon cans to their chests to keep them afloat. He also learned to wrestle there.

In junior high school, Dennis met a boy named Bill Peterson. They became friends, often hung out in the same crowd. They would swim together at a place called Blue Hole. Sometimes, along with other kids, Dennis was invited to the Peterson home, a palace compared with his own family's working-class house. The fact that Bill Peterson's grandfather, P. A. Norris, owned the bank where Dennis Smith's father swept the floors did not seem to impede their friendship; it lasted well into high school. Then they began to drift into separate crowds. No one could know then that Dennis Smith one day would become Ada's detective captain, and Bill Peterson its district attorney.

When Smith graduated from Ada High, he enlisted in the Marines. He was stationed in California and in Okinawa. This was after Korea, before Vietnam. He thought for a time of making a career of the Marines, because of the Corps' excellent retirement plan after twenty years; but he didn't. Instead he returned to Ada, went to East Central, and joined the police force. He does not pretend he became a cop to make the streets of the town safer, or to help combat evil; he became a cop when he learned that the Ada police department also had an excellent retirement plan after twenty years: half the pay of your highest annual salary.

For nine years he was a uniformed officer, patrolling the town in a squad car; then he became a detective, attended OSBI seminars in detective work. He would reach his twenty-year plateau for possible retirement in January 1986. In the interim he was married, divorced, remarried. He had two boys, now teenagers, James and Shawn. His bull chest, round face, bald pate, "hard eyes" became familiar in the town as he probed the burglaries, the drug traffic that were increasingly common in Ada.

About every two years there was a murder. Most of them were family-related, and were solved fairly quickly.

Main Street terminates abruptly at the campus of East Central University. It is a pleasant campus, the administration building off to one side, the library dead ahead, the education building behind it to the right. Walkways connect the buildings between grassy, tree-shaded lawns. Behind the library the land slopes sharply downward. Set into the slope is the science building. Across a roadway at the bottom of the hill is the football stadium: Norris Field.

Founded in 1909 as East Central Normal School, the institution had expanded through the years to become East Central State Teachers College, then East Central Oklahoma State College, and finally East Central University. By 1984 it was serving about 4,000 students. Most of them had grown up within a fifty-mile radius of the campus. Others came from all over the state.

The education department had long been the mainstay of the school. The director of elementary education was Norman Frame, who had been at the college for twenty years. As an elementary education major, Denice Haraway had taken several of Frame's classes; he also had been, for the past three years, her faculty adviser. During the first two years her name was Denice Lyon. She struck Norman Frame as a very beautiful girl, the kind whose presence brightened your day—although not all that serious about her work, about average.

Then, having married in August, she turned up for her senior year as Denice Haraway. Frame noticed a change. Her marriage seemed to have matured her; she worked harder, was more serious about wanting to become a teacher.

In his early days in Ada, Norman Frame had been active in the First Christian Church. So, too, had Dr. and Mrs. Haraway. He and the Haraways had become friends, had visited each other's homes; he'd known Steve Haraway then as a nice little boy, a bit shy but coming out of it. He remembered this when he heard the news of Denice's disappearance on Sunday, on television, and he recalled his last conference with Denice. It had been in late winter, when she had completed her classes, just before she'd started her student teaching. He'd given her a grade of 90 in his class. No one was more surprised than he at how well she had done; it was a tough course. When he told her that, in his narrow office in the education building, she smiled slightly. He could tell that she was pleased, very proud of what he was saying; but she was trying to maintain her ladylike decorum, trying, in that way she had, to retain control of her emotions.

The moment he heard the news, Norman Frame felt something terrible had happened to Denice. Other students that he knew might suddenly take off on a lark, an impulse, and not say where they were going. But not Denice.

Donna Howard, the teacher under whom Denice had been practice teaching, was out of town that weekend. When she got home late Sunday, she got a call from a friend who told her about the disappearance. She watched the ten o'clock news on television, saw the report there. She, too, felt from the start that something terrible had happened. Denice was not the kind of person to run away.

Denice had been assigned to Mrs. Howard's classroom in early February. For eight weeks, every Friday, instead of going to the college, she came to Hayes Elementary, sat at the rear of the class, and watched Mrs. Howard teach. She was quiet; she rarely had any questions. In late March she began the required eight weeks of full-time practice teaching. At first, still shy, she had trouble making her voice heard by the entire class. Mrs. Howard worked with her on voice projection. As second-graders will, some of them began to test the student teacher, acting wise, disrupting the class. Denice was surprisingly firm with them; she quickly got them into line; not once did Mrs. Howard have to step in and help her out. When the pupils were at music or physical education, Denice and Mrs. Howard would sometimes chat, have coffee. Mostly Denice talked about teaching. After graduation, she told Mrs. Howard, Steve hoped to get a job with a pharmaceutical firm, as a salesman. They wanted to live in a metropolitan area—Oklahoma City or Tulsa. She would wait till Steve got a job, see where they would live, then apply for a teaching job there. She was hoping it would be Oklahoma City, which was a lot closer to Purcell, where her mother lived.

Classes at Hayes ran until 3:30. Denice would drive to the school each morning, park on the street outside—the school lot was reserved for the regular staff—and teach the class. She would wear dresses, or skirts and blouses, to teach. About 2:30 she would change into blue jeans, and leave, to go to her job at McAnally's. Sometimes, if she was going to be late, she would call the store to let them know.

On Monday morning, Denice's car was not outside the school. The early arrivals among the twenty-two second-graders in the class whispered among themselves. Some of them had heard on television that Mrs. Haraway had disappeared. The others were quickly being filled in. When Mrs. Howard entered, they pressed around her, asking questions. Mrs. Howard told them to return to their seats, that she would talk about it when all the children had arrived.

When the bell rang and the class started, the teacher told them all that she knew: that Mrs. Haraway had disappeared from the store where she was working Saturday night; that police thought she may have been taken away by two men driving a gray pickup truck; that that was all anyone knew. Most of the students chattered for a bit, then settled down. One little girl started crying and couldn't stop. She cried most of the day. She had not seemed especially close to Denice Haraway—just more sensitive, perhaps. Mrs. Howard taught the class herself that day.

As the second-graders buzzed, Steve Haraway and six or seven of his college friends gathered at police headquarters. The police had obtained from the college a photograph of Denice. They were mimeographing it onto flyers with her description—twenty-four years old, five-feet-five, 110 pounds, brown eyes, dark blond hair, a light complexion. The description indicated that her hair had been cut to shoulder length since the picture had been taken. The flyer also contained descriptions of the gray pickup and of the two possible suspects. The Ada police would distribute the flyers in town, get them into store windows. The sheriff's department and the highway patrol would do the same out in the county. Steve and his friends volunteered to take them into neighboring counties, where no searches had been conducted the day before.

One of the volunteers was Gary May, Steve's friend and fraternity brother. Gary took a stack of flyers and headed north, toward Seminole County and the city of Seminole.

The first place he stopped was the Circle K, on Strothers Street. The people there were very cooperative. They put a flyer in the window. The place had recently changed hands, they told Gary; it used to be called U-Totem. It was the same store from which Patty Hamilton had disappeared.

Gary, an Ada native, good-looking, well-mannered, thanked them and drove up the road. He came to another convenience store, took a flyer in. A young woman was behind the counter. She, too, was very cooperative. She had heard about the disappearance on the news.

"The same thing happened to my sister," she said.

Gary could hardly believe it. She was the sister of Patty Hamilton. He was afraid the woman would go to pieces, being reminded like this. But she didn't. Instead she became supportive of him.

"Don't worry, they'll find her," she said. "My sister's been gone for a year now, but I know she's okay. I know she'll turn up okay one day."

Shaken by the coincidence, Gary returned to the car, sat for a moment Then he drove on up the road, stopped at the next convenience store. A young woman clerk was tending that store, too. Gary made his request about the flyer, handed her one. The woman looked at it.

"Oh, my God!" she said. "Denice? Denice is missing? She's my cousin!"

The cousin had not yet heard about the disappearance.

They talked for a bit. Then Gary returned to the car. In Oklahoma, he realized, news often travels slowly on Sundays. He felt shaky. Encountering them one after the other like that—first the store where

Patty Hamilton had worked, then Patty Hamilton's sister, then Denice Haraway's cousin, both working in convenience stores—was the most startling experience of his life.

Harvey Pratt was a cop—part Cheyenne-Arapaho Indian, part Sioux, a little French. By night he was an artist, painting detailed watercolors of winter scenes on the plains, of sacred scenes from his ancestors' tribal past. His paintings were on display in galleries in Oklahoma City, Chicago, and Santa Fe. By day he was an agent for the OSBI, supervisor of the organized crime and criminal intelligence division. One of his jobs, when necessary, was to make composite drawings of suspects.

On Monday morning, April 30, Pratt drove to Ada. He met at the police station with Karen Wise. From her descriptions, he drew sketches of the two men she had seen "acting weird" at J.P.'s. The sketches would later be shown to Lenny Timmons, who would agree that the one on the right was a reasonable likeness of the man he had passed in the doorway, that it was at least "in the ballpark." New flyers were Xeroxed, bearing the sketches of these suspects as well as Denice Haraway's photograph. The sketches were distributed to the news media.

They arrived at the Ada *Evening News* too late for inclusion in Monday's edition. The paper's deadline is about 11 A.M. When it hit the newsstands about 1 P.M., the disappearance of Denice Haraway was the lead story.

MISSING, LOCAL CLERK ABDUCTED

the headline said. Beside it was the college photograph of Denice, smiling, a delicate chain necklace over her sweater.

Under the byline of a reporter named Dorothy Hogue, the story recounted all the information the police had obtained at that point about the disappearance. It said that Mr. and Mrs. McAnally had offered a $1,000 reward for information leading to the whereabouts of Mrs. Haraway. For further information, the story said, Detective Dennis Smith should be contacted.

By late Monday, the composite sketches were being shown on

KTEN, the local TV station. On Tuesday they were printed on the front page of the *News*. And the phones at police headquarters were ringing; people were calling in the names of young men they felt might be the ones in the drawings: *Billy Charley. Tommy Ward. Randy Rogers. Tommy Ward. Billy Charley. Marty Ashley.*

The department's four detectives—Smith, Baskin, Danny Barrett, and James Fox—took calls; when they got too busy, uniformed officers helped out.

Bob Sparcino. Billy Charley. Tommy Ward. Billy Charley. Tommy Ward.

Smith soon realized that the detectives were so busy answering the phone calls that they weren't out doing detective work. He got some of the department's seven civilian clerks and secretaries to answer the phone. The names of the people calling in were not taken, just the names of the possible suspects.

More than a hundred calls were taken in those first few days. More than twenty-five different names were given. The police were familiar with some of the names—young men they had arrested in the past. Others were new to them. Some of the names had been given by only one or two callers. But two stood out glaringly. The name Billy Charley had been given by more than thirty callers. They said he resembled the sketch on the right-hand side as they appeared on the flyers and in the *News*. The name Tommy Ward had also been given by more than thirty callers as resembling the same sketch.

The police were familiar with Billy Charley. They called him in for questioning. He showed up at headquarters with his parents, who said he had been at home with them Saturday evening. The police believed the parents. Charley was pretty much eliminated as a suspect.

They called in Tommy Ward, whom they also knew. He'd been arrested several times in the past—for misdemeanors such as being drunk and disorderly, though never for anything violent. Like Charley, he came in voluntarily. Dennis Smith and Mike Baskin questioned him about where he had been Saturday night. He said he'd been fishing with a friend, Karl Fontenot; then they had gone to a party at the home of another friend. He'd stayed at the party till about 4 A.M., he said, and then had walked home.

The detectives noticed that Ward's blond hair was cut real short, above his ears, unlike the suspect in the sketch, who had longish hair. They noted, too, that it was sort of choppy in the back—an unprofessional haircut. They took a Polaroid picture of Ward, and wrote the date on it: May 1.

Mike Baskin went to talk to Karl Fontenot, who had no prior record. When he arrived at the address, he encountered a dark-haired young man coming down the stairs. Baskin asked the youth if he knew where Karl Fontenot lived. The youth said that he was Karl Fontenot. Baskin identified himself, asked if Fontenot would come down to headquarters and answer a few questions. The youth said he was on his way to his job at Wendy's but would come in after work. Baskin said that would be okay.

Fontenot never showed up for questioning. The police did not pursue the matter. They had no reason to arrest him. Besides, Fontenot had dark hair; the two described suspects had light hair.

There were other names to check out, and one by one in the ensuing days the detectives went down the list, questioning all of those they could locate; a few no longer lived in Ada, and could not be found. They got calls about pickup trucks that might have been used in the crime, and checked those out. They found no evidence that linked any of the men whose names had been called in, or any of the trucks, to the disappearance of Denice Haraway.

A man was arrested in Shamrock, Texas, near the western Oklahoma border, for abducting a woman in Amarillo. His description fit one of the suspects in the Haraway case, and there was evidence in his car that he may have been in Oklahoma on Saturday. But further investigation cleared him of any involvement.

The name and description of Donna Denice Haraway was put into a nationwide, computerized missing persons network, as well as into missing persons bulletins that go to law enforcement agencies in all fifty states. No information of use turned up. When the detectives were not busy interviewing people, they and uniformed officers and sheriff's deputies continued to search the county in places they thought a body might have been dumped: under bridges, in ravines, at dump sites. They found no body, no murder weapon, no bloodstains, no clothing that could be linked to Denice—nothing to indicate if she was dead or alive.

In the apartment above the dental office, Steve Haraway was kept company by his closest friends when they were not out distributing flyers or searching. The phone kept ringing there, too, and with each ring there was the momentary flicker of hope that it might be Denice, that she might be alive. But most of the calls were from the ministers of Ada's scores of churches, wanting to offer comfort, wanting to come over and say a prayer for Denice. Other ministers came and knocked on the door. Steve did not want to talk to any of them. His friends began taking the calls, answering the door, shooing the ministers away. It got so bad that an answering machine was put on the telephone, to screen the calls.

The disappearance was the talk of Ada: at the feed mill and the factories, on the farms and in the oil fields, in the stores and in the homes. As each new day passed with no body turning up, no evidence, no suspects, new rumors blew through the town: that Denice had faked her own disappearance, to run away with a lover or because she was involved in drug trafficking. People didn't just vanish into the air.

Where the rumors didn't take, where people believed that Denice had probably been kidnapped and killed, there was fear. This kind of thing might go on in Tulsa, in Oklahoma City, in Chicago, in New York. But in Ada?

At the Ada Trading Post on Main Street, a large pawnshop with a gun display on one side, pistols in glass cases, rifles and shotguns on the walls, business was brisker than usual. People kept coming in—mostly young couples—to buy handguns. In Oklahoma it is legal for almost anyone to buy a gun, though it is illegal to carry one loaded; all anyone needs is a driver's license. The most popular model was an Italian-made X-cam .25-caliber pistol, very small. They retailed new for $50 but were available used for $39. "It'll jam half the time," the proprietor, Gene Matthews, would tell them. He would say that the most effective weapon at close range was a shotgun. But the women were afraid to handle shotguns; they bought the inexpensive pistols.

The only other time there had been fear like this, in most people's memories, had been sixteen months before, in December 1982: the time of the last murder in Ada. The name of the victim still came easily to the lips of the people: Debbie Carter.

To Dennis Smith, sitting at his desk at police headquarters, placing a bit of smokeless tobacco along his gums, spitting out tobacco-colored saliva, the name, the crime, burned like an ulcer in his gut.

Debbie had been twenty-one years old, beautiful, with the kind of figure that turns men's heads. She was working as a waitress at the Coachlight Club, which later became Buzzy's nightclub. On the night of December 8, 1982, when she got home from work, she was brutally raped and strangled in her apartment. Police found the apartment a gory mess. Debbie's body was naked. An electric cord was around her neck. Bottles were strewn about—including a ketchup bottle with which she had been raped. On her stomach, the word DIE had been written with nail polish. Other words had been written with lipstick, on her back and on the walls.

Dennis Smith seethed with rage when he saw the body, the apartment. He had known Debbie Carter; she used to live down the block from him. He had known her parents. He was determined to find the killer.

There were no witnesses. A case would have to be made with physical evidence: with hairs found at the scene, with fibers. These were sent off to the OSBI laboratory in Oklahoma City.

Through his investigation, Smith quickly became convinced who the killer was. But he couldn't prove it. There was not enough evidence. Most of the town soon knew there was a single suspect in the case. But he had never been brought to trial.

Debbie had lived not far from the college. The dormitories had been locked up for a time after her death, with a mad killer on the loose. There was pressure on the police to make an arrest. But they never had.

The town for a time had lived in fear. Then it had subsided, as it always does.

Now it was back again.

The Debbie Carter case remained unsolved. In a town that small, it was a lingering cloud, perhaps in the shape of a murderer's hand, over the police department.

One day Detective Smith pulled a manila envelope from a cabinet in his small basement office. In it were the photographs from the Carter case: black and white, eight-by-tens. He arranged them in a certain sequence. First, distant shots of the street, the house, the garage, her car. Then, the interior of the apartment: the mess; the writing on the walls; the nude body—first the back, the way she had been found, face down; then the front, the cord around the neck, the wasted beauty. He had done this many times before. Every time, the images burned his gut, renewed his rage.

Unlike the disappearance from Seminole of Patty Hamilton, which bore a strong resemblance to the Denice Haraway case, the Debbie Carter murder did not. They were not connected—except in two ways: in the fear they brought to the streets of Ada; and in the extra pressure the ghost of Debbie Carter put on Ada police to solve the Haraway case.

Sitting at his desk, a copy of the Haraway flyer always prominent on it, Detective Smith would suddenly think of a place out in the country that was a likely spot for a body to be hidden, a place that might have been overlooked by the searchers. He would get into a car and drive out there and look around. Ninety percent of his working time was being spent on the case, and much of his personal time as well. Often he would not get home till after dark; then, to relieve his frustration, he would mow the two acres of grass that surrounded his house; and in the morning, going out early to deliver the newspapers, he would see tufts of grass that he had missed in the dark sticking up from the lawn here and there, like a bad haircut.

By mid-May, most of the more than twenty-five possible suspects—the names produced by the composite sketches—had been interviewed; several dozen pickups had been checked out. Nothing had been discovered to connect any person or any truck to the disappearance, though the McAnallys had increased their reward offer to $5,000, and the OSBI had offered another $5,000, and a private donor had put up $100.

One night about ten o'clock, when Smith was at home with Sandi and the boys, he got a phone call from Mike Baskin. A member of the

Haraway family had contacted a psychic in northern Oklahoma in an attempt to discover where Denice was. The psychic had visualized a scene; the information had just been relayed by the family to Baskin. According to the psychic, Denice's body could be found about eight miles east of Ada, near a government installation; there would be a water tower, a creek, a bridge; old stoves and refrigerators would dot the creek; the number 7 would somehow be hanging symbolically over the scene.

Baskin wanted to go out and look right away, in the dark.

Dennis Smith did not believe in psychics. He preferred hard-nosed logic, tough police work. But he had read of cases where bodies had been found by psychics; he felt he could not disregard the information; if he saw it work for himself, he felt, he would even become a believer. He told Sandi what Baskin had said. "Let's all go look," Sandi suggested.

Smith felt it was bizarre, taking the whole family out to look for a body. But they went, he and Sandi and the boys, carrying flashlights. They picked up Baskin and drove out Highway One, heading east, past McAnally's, past Deer Creek Estates, past the village of Homer, past the turnoff to a cemetery and to a village called Happyland. Just when they had gone about eight miles, they saw a water tower; Smith realized it was for Rural Water District Number 7. It was on the Kallihoma Indian Reservation—a government installation. They came to a bridge over a creek, pulled off the road, got out, looked around; down in the creek they could see, in the yellow circles of their flashlights, a bunch of junk—old stoves, refrigerators.

As they moved down, flashlights illuminating the grass and sand at their feet, they smelled something foul, the smell of death. Holding their breaths against the smell, and perhaps in anticipation, they poked around in the debris—and found the rotting carcass of a calf.

In the days and weeks after the disappearance, McAnally's became something of an Ada shrine. People would stop by and look around, and ask the clerks about the Haraway case. The constant questions took their toll on some. James Watts, who worked the morning shift, who had been relieved by Denice at 2:30 on April 28, quit in early May. On May 19 the manager, Monroe Atkeson, quit. It was one year to the day since Denice Haraway, then Denice Lyon, had started work there.

A new manager was hired, and a new clerk. The McAnallys looked around their now notorious store. Their eyes fell with displeasure on the magazine rack, with its large selection of naked girls on the covers. The store did between $80 and $90 a day business in these adult magazines; the McAnallys decided the pictures might be inciting young men to crimes of sex. They decided to ask their distributor to stop bringing in such trash.

With only a few weeks remaining to the end of the semester, Steve Haraway did not return to classes at East Central. He arranged to get I's—Incompletes—in all his courses; to take the final exams, to qualify for graduation, later on. When he was not out searching the countryside with friends, he sat in the lonely apartment, morose, waiting. Formerly gregarious, he was now quiet; he did not talk about what had happened, he simply waited.

For two weeks, he, Monty Moyer, Gary May, Brad Goss, and a few other friends distributed flyers. They drove in every direction within a 150-mile radius of Ada, stopping at gas stations, grocery stores, small-town police departments. Several of his friends owned four-wheel-drive vehicles; they went searching for Denice's body in otherwise inaccessible places. The police would get calls that someone thought they had heard or seen something the night of the disappearance. They relayed some of these to Steve and his friends, who checked them out.

In the first few days, it had seemed better not to find anything; with the passing weeks it seemed, at least to Steve's friends, that it was time to find something, to learn what had happened to Denice.

On Memorial Day weekend his friends convinced Steve to get away from this for a while. He agreed to join Monty, Gary, Brad, others on a boat trip down the Illinois River. It was their first time away from the case in the month since Denice had disappeared. The water swirled beneath them. The wind whipped through their hair. Steve remained quiet most of the time, alone with his thoughts.

One day he went to the financial office at the college. A hush fell over the clerks. Everyone seemed to know what he was there for: to pay off his wife's student loan.

Spring became summer in Ada. The fields in the outlying areas were green. Lilacs and hollyhocks and roses took turns blooming on the small lawns that front most of Ada's houses. They bloomed on the large ranches surrounding the town, and near the small working-class houses, and in colored town, which is what the small black section is still called. Colored town used to be right downtown; but a few decades back, as Ada grew and downtown real estate became more valuable, the city fathers razed colored town and built a new one out on the highway, across from the small airport at the northern edge of the city.

Stories about the case in the Ada *News* stopped in mid-May; but members of the Haraway family called the police frequently—every day in the early weeks—to see if there was any news.

Every few weeks, a bright new lead seemed to flare briefly, tantalizingly, before the eyes of the police, and then die. In mid-summer, a man named Gary Allen Walker was arrested in Tulsa. He allegedly had killed nine or ten women, leaving a string of bodies through several states. His method of operation did not seem quite the same as in the Haraway case, but Gary Rogers and Danny Barrett went hopefully to Okmulgee to see his parents. They found that Walker had been with them the night Denice Haraway disappeared. He later confessed to other killings, but not to killing Denice Haraway.

A man was arrested in Texas and accused of killing several women there. OSBI agents went to interview him, to determine his whereabouts on April 28; he had not been in Oklahoma. Another man was arrested in Texas, accused of kidnapping and raping a woman. OSBI agents went down to check out his clothing, his car, to see if they could find any evidence that would tie him to Denice Haraway. They couldn't.

The police and the OSBI got frequent calls from other states where unidentified female bodies had been found. None of them matched Denice's description. One that stuck in Dennis Smith's mind was from Missouri, where the lower half of a woman's body had been found in a parking lot. There were tattoos on the thighs. The police checked with the family, to make sure Denice had none. The dead woman was later identified as coming from the northern Midwest.

   With each new lead Dennis Smith felt a small flicker of hope. When the leads did not check out, he felt a new sense of frustration. He was back to square one: what to do now?

The days grew hotter, more humid. Summer reached its peak. String beans and broccoli and tomatoes and yams and okra—lots of okra— sprouted in the gardens that many Ada residents tend behind their homes. The rodeo made its annual visit to Ken Lance's sports arena, and for a few days Ada's motels were crowded. The county fair was held at the old rodeo grounds. The husks of the pecans on the leafy trees all over town began to shade from green to brown.

   On Labor Day, Ada broke into the nation's sports news; the million-dollar All-American Futurity at Ruidoso Downs, New Mexico, the richest quarter-horse race in the world, was won by Eastex, whose owner was an Ada dentist named H. D. Hall; he had an office right there on Arlington. Eastex was the second Ada horse in three years to win the Futurity. Local horsemen strutted with pride.

   Dennis Smith did not have to work on Labor Day. Neither did his wife. Dennis asked her how she would like to spend the holiday.

   "Let's go look for Denice Haraway's body," Sandi said.

   The detective agreed. They got into the family car to search, as they had done together once before, the night of the psychic's vision. They drove this time, for no particular reason, to an area near the Reeves Packing Plant, on the western edge of town. They climbed out and looked in fields and woodlands, creeks and ravines. In time, at the edge of Sandy Creek, amid a site common in Ada—old stoves and refrigerators and mattresses dumped where they should not have been—Smith saw a cardboard box with bloodstains on the lid. The blood, to his practiced eye, looked too fresh; Denice Haraway, he felt fairly certain, had been dead for four months.

   "Well, take the cover off!" Sandi urged.

   The detective removed the lid. Inside the box, peering up at them with mournful eyes, was the severed head of a deer.

Smith had run out of ideas, had run out of places to search. In his office during the next few weeks, he could only put shreds of tobacco in his mouth and spit the brown juice and try to accept the fact that the

mystery of Denice Haraway's disappearance was going to remain unsolved. There were no more leads to check out. The file would remain
open, but in the public mind it would be another case that the local
police and the OSBI couldn't handle—like the disappearance of Patty
Hamilton up in Seminole, like the murder of Debbie Carter.

Then, one day in early October, a young man named Jeff Miller
walked into police headquarters. He wanted to talk to Dennis Smith,
he told the officer at the desk; he had some information about the
Haraway case.

3

SUSPECTS

In Ada, despite its Bible Belt moorings and its pastoral locale, there is a substantial underclass of young people whose roots are in the town but whose daily existence drifts with the passing breeze. Mostly high school dropouts, they tend to find employment in the local factories, work for several weeks, then stop showing up at work, often after an all-night party. Between sporadic employment their primary activity is "running" together: cruising the area in whatever pickup is available, getting hold of a keg of beer or a few six-packs and partying—out by a creek or river in the warm months, in someone's pad in the cold—smoking or snorting whatever dope is available. The pushers among their number, coming into a good supply, will rent a room in one of Ada's nine motels. Word will spread through the grapevine like a brushfire: there's dope at room 52 of the such and such motel: the Village Inn or the Holiday Inn, the Rainbow Motel, the Indian Hills Motel—whatever. A steady stream of beat-up cars and pickups will arrive at the motel in search of the room in question. Or long-haired youths will stop at the front desk and ask what room so-and-so is in. The clerks understand what is going on. They do not call the police, because they don't want a scene at the motel; they don't want the place to get a bad reputation. On the contrary, they hope the pusher does well, that he exhausts his supply quickly; then he will be gone in a few hours. Usually he is. The dope fuels a few more nights or weeks of partying, until, flat broke, with no money for the two indispensable needs of running together—beer and gas—the runners will surrender to the society around them, get a job for a while, confine their partying to nights and weekends—till the job pales in the torpor of a late binge, a new person to shack up with, and they don't show up at work again. The town points with pride to the solid achievements of its sons and daughters at Ada High and nearby Byng High, to the future professionals at East Central; the running underclass is acknowledged mostly by the police. Some never come in contact with the law; those who do are viewed by the authorities as the town's inevitable quota of "trash."

From this milieu came Jeff Miller's information, which was not surprising to Dennis Smith; you don't get tips on street crimes from the parsonage. Jeff Miller sat in police headquarters and told the detective that two young women in the town—he gave their names—had been at a party down by Blue River, about twenty-five miles south of Ada, on the night Denice Haraway disappeared; that the women had told him Tommy Ward had been at the party with a group that included a woman named Jannette Roberts; that midway through the party, with the beer supply running low, Tommy Ward had offered to go get some more; that he had borrowed Jannette Roberts's pickup and left; that he had been gone for some time; and that when he returned he was crying. When asked why he was crying, he told friends he had gone back to Ada, had taken a girl from a store and had raped her and killed her; and now he felt terrible about what he had done.

All this Jeff Miller told the police. He had not been at the party himself, he said; his information had come from these two women, who said they had been there when it happened. Why the women would tell this to Jeff Miller, instead of to the police, remained unclear. So, too, was the question of why they would remain silent for five months, then speak of it.

The detectives asked Miller if he knew where Tommy Ward was. Miller said he had heard that Ward and his friend Karl Fontenot had been living in Norman with Jannette Roberts and her husband, but that Jannette had thrown them out because they weren't contributing to the rent. He didn't know where Ward was now, Miller said.

The detectives thanked Miller for coming in. This was only hearsay; proof might be a long way away. Still, for the first time in months, they had something to go on; they might solve the Haraway mystery after all.

The first step was to find the two women Jeff Miller had quoted, to get the story from them firsthand; they might also know where Tommy Ward was. But the women had moved from their last known address. They were part of the running underclass. Smith couldn't locate them.

The next step was to contact Jannette Roberts. She had been at the party at Blue River, according to the Ada women as quoted by Jeff Miller; she had loaned Tommy Ward her pickup; she had kicked him out of her house; she might know where he had gone. Smith obtained an address for her in Norman. He tried to call her, to set up a meeting. She didn't have a telephone.

On October 12, a Friday, Dennis Smith and Mike Baskin decided to drive to Norman, eighty miles away, to drop in on Jannette Roberts, to question her about the party at Blue River, about Tommy Ward. Though she was married to a fellow named Mike Roberts, in the minds of the detectives she was Jannette Blood. That was her name from a previous marriage. It was the name under which she had been convicted years before for forging a drug prescription, the name under which she had spent six years in prison.

As the detectives drove through the countryside, out Route 3W, the trees and woodlands were rich in their autumn colors: reds, yellows, oranges. The mood of the officers was equally bright with the excitement of the chase, of a possible solution after all these months. On the pecan trees beside the road, the husks were a deep brown; they soon would be ready for cracking.

Jannette Roberts was thirty-eight, a pretty woman with reddish-brown hair, but you could almost read the contours of her life in her face: three marriages, six children, two convictions for forging drug prescriptions, a six-year term for the second one. When she got out of prison in 1982, she came to Ada to start a new life. She got a job at Taco Tico, a fast-food Mexican place, worked her way up to assistant manager. One day the eldest of the children living with her, Niki Lindsey, a teenager, said she had met a fellow in town who lived on the streets, who didn't have any home, any family. He was real nice, real gentle, Niki told her mother. Would it be all right to bring him home?

Jannette had always been softhearted about taking in strays, animal or human. She told Niki to bring him home. Niki did—he was a dark-haired youth, seventeen years old. His name was Karl Fontenot. They gave him a place to sleep; he became like part of the family. Karl had a friend named Tommy Ward, four years older, who came to visit sometimes. They all got along well together, Jannette and her husband Mike, Karl and Tommy and the kids. Often, after a late party, Tommy would stay over as well instead of walking back to his mother's house on the edge of town. Sometimes Tommy and Karl would babysit while Mike and Jannette were out.

The Roberts family lived in a small apartment at 509½ South Townsend, in downtown Ada. But the building was condemned. One by one the other tenants moved out, until the Roberts clan were the only ones left. When the water was turned off, they, too, were forced to move. Mike Roberts took a job in Norman, installing aluminum siding. The whole household followed. Mike taught Tommy Ward how to install siding, got him a job with the same company. Karl, who had worked for a time at Wendy's in Ada, got work with another fast-food place. Tommy helped with the rent, Karl with the groceries. The siding business was good that summer and fall. Mike and Tommy worked till dark most days, coming home at times with bad sunburns and blistered fingers.

When Detectives Smith and Baskin arrived in Norman on October 12, they found Jannette at home. They asked if she would come to Norman police headquarters; they wanted to ask her some questions. Jannette said she couldn't do it, that her daughter Jessica, who had just turned seven, would be coming home from school soon. The detectives said she should come anyway; that if they weren't back in time, a police car would pick up Jessica. Reluctantly, Jannette went.

At the police station, the detectives asked her about the information they had received from Jeff Miller. Jannette said that she and her husband and Tommy and Karl and various friends and neighbors used to party together a lot. Yes, they had partied at Blue River a number of times, she said, but she didn't think the night the Haraway girl disappeared was one of them. Yes, she said, she sometimes let Tommy borrow her pickup. But this she was sure about, she said: Tommy had never borrowed her pickup and left a party at Blue River and then come back crying and said he had kidnapped a girl and raped her and killed her. That had never happened, she said.

Jannette was getting anxious about the time. Jessica would be coming home soon. The detectives sent a squad car to Jessica's school; it picked her up and brought her to the police station. In their minds this was a kindness they had provided; in the mind of Jannette, it stank—bringing her little girl into the police-station atmosphere.

The detectives resumed their questioning. About Tommy and Karl: did she know where they had gone?

Karl had moved to Hominy, near Tulsa, Jannette said; he was staying with Tommy's sister and brother-in-law, Joice and Robert Cavins. He'd gotten a job up there, installing fencing.

And Tommy? Did she know where Tommy had gone?

Tommy hadn't gone anywhere, Jannette told the detectives. He was still living with her and Mike; still working with her husband at All-Siding. They were at work right now, but they would be home after dark—maybe around eight, she figured.

Smith and Baskin were surprised and delighted. They decided to stay in Norman, to talk to Tommy Ward. They told Jannette to give Tommy a message when he came home from work: that they would like him to come down to the police station, to answer a few questions.

As the detectives killed time in Norman, waiting for Tommy Ward, they were convinced they had gotten good information from Jeff Miller. Jannette had confirmed that she and Tommy and the others used to party together, sometimes at Blue River, and that at times she had let Tommy borrow her pickup. She had denied the key incident about the crying, the confession; but perhaps she had not been within earshot of that, or perhaps she was protecting her friend. The fact that Tommy was still living in Norman, they felt, was a stroke of luck.

When Tommy and Mike got home from work, Jannette gave Tommy the message: two detectives were waiting for him at the police station, wanting to talk to him.

"What about?" Tommy asked.

"They think you had something to do with that girl who disappeared from McAnally's," Jannette said.

Tommy told Jannette and Mike that when the girl disappeared, and they put the drawings of the two suspects in the newspaper, people used to hassle him that he looked like one of the pictures. That was one reason he was glad they had moved to Norman, he said. So people would stop hassling him. The cops had already questioned him once. Why didn't they leave him alone? He wasn't sure he wanted to go.

"They're waiting for you at the police station," Jannette said. "If you didn't have anything to do with it, go down there and tell them that."

Tommy agreed that that was the best course. Mike drove him to the station. Inside, he told a clerk who he was. Detectives Smith and Baskin came out of an inner office. They led him downstairs, to a room with videotaping equipment set up. They told him they were going to make a tape of the questioning, asked if that was all right with him. He said it was. The machine was turned on by Eddie Davenport of the Norman police department. The detectives read Ward his rights under the Miranda Act: that he had the right to remain silent; that he had the right for a lawyer to be present; that he was free to go at any time; that if he did answer questions, he could stop answering them at any time; that if he did answer their questions, anything he said could be used against him in a court of law.

Tommy sat in a wooden chair, listening. He had not changed clothes after work. He was dressed as he usually was, in blue jeans, an athletic shirt, tennis sneakers. He told the detectives that he understood all of that, that he would answer their questions.

As the tape rolled, Dennis Smith recalled to Tommy the previous time he had been questioned, shortly after the disappearance: how Tommy had told them he would help them in any way he could to find out what had happened. Tommy said he remembered saying that.

Mike Baskin asked him what he had done the day Denice Haraway "was kidnapped." Tommy said he had installed plumbing at his mother's home with his brother-in-law, Robert Cavins. Then he had showered and walked to Jannette's, about 9 P.M. Karl Fontenot was there, he said, and some other people, and they had a party.

The detectives told him that when they had questioned him the last time, he had told a different story. Tommy replied that the first story he had told them had happened the day before the disappearance. He had realized this later, he said.

"What was the statement you gave us?" Smith asked.

"I don't remember," Tommy said.

"When did you realize you hadn't told the truth?" Baskin asked.

"I got mixed up the days," Ward said.

The red light of the taping machine remained on. Smith asked Tommy if he was nervous. The detective then refreshed his memory about his previous story—about going fishing and then to a party.

"Yeah, that's what I did the day before it happened," Ward said. "I told you the twenty-seventh instead of the twenty-eighth."

"Are you telling us the truth now?" Smith said.

"Yes, sir," Ward said.

The voices of the detectives were soft as they asked the questions. Ward sounded almost bored as he answered them.

"You haven't told us the truth," Dennis Smith said. "We have a statement from Jannette about where you were at that night. We know more than you're telling us."

"About what?"

"About where you were at that night. About what you did that night. We have a witness. You're getting yourself in more trouble . . . We have a person that will testify that that wasn't what happened."

Tommy insisted he was telling the truth.

"You're getting yourself in more serious trouble . . . That particular night you and Karl and Jannette went to the Blue River."

"I didn't go to the Blue River that night."

"You didn't?"

"No, I didn't."

The detectives kept telling Tommy that he and Karl and Jannette and others were at the Blue River that night. That had been Sunday night, Tommy insisted.

They told him he had borrowed a pickup and left the party.

"I still don't understand what you're getting at," Ward said. "Sunday night is the night she's talking about."

"Tommy," Mike Baskin said, "are all these people mistaken about the day?"

"I guess so," Tommy said.

The questioning continued. Dennis Smith tried a new approach. A bluff.

"Karl this morning gave us a statement that you were at the river," he said. "You ran out of beer. You took her pickup and went into town to get beer."

"I'm sure we wouldn't come all the way back into town to get beer," Tommy said.

"Isn't it true you were going to rob McAnally's?" Smith said.

"No."

"We've got people who are going to testify that you and Karl said that," Smith told him. "You and Karl left the party and were gone a long time, and then came back."

Tommy Ward said no such thing had happened. He said that on Friday he had gone fishing; on Saturday he had installed plumbing with his brother-in-law; on Sunday they had gone to Blue River.

Dennis Smith reached for an envelope. He pulled out a large photograph. He held it perhaps three feet from Ward's face.

"Do you know that girl?" he asked.

"I don't know her. I've seen her."

"Would that be Donna Denice Haraway?"

"I guess."

"Did you kill that girl?"

The detective's voice was still soft, gentle.

"No, I didn't. I wouldn't take nobody's life away from them."

"Who did kill her?"

"I don't know."

Smith continued to hold the photograph close to Ward's face.

"Was she a pretty girl?"

"Yeah."

"Is she still pretty?"

"Yeah."

"This girl's family would like to bury her," Smith said. "They'd like to know where she's at so they can bury her."

"I don't know where she's at."

Smith continued to hold the picture of Denice Haraway in front of him.

"Would you tell me where she's at, so her family could bury her?"

"Yeah, if I did it. But I didn't do it."

"What do you think happened to this girl?"

"I don't know."

"Use your imagination," Smith told him. "Two guys took her, got her in a pickup, took her away. What do you think they did with the body?"

"No telling."

"Use your imagination. What do you think?"

"She could still be alive for all I know, for all you know. For all anyone knows."

"You think they hid her under some rocks or something?"

"Could be. No telling."

"Are you telling the truth?"

"Yes, I'm telling the truth. I wouldn't do nothing like that. I'm not that kind of guy . . . I feel sorry for whoever did it."

"Her family would like to have a Christian burial for this girl," Smith said. The picture was still smiling at Ward. "A funeral service. And put her in the ground the way she's supposed to be."

"If it were my daughter, I would too," Tommy Ward said.

"So what do you think happened? What happened to this girl? You think they did it because she recognized them?"

He continued to hold up the picture.

"She was a beautiful girl," Dennis Smith said.

"Yes, she is," Tommy Ward replied.

The questions continued.

"If I thought I did something like that, I'd kill myself," Ward said.

"Were you on drugs that night?"

"I was drinking some beer."

"Steve Haraway wishes she would come back," Smith said. "He lays awake at night, wondering where she's at. Her family lies awake at night, wondering where she's at. They would like to give her a decent burial."

"Do you think she screamed?" Mike Baskin asked. "I bet whoever did it can still hear her screaming. What do you think?"

"I didn't do it," Ward said.

"Tommy, have you prayed about this?" Smith asked. "Are you a religious person? Do you believe in God?"

"Yes, I do."

"Do you know that a person that asks for forgiveness and confesses their sins is forgiven?"

"The Bible says in the Sixth Commandment, 'Thou Shalt Not Kill,' " Ward replied.

He crossed his legs occasionally; otherwise he remained almost motionless. So did Dennis Smith, leaning forward, holding up the picture of Denice Haraway.

"That's why God's son Jesus was killed," Mike Baskin said. "Remember what He said just before He died. God forgive them, for they know not what they do."

Tommy Ward waited.

"You think it would take a person under the influence of drugs to do something like that?" Baskin asked.

"They'd have to be crazy," Ward said.

Smith set the picture of Denice aside for a time. They asked Ward about the composite drawings.

"Several people asked me if I did it," Ward said. He said he never thought the picture looked like him. They asked if he had any mental problems. He said he didn't. He said he had quit school, which he should not have done. Baskin agreed that that was not a mental problem.

Smith held up the photograph again. He asked where Tommy would have buried her if he had done it. Ward said he hadn't done it. Baskin asked what if he had accidentally killed her, but hadn't meant to. "It would be an accident," Tommy said.

Baskin asked him what he would do if another person had committed a crime, and he knew about it.

"I'd tell the police," Ward said.

"Can you imagine the burden they're carrying around?" Smith asked.

"I can imagine."

"If they don't tell the police," Baskin said, "they're gonna file first-degree murder on 'em, which carries the death penalty."

"It's terrible," Ward said.

"If they don't come up with an explanation," Baskin said again, "it's gonna be first-degree murder, which carries the death penalty."

Baskin began to speak of the Haraway family's suffering. "They need to find her so they can get on with their lives," he said. "Knowing she's laying out there somewhere, winter's coming on, it's fixing to get cold. Imagine how they feel, knowing she's lying out there . . . All it would take to end their suffering is to tell where she's at. She could be taken to a funeral home, be fixed up for a Christian burial."

"I feel sorry, you know, for the girl," Tommy said; he would help the family if he could.

"She was a pretty girl, wasn't she?" Dennis Smith said.

"Yes, she was," Tommy replied.

"Can't you use your imagination?" Smith asked.

Baskin said, "I wonder if she cried."

Smith still was holding the picture.

"Tommy, did you kill this girl?"

"No, I didn't."

"Do you know who did?"

"No, I don't."

"Her body's probably deteriorating out there . . . ," Smith said.

The questioning continued. The detectives asked Ward if he would take a polygraph, a lie-detector test, in a few days, to prove he was telling the truth. Tommy said he would.

The interview lasted for an hour and forty-five minutes, all of it taped. Ward maintained to the end that he knew nothing about the disappearance of Denice Haraway.

The tape machine was turned off. They all stood up. Ward went outside, to where Mike Roberts was waiting to take him home.

Smith and Baskin walked to their car. It was late. The roads were almost empty as they made the eighty-mile drive back to Ada. Their headlights splayed the blacktop. There were no streetlights along the roads; the only light in the car was from the dashboard; it illuminated the satisfaction in their faces.

The detectives were now convinced that Tommy Ward had killed Denice Haraway.

There was the composite sketch that looked like him—a little wide in the jaw, Smith felt, but otherwise it was him. More than thirty callers had said it looked like him. Now this interview: he had seemed nervous. And the most important thing, the clincher: he had changed his story about what he had been doing the night of the disappearance. There was no reason to do that if he wasn't guilty.

They had gotten lucky, Dennis Smith felt. Jeff Miller coming in, Ward still being in Norman. But that's what it took sometimes.

They rolled into pools of light, the streetlights of Ada. The search was over, they had found the killer, they believed. All they had to do now was find the evidence; all they had to do now was prove it. Or get Tommy Ward to confess. Ward had agreed to take a polygraph. The detectives were hopeful it would trip him up.

The test was to be administered at OSBI headquarters in Oklahoma City. Smith and Gary Rogers would go up there to talk to Ward; Baskin would stay behind in Ada.

Mike Roberts is a brown-haired, wiry young man with a wisp of a beard. As he drove Tommy Ward home from the police station in Norman, Tommy told how the questioning had gone. When he was through, Mike asked if he'd had anything to do with Denice Haraway's disappearance, if he had killed her.

Tommy assured him he'd had nothing to do with it, that he enjoyed life too much to kill anyone.

Mike Roberts was relieved. He told Tommy he hadn't believed he'd done anything wrong; it was just that with the police suspecting him, he had gotten worried.

At home, Tommy told Jannette about the questioning; he'd agreed to take a polygraph, he said, to prove he was innocent. He was in high spirits. Soon the police would stop hassling him.

But his mood didn't last. In the next few days he told Jannette he was having dreams about the case, because of all those people who had told him the drawing looked like him; because of Dennis Smith questioning him. He began to get worried about the lie-detector test.

Tommy didn't much like the police; he felt they didn't like him. He'd spent a few nights in jail, arrested on minor charges, but was always bailed out by his mother or a sister or a brother. One time about a year earlier he had been involved in a traffic accident. The police at the scene accused him of driving while stoned; Tommy told them he wasn't the driver. The officers, uniformed ones, told him they would get him one day.

The recollection made him nervous. On Monday night, October 15, he telephoned his mother. He told her what was going on, that he was going to take a lie-detector test to prove he was innocent.

"I'm scared to death," he said. "I'm afraid they'll try to make me say something I'm not supposed to say."

His mother tried to calm him. "Just tell the truth," she said, "and everything will be all right."

The polygraph was scheduled for Thursday morning. Tommy told his boss about it, explaining he would need the time off.

Mike Roberts took Tommy aside. He told him that he still had $3,000 from their last siding job. If Tommy was afraid, Mike told him, he could have the money. He could use it to leave Norman, to leave Oklahoma, so the police would stop hassling him. Tommy declined the offer. If he ran, he told Mike and Jannette, then the cops would be convinced he was guilty,

On Thursday morning, Mike drove Tommy to Oklahoma City, fifteen miles north of Norman, to the headquarters of the OSBI. He told Tommy he would wait for him in the parking lot. Then they would drive to work.

Tommy walked into the building. Mike leaned back to wait. Half an hour passed, an hour, two. Afternoon came, and still Mike waited; Tommy would have no other way to get home; you didn't desert a friend. Three hours passed. Four. Five. Mike Roberts waited in the parking lot. He didn't know what was going on; he didn't think the OSBI would appreciate it if he went in to find out.

They had arrived in the parking lot at ten in the morning, right on time. It was after five o'clock when an OSBI agent came out of the building and asked Mike if he was waiting for Tommy Ward. Mike said he was.

"They still have more questions to ask him," the agent said. "We'll give him a ride home when they're through."

Mike was upset. He didn't know what they were doing in there for so long. But there was nothing he could do about it. He drove on back to Norman.

When Tommy Ward entered the building, Dennis Smith greeted him, shook his hand, led him into an office. Then Smith disappeared. Ward was made to wait for perhaps half an hour; to Ward it felt like two hours. This is common police procedure prior to the questioning of a suspect: let him wait, let him think about it; let him get nervous.

Tommy looked at the walls, looked at his hands, looked at the walls again.

About 10:30 A.M., by police accounts, Gary Rogers came out of an inner office. He introduced Tommy to agent Rusty Featherstone, who would administer the polygraph. Featherstone was a large man, neatly dressed, with reddish-brown hair, a neatly trimmed red beard, glasses. He looked more like a scientist or a professor than a cop. But he had been a cop before joining the OSBI three years earlier. He held the title of deputy inspector.

Featherstone explained to Ward how the polygraph worked. He hooked him up to it. Electrodes would monitor Tommy's pulse, his perspiration level, as he answered the questions. The agent sat behind his desk, Ward to the side of it. The agent ran some simple question-and-answer tests on the machine. He asked Tommy his personal history, his medical history. At 11:05 A.M., according to the agent, he read Ward his Miranda rights. Tommy said he would answer all questions, that he did not need a lawyer.

The agent questioned Ward about his activities on April 28. As paper moved through the machine, as the moving arm charted his biological responses, Ward repeated what he had told Smith and Baskin three days earlier. He said he had worked on plumbing at home with his brother-in-law, Robert Cavins. Then he had showered, he said. About 9 P.M. he had left the house and walked over to Jannette and

Mike Roberts's place, about a twenty-minute walk. They had gone to a party over at one of Jannette's neighbors, Gordon Calhoun. Karl Fontenot was at the party as well. They had partied till about four in the morning. Then he had walked home.

The moving finger moved across the paper, scrawling its ups and downs, its two-sided triangles. Rusty Featherstone repeated the questions. Tommy Ward repeated the answers. On and on the questioning went, without a break, until 1:30 P.M. The entire time, Ward denied any knowledge of what had happened to Denice Haraway.

The agent unhooked the machine. He told Ward he would be back soon, and he left the room. Tommy felt elated. He knew he had done well. There would be no problem.

The agent returned about five minutes later. He looked over the test. He asked Tommy what he thought. Tommy replied that he knew he had passed the test, that perhaps now they would believe that he hadn't done anything to Denice Haraway. Tommy began to stand, preparing to leave.

The agent said he was afraid not; he was afraid Tommy had flunked the test. He told him to remain seated.

At first Tommy didn't believe him. But Rusty Featherstone insisted that he had failed the test, that he was involved somehow in the Haraway kidnapping. He asked if Tommy wanted to talk about it.

Tommy said there was nothing to talk about, that he hadn't done it.

The polygraph doesn't lie, the agent told Tommy. It was right there on the paper: Tommy was holding something back; he knew something about the case that he wasn't telling; he was carrying some kind of burden that he needed to rid himself of; he would feel a lot better if he talked about it. Didn't he want to talk about it?

In a nearby room, Gary Rogers and Dennis Smith were waiting.

In Ada, eighty miles to the southeast, Mike Baskin, too, was waiting. He could not be certain what for. He would have preferred to be up there in the city, taking part in the questioning. He had been in Norman with Dennis last Friday; he had been the first—the only—detective on the scene at McAnally's.

At three in the afternoon, the phone rang at headquarters in Ada.

It was Gary Rogers calling. Ward was talking, Rogers said. He told Baskin to go out to the power plant west of town, to make a quick search of the area, to look there for the remains of Denice Haraway.

Baskin got into a squad car, drove out past Latta, a community of a few square blocks on the western edge of Ada. He circled under Richardson Loop, a highway bypass of the town, drove up a slope to where the power plant rested on a level site. He parked beside the gray gridwork, the network of wire cables that kept the lights on in Ada, the refrigerators working, the television sets, the machinery at the factories. He got out and looked around. There was a wide area of dirt, with gravel ground into it. Off to the right were grassy fields, trees, woodlands that sloped away. It was an open space, a lot of area to cover. He made a brief search but could find nothing. You would need a lot of people to cover this area thoroughly. He returned to his car and drove back to headquarters.

He had been back only a short time when Gary Rogers called again. Tommy Ward was giving more information, Rogers told him. According to Ward, there is a burned-out house in the woodland to the right of the power plant as you approach. Go on back out there, the OSBI agent told Baskin. Find that house. Search it for the remains of Denice Haraway.

Baskin drove back to the power plant. He parked and walked off into the yellow autumn grass, circling about, looking for the burned-out house. He could only imagine what the remains of the girl would be like after five months out in the rain, the summer heat, fair game for foxes and other small animals. It would not be a pretty sight.

He found the house. There was nothing left of it but a foundation, about twenty-five feet square; there was burned timber scattered about. One area—it must have been a bathroom once—contained mounds of broken tile. The detective poked about in the rubble, looking for the remnants of a body.

He found none.

He drove back to headquarters.

Gary Rogers called a third time. Baskin told Rogers he had looked near the power plant and in the burned-out house; he hadn't seen a body. Go back, Rogers told him, to the same area. Find a concrete bunker. Ward had said the body was in the bunker.

The sun was low in the sky; it would soon be dark. Baskin drove to the area a third time. The power plant was only a silhouette now. He found the bunker, a concrete vat in the ground. It was deep, filled with garbage; there was no telling what was under there. He returned to headquarters, called Rogers, told him he had found the bunker. But it was huge, he said, and it was getting dark. There was not much he could do out there by himself.

Get help, Rogers said.

Baskin got the Ada police chief, Richard Gray, and Sergeant James Fox to go out to the bunker with him. They searched it as best they could. They were still searching the area, under floodlights, finding nothing, as night descended on the town.

Shortly after Rusty Featherstone told Tommy Ward he had flunked the lie-detector test, Gary Rogers and Dennis Smith came in and took over the questioning. The mood in the room had changed. It was no longer an interview. It was an interrogation. The manner of the interrogators was no longer gentle. For five hours this new questioning continued, interrupted only by visits to the bathroom or by the phone calls Rogers made to Ada.

At 6:58 P.M., Ward sat in a chair in front of a video camera. Arrayed around him were Rogers, Smith, and Featherstone. An agent named Dee Cordray switched on the camera. Featherstone read Ward his Miranda warnings. Ward indicated that he understood them, that whatever he was about to say he was saying voluntarily.

For the next thirty-one minutes the three officers asked Ward questions while the videotape rolled. In the tape Ward is slouched in a chair, drinking a Coke, puffing on a cigarette, telling in grisly detail, his voice flat, almost bored, how he and Karl Fontenot and an ex-con named Odell Titsworth had kidnapped Denice Haraway, driven to a power plant on the outskirts of town, and raped her and cut her; and how he, Tommy, had then left, and the others had killed her and tossed her off a concrete bunker near Sandy Creek. The knife used was described several times as Titsworth's five- or six-inch lock-blade knife.

At 7:29 the camera was switched off. Handcuffs were placed on

Tommy Ward. Smith and Rogers drove him back to Ada. They locked him in the windowless, one-story cement building that is the Pontotoc County Jail.

They did not charge him with anything.

No one informed Mike or Jannette Roberts that Tommy Ward would not be coming home that night.

The next morning, Smith and Rogers called a news conference. They told the local press that they believed they had solved the Haraway case. They said that Tommy Ward, twenty-four, of Ada, had confessed to the robbery, kidnapping, rape, and murder of Denice Haraway, and had been arrested. They said he had implicated two other men, who were being sought. The names of the other suspects would be withheld pending their apprehension.

The officers asked that the story be withheld until the other arrests were made. Dorothy Hogue of the Ada *News* complied with the request; the 11 A.M. deadline for Friday's paper passed with no story written. But a television reporter called the OSBI public information office in Oklahoma City, which apparently did not realize that the story was supposed to be withheld. The TV reporter got confirmation; the news went out over the air: Tommy Ward of Ada had confessed to killing Denice Haraway, according to the police, and had implicated two other suspects.

In the early afternoon, two officers went to the home of Joice and Robert Cavins in Hominy, Oklahoma, near Tulsa, about three hours north of Ada. They found Karl Fontenot there. They asked him to step outside so they could ask him some questions. When he did, they thrust him against a squad car, frisked him, and placed handcuffs on him. They brought him back to Ada. At police headquarters, Rogers and Smith questioned Fontenot about the Haraway case for an hour and a half. For a brief period Fontenot, a twenty-year-old, dark-haired youth with a slightly pudgy face, denied any involvement. Then he, too, made a videotaped statement. On it, in answer to police questions, he said that he, Tommy Ward, and Odell Titsworth had raped and killed Denice Haraway.

When the video machine was turned off, Fontenot was placed in a cell in the city jail, in the basement of police headquarters, across the street from the county jail, where Tommy Ward was being held. Fontenot had never been in jail before.

The Ward tape and the Fontenot tape were in agreement that Odell Titsworth had been the ringleader, had had the pickup and the lock-blade knife, had done the actual killing. But there were a number of discrepancies between the two tapes as to how the crime had been committed. The biggest discrepancy concerned the disposal of the body. Fontenot's tape, unlike Ward's, said they had burned the body in the abandoned house near the power plant, and then had burned down the house.

"What portion of the house was this in, Karl?"

"It was in one of the bedrooms."

". . . Did you go through the front-door portion of the house?"

"Yes."

". . . And then what did you do after you poured the gas on her?"

"We lit the house. We lit the gas and burned the house and her."

"Did the whole house catch on fire or just part of it?"

"It just more or less built itself up, flames built up."

". . . Who lit the match to start it?"

"Odell."

In early evening, in a town called Tallequah, headquarters of the Cherokee Nation, Odell Titsworth was arrested. He was brought back to Ada. In the basement of police headquarters, he was subjected to questioning far more aggressive than that of Ward and Fontenot, because the police knew him as a "cop-hater" with four felony convictions. No videotape was made. Titsworth, with black hair that hung to his shoulders, insisted throughout that he was innocent, that he knew nothing about the Haraway case.

He, too, was locked in a solitary cell in the city jail.

The police fleshed out the story for the press. They said they believed Tommy Ward, Karl Fontenot, and Odell Titsworth had raped and murdered Donna Denice Haraway, and had disposed of her body in an area west of Ada. They said state crime laboratory officials were searching the remains of a burned-out house. They said the initial search had turned up pieces of what appeared to be a jawbone. The medical examiner had not yet determined if the bones were human.

The three suspects would probably be charged with the crimes on Monday, the police told the press.

Tricia Wolf was at home Friday morning, in the living room with the large painting of Jesus in it, done by her father-in-law. She had already completed her morning rounds: had driven Bud to work at the feed mill, for the eight o'clock shift, then gotten the five kids to three different schools by 8:30. Three of the kids were hers and Bud's; two were foster kids they had taken in a few weeks before.

The foster kids were Indian boys: Vernon, eight, and his brother Thomas, seven. Unlike some Ada residents, Tricia and Bud did not look down on Indians; kids were kids. Though the house was already crowded, when the welfare department called about the two boys, they had converted their small laundry room into an extra bedroom. The boys had been removed from their family, the social worker told them, because their father used to beat their mother, and their mother cried a lot and drank a lot.

Tricia was particularly concerned about Vernon. A few days earlier, a psychologist had asked him to draw a picture of the devil. He drew a man with holes all over his body, with bright red blood spewing out of all the holes. The psychologist told Tricia this was a common symbol among children who had been beaten and abused by their parents.

The house was a mess that morning, as it too often was with five kids between the ages of five and nine, playing, eating, sometimes fighting. Tricia turned on the small TV in the cluttered living room, sat for a bit, pondering which room to tackle first. She was barely paying attention when a news report came on: Ada police and the OSBI had arrested a suspect in the Denice Haraway case. The suspect had been identified as Tommy Ward, twenty-four, of Ada. Police were seeking two other men . . .

The words leaped at Tricia.

. . . were searching a burned-out house where they believed the missing clerk's body had been disposed of . . . several bones which might be Haraway's . . .

Tricia slumped in her chair. It couldn't be! Tommy couldn't have done something like that. Tommy was her baby brother!

Memories ran wild through her mind . . . Tommy at eight years old, playing by the power plant, a couple of blocks from their house in Latta. He got his hand caught in a machine. He couldn't get it out. The moving gears were dragging him along, pulling him into the machine. By the time he was pulled free, the bones in his hand were crushed . . . Tommy at ten, that big concrete bunker filled with mud. Tommy fell in. The mud was like quicksand, pulling him down. It was almost up to his neck when Mama got there. She threw him a fishing line. He held onto the line, stopped sinking. But it wasn't strong enough to pull him out with. He clung to the line down in the bunker, in the mud, Mama holding to the pole on top, till rescuers got there with strong ropes and saved his life . . . Tommy at twelve years old, climbing a tall tree near the house. It was about forty feet high. He fell, slammed into the thick lowest branch with his stomach. Then he hit the ground. He wandered around dazed, spastic, choking on his tongue. The family rushed to him, was certain he would die. But he had recovered.

"He's spent his life getting into situations where he was going to die. And then somehow getting out of them."

The thought burned itself into Tricia's brain.

Tommy Ward, twenty-four, of Ada . . .

It couldn't be. He couldn't kill someone. Himself, maybe. But not someone else.

She would not remember clearly if a lot of time passed or none at all. The telephone rang. Tricia grabbed the phone. It was Tommy. He was crying.

"Tommy! What's going on?"

"I'm in the county jail. They say I killed that girl . . ."

"I know. I heard on the TV . . ."

"They told me I killed her and that I'll get the death penalty. But I didn't do it!"

"What do you mean they told you? How could . . . they said on TV you confessed."

"I didn't confess," Tommy said, still crying. "I told them a dream I had. It was only a dream. But they say it's true. They say I done it."

"But they found her bones out there!"

"Well, they can't be her bones, because I made it up. It was only a dream."

Tricia's mind was whirling. None of it made sense—not Tommy killing that girl, not the police saying a dream was true.

"What kind of a dream?" she asked. "They say you confessed!"

"I didn't confess. It was only a dream, I told them. And then they said I done it. And that I'll get the death penalty."

"I don't understand," she said, again, again. "You told them a dream you had, and they say you done it?"

Tommy was still crying. "You better get me a lawyer," he said.

When she hung up the phone, Tricia was crying, too.

Two detectives came to the house. Tricia let them in. They sat on the sofa and asked her questions; they wanted to know where her mother—Tommy's mother—was; her mother was staying in Tulsa, with their brother Joel. The rest of the questions were a blur; they faded quickly from her memory. All she would remember later was that one of the detectives had a fly perched on his head; all through the questioning, she couldn't take her eyes off the fly.

4

THE PECAN TREE

In the early part of the century the American Casket Company built one of the largest factories in Ada. Glass coffins were manufactured there. The site was chosen because of sand deposits in the region that could be used in the manufacture of glass. The coffins made in Ada were not very practical; they were so heavy that pallbearers could get hernias. But glass coffins were attractive at funerals. And they were very good at preserving remains.

The plant was taken over in the 1920s by the Hazel-Atlas Glass Container Company, which specialized in making canning jars, to preserve fruits and vegetables. The making of caskets in Ada ceased. According to local legend, the last batch of glass coffins, four or five in number, were too few to be shipped away, and too pretty to be destroyed. Instead, legend has it, the empty coffins were buried in the earth somewhere near the factory.

The glass plant remains in operation today, having changed hands through the decades from Hazel-Atlas to the Continental Can Company to the Brockway Corporation. Three hundred and twenty of Ada's citizens work at the glass plant, on round-the-clock shifts, producing the 1.3 million bottles and jars a day that will be filled elsewhere with Coke, Pepsi, Miller beer, Gerber's baby food, salad dressing, pickles. Until his death in 1979, Jesse Ward, Tommy's father, had spent most of his working life at the glass plant—thirty-two years wearing earplugs and safety glasses amid the noise and searing heat of the furnaces.

Jesse Ward was born and raised in a village ten miles north of Ada, which later would be named Oil Center because of the pumps nodding and rising in the fields. When he was still young his family bought a frame house, with no indoor plumbing, at 1609 Ashland Avenue, on the western edge of Ada. Susie Dismukes lived in a house a block away that had once been a grocery store. Jesse Ward and Susie Dismukes met at a friend's birthday party in December 1937. They were married on April 9, 1938. Jesse was twenty-three, Susie was seventeen. On the day they were married and moved into his father's house, Jesse planted a pecan tree in the front yard.

Jesse was a musician in those days, playing guitar in a local string band called Ragtime. The band played at parties and in local clubs and did concerts over the local radio station. One band member, the banjo player, lived behind a cafe. One night while he was asleep, the cafe caught fire and burned. The banjo player died in the blaze. His death marked the end of Ragtime.

His music gone, Jesse moved from one job to another for a few years. Then he was hired at the glass plant. He became a machine operator, working rotating shifts, one week the 8 A.M. shift, the next week the 4 P.M. shift, the next week the midnight shift: oiling and swabbing the equipment as sand and limestone and soda ash and cullet, which is smashed recycled glass, were melted in a huge furnace into 300 tons of glass a day, were spewed in molten liquid form, bright white and orange flashes in the dark plant, into molds, to cool into the bottles and jars that would be hauled away by trucks. While he worked, Susie stayed home; few married women held jobs in those days, and the glass plant was the best-paying blue-collar employer in town. To this day, while not the largest employer, it has the largest payroll in Ada; unionized, entry-level jobs start at nine dollars an hour.

Jesse and Susie Ward wanted children. But year after year passed without Susie getting pregnant. She went to see a doctor; he told her that her pelvic area was too small to bear children. They both were deeply disappointed. Jesse began to drink some. He also became a self-taught expert on pecans. He learned how to graft shoots of different kinds of pecan trees onto one trunk. He did that with the lone pecan tree in the front yard, the one he had planted on his wedding day. After several years, the one tree was producing many different kinds of pecans. One year Jesse entered his different varieties in the Oklahoma State Fair. He won a prize. He received a letter from fair officials, asking how many trees he had in his orchard. He only had the one.

For twelve years they lived that way, childless, Jesse working, Susie at home, drawing cold water from a spigot in the yard, which was the only plumbing; an outhouse stood out back. Then Susie became pregnant. Her only explanation was that she suddenly grew up. She was thirty years old when she was delivered of her first child, a boy. They named him Jimmy.

Three years passed. They thought Jimmy was all they would have. Then a daughter was born. They named her Latricia. (She would be called Tricia most of the time.) Children came in rapid succession after that: a boy, Joel; twins, Melva and Melvin; a daughter, Joice; then a seventh child, a boy, the only one they would name after his father: Thomas Jesse Ward.

Six years passed; they thought their family was complete at seven kids. Susie got pregnant again. She had to spend the last three months of her term in the hospital. She bore a healthy daughter, Kay, making four boys and four girls. The doctor told her not to get pregnant again, that it might endanger her life; she didn't.

Despite the differences in their ages, the eight Ward kids grew up in only two bedrooms, the four boys in one, the four girls across the hall. Jesse was the patriarch of the family, but his wages at the glass plant were stretched thin by a household of ten; once food was put on the table there was little money for anything else. The kids wore hand-me-downs to school; their classmates knew they were poor. Sometimes they were teased about this, or about their name, which the other kids transformed into Wart, or Warthog. A large, poor family who lived without plumbing on the edge of town: that was all the town knew about the Wards; their very numbers made them visible. But the kids themselves were as varied as the pecans on the tree out front. Some took the slights of the other children personally, and carried the hurt inside them long after. Joice was one of these; Tommy was another. Others with more inner strength, such as Tricia and Joel, absorbed the hurt, somehow understood the natural cruelties of childhood, and let it go.

Jimmy, the oldest boy, started smoking marijuana in his teens. Tricia, three years younger, heard about this from a friend. She was at an age, fourteen, when tattling on your big brother seemed a lovely thing to do. She told their dad about it. Instead of scolding Jimmy, their father called Tricia a liar; he told her he did not want to hear anything like that again. Tricia would think years later that if her father had put a stop to Jimmy's drug use right then, all that followed might not have happened. But he didn't; perhaps he sensed that he couldn't. Jimmy got in with a bad crowd. He was never in serious trouble with the law, but he got a reputation in town as a lowlife, a drinker, a troublemaker; a reputation that would settle indiscriminately over all of the family: "those Wards."

Jimmy in time went off to Vietnam to serve his country, came back with a nervous condition, was in and out of hospitals as he went through marriage, fatherhood, divorce. While on tranquilizers prescribed by doctors at the Veterans' Administration Hospital in Oklahoma City, he would move through Ada quietly, a tall, pale specter, seeming invisible, living on disability payments.

Tricia, the oldest girl, was, perforce, her mother's helper. After school she would take care of the little ones, Tommy and Kay. On Sunday mornings she would go to church with her mother and Joice. During periods when the others lapsed in their devotion, Tricia would go by herself, or take Tommy along, getting a ride with the preacher and his wife. One day when she was in the ninth grade, a boy in her class started pestering her, and grabbed her shoe. She threw a stick at him. He dropped her shoe into a sewer. She punched him in the eye, blackening it. His name was Charles L. Wolf Jr. He went by Bud. They didn't speak for a year after that. She would go to her locker and find gross things in it, placed there by Bud. But when he asked her out on a date, she accepted. Attention turned to affection. They were married before graduation, while still in their teens, on St. Patrick's Day.

They had no goals higher or lower than to raise a family and live their lives in Ada, with the blessing of Jesus their Lord. So they both desired it; so it would be.

Tricia was tall and thin and big-boned with blond hair worn long and straight in the high school fashion of the time, big-boned in a way that would soon accommodate a certain earthy fleshiness, which, if Bud ever complained about it, he did so only in jest; there was, as they might say at the feed mill later on, more to grab ahold of. She had an easygoing wholesomeness that brooked no ill will toward any fellow creature. She moved through the days of her life poorer than she might have liked, but with the inborn certainty that her contentment and salvation would come not through riches or book learning, to which she was not partial, but through her husband, and through the children her body had been created to create, and through a simple, unquestioning faith in the teachings of Jesus, as related by the Baptist church.

Bud, for his part, in high school had worn his hair long in the protest fashion of the time—more for the fashion than for the political protest it then implied—and had drunk his quota of high school beer; but he turned short-haired and straight by his wedding day. At times he would simmer with some inner rage which after a marital squabble early on would lead him to storm from the house in silence, hunting rifle in hand, not saying where he was going—leaving Tricia to wait and wonder whether she had misjudged the man she'd hoped was hidden in the boy, to wonder whether he would return at all, whether he might, to quiet some demon beyond her ken, even turn the rifle on himself. But then he would return. With the passing years the rifle walking happened less and less, and then stopped altogether, except for genuine hunting, as the calm in the man overcame the frenzy in the boy. Bud worked for the city of Ada for two years as a bookkeeper, of all things—book learning might have been a path open to him had he chosen to follow it—and then signed on at the feed mill, a solid provider. With the help of Bud's parents, they purchased a frame house on Ninth Street, a house with a hole in the porch that Bud eventually repaired. There, they started a family: Rhonda was born in 1974. She grew up blond as her mother and thin as a beanpole and pretty as a far-off New York model, with one troublesome freckle smack at the point of her otherwise perfect nose. Then came C. L. Wolf III, in 1977, called "Buddy," a boy with a bowl haircut and a gap between his two front teeth, a boy who always had a frog in his pocket, real or imaginary. Then there was Laura Sue, in 1978, cute and loving and most likely of all to curl up trusting as a puppy in the nearest available lap. This Bud and Tricia had, along with the assorted foster children and Tricia's brothers and sisters crashing in their house from time to time—taking advantage of them, others would say. But this was a view that never seemed to cross Tricia's mind—her family was as her flesh—and Bud, having married both spirit and flesh, was willing to put up with all of them as his own. If on occasion their telephone was disconnected because the relatives ran up bills that Bud's paycheck couldn't cover, this and other material discomforts would usually be numbered among the minor testings of the Lord. No sweat—or not too much sweat, most of the time.

Joel, the next oldest after Tricia, was the most ambitious of the Wards. He attended Oklahoma State Tech, a vocational college near Tulsa, for two years, became an auto mechanic, developed the most solid earning capacity in the family. He went to work in Tulsa, bought a house there. After Jesse Ward died in 1979, Susie, as the family called her, or Miz Ward, as everyone else did, came to rely on Tricia and Joel as the two sturdy rocks of her family.

Melva, one of the twins, also tall and solid, married an Army man; she moved to Lawton, Oklahoma, where her husband was stationed. Melvin, the other twin, blue-eyed bearer of his own rowdy streak, saw Jimmy getting into trouble, felt that if he stayed in Ada the same would happen to him. He enlisted in the Navy, was stationed in Virginia. Joice, the stocky street runner among the girls, married a heavy-set fellow named Robert Cavins. They had three kids, moved from job to job in the Ada area, Joice exhibiting a boisterous, inflammable personality that perhaps was a cover for insecurity. Kay, by six years the youngest, pretty and quieter than the others, graduated from high school in June 1984. She married her sweetheart, a local boy named Billy Garrett, in August.

And then there was Tommy, Tricia thought, sitting alone in the living room, stunned by his call from the jail. He'd been the baby of the family for six years, till Kay came along. The other boys used to tease him. "The runt of the litter," Tommy was smaller than Jimmy and Joel and Melvin, even when he reached his full height of five-feet-eight-

and-a-half. As a kid he was sweet, polite. He loved going to church with her; when she and Bud started dating, Bud took a liking to Tommy, would take him hunting, fishing. He was eleven when they got married; in their wedding album, starting to fall apart now after thirteen years, there were pictures of Tommy at the wedding, cute in his new blue suit.

Then had come the turning point: the death of their father. Of all the kids, Tommy had been the closest to Jesse; he took it the hardest when their dad developed cancer. The doctors operated, found it had spread all through him. They sewed him up and sent him home to wait for death. For three months Jesse Ward lay in the house on Ashland Avenue that he had inherited from his father, the pecan tree he had planted still bearing fruit out front. The last few days they took turns sitting at his bedside, Miz Ward and all eight of the kids, and Bud. Two of them, Melvin and Tommy, couldn't bear it; they would disappear for days at a time, unable to watch their father waste away.

To ease the pain of his father's death, someone gave Tommy a joint to smoke. Some say it was Jimmy; some say it was Robert Cavins; some say it was a friend. Whoever it was, within a week the family could see that Tommy was doing a lot of dope. Perhaps Jesse Ward could have stopped him if he were alive, perhaps not. Susie Ward couldn't. Tommy quit high school, grew fond of beer, of cheap wine. He began to run with a bad crowd in the streets. He got arrested occasionally for misdemeanors, had to be bailed out, might sass the police in the process; he was another one of "those Wards," in the eyes of the town.

But would he kill somebody? It was impossible, Tricia thought, pacing the living room, unable to sit still. Jut-jawed, Tommy had a temper; he would get angry sometimes; but when he did he would punch a wall, or the refrigerator, and hurt himself, not the person he was angry at. The house on Ashland had plenty of holes in the walls to prove it. The time his former girlfriend, Lisa Lawson, broke up with him, Tommy had gone out and banged himself up on his motorcycle; he'd never laid a finger on Lisa. Then he had come home and put his head in Tricia's lap and cried.

Now the police were saying he killed the Haraway girl. Tricia didn't believe it, not for a minute—not if Tommy said he didn't. She knew he might do a lot of things, but not kill.

Get a lawyer? Thanksgiving was only a month away; she'd been wondering how they were going to afford a turkey; Bud was planning to go to a loan company to get money to pay the October bills. How could they afford a lawyer?

She thought of Susie. Of Mama. She would have to tell Mama, though it would break her heart.

Miz Ward was staying in Tulsa at the time, to help Joel, who had hurt his leg at work and was having trouble getting around. Tricia had to summon all her self-control to get her fingers to dial the number correctly.

Crying, she told her mother about Tommy's arrest. Miz Ward listened with a quiet bewilderment. It wasn't so; Tommy wouldn't do such a thing.

She remembered the time the police came looking for Tommy, a few days after the girl disappeared. He had gone down and talked to them. There had been no problem. They had let him go. Why would they arrest him now, six months later?

It was all a mistake, Susie Ward thought. Things would get straightened out.

"We have to get him a lawyer," Tricia said.

"Yes, I guess we do," Miz Ward agreed, in the soft, laconic way she had of speaking; such emotion as she might be feeling rarely was evident in her voice.

Miz Ward talked to Joel; Joel talked to Tricia. Being the two strongest ones, Tricia and Joel sometimes butted heads, got into arguments. But now they would need each other; Tommy would need them both. Joel and Miz Ward drove to Ada from Tulsa.

Tricia called Bud's mother, Maxine, who lived ten blocks away on Seventeenth Street. The two sets of in-laws, the Wolfs and the Wards, were not close, did not always get along, but Maxine loved Tricia, her daughter-in-law, mother of three of her four grandchildren. Why, that's crazy, Maxine told Tricia. Tommy wouldn't do such a thing. Whenever she had met him, he had always been nice, polite. She was thinking, but not saying: *unless he was on drugs, and it was the drugs that made him do it; you never knew what someone might do on drugs.* But mostly not believing it.

When Maxine hung up the phone, it was Tricia she was concerned about. She telephoned Reverend Larry Jones, the preacher of their church, the Unity Missionary Baptist; the preacher went to Tricia's house, to offer her such comfort as he could.

Tricia did not know much about the legal system, had never been in trouble that way. All she knew was that lawyers cost a lot. They would probably have to get one of those public defenders, she thought—not knowing a technicality, that in Oklahoma there are public defenders only in the major cities; in the smaller towns the right-to-counsel for the poor is granted through court-appointed private attorneys.

She called some friends, spoke of Tommy's plight; told them he said he didn't do it, despite what the TV was saying about a confession. Don't settle for a public defender, her friends told her. They're not experienced, they don't try very hard; that would be signing Tommy's death warrant.

Bewildered, not knowing where to turn, Tricia called the office of the state attorney general in Oklahoma City. The advice was similar: in a capital case it would be better to hire a private attorney, if that were at all possible.

Tricia hung up, frightened. She did not see how that would be possible.

In its Wild West days, Ada had been renowned as an open city, a haven for outlaws. Belle Starr used to hang out in a hideaway called Devil's Den, about thirty miles from Ada, a lichen-covered rock canyon that later would become a tourist attraction, a place for picnicking. According to legend, the Jesse James gang once held up the bank at Francis, a few miles northeast of Ada, and found only eleven dollars in it, and, encountering the sheriff as they were leaving, ridiculed the place for its slim pickings. Outlaws who had fled from the States into Indian Territory walked the streets of Ada with impunity. Until 1909. That year a local man named Gus Bobbitt was shot dead. Four itinerant outlaws were arrested for the murder. As the men were being held in the local jail, the citizens of Ada rose up in wrath. They stormed the jail, took out the men before they could be tried, and hanged them in a nearby barn. The lynching of the four suspects—Jim Miller, Joe Allen, B. B. Burwell, and Jesse West—is the moment in its history of which Ada is most proud. It was, in the words of a history book published by an Ada bank, "one mob action in America entirely justified in the eyes of God and man." At the Ada Chamber of Commerce, situated in an old railroad depot on Main Street, there is available only one picture postcard of the town. It is a faded black-and-white photograph of the lynching: the four suspects clearly visible, dangling simultaneously from ropes affixed to the barn's rafters, while in the background morning sun filters in over the heads of onlookers, and to the right, beside the dangling bodies, a white horse grazes peacefully.

Now the town was in a lynch mood again.

Tommy Ward had confessed, according to the news reports. Karl Fontenot had also confessed. Odell Titsworth had not confessed, but both Ward and Fontenot had implicated him. Two confessions and Odell Titsworth—who was known in the town as a bad guy, with four convictions for things like assault and battery. Few in Ada had reason to doubt that all the suspects were guilty. The murder of Denice Haraway was the angry talk of the factories and the stores, the homes and the 3.2-beer bars, much as her disappearance had been the curious talk five months earlier.

At the feed mill, Bud Wolf operated a computer that mixed different grains into the proper proportions for different feeds. He had been working at the mill for six years; his coworkers were well aware that Tommy Ward was his brother-in-law, that Tricia was his wife. "Those Wards," one worker said, making sure that Bud could hear him. "They're all no good. They ought to kill them all."

At Latta Elementary School, Rhonda was taunted by her fifth-grade classmates every day about how her uncle had killed that girl. Every day she came home in tears; she loved her uncle Tommy. The taunting was led by the daughter of a policeman.

Odell Titsworth's sister Judy worked at Blue Bell jeans. Every weekday morning after the arrests, she came in and sat at her machine with her head down. The other women perched at their sewing machines under the fluorescent lights, and gazed at Judy, and said nothing—

aware, perhaps out of personal experience, that women were not responsible for the violence of the men in their lives.

Call after call came into police headquarters and the district attorney's office warning that the suspects in the Haraway case would be killed. It is only forty-three steps across a neat green lawn beneath a pecan tree from the county jail to the county courthouse, but because of the death threats District Judge Jesse Green moved a scheduled hearing on Monday from the courthouse to the jail. At the hearing the men were told they were being held in connection with the Haraway case—but no formal charges were brought.

The next day, District Attorney Bill Peterson asked that formal arraignments be postponed until Thursday. "They have admitted it, but we don't have the rest of the evidence yet," he told the Ada *News*. "What we're trying to prove is if they are the ones. It's not as easy as it appears."

On Thursday, the state medical examiner's office announced that the charred bones found in the burned-out house during the initial search were not human bones. A jawbone found was the jawbone of a possum. "This puts us back to square one in the search for the body," Paul Renfrow, a spokesman for the OSBI, told the press. The scheduled arraignments were delayed again; the men had been in jail for a week without any charges being brought.

The town still seethed with dark threats, with a desire for revenge. One night the phone rang in the county jail. The jailer was told that he had better leave, because the jail would be blown up that night, to kill Tommy Ward. The call was anonymous, but the jailer believed he recognized the voice as that of a local thug; even the running underclass was outraged. The jailer stayed where he was. There was no bombing.

Day after day the police continued to search for Denice Haraway's body in the area west of town. Tommy Ward had mentioned in his taped statement Sandy Creek; the police prowled its edges, poked its muddy depths in search of the body. They didn't find it. Tommy had also mentioned the concrete bunker. There was fifteen feet of garbage in the bunker. Police went down into it, hauled out the garbage. They found no body. OSBI technicians went through the remains of the burned-out house described by Fontenot, using window screens to sift the debris, looking for bone fragments or teeth. They found none. They used metal detectors to try to unearth dental fillings; they came up with many rusty nails, but no fillings, no evidence.

The 200 acres of land just west of Ada, in the area of the power plant, were owned by a gentleman named Forrest Simpson, the manager of the Southern Oklahoma Livestock Auction. On his land stood the house in which he lived, plus five barns and an older, unoccupied house. There used to be two old houses. But one day in June of 1983, Forrest Simpson decided to get rid of one of the old houses, which was an eyesore on the land. He tore out what scrap lumber in the house he thought he might be able to use; he tore out the floor. The house had been four rooms, each exterior wall about twenty-five feet long. What lumber he didn't want he tossed inside the foundation. Then he lit a match and set it to the old, dry wood, and he burned the entire house to the ground.

After the arrests in the Haraway case, Forrest Simpson was told on the telephone that a bunch of police were out on his land, poking around in the remains of the house. He went over and saw the police at work, sifting through the sticks of charred wood that remained, and the broken tiles. He asked what they were doing. They told him they were looking for the body of Denice Haraway, the clerk who had been kidnapped from McAnally's. One of the fellows who'd confessed, Simpson was told, had said they had brought the woman's body to this abandoned house, and poured gasoline over it, and burned it, and then burned down the entire house.

That was last April, wasn't it? Forrest Simpson said.

He was told that that was correct.

Well, that couldn't be, Simpson told the police, because he himself had burned down the house in June of '83, ten months before the woman disappeared.

Are you sure about that? Simpson was asked.

Yes, he was quite sure. The night in question there'd been nothing here but the foot-high foundation in front of them now.

This development would be a problem, Dennis Smith understood, unless they found the body somewhere.

The news provided by Forrest Simpson was not made public. The police continued to search the burned-out house, while cattle watched dumbly from behind a barbed-wire fence.

Detective Mike Baskin, too, had a problem; it wouldn't go away. He was glad that Dennis Smith and Gary Rogers had obtained a confession from Tommy Ward; he was glad that Rogers and Smith had obtained a similar confession from Karl Fontenot. Odell Titsworth had not yet confessed, despite intensive questioning, but Titsworth, he knew, would be harder to crack; he'd been through rough questioning before. But Titsworth had to be guilty. There it was on Ward's tape: the robbery, the kidnapping had been Titsworth's idea; they had left a keg party in Titsworth's pickup; Titsworth had taken the girl from the store; Titsworth had the knife; Titsworth raped her first; Titsworth did most of the stabbing; Titsworth kept the money from the cash register.

It was pretty much the same on Fontenot's tape: Titsworth's idea, Titsworth's truck, Titsworth's knife. Titsworth the murderer.

The case was pretty much solved, would be finished once they found the body, it seemed. Just a matter of all the courtroom stuff from now on.

Still, something was bothering Detective Baskin, niggling at his brain. He went back in his mind to the night of the disappearance—April 28. He remembered how he had gotten the call in the squad car, how he had gone to McAnally's. He remembered what he had been doing just before the call came in, why he was working that Saturday night. He had gone to Valley View Hospital that night to get a statement from the staff at the emergency room, because . . . because two nights before, in an altercation, the police had broken Odell Titsworth's arm!

Baskin checked the records. There it was. The altercation at Marie Titsworth's house: April 26, 1984.

Baskin told Dennis Smith of his recollection, and Gary Rogers. The same thought was in all of their minds: how much could you do with a broken arm?

The next morning, Detective Smith called Dr. Jack Howard, the physician who had set Titsworth's arm. It had been a spiral fracture, between the elbow and the shoulder, the doctor told the detective after checking his records; such things are very painful; Titsworth would have had to sleep sitting up, his cast in a sling; there was no way he could have removed the cast and then put it back on again, the doctor said. No way he could have carried a body, as was described in the confessions. No way he could have committed a violent rape. No way.

Dennis Smith thanked the doctor, the tapes running wild in his head. This, too, was going to be a problem, unless they found the body.

Smith gathered eight mug shots together. He showed them to Karl Fontenot, asked him to pick out the picture that was Odell Titsworth; Fontenot couldn't. Smith reduced the number of pictures to four, asked him to pick out Titsworth; Fontenot couldn't. He reduced the photos to two. Which one was Titsworth? Fontenot didn't know; he didn't know what Odell Titsworth looked like.

What about markings? Smith asked Fontenot. Did Titsworth have anything on his arms?

No, Fontenot said.

Whereas Odell Titsworth's arms, like most of his body, were covered in dark tattoos; and according to the taped confessions, he was wearing only a T-shirt that night; and, according to the doctor, he was wearing a cast that night.

Reluctantly, Smith, Baskin, Rogers, Bill Peterson had to agree: Odell Titsworth was telling the truth: he had not been involved, despite the stories on the tapes.

Titsworth, in his cell, also remembered that his arm had been broken at the time. He told this to the police. He'd been at his girlfriend's home that night, nursing his painful arm; there were witnesses, who backed him up.

This information was not made public just then. Ward, Fontenot, and Titsworth were kept in jail; no charges had yet been filed against them.

If only he had been in on the questioning of Ward, Mike Baskin could not help thinking, he would have remembered right away that Titsworth had had a broken arm that night; the final taped statement might have turned out differently.

Not long after the tapes were made the detectives finally located the two women who allegedly had seen Tommy Ward return to a party at Blue River the night of the disappearance, crying, and allegedly had heard him confess to killing a woman, and allegedly had told of this to Jeff Miller. Both women denied to the detectives having been present at any such scene, or having told Jeff Miller about any such scene. The origins of the story, and how and why Jeff Miller came to tell it, remained uncertain. All that appeared certain was that the story was not true—and that it had led the police to Tommy Ward.

Miz Ward, Tommy's mother, owned a bird. It was a cockatiel, a crested parrot, native to Australia. It had a yellow head, a multicolored, bluish body. She called it Pretty Boy. A few months before Denice Haraway disappeared, Tommy was playing with the bird at the house on Ashland Avenue, as he often did. He had opened the bird cage and was allowing Pretty Boy to fly around in the house, perching wherever it wanted, in the living room, the bedrooms. Flying into the kitchen, it landed on the electric range—on a burner that had accidentally been left on. The bird screeched; its claws were seared to the burner.

When Tommy saw what had happened to Pretty Boy, he cried. He placed Vaseline on its burned claws, wrapped them in gauze. He placed cloth at the bottom of its cage, so the bird would have someplace soft to rest. Every day for months he changed the dressings—new Vaseline, new gauze—until the bird recovered.

At the time of Tommy's arrest, Miz Ward still had the bird. It would talk somewhat, saying "Kiss me, Pretty Boy, kiss me, Pretty Boy," and would make small kissing sounds. It seemed as healthy as ever—except that instead of four claws on each foot, it now had two claws on one foot, one claw on the other. Also, it no longer flew freely around the house; it remained in its cage, even when the door was opened.

This was the Tommy that was in Miz Ward's mind when she heard of his arrest. She had seen his temper in action, the times he had put his fist through the walls of the house. But it was only himself he would hurt. If there had ever been anyone he wanted to kill, Miz Ward thought, it was Lisa Lawson, that time she broke up with him. Instead he had gone out and wrecked his motorcycle. He would kill himself before he'd hurt anyone else.

She knew Tommy had some trouble inside him, ever since his father died. He had started having his dreams around then—bad dreams. He would have one every few weeks, every few months. Miz Ward would hear him screaming in the middle of the night. She would rush into his room to see what was wrong, and he would be sitting up in bed, crying. He'd had a terrible dream, he would tell her, a real bad dream. But when she would ask what the dream was about, he wouldn't tell her. He would say it was too horrible to talk about. Instead, he would get some paper and a pencil, and he would draw pictures—pictures of animals, strange, weird animals that she had never seen. Then he wouldn't be afraid anymore—not till his next dream. But dreams were different from killing.

She remembered the time the Haraway girl disappeared. She and her daughter Kay had gone to Lawton that weekend to visit Melva, who had invited them to a Tupperware party on Saturday night. They had gone not so much for Tupperware as for the visit; Melva's Army husband had been reassigned to California, and then would be shipping off to Germany. He and Melva and their three kids would be leaving Oklahoma soon; Miz Ward did not know when she would see them again. So they had driven down there, she and Kay, and had come back Sunday night and found everyone talking about the clerk who had disappeared from McAnally's. Miz Ward had a job back then, the first job of her life outside the house, working nights at Love's Country Store on Main near Oak. She remembered that on Tuesday night, the day the drawings of the two suspects appeared in the Ada *News*, someone had come into the store and showed her the paper and told her that the picture looked like Tommy; she'd told whoever it was who brought the paper that she didn't think it looked like Tommy.

Now Tommy was in jail. She still didn't think the picture looked like him. Also, the caption said the man had been wearing a white T-shirt. Tommy didn't wear white T-shirts, only black ones or Navy blue; the only white T-shirt he owned had a picture of Lisa on the front, and his own name, Tommy, on the back. He didn't wear the shirt with the picture of Lisa anymore, she knew.

The other picture didn't look like Karl, either, Miz Ward thought. The caption with the picture said sandy hair, and Karl's hair was black.

She knew Karl Fontenot. When Tommy was working nights over at Davis's garage a couple of years back, fixing motors, Karl started hanging around there to pass the evenings. He was the kind of person who often would hang around people, looking for friends, until they shooed him away. But Tommy didn't shoo him away, he let him hang about, became his friend. On nights when Tommy wasn't around, Karl would walk over to Love's where Miz Ward was the clerk, and would sit in one of the plastic booths, fold his arms on the table, and lay his head on his arms and go to sleep. He would sleep that way all night. Miz Ward would leave him be. Sometimes, if there was an extra sandwich that had been made up and not bought, she would give it to Karl; he never had money to buy one.

Still seeking the body, the police announced that a citizen search would be held in the area west of town on Sunday, November 4. About eighty-five people turned out: members of the National Guard, the Amateur Radio Club, the Rifle and Pistol Club, other private citizens. Under the direction of the detectives and the OSBI, they lined up shoulder to shoulder along a fence line. They walked slowly through the tall, dry grass, up hills and down ravines, looking. When they reached the fence line opposite, they moved over a few yards, stood shoulder to shoulder again, and walked back, peering at the earth.

The district attorney, Bill Peterson, stood watching. He knew the gory content of the confessions; but to bring murder charges without a body would be highly unusual. Trying a murder case without a body was not something he would relish. As he watched the searchers, one thought ran through his mind, over and over, like a prayer: "Find me a bone! I want a bone!" He didn't need an entire body; one of Denice Haraway's bones would be enough. Any human bone would help.

The search went on from nine in the morning till five in the afternoon. Police climbed down into wells in the area. Volunteers searched dump sites. Several more bones were found, were sent off to the medical examiner's office to be studied. None of them were human bones.

In the Pontotoc County Jail there were cells made of bars, which fronted on a small common area in which inmates released from their cells could sit at tables and play checkers or read magazines. Tommy Ward was not in one of these. He was kept in a solitary cell, with cement walls on all sides. The only opening was a small, barred window in the steel door. There was no television in the jail, and he was allowed no magazines, no books except a Bible. There was nothing he could do but sit or lie on his bunk, and think, or cry, or pray.

Alone on his bunk, his mind went back to the day he took the polygraph, to the questioning that had followed. A Thursday, he thought it had been, but he was no longer sure; time stood still in the jail. The days blended together, with absolutely nothing to do; the mind played tricks. He was not good with names, words, spelling. He'd been in slow-learner classes all through school. This was evident a few days later, when he put down on paper, at the request of a lawyer, his version of what had transpired during the questioning. He wrote his account with a ballpoint pen on lined notebook paper, on both sides of the page. The most notable misspelling was that of the first name of his friend, Karl Fontenot. He spelled it repeatedly as "Carol."

This is part of what he wrote:

Mr. Smith shuck my hand when I came in the door and had me to wate. I waited for about 2 hours wile they was back in the back room talking. Then they came and got me and a OBI agent ask me if I had anything to drink or taken any drugs in the last 24 hours. I told him I drank a cuple of beers last night. Then he said, did you take any dope. I said, I don't do dope. Then he gave me the number test. Then he told what number it was then showed me the test. So then he ask me the questions about the girl missing and I answered him no on all of them. Then he ask me some more questions about the girl missing and I answered no on them. Then he told me to go back in and have a seat that he would be in, in a minnit. So I went back in the room and then about 5 minits later he came back in. Then he checked the test. Then he said, what do you think. I said, I know I passed. And now they can see I didnt do it. Then I started to get up to leve. Then he said fraid not you flunked the test. I about fell out of my seet. Then he said do you want to talk about it. I said, thers nothing to talk about cause I didn't do it. Then he said the looks of these test you know something. I said I know I didnt do it. Then he went to the door and got Mr. Smith and the OBI agent. Then the OBI agent said, what do you know about it. I said I dont know nothing I didnt do it. Then he said, you do to know something about it or you wouldnt have flunked the test. Then he said, you did it, or you played a part in it. I said no I dont know nothing about it. Then he said, you do know something. Then I said, after people comming up to me I had a dream. And Mr. Smith questioning me. Then he said when did I have this dream. I told him after Mr Smith questioning me that was the night I had a dream. Then OBI he ask me what did I dream about. I told him.

I had a dream that I was at a keg party then poof I was sitting in a pickup with two guys and a girl. Then this one guy started kissing this girl, and she told him to leve her alone. Then I told him to leve her alone then he said if you dont like it you can go home. Then I looked out the window and we was at the power plant then I looked back at him and one of the guys was gone. Then I told him to take me home. Then he said you are home. Then I looked out the window and I was home. Then poof I was at the sink trying to get something black off my arm and I couldn't get it off then I woke up. . . .

Then the OBI agent said, your dream dont make since. I said, what dream dose make since. Then Mr. Smith said, it was Odell Tittsworth and Carol Fottno in your dream wasn't it. I said no I dont know who it was. Then he had me to take another test. Then he had me to go back in. Then about 5 minits later he came back in and checked the test. Then he had me to singg [sign] them. . . .

Then he said, do you want to tell the truth. I said, the truth is I didnt have nothing to do with it. Then he said, OK. Then he went to the door and got Mr. Smith and the OBI agent. Then the OBI agent said, you and Carol and Odell went out to the store and kiddnaped that girl and took her out to the power plant and killed her. I said, no I didnt have nothing to do with that girls dissiperence. Then Mr. Smith said were did ya'll go to discuess it at. I said, we didn't discuss it no were cause I didnt do it. They they cept on at me about Carol and Odell being in my dream. So then I thought I would play there little game so they could see themselves it was a bunch of bull thats were I made my mestack. So then I told them that Carol and Odell was in my dream and we left the keg party then poof we was at ET [Evangelist Temple] and smoked a joint. Then the OBI agent said, yall went out to the store and kidd-naped her. I said, no. Then he said, you did to and what did Carol do. I said, nothing. Then he said who went in you and Odell. I said no. Then he said, you did to. Then he said what did Carol do wile you and Odell was in the store. I lied and said he jumped in the back of the pickup. Then I said, no that it wasnt in my dream.

So then Mr Smith said: you was at the keg party and Odell came in and ask you if you wanted to go smoke a joint then you went out to E.T. and ya'll discused it and ya'll went out to MacKanalies and ya'll went in and took her out and then did you see any one. I said no cause it wasnt in my dream. Then they cep on at me about it. So I lied and said I seen a guy lean-ing up aginst the Ice Mechine. Then he said, Then yall left and went down Arlington to Mississippi and turned off to Richardson loop. Then went to the power plant. Then I said we stoped on Mississippi then Carol jumped out. Then the OBI agent said Carol did not jump out he was there all the time. Then he said then what did we do when we got to the power plant. I said that Odell was kissing her and she told him to quit. Then I told him to leve her alone. Then he said If I dont like it I could go home. Then I said for him to take me home. Then he said you are home then I looked out the win-dow and I was home. Then the OBI agent said come on now.

You staid at the power plant and you and Odell got out and Carol got out of the back of the pickup and you'all started to rape her.

Then he said who raped her first Odell. I said nobody raped her cause it was a dream. Then I told them again that Carol jumped out on Mississippi and we was at the power plant then Odell started to kissing her then I told him to leve her alone then. He said If I dont like it I could go home. Than Mr. Smith stoped me and said, Carol didnt jump out on Mississippi that he was in the back of the pick laying down wasnt he. I said no that he got out on Mississippi. Then the OBI agent said Odell raped her and you helt her didnt you. So they cep on at me and finly I said, I lied again I helt her down and Odell raped her and that he cut her on her side. Then Mr. Smith said why didnt you try to stop him. Then I said, I couldnt cause this was just a dream. Then the OBI agent said after Odell raped her who wraped her next. Then Mr. Smith said you raped her didnt you. Then I said I didnt rape her cause it wasnt in my dream. Then the OBI agent said come on now you did to rape her didn't you. So then I lied again and I said I couldnt rape her. Then Mr Smith said you couldnt rape her cause you new she new you. So then Mr. Smith said, you cut her didnt you. So I lied and said, I couldnt rape her then she broke away from me and I coaght her and we fell on the ground and I bit her on the tit. I just said it to see there expreshens on there face.

Then Mr Smith cep on at me about cuting her. So then I lied and said that I cut her on her arm and on her side but they were jest scratches. Then I said she broke away from me and she ran and I cought her and bit her on her tit then Odell and Carol grabed her off me and took her back to the pickup. Then Mr Smith said that is when Carol raped her wasnt it. So I lied and said yes. Then he said what did you do. I said I went home. Then the OBI said, you watched and you didn't go home. So then I said, this is a bunch of bull this was only a dream. So then Mr Smith said you went home and you came back then what was they doing to her. Then I thought up a

funny lie and I told them that Carol was raping her and Odell
was standing at the side of the pickup and Odell was laughing
saying Carol is scruewing a dead corps. I said it to see the ex-
preshons on their face. Then Mr Smith said what did you do
with her. So I lied and said I helped put her on Odell's sholder
and Carol grabed her legs and they started walking down
twards the woods and I went back home. So then Mr Smith
ask me if we ever discussed it. I told him no that it was just a
dream.

Then he said I bet its been eating your heart out wondering
what they did whith her. I said, no that its never botherd me
cause I knew it was just a dream. So then I told them about
standing at the sink trying to get something black off my arm
and it woke me up. All the time they was going along with me
about a dream. And they know they had me to lie and add on
to my dream cause they told me what to say. Then Mr. Smith
said it was blood wasnt it. I said, no I dont know what it was
but it was scaring me that's what woke me up. Then I said,
cant you see that this was only a dream I had. Then the OBI
agent said, It was to blood wasnt it. So I lied and said, I guess
so, but whatever it was I was having a heck of a time getting it
off!

Then they went out and got a man. And he came in with a
projector. Then they started sitting it up. Then Mr. Smith said,
soposen were did they take her. I said, they didnt take her any-
were cause it was a dream. Then he said, suposenly were they
might have taken her. So I thought I would lie and tell them
that they might have taken her to the house or to this concreak slab. So they could see that it was a dream and let me go.
So I told them she might be at that house or that concreak
slab down by Sandy. So then the OBI said, what concreak slab
so I told him were it was and he said a concreak bunker. I said,
I guess that is what you call it. Then the OBI agent got on the
phone and called the Ada p.d. and told them to go look down
there. I thought for surley they would let me go when they
seen she wasnt down there and see it was a dream and run me
out. So then they got the projector hooked up and I ask Mr.

Smith what day this was. I was refering what day he came and talked to me, and that was the night I had my dream. So then he said, Sat. Apr 28. So then the OBI agent said, I'm tired of hearing this dream B.S. I just want you to tell what happend in your dream. So then I said, OK if that is what you want to know about. So then I gave my statement. Then during my statement I know I did say this was just a dream. They must have cutten it out cause I was looking down at the mick when I said it or I might not of said it lowed enough cause I didn't want them to hear me say it. Then when I said, I wouldn't have done it if I wasnt doped on or something It was an ex-presohn, verifying that they would see my statement was a lie cause I don't do dope and they could check me and I dont have anything wrong with me.

They can see that Im not nutts. God knows that I didnt do it. And that I'm not the kind of guy to do something like that. He knows I dont have the heart, or dont have the gutts to do something like that. I just give the statement so they could see that it was a dream and let me go.

So getting back to what happened. Mr. Smith said, after I give the statement, you just wished that this was a dream it realy happened. I about laughed in his face. But I said, I know it was a dream and you will find that out. Then Mr Smith ask me if I would come to Ada with them and show them that this was a dream. So I said, OK. So then he started to put hand-cuffs on me. I ask him why he was putting them on me for. He said for your protection just in case someone sees you that they would think you was a prisoner instead of a snitch. So I thought that was well enough excuse. So then he put them on me. So then we was on our way back to Ada when I started talking to them about it and I said, I will show you that this was a dream. I also told him that I was lieing adding on my dream so they could see it was a lie. Then the OBI agent said, I don't want to hear this dream B.S. If you got something to talk about talk about something else.

So then we got back to Ada. And Mr Smith said, show me that this was just a dream. So then we went to the power plant. And I showed them. I said were they caried her there was no road. And were she ran from me theres a fince their. So I said see this was just a dream. Then I thought I had them convinsted that it was a dream. Cause they was acting as if they seen it was a dream. Then the OBI agent said, well see what Odell and Carol has to say about this. Then I said, they wont have anything to say about this cause it was a dream. Then he said, we'll see. Then they brought me to jail I about died when they brought me here. I thought that we was going to come down and I show them that it was a dream and they let me go. Then they brought me and put me in jail. So then I called my sister and told her I was in jail and not to worie I will be out tomarow when they see that this was a dream. So then I came back and they locked me up. They never did tell me I was under arest for the murder of that girl. I still to this day dont understand why they think I might of done it.

On and on he wrote, filling page after page. When he was through, he went back and wrote across the top of the first page: "This statement is the truth nothing but the truth so help me God."

The fact that the police had taped confessions from Tommy Ward and Karl Fontenot had been well publicized; the fact that the two young men had repudiated the statements almost immediately had not yet been made public. Since they had not yet been formally charged with any crime, they had not had an opportunity in public to plead not guilty. With all the problems with the tapes—the fact that Odell Titsworth could not have been involved, the fact that the burned-out house had been burned down long before—the police knew they would have a much stronger case if they could find physical evidence to substantiate the tapes: Denice Haraway's body or her bloodstained clothing, or a murder weapon—something. So they searched continually, mostly in the area west of town, and found nothing. Dennis Smith would be sitting at his desk when suddenly a place leaped into mind that they had not searched. He would get into a squad car immediately and go out there and look. And would find nothing. Mike Baskin would lie awake at night, wondering where the body could be, and would get an idea. The first thing in the morning, he would go to the site—and would find nothing. With six months gone since the disappearance, the detectives began to feel they would never find the body unless Ward or Fontenot told them where it was.

One day they got an idea. They went to see Ward in the county jail, Baskin carrying a plastic garbage bag. Confronting Tommy, the detective reached into the bag and pulled out a skull, then a femur, then another bone. He said, or implied, that these were Denice Haraway's. He asked Tommy to tell them where the rest of her bones were, so her family could bury her.

Tommy said it wasn't her. Or that if it was, he didn't know anything about it. He did not crack under the eerie pressure and tell them where the body was, as the detectives had hoped.

They had borrowed the bones from the biology lab at East Central University, where Denice Haraway may at one time have studied them; where her husband, a sometime biology major, almost certainly had.

5

MURDER IN THE FIRST DEGREE

The police were not the only ones obsessed. Denice Haraway's missing body—assuming that she was dead—began to invade the darkening dreams of Ada.

One woman saw vividly in a dream where the body lay. She did not want to get involved in the case. But her dream gnawed at her. She telephoned her lawyer and told him of her dream; she asked the lawyer to relay the information to the police, without revealing her name. The lawyer called Dennis Smith. Though the place the woman had dreamed about had already been searched several times, Smith dutifully went out there and looked again. He found nothing.

A school teacher named Arlene Cameron dreamed she saw Denice Haraway's body lying on wooded slopes a few acres from her home, in a nearby village called Happyland. She told her dream to her neighbor in Happyland, Maxine Wolf—Tricia's mother-in-law, who was building a small makeshift farm out there. Arlene asked Maxine if she should tell the police; Maxine advised against it. "Look what happened to Tommy when he told the police a dream," she said. For Maxine had told Arlene the family's view of the case.

Arlene was well acquainted with the police view; her boyfriend at the time was a deputy sheriff.

Maxine suggested that the two women go over and look for the body themselves. And they did. They put on pants and shirts and spent a long autumn afternoon tramping through the foliage, kicking aside the fallen leaves, looking for a body which, if they found it, would be greatly decomposed. Arlene was convinced from what she had seen in the newspaper and on television, and from what she had heard from her boyfriend, that Tommy Ward was guilty; Maxine Wolf wanted very much for him to be innocent, because she loved Tricia; Tricia had been good for Bud. Side by side with conflicting involvements, the two women searched, their arms and legs whispering through the leaves. They found no corpse in Happyland.

In town, Tricia Wolf was having different kinds of dreams. She dreamed one night that she saw her brother Tommy being strapped into a chair. She watched helplessly as he was injected with a lethal poison, which is the prescribed method of execution in Oklahoma. She saw him slump over in the chair. He was dead.

She woke up, her heart thumping wildly; she was in her own bed.

Two nights later she had the same dream again. It seemed just as real the second time.

For Tricia, if not for the others, the dreams of the night were rivaled by the nightmares of the day. Her daughter Rhonda came home from school screaming every day because of the taunting of the other kids. Bud came home from the mill with new stories of slurs by the other workers. And there was the incessant ringing of the telephone. People they hadn't seen for years kept calling to ask if the Tommy who had been arrested was their Tommy, if the Tommy who had killed that girl was their Tommy. Yes, she would tell them, Tommy had been arrested. But no, she would say, he hadn't killed that girl.

One woman called to gossip about the strange rumors floating around town about what might have happened to the body: that it had been buried in a wet cement wall out by the Ideal Cement plant; that it had been placed in an acid pit at the Reeves Packing Plant, near the power station, and had been dissolved. Tricia did not care to hear these tales.

The acid-pit theory would soon be the most persistent story in town—this despite the fact that there is no acid pit. There is near the packing plant a pit into which the blood of the slaughtered animals runs. There is no acid in it, nothing that would dissolve a body.

The case made some people wish that Nigger Sairy were still alive. A gnarled black woman who lived at Fourth Street and Broadway in the old colored section, Nigger Sairy had been feared by the children of Ada, who believed that she kidnapped kids and killed them and sold them for chopped meat. This they could prove by the mysterious letters painted on the three posts in front of her house: R, O, E. In fact, that was her name—Sarah Roe. But Nigger Sairy had the respect of many adults because she was a seer who specialized in envisioning where lost objects or animals could be found. Many is the Ada farmer who will swear he braved the mysteries of Nigger Sairy's house, which contained her own self-made coffin, and was told precisely where he could find his missing hog or heifer. If Nigger Sairy were still alive, some people believed, she could tell the police where Denice Haraway was. But Nigger Sairy was long since dead.

Tricia's own fervent belief was that Denice Haraway was still alive: that she had run off somewhere, perhaps with a lover, perhaps for some other reason. Just because nobody had heard from her, that didn't mean she was dead. Rumors to that effect were floating through the town as well: that she had been seen in Oklahoma City; that she had been seen in Texas. Sometimes Tricia's sympathetic friends would call to report these rumors. These gave Tricia hope.

Strangers, too, called. One day an old woman on the phone asked Tricia if she was the sister of that Thomas Ward who killed that girl. Tricia didn't know who the woman was, or how she knew she was Tommy's sister, since her name had been Wolf, not Ward, for eleven years.

"Are you his sister?" the woman persisted.

"It hasn't been proved. He didn't do it," Tricia said.

"It's terrible that he killed that girl," the woman said.

"This isn't funny," Tricia said.

"I don't think it's funny that he killed that girl," the woman said.

Tricia hung up the phone, wondering what she was doing even talking to this woman. She went over to Maxine's, to get away from the ringing phone. For days afterward she burst out crying every time she heard in her mind the old woman's voice.

Maxine, soon after, got a different kind of telephone call. It was from a friend and fellow churchgoer, Mildred Gandy, who lived in a trailer at the Brook Mobile Home Park, a large trailer court off Country Club Road, about a mile from McAnally's. Mildred Gandy told Maxine she had seen Denice Haraway out at the trailer court, just a few trailers away. She was standing there with two guys, Mrs. Gandy said. This had been back in the spring, Mrs. Gandy told Maxine—but it was two days after the Haraway girl supposedly was killed. She hadn't told the police, she said, because she did not want to get involved. But since Tommy had been arrested, she thought she ought to tell Maxine.

Maxine excitedly told Tricia of the call. It reinforced their belief that Denice Haraway was still alive. It was something else to tell Tommy's lawyer—as soon as they could find him a lawyer.

Barney Ward—no relation to Tommy Ward or his family—grew up in Ada. In high school he was in an accident that left him permanently blind. Despite this, he went on to graduate from East Central—where as a stunt he flew an airplane one day—and then from law school. He set up shop in Ada as a criminal attorney. In thirty-three years at the bar he had earned a reputation as the best criminal lawyer in town. A large, stocky man, he was a familiar figure at the courthouse, always walking slowly on the arm of his female legal assistant, black glasses shielding his eyes. His office was in the American Building, diagonally across the street from the courthouse; there his assistant read to him whatever material he needed in the preparation of his cases. He was known to be sympathetic to poor people in trouble.

Barney Ward was the first choice of Tricia and Joel to defend Tommy. Joel called the lawyer's office from Tricia's house; his legal assistant took the call. For many long minutes Joel explained the situation—Tommy's tale of his dream, all the information that had not been in the news accounts. The assistant asked Joel to hold on. He held while for many more long minutes the assistant relayed the information to the attorney. Then she got back on the phone. She said that Mr. Ward was sorry, but that he would not be able to take the case.

Barney Ward did not know the defendants. But he had heard the scuttlebutt: that they were not very bright, that they had repudiated the confessions. And it was public knowledge that no body, no physical evidence whatever, had yet been found. Unlike most of the town, he was not convinced that they were guilty. But he had his own problems about taking the case. One was financial. The case gave every promise of being long and arduous and time-consuming, of being a losing proposition financially. More important, he knew Dr. Haraway, who was a familiar figure around town. Whoever defended these boys would earn the undying bitterness of the Haraway family. And in a town that small, he would continue to run into the Haraways. In his younger days Barney Ward might have sacrificed such considerations to his desire for legal and social justice. But now he felt he was too old for that sort of strain. So he turned it down. There were other attorneys who could defend the boys.

The second attorney Joel called reflected a different attitude, the one that pervaded most of Ada's legal community. "Frankly," the lawyer told Joel coldly, "I'd rather prosecute."

Though they did not want to settle for a court-appointed attorney, Bud and Tricia went to see Assistant District Attorney Chris Ross, to find out how the system worked, should it become necessary. They knew Chris Ross; they had been in the same foster-parent class. The visit sent a shudder of apprehension through the law offices of Ada. No one wanted to defend Tommy Ward. One consideration was money. The fee an attorney received from the state, if appointed in a capital case, was only $2,500—chicken feed, in the eyes of most of the lawyers. And defending Tommy Ward, most of the lawyers feared, would be devastating to their livelihoods. They received most of their income not from criminal cases but from civil suits: divorces, accident and injury cases. The town was convinced that the suspects were guilty; the town was outraged about what, according to the taped confessions, had been done to Denice Haraway. Whoever defended these boys was likely to see much of his civil practice drop away.

That was the scuttlebutt in the law offices and in the courthouse and in the restaurants near the courthouse where the lawyers and the judges often ate—the Feed Store, Mercy's sandwich shop. Several attorneys said they would quit the bar before they would defend Tommy Ward or Karl Fontenot.

For several days, Tricia and Bud and Joel and Miz Ward did not know what to do. Then, at the feed mill, Bud heard about Don Wyatt. He heard it from several people: Don Wyatt had represented them in accident cases, workmen's compensation cases, and had won. He was not afraid to take on the big factories, the big insurance companies.

They needed someone who was not afraid. Why not give Don Wyatt a call, over at Wyatt & Addicott?

Joel did. Don Wyatt told him over the phone that his fee to represent Tommy would be $25,000, that $3,000 would have to be paid as a retainer; the rest would have to be paid within a year.

Joel called Tricia, told her what Wyatt had said. The fee seemed enormous. But they had to get Tommy out of this trouble; they were sure he was innocent. Perhaps, if they couldn't raise $25,000, the lawyer would take Miz Ward's house on Ashland Avenue. Joel wired Tricia some money from Tulsa. They got in touch with their sister Melva out in California, told her what was going on. Melva, too, was convinced that Tommy could not have done such a thing. She wired the rest of the money. Tricia took the $3,000 to Don Wyatt's office on Arlington.

The lawyer wasn't in. She left the money with his receptionist. A few hours later, Wyatt phoned her. There had been some misunderstanding, he said. He would need a $3,000 retainer if he agreed to take the case. But he had not yet agreed to take it. First he wanted to talk to Tommy, he said. Then he would decide. Meanwhile, she'd better come and get the money.

Tricia went and got the money and drove back home, at a loss as to what to do next.

In their taped statements, both Tommy Ward and Karl Fontenot said the crime had been committed with Odell Titsworth's truck. Since the police were convinced within a matter of days that Titsworth could not have committed the crime, they were left with yet another problem: what pickup had been used? And where was it now? Neither Ward nor Fontenot owned a truck. A check of motor vehicle records indicated that Titsworth did not own a pickup, but that one of his sisters, Melba, did. The police obtained a search warrant for it. On the Monday after the arrests they located the pickup. It was parked outside a sumptuous two-story sprawling home at 110 Mayfair Way; the home of Don Wyatt, attorney.

Marie Titsworth, Odell's mother, had been cleaning the houses of well-off Ada residents for eight years. For six of those years one of her employers had been Don Wyatt. On Wednesday evenings and on Saturdays she dusted and vacuumed his large suite of offices. On Mondays she cleaned his home. The relationship between the busy attorney and his wife, and the small, gentle Indian woman, had become through the years one of total trust and affection.

That Monday, Mrs. Titsworth had borrowed her daughter's truck to get to work, as she often did. Midway through the day, as she was cleaning the lawyer's house, with the Wyatts away at work, she happened to glance out the front window, and noticed a police car parked outside; parked right behind her truck, blocking it. As she continued with her cleaning, her vacuuming, she glanced frequently out the window. The police car remained where it was. Finally she went outside, to see what the problem was.

The patrolman in the squad car asked if it was her truck. She said it belonged to her daughter. Since it wasn't hers, the officer said, he could not tell her what this was about, except that the truck was being impounded in an investigation. The investigation, she would later recall him saying, had to do with narcotics trafficking.

Marie moved toward the front of the truck, to get a sweater that she had left on the seat. The officer stopped her. He told her she could not take anything from the truck.

Mrs. Titsworth returned to the house, embarrassed that the patrol car was parked there, in front of Mr. Wyatt's, for all the neighbors to see. She phoned Melba, who got a ride over. For more than two hours the patrol car was parked behind the pickup, till a tow-truck arrived and towed it away. Before they left, the police allowed her to get her sweater.

Marie asked her friend and employer, Don Wyatt, for help. Mrs. Titsworth told Wyatt that her boy could not have hurt the Haraway girl; that the police had broken his arm two nights before, in her own home.

Wyatt informed the district attorney's office of this. The authorities already knew it. Odell Titsworth, they said, was being held on an outstanding warrant for his assault on a policeman the night his arm was broken, not for the Haraway case.

It was nearly a week before Marie Titsworth got her daughter's truck back. The OSBI had treated every inch of it for hairs, fibers, fingerprints, anything that might connect it to Donna Denice Haraway.

They found nothing. When the truck was returned, it was covered with a film of black soot used in the analysis. Marie Titsworth felt that the least they could have done before returning the truck was to clean up the mess they had made. Don Wyatt agreed with her.

Wyatt was a maverick among the attorneys of Ada. A loner by nature, he did not belong to the Rotary Club or any other civic organizations at whose functions other attorneys hobnobbed with clients or prospective clients. His own clients were mostly poor criminals, or poor factory workers engaged in claims against management. For him to mingle socially with the opposition would have made both sides uncomfortable.

Born and raised in Oklahoma City, Wyatt moved to Ada after O.U. law school, because of its quiet beauty. There was an aura about him of a city slicker in the country, an aura fraught with contradictions. His city upbringing was reflected in the pale gray suits and ties and white shirts he favored in court, in the gold watch he wore with its face turned toward the inside of his wrist, as if he were guarding the privacy even of his time. He was mildly stocky, had a full moustache, was not tall but somehow gave the forceful impression of being taller than he was. He spoke in a soft, well-modulated voice, but his words were usually direct, sometimes even brusque. His rural side was reflected in the dark plaid wool or cotton shirts, open at the neck, that he wore when he did not have to go to court; in the green and cream–colored Ram Charger he drove; in the spent buckshot shells that littered the rear of the Charger, hunting pheasant and shooting skeet being his favorite ways to relax.

He came to Ada in the 1970s as an assistant district attorney. After several years he quit to practice criminal law. In the view of some of Ada's law enforcement people, that switch was almost like a police-man quitting to become a burglar. At first he handled only criminal cases; some of his first clients were people he had helped to convict, who, in trouble again, wanted him to represent them now. Gradually he branched out into civil suits. His firm, Wyatt & Addicott, was one of several law firms in the state that advertised on television at times for accident or personal injury cases; in the eyes of the town's upper classes, this made him an "ambulance chaser." Yet it was of these same injury cases that he was most proud. On a wall in the stunning law building he had designed for himself was a state map dotted with clusters of light blue and dark green pins; there were large clusters of pins around Ada, around Oklahoma City, around Tulsa, and individual pins scattered through the state; the pins represented more than 400 workmen's compensation cases and 300 civil suits—personal injury cases, automobile accidents—that were pending in his computerized files at any given time, in addition to 40 or 50 criminal cases.

The success of his practice was evident in the size of his staff—the firm had nine employees—as well as in the office building itself, which some passersby thought, while it was being built in the summer of 1984, would be Ada's fifty-first church. Made of red brick, it had a peaked roof, vaulted windows, beautiful wood parquet floors, handcrafted wooden chair railings, thick carpets, soaring ceilings and skylights, a library, a conference room with stained glass in the doors, a computer room, a kitchen, a large parking lot out back, manicured lawns that sloped to Arlington Boulevard in front. The building was a monument to Wyatt's taste, to the 20 to 33 percent fees he got for winning civil cases, and to the number of cases he won. His business card listed phone numbers in Tulsa and Oklahoma City, where the industrial courts were located, as well as in Ada; all of the toll-free numbers rang in Ada, but the clientele was statewide.

Because of all this, Don Wyatt did not have the fears other Ada attorneys had about representing the defendants in the Haraway case. By the time he was asked to represent Tommy Ward, his hackles had already been raised by what he viewed as police mistreatment of his cleaning lady, Marie Titsworth. There would be no conflict of interest, he was confident, because Odell Titsworth was not likely to be charged in the case.

Wyatt had heard of Tommy Ward's confession. He did not want to take the case merely to enter a plea of guilty. He knew the Ward family was poor; a court-appointed attorney could do that. So he went to talk to Tommy Ward. He went back several times, questioning Tommy in the jail about why he had made the taped confession. Tommy told him his account of the dream, of the questioning by

Gary Rogers and Dennis Smith. He insisted that he hadn't done it. After three or four visits, Wyatt was not totally convinced that Ward was innocent. But he felt there was a strong possibility that he was. He decided to take the case.

Tricia, Miz Ward, and Joel went back with the $3,000 retainer. Wyatt repeated that his services would cost $25,000. He agreed that if they could not pay him in full within a year, he would take the old Ward house on Ashland Avenue, and the three acres on which it stood, in lieu of cash. The date the house would change hands, if the fee was not paid in full, would be one year to the day, on October 29, 1985.

Soon after, Don Wyatt filed a writ of habeas corpus. The suspects had been in jail for eleven days, with no charges brought against them. The district attorney would have to file formal charges, body or no body, or set them free.

The first response of the D.A.'s office was to claim that the men were being held as material witnesses in the case. But that didn't hold up in court. On November 7, twenty days after their arrests, Tommy Ward and Karl Fontenot were formally charged with robbery with a dangerous weapon; with kidnapping; with rape; and with the murder, in the first degree, of Donna Denice Haraway.

There was still no body.

TWO MEN CHARGED
IN HARAWAY CASE

announced the Ada *News* the next day.

Odell Titsworth was still in jail, but he had not been charged. District Attorney Bill Peterson went to great lengths to explain to the public why.

"After an extensive investigation by the officers of the Ada Police Department, the Pontotoc County Sheriff's Department, the Oklahoma State Bureau of Investigation, and the District Attorney's Office, Odell Titsworth has been eliminated as a suspect in the Donna Haraway case," Peterson stated. He said Titsworth was still being held in jail on charges in an unrelated assault-and-battery case.

A broken arm suffered by Titsworth in the unrelated incident two days before the disappearance of Denice Haraway was one of the main factors used to rule him out as a suspect, the *News* reported to the people of Ada. According to Peterson, although both Ward and Fontenot implicated Titsworth as having a major part in the crime, Titsworth had been ruled out for three main reasons.

"First, Ward and Fontenot said Titsworth had on a short-sleeve shirt the night of the crime and had no scars or tattoos or anything wrong with his arm, when in fact he is heavily tattooed on both arms from his knuckles to his elbows. Titsworth had a cast on his left arm from wrist to shoulder at that time. Medical records and police reports show his arm was broken two days prior to Haraway's abduction," Peterson said.

"Secondly, statements by Ward and Fontenot implicating Titsworth include actions allegedly done by him which would not have been physically possible with an arm in a cast or with a broken arm had the cast been removed. Third, Karl Fontenot was unable to pick Titsworth out of a photo lineup.

"Titsworth's medical record, along with witnesses' statements, establish his whereabouts, his actions, and his physical condition on April 28, 1984. All these facts and other factors which cannot be released at this time indicate Titsworth is not a suspect in the commission of this crime," Peterson said.

The news of the murder charges swept Ada like a verbal tornado, swirling, doubling back upon itself. Some people wondered why it had taken so long to bring the charges. "Because they can't find the body," other people answered, and wondered how you could even bring murder charges without a body. Still others, aware of Odell Titsworth's reputation, felt the police had cleared the wrong man. But most of the town could only assume the police knew what they were doing: that Ward and Fontenot were the guilty ones, because they had confessed.

The formal charges filed against the pair read as follows:

In the name and by the authority of the State of Oklahoma, William N. Peterson, District Attorney for the 22nd District, comes into court and states upon this affidavit that the above-named defendants, Thomas Jesse Ward and Karl Allen Fontenot, on or about the 28th day of April, 1984, in Pontotoc County, State of Oklahoma, did commit the offense of:

COUNT I

ROBBERY WITH A DANGEROUS WEAPON: That is to say, the said defendants, Thomas Jesse Ward and Karl Allen Fontenot, acting together and in concert each with the other, on or about the 28th day of April, 1984, in Pontotoc County, State of Oklahoma, did unlawfully, wrongfully and feloniously rob one Donna Denice Haraway, by wrongfully taking and carrying away certain money belonging to McAnally's and in the possession of said Donna Denice Haraway, and in her immediate presence, without her consent and against her will, said robbery being accomplished by said defendants with the use of a certain dangerous weapon, to-wit: a knife with a long, sharp pointed blade, and which they used to menace and threaten the said Donna Denice Haraway, with harm if she resisted, and by said assault, threats and menace did put the said Donna Denice Haraway in fear of immediate and unlawful injury to her person and overcame all her resistance, and while so intimidating her did wrongfully take and obtain from her the money aforesaid, and

COUNT II

KIDNAPPING: That is to say, the said defendants, Thomas Jesse Ward and Karl Allen Fontenot, acting together and in concert each with the other on or about the 28th day of April, 1984, in Pontotoc County, State of Oklahoma, did unlawfully, willfully and feloniously, without lawful authority, forcibly seize, kidnap and confine one Donna Denice Haraway from a place in Pontotoc County, Oklahoma, to-wit: 2727 East Arlington, in the City of Ada, with the unlawful and felonious intent on the part of the said defendants to cause the said Donna Denice Haraway to be secretly confined and imprisoned in this State against her will, and

COUNT III

RAPE, FIRST DEGREE: That is to say, the said defendants, Thomas Jesse Ward and Karl Allen Fontenot, acting together and in concert each with the other on or about the 28th day of April, 1984, in Pontotoc County, State of Oklahoma, did unlawfully, willfully and feloniously with the use of force and violence and by means of threats of immediate and great bodily harm to one Donna Denice Haraway, a female person not the wife of the said defendant, overcome all resistance on the part of said Donna Denice Haraway, and did rape, ravish, and carnally know and have sexual intercourse with the said female, against her will and consent, said defendants being over the age of 18, and

COUNT IV

MURDER IN THE FIRST DEGREE: That is to say, the said defendants, Thomas Jesse Ward and Karl Allen Fontenot, acting together and in concert each with the other on or about the 28th day of April, 1984, in Pontotoc County, State of Oklahoma, did unlawfully, willfully and feloniously, with malice aforethought, without authority of law, effect the death of Donna Denice Haraway by stabbing, slashing, cutting her with a certain knife, to-wit: a 5 to 6" lock blade knife, thereby inflicting certain mortal wounds in the body of said Donna Denice Haraway, from which mortal wounds the same Donna Denice Haraway did languish and die on the 28th day of April, 1984, contrary to the form of the statutes made and provided and against the peace and dignity of the State of Oklahoma.

The charges were signed by the district attorney, and by Gary Rogers of the OSBI.

The next day a short bill of particulars was added to the charges. It stated that

1. The murder was especially heinous, atrocious, or cruel;
2. The murder was committed for the purpose of avoiding or preventing a lawful arrest or prosecution;

3. There existed a probability that the defendants would commit criminal acts of violence that would constitute a continuing threat to society.

The purpose of this list of aggravating circumstances, under Oklahoma law, was to permit the district attorney to seek the death
penalty.

For three weeks the family of Tommy Ward had been hearing that this
day might come; Tommy had told Tricia in his first phone call from
the jail: they said he would get the death penalty. Still, Tricia and Bud,
Joel and Miz Ward, Bud's parents Maxine and C.L., all the others,
could not believe it. Over and over the question rattled through their
minds, like the freights going in and out of the feed mill: there was no
body, no weapon, no bones, no bloodstains; nothing. How did they
know for sure that Denice Haraway was dead?

On Thursday, November 8, at 2 P.M., Tommy Ward and Karl Fontenot
appeared in court before Special District Judge John Miller, to plead
to the charges.

Ward, accompanied by attorney Mike Addicott of Wyatt & Addicott, pleaded not guilty to all counts.

Fontenot, who still did not have a lawyer, did not plead, pending
the appointment of an attorney by the court.

Both men were ordered held without bail.

Don Wyatt moved to have Ward released on bail. It was largely a
pro forma motion, in behalf of a client who had pleaded not guilty;
the attorney knew that the Wards had no money with which to post
bond; he knew, too, from the talk of the town, that if Tommy Ward
were released, he might very well be killed by one or more of the angry people of Ada.

The bail hearing was held on Thursday, November 15—a week before Thanksgiving. Judge Miller denied bail. The story was the lead
headline in the Ada *News* on Friday. Beside the headline was a large
photograph of Tommy Ward being led from the county jail to the bail
hearing. He was wearing white prisoner's coveralls. His hands were

handcuffed behind him. His arms were being held by two armed sheriff's deputies in uniform.

The second paragraph of the story quoted attorney Wyatt indirectly, as follows:

> Wyatt said at this time no body has been found to be in existence and no evidence has been produced indicating a crime has been committed. Ward is being held solely on his recounting of a dream which the prosecution is calling a confession, Wyatt said.

That was the first mention in the *News* of the word "dream" in connection with the Haraway case. The police had never mentioned it to the media. The reporter writing the story pressed no further for an explanation.

Tricia and Bud were at home when they read the story in the paper that evening. They had not expected Tommy to get bail; the denial was no surprise. Suddenly, without warning, Tricia, in a rare outburst of temper, swung around and punched Bud viciously in the shoulder.

Bud grabbed his throbbing shoulder and stepped back. "What was that for?" he wanted to know.

Tricia was in a rage. She showed him a sentence farther down in the story; it was quoting Assistant District Attorney Chris Ross.

"Ward should be denied bail because of evidence against him, the fact he has not been permanently employed in years and no one has come forward to claim his reliability, Ross said."

Tricia apologized to Bud. She hadn't been angry at him. She had just exploded in frustration.

"No one has come forward!" she said. "How can he say that? We put up the house! We hired a lawyer for twenty-five thousand dollars!"

The story went on to describe how Don Wyatt had asked the judge to place a gag order on the prosecutor, because, "He is trying the case in the papers and on television." The judge refused the gag order, but instructed the prosecution to review the code of ethics and to follow it.

The judge then denied bail: because the charge was murder, and because the district attorney had said he would seek a sentence of death.

The new Pontotoc County Jail, built in 1972 to replace the former one on the top floor of the courthouse, was situated across the lawn from the courthouse, across the street from City Hall and the police station. The jail was built one story high, a long, narrow rectangle, with walls of solid cement. There were no windows. There were two doors, made of steel. One door was at one end of the rectangle, facing onto a small side street. It was for the use of sheriff's deputies, the jailers. The other door faced the lawn and the courthouse. This was the door for visitors.

Visitors sat in a small, dark room the size of a clothes closet; inmates were brought from their cells and led into a similar closet-sized room on the other side of a wall; between the two rooms was a narrow glass window, about four inches across, ten inches high. Through this thick-paned window the prisoner and his visitor could see each other. Beneath the window was a small opening covered on both sides by metal strips with holes in them. Through these holes the inmate and the visitor could talk; they usually had to half shout to hear one another.

Visiting was allowed only on Sunday, from 1 P.M. to 3 P.M., and only for ten minutes. There was only the one visiting room. People who came to visit an inmate had to give the inmate's name, and their name, and their relationship, to a jailer, speaking through a door that led to a jail office. They then had to wait their turn. The waiting room was a cubicle about four feet by five feet. In it was a small metal table and two folding chairs. Most of the people who came to visit were women and children whose husbands or fathers were in the jail; or the mothers and girlfriends of young men who had been picked up for being rowdy on Saturday night. Often, by one o'clock Sunday afternoon there were ten or twelve people waiting to see someone in the jail; often, many of them were pregnant. There were only the two seats in the waiting room; the others could stand against the walls, or outside, or sit on the pavement or the lawn, if it wasn't too cold or too hot or raining or snowing. Between the small waiting room and the small visiting room was an orange metal door that ended two inches above the floor. Through this two-inch gap the words being shouted to the inmate by the visitor could easily be heard. There was no privacy.

On the day she first heard Tommy had been arrested, Tricia tried to see him at the jail. She was told by Bob Kaiser, a former major league baseball pitcher who was the Pontotoc County sheriff, that Tommy could not yet have visitors. Tricia, Bud, and Miz Ward went to the jail that first Sunday, visiting day. Again they were told that Tommy could not have visitors. Not until the charges were filed against him were they allowed their ten minutes a week.

The first time they saw him, peering out through the narrow glass window, his whole body was trembling uncontrollably; he resembled an animal in a shelter. He could hardly speak. He cried most of the time. They could only look at him, tears in the eyes of Tricia and Miz Ward as well: at his long hair, grown back since his haircut in the spring; at the white prison coveralls. When he could mumble coherent sentences, it was to repeat what he had said from the beginning: that he hadn't done it; that he had told the police his dream, and they had said it really happened; but that it wasn't true, all it was was a dream. Then there was a knock on the door behind him, and he was taken away; the ten minutes were up.

The second visit was much the same, Tommy sobbing most of the time. They brought him cigarettes; that was all he wanted from the outside world. The third time, he talked more. He made a statement that made Tricia feel a little better. "They may kill me," he said. "But they can only kill my body. The Lord will have my soul."

To Tricia this meant two things: it reaffirmed her belief in his innocence; and it comforted her that, with that outlook, he would not do something foolish in jail; he would not try to kill himself.

While the entire Ward family rallied around Tommy—letters of faith arriving from Melva in California, from Melvin stationed in Virginia, Miz Ward driving down from Tulsa every Sunday to visit him, three hours each way, sometimes with Joel, sometimes with Joice—such was not the case with Karl Fontenot. His family deserted him.

He had been born in Ada twenty years before, the second youngest of five children; he grew up in filthy poverty. His father, an alcoholic, left the family when Karl was twelve, going off in the direction of Texas and Louisiana. Karl had not heard from him in eight years, did not know if he was alive or dead. To feed her family, his mother, Dottie, would go to a fast-food restaurant where she knew the owner—it sold kiddie hamburgers five for a dollar in those days—and would buy five hamburgers, and then ask for credit for the dollar.

One day when he was sixteen, Karl and his mother were in the car, his mother driving. They got into a minor accident. Dottie Fontenot got out to look at the damage. As she did, she was struck and killed by a speeding car, in front of Karl's eyes.

The death of Dottie Fontenot led to the breakup of the family. Karl dropped out of high school, began to live in the streets, to sleep wherever he could. One of his brothers moved to California. Another of his brothers went to jail; his sister-in-law remained in Ada, but wanted nothing to do with Karl. Neither did his older sister, who was married. Karl liked his younger sister, who was going to high school at nearby Byng, but the older sister kept them apart.

His reputation on the streets was that of being "weird." Few could explain what they meant by that, except that it didn't mean violent. No one who knew him thought he could hurt anyone. Some said he was "weird" in that he would suddenly laugh at the wrong things, laugh when nothing was funny. But nothing worse than that. He was like a puppy dog who hung around looking for friends, people said.

And Tommy Ward, always eager to find fishing companions, had become his friend.

When Karl was arrested in the Haraway case, no one came to see him. Instead, his two sisters moved away from Ada, to California, without a visit, or a phone call, or a note.

Alone in his cell in the city jail, Karl hailed any policeman passing down the corridor and struck up a conversation, in an attempt to pass the time. He made up stories about where Denice Haraway's body was. When the police went to look, he said he was only making it up;

he didn't know where the body was; he didn't do it. The police felt he was enjoying whatever attention he could get.

An Ada woman who was a social worker when Karl was a child recalled what his early home life had been like. "They came up here from Louisiana," she said. "His father was a killer at Wyckham packing plant. A lot of those killer guys are pretty demented. At that time the way they would kill the animals, they would just hit them on the head and slit their throats and wade around in the blood. I had occasion to go to their home a number of times, because they were turned in for child abuse, child neglect. The home was utter chaos. Absolutely filthy. About as many dogs in the house as there were people. The whole place was full: a small apartment over in the north side of Ada, down an alley; a typical welfare village. They didn't have a chance in the world, the kids. They were born into deprivation and nobody gave them anything. The mother was young; she had no skills as a housewife. I remember going over there and her crying about how mean the husband was to the children. He was sadistic. There were incidents involving animals. Sexual relationships with animals in front of the family. Dog feces, kitten feces all over the place. The mother would leave all the time, and then come back. I guess she had no place else to go. It was as bad a situation as I had ever seen. I recommended to the court that the children be removed from the parents. The court didn't see fit to do so."

Nearly twenty years later, because he had no money, and no family to put up money, a different court assigned Karl Fontenot a lawyer.

The attorneys of Ada had made it clear that they wanted no part of the case. Judge Miller chose an experienced criminal lawyer from adjacent Seminole County, George Butner, to represent Fontenot. Butner visited Karl in the jail; Karl told him he was innocent; that he knew nothing about the Haraway case, despite the tape he had made.

In court, Fontenot, too, pleaded not guilty. Judge Miller set January 7, 1985, as the date for a preliminary hearing. It would determine if there was enough evidence to bring Tommy Ward and Karl Fontenot to trial.

The Ada *Evening News* is housed in a two-story white stone building on Broadway, a block from Main Street. On the street level are the cir-

culation offices and the advertising offices. To find the news department you walk up a flight of stairs, and turn left.

At a desk near the middle of the newsroom sits Dorothy Hogue. She
is a young woman, a reporter. She has written all the stories in the Ada
News concerning the Haraway case, from the night of the abduction, to
the arrest of the suspects, to the denial of bail for Tommy Ward.

If you ask her, she will tell you that she believes the suspects are
guilty.

"They confessed," she says, "so they must be guilty."

A few days before, a request had come in the mail for a set of Xeroxed clippings of all the stories the paper had printed about the Haraway case. Enclosed with the request was a twenty-dollar bill. Ms.
Hogue had shown the letter to her managing editor, Tony Pippen,
who instructed her to send the clippings. The return address was to a
man in the state of Washington.

"We assumed it was a friend of the family, who wants to know
what's going on," Ms. Hogue said. "But who knows? It could be the
girl herself."

She said this not sixty seconds after she said she believed the suspects were guilty of murder.

The reporter thought a moment about what she had said. Then
she added, "Even if Tommy Ward gets off, he can't live in this town
anymore. People believe he did it. If he shows himself in the streets,
he'll probably be killed."

As a precaution, Ms. Hogue told the police about the request for
clippings from the man in Washington. Dennis Smith queried the
Washington state police about him. No response came back, meaning
that the computers in Washington state had no criminal information,
under that name, about the man. How he had heard about the case,
why he was so interested remained unknown.

Two years earlier, a new business had begun to boom in Ada—the
small-loan business. In Oklahoma, loans of $1,000 or more, known as
Grade A loans, are handled by banks. Grade B loans, of $500 or less,
are made by finance companies. Until the early 1980s there were no
finance companies in Ada; now, suddenly, there were eight: walk-in

storefronts where a person could borrow $50 or $100 or $300, some-
times with a cursory credit check, sometimes on a signature. The interest on these small, short-term loans was high. But they were a
useful source of quick money when the rent was due and the month's
wages had been spent; when a tuition payment was needed at the college; when an elderly person had unexpected medical bills. All at once
a number of companies had found Ada to be a fertile field for the
quick-loan business.

One new and frequent visitor to the loan companies was Bud Wolf.
He found them useful when his paycheck at the feed mill ran short.
November was one of those times; some of October's bills had yet to
be paid, what with the Indian foster boys making two more mouths
to feed. Bud went to his favorite company and got a loan. While he
was there, the clerk asked him to fill out an extra form.

"We're holding a lottery," she said. "We're going to give away a
Thanksgiving turkey to the lucky winner."

Bud filled out the form, as he had the loan application, with his
real name, Charles L. Wolf Jr. The woman looked at it. Across the top,
she wrote: "BUD."

"I hope you folks win the turkey," the woman said. "You're the
most deserving people in town."

It was not a sentiment they had been hearing much lately.

On the Monday before Thanksgiving, Tricia got a call from the
woman at the loan company. "Congratulations!" the woman said.
"You just won our lottery."

"Do I get a hundred thousand dollars?" Tricia asked.

"I'm afraid not," the woman said. "But you do get a free turkey."

Tricia was very pleased to win the turkey.

She did not believe that luck had had much to do with it.

The next day, Bud and Tricia received their monthly telephone bill.
It was $200. All those calls to Tulsa, to talk to Miz Ward and Joel about
Tommy's case. The loan money would not cover it. They decided to
sell their microwave in order to keep their telephone.

Thanksgiving Day in Ada was sunny and mild. Some of the trees still
were clinging to red and brown and orange leaves. Not a single car

was parked on Main Street; everyone was at home, cooking, preparing to feast, or to visit relatives.

In the morning, while the loan company's gift turkey was roasting, Tricia took the foster boys to the social worker, who would return them to their real mother for the holiday. Then she and Bud and the kids piled into the car with the warm turkey and went to Bud's parents' house, as they did every year.

Maxine had spent most of two days cooking. The table was laden with a ham in addition to the free turkey; with yams from Maxine's garden at the budding farm in Happyland, with mashed potatoes, corn, string beans, dressing, pickles, sweet iced tea—all the Wolfs are serious Baptists; they don't touch alcohol—and half a dozen homemade pies in three flavors: cherry, apple, and peach. On the floor in a corner of the kitchen where the whole family ate—the small house had no dining room—was a large brown paper sack filled with eighteen pounds of pecans that C.L. had had cracked by the pecan cracker. Maxine had had too much to do; she never got around to making pecan pies.

The three Wolf children—Rhonda, Buddy, and Laura Sue—took turns saying grace, thanking the Lord for the food. Little Laura Sue asked God in her prayer to watch over Uncle Tommy.

After dinner, as they called the afternoon meal, they all rode out to Happyland—unavoidably passing McAnally's on the way—so Maxine and C.L. could feed the chickens, the two sheep, the five goats. Then they returned to the house and ate some more, buffet style.

In mid-afternoon, Bud and Tricia excused themselves; they were going over to the jail, they said, to see if they could get to visit Tommy. It being Thanksgiving and all.

They returned after fifteen minutes. They had not been allowed to see him. Only on Sundays, they'd been told.

The conversation turned, as it had on and off all day, to Tommy. Then Maxine asked about Karl Fontenot; she didn't know him. Tricia said she had met him only once. It was one night early that fall, she recalled. Tommy and Karl were riding down to Ada from Norman when Tommy's motorcycle broke down. Tommy and Karl walked several miles, then knocked on the door of a house near the road and asked if they could use the phone. Tommy telephoned Tricia, asked if she could come and get him. They all piled into the car. It was almost midnight when they got to the place. Tommy was in the house, chatting amiably with the man who had let him use the phone.

When they got back to Ada, Tommy asked Tricia if it would be okay for his friend Karl to spend the night. Tricia had an instant, funny feeling about Karl; he seemed strange to her somehow, though she could not say why. But he was Tommy's friend, so she said sure, he could sleep on the living room sofa.

Soon the household was asleep. And Tricia had a nightmare. She dreamed that Karl Fontenot was standing at the foot of her bed, looking down at her eerily. She woke up and opened her eyes. There was no one at the foot of her bed.

She went back to sleep. She had the same dream again: that Fontenot was standing there, staring at her. She woke up with her heart pounding. Again there was no one there. This time she got out of bed, walked quietly to the door, peered into the living room. Karl was fast asleep on the sofa.

Tricia had no idea what was causing the dreams. There was something weird about Karl, she felt, but she couldn't say what it was.

Now on this Thanksgiving afternoon they talked of Tommy again, recounted for each other again all the discrepancies they saw in the case against him: how Odell Titsworth had been cleared; how the house had been burned down the year before; how there was no body, no proof that the girl was even dead.

"I keep hearing she's been seen in Texas, or Oklahoma City," Tricia said. "Mildred Gandy told Maxine she'd seen her alive out at the Brook Trailer Park two days after she disappeared."

They spoke of what they felt was the clinching argument: that they knew where Tommy had been on the night of April 28, that Tommy had been at home.

"Joice says he was at home with her and the kids all night," Miz Ward said in her soft voice.

Home at the time was the house on Ashland Avenue. In the spring, at the time of Denice Haraway's disappearance, not only had Miz

Ward been living there, and Tommy, and Kay, who was not yet married, but also Joice and Robert Cavins and their three small children.

"Joice says she remembers she had a headache that night," Miz Ward said. "She asked Tommy to help her put the kids to bed. That was about eight o'clock. And she stayed up for a while and then went to bed, and Tommy never left the house."

"Robert says he come home from work about eleven-twenty that night," Tricia put in. "And he found Tommy asleep on the sofa. So how could he have done what they say he done?"

"Robert remembers it was that night," Miz Ward said, "because after he was home for a while he heard water running somewhere. He checked all the faucets and none of them was on. But still he heard water running. So he checked under the house and there was a leak. They'd put in new pipes the week before, and they was leaking."

"He didn't know where the switch was to turn off the water," Tricia said. "So he woke up Tommy to show him where it was. And then the two of them worked under the house till four in the morning, getting them pipes fixed."

"When we come back from Lawton Sunday night," Miz Ward said, "me and Kay, there was water all over the yard from where the pipes had broke. And up in the bathroom sink there was Tommy's jeans and T-shirt all balled up, all wet and covered with mud from crawlin' under the house."

"So how can they say he killed that girl?" Tricia said. "I don't see what they even got him in jail for. Them tapes don't check out, and he was at home that night, and that girl could be alive somewhere. It just ain't right."

Suddenly she quieted. "Listen to me," she said, "runnin' my mouth at ninety-to-nothin'."

It was her favorite expression, a description of out-of-control activity. When her kids were acting up, they'd be running through the house at ninety-to-nothin'. Joice's kids were always going ninety-to-nothin'. When she woke up from a nightmare, like the one about Karl looking down at her, she could feel her heart inside her going ninety-to-nothin'.

"But it makes me so mad!" she said. "You know?"

As she talked, the message board of the Church of Christ, directly across the street from Maxine and C.L.'s house, was visible through the glass storm door. It proclaimed, in black capital letters, the sermon that would be delivered on Sunday:

ALL THIS AND HEAVEN PLUS

6

GHOSTS

On April 28, 1909—seventy-five years, to the day, before Denice Haraway disappeared—a woman named Nettie V. Brown set off on a journey across the rugged new state of Oklahoma. She was accompanied by her husband, her stepson, and her niece. The journey, made in two wagons drawn by teams of horses and mules, was to prove vitally important to those involved in the Haraway case.

Nettie Brown was married in Shelbina, Missouri, in 1904, to T. H. Brown; she was twenty-nine years old; her husband was fifty-three; he had had several children by a previous marriage; one of these was A. P. "Pete" Brown, who was fifteen. After five years, the marriage began to come apart; Nettie Brown instituted divorce proceedings against her husband.

While the divorce proceedings were pending, Nettie went to Arkansas City, Kansas. So, too, did her stepson Pete, now twenty. They were arrested in bed together, at night, by the police. They pleaded guilty to charges of illegal cohabitation, and they paid a fine.

Nettie Brown was advised by her attorney that her adultery in Arkansas City would defeat her divorce suit, would make it impossible for her to win any money from her husband. Soon after, Nettie and her husband were reconciled; Nettie withdrew her suit for divorce; they lived together again as man and wife. They decided to move from their home in Osage County, Oklahoma, to Missouri. T. H. Brown converted all his property into money, except for some household goods, wagons, horses, and mules. On April 10, 1909, he drew all of his money out of the bank—a bit over $2,500. On April 28, Nettie and T.H., along with his son Pete and her niece, Ruby Waters, fourteen, left home.

On the third night of the journey they camped at a place called Aikens's ranch. Strangers visited the camp that night. They saw all four of the travelers alive and well. After the strangers left, no one besides his wife, his stepson, and the niece ever saw T. H. Brown again.

When they awakened the next morning, T.H. was nowhere to be found. Ruby asked Pete where his father was; Pete said he didn't know; he seemed to have left in the night. He would have had to have walked, because both wagons and all the horses and mules were there. When they resumed their journey, Nettie told her niece to tell people T.H. had gone to Kansas to look for a place for them to live. Along the way, she told other people that her husband had run off, and had left her destitute. But she began to make a series of bank deposits under assumed names. The money added up to about $2,500.

Some months later, Nettie Brown was accused of murdering her husband, despite the fact that his body had not been found, and there was no definitive proof that he was dead.

Pete Brown turned state's evidence. He said that when they learned Nettie would not get her divorce, they decided to kill his father. He took law officers, in August, to the site where they had camped the third night of the journey. The place was grown up with grass and weeds, but they found a spot where there had been a fire. The spot had been covered with loose dirt about six inches deep; the dirt extended for five or six feet. Beneath the dirt they found ashes; in the ashes they found bones, teeth, suspender buckles. There they had killed his father, Pete Brown said.

At her murder trial, Nettie Brown denied that she had killed her husband. Technology at the time was not advanced enough to determine if these were in fact his bones; there was no definitive proof that T. H. Brown was dead. Yet Nettie Brown was convicted. Her attorney appealed, on the ground that the state had failed to prove the corpus delicti.

There is a common misconception that the phrase "corpus delicti" in a murder case refers to the presence of a body. It doesn't. The phrase means "body of the crime"; it refers to the criminal act and those involved in it. Nettie Brown's attorneys argued that in the absence of definitive proof that T. H. Brown was dead, the state had not proved that the crime of murder had been committed; had not proved the corpus delicti. Such proof is a requirement for every conviction.

The appeal in the case of Nettie V. Brown vs. the State of Oklahoma was ruled on, on May 18, 1913. A judge named Furman wrote the opinion, which was concurred in by Judges Doyle and Armstrong. Judge Furman wrote, in part:

> Counsel in their brief say: "The facts testified to in this case are not sufficient in law to establish the corpus delicti of the crime charged." This contention is based upon the rule of the common law that there can be no conviction for murder unless the body of the deceased or some vital part thereof has been found and identified. This rule is based upon an ancient arbitrary act of Parliament. It was brought to America in the days of the colonies . . .
>
> The law in Oklahoma upon this subject is as follows . . .
>
> No person can be convicted of murder or manslaughter or of aiding suicide, unless the death of the person alleged to have been killed and the fact of the killing by the accused are each established as independent facts beyond a reasonable doubt . . . A conviction cannot be had upon the testimony of an accomplice unless he be corroborated by such other evidence as tends to connect the defendant with the commission of the offense . . .
>
> To prove corpus delicti, it is not necessary that the corpus delicti should be established by direct and positive proof. It may be proved as well by circumstantial evidence, if on all the evidence the jury are satisfied of defendant's guilt beyond a reasonable doubt . . .
>
> It has been considered a rule that no person should be convicted of murder unless the body of the deceased has been found; and a very great judge says, "I would never convict any person of murder or manslaughter, unless the fact were proven to be done, or at least the body be found dead." But this rule, it seems, must be taken with some qualifications; and circum-

stances may be sufficiently strong to show the fact of the murder, though the body has never been found.

Having cited these assorted legal opinions, the court then turned to the specifics of the Nettie Brown case.

The evidence is positive and direct that T. H. Brown was last seen by disinterested persons in company with appellant and A. P. Brown at night at a camp near Aikens' ranch in Osage County. There is not a scintilla of evidence in the record that he has ever been seen or heard of since. The statement that he went away during the night and left appellant is an insult to human intelligence and human experience. He only had about $2,500 . . . Appellant is proven to have had this amount of money in her possession when she reached Missouri. Where did she get this money? Why would T. H. Brown leave the camp at night in a penniless condition and on foot? . . . There is not a semblance of reason in the statement that T. H. Brown walked off at night and mysteriously disappeared and has never been heard of since. No possible cause for his leaving in any manner appears in the record . . .

The court went on to question why a six-foot fire would have been built at the campsite on an April night, were it not for the purpose of burning the body. It continued:

Even under the strictest rule of the common law requiring the identification of the body of the deceased, this was never necessary where the deceased had been killed by being burned to death. We are not willing to establish the doctrine in Oklahoma that there can be no conviction for murder in any case unless the body of the deceased is recognized and identified by direct and positive evidence. Such a rule would make murder safe and would place a premium upon the most vile and brutal kind of assassination. All that the murderer would have to do to escape punishment would be to so mutilate and disfigure the body of his victim, which could easily be done, as to make identification impossible . . . This court will never consent to the establishment of a doctrine in Oklahoma which would result in such monstrous consequences.

The only just and logical position consistent with the safety of society and the sanctity of human life which courts can assume is that the corpus delicti may be proven by circumstantial evidence.

District Attorney Bill Peterson still wanted the police, the OSBI, civilian searchers, *somebody*, to find Denice Haraway's body; between the body and the confessions of Ward and Fontenot, a conviction would be easy, despite the apparent falsehoods on the tapes. But there it was in the austere lawbooks: you didn't need a body. Not if the circumstantial evidence was strong enough. It was a wonderful opinion, the Nettie Brown case, he felt. Sensible. Logical. Two qualities Bill Peterson felt were the tenets of his own work, the underpinnings of his own approach to the law.

There were parts of the opinion that were eloquent—"grandiloquent" would be a better word—in an old-fashioned way. So fond of the case did Peterson become that he at times read aloud from the opinion to his fellows, once uncharacteristically proclaiming it loudly in the courthouse halls.

Peterson did not find any "no-body" cases occurring in Oklahoma in the succeeding decade; nor in the next six decades thereafter. Not until 1983 did another "no-body" case turn up in Oklahoma law.

It was called the Rawlings case. He knew of it; many people did. A man in Oklahoma County had been accused of killing his wife, transporting her body in his car to an airplane, taking it up in the airplane, and tossing it into the ocean. Her body had never been recovered. Despite this, he was convicted of murder.

The major evidence was traces of blood found in the trunk of his car and in the airplane. It could not be proved that the blood had been his wife's. Still, the jury had convicted. The Brown case had laid the groundwork.

Sitting at his desk amid the lawbooks, Bill Peterson realized that the Haraway case was different from both of those earlier cases. In the first there had been bones; in the second there had been blood. In the Haraway case, thus far, no physical evidence whatever had been found. He desperately wanted a bone, a hank of hair, something. Still, ". . . the corpus delicti may be proven by circumstantial evidence."

"We know you didn't do it," a uniformed Ada police officer said to Tommy Ward in the county jail, "but we're going to nail you for it anyway."

This according to Tommy, who told of it to Tricia during one of her Sunday visits early in December.

Tommy went on to say that the officer's remark had been overheard by a black inmate in the next cell; and that the inmate told Tommy he would testify to what he had heard. But, Tommy said, this second comment was overheard by police, who took the black inmate away for a few hours. When he was brought back, he told Tommy the police had warned him that if he repeated what he had heard, he would never see the light of day.

Soon after, the black inmate was removed from the county jail: to freedom or to the state prison at McAlester, Tommy didn't know.

What Tommy said stoked the bile burning in Tricia's belly, in Bud's, in Miz Ward's, in all those in the family and close to it who believed Tommy was innocent. It reinforced their belief that the police were out to "get" Tommy.

Kay Ward Garrett's new husband was a pleasant, blond young man named Billy Garrett. Just out of high school, he worked at his parents' grocery store, hoped one day to go to art school. His simple drawings and washes showed a strong sense of color and design. Whether he would ever be able to afford art school was another matter. He entered a competition for an art scholarship in a neighboring county; he won high praise from the judges, but no scholarship.

One day Billy was sitting in a diner with a guy he knew. The guy had a relative who had been convicted some time before of writing bad checks. Now she was facing similar charges again. Her name was Terry McCartney. According to the relative, Terry had been approached by the police regarding the Haraway case; she had been told the charges against her would be dropped if she testified against Tommy Ward; but she would get fifteen years in prison if she refused to cooperate.

Billy told of the incident to Tricia and Bud and Miz Ward, who relayed it to Don Wyatt. The relative apparently didn't know that Billy Garrett was now Tommy Ward's brother-in-law.

The family's emotions boiled again at the apparent tactics of the police; what Terry McCartney might have to say about the Haraway case, they had no idea.

Where was Denice Haraway? What had they done with her body? The question still plagued Dennis Smith as he sat at the desk in his office, the walls bare except for framed certificates from detective courses he had taken; the only color was provided by a plaque someone had made for him; pasted on it, from a magazine photograph, were the characters from *Hill Street Blues*.

They had the taped confessions; the charges had been filed, all of them: robbery, kidnapping, rape, murder. Still, he wanted the body.

Suddenly he had an illumination. He climbed into an unmarked squad car parked behind the station, and he drove out to the area of the power plant and the packing plant. Sure enough, there were sewer lines there. He pulled the tops off several manholes, and peered in. They were deep enough to hold a body.

He leaned down into an opening, peered closer. A ten-inch-wide sewer pipe ran beneath the surface, its openings in the manhole pits. A body could not pass through that pipe.

Discouraged, he replaced the manhole cover. He returned to the car and drove back toward the station. As he did, he had another thought. More than seven months had passed. The body would have decomposed long ago. Perhaps, hidden in the manhole, the body could have lain there till it decomposed, then been flushed through the sewers.

Back at his desk, his excitement rising, he telephoned the sewer department. He explained his theory. He wanted to know where the decomposed remains would have emerged if that had happened.

That could not have happened, he was told. If a body had been shoved down a manhole, it would have blocked the lines, clogged up the system. The water and other effluents would have backed up. The blockage would have shown on the gauges at the sewer department. An inspector would have been sent out to see what the problem was. None of that had occurred.

Disappointed, Smith hung up the phone. He was back to square one yet again with regard to the body. And the preliminary hearing was only weeks away.

Still in solitary confinement at the county jail, Tommy Ward began taking comfort in religion. As a boy he had gone to church often with Tricia and the others; sometimes he had even gone alone. As a young teenager he was still a churchgoer. Then he had fallen away from religion. Now, allowed nothing to read but a Bible, he began to read it regularly, to find in it the strength with which to endure his imprisonment.

He also spent time drawing and writing. Don Wyatt had asked him to set down his account of everything that had happened with regard to the case. The attorney did not know how trustworthy, how useful, the account would be. But he thought it might help. So Tommy wrote. He wrote his account of the questioning by Dennis Smith and Gary Rogers the day he made the taped confession. He continued with his account of what happened next.

> I bet the guys that did do it is setting back laughing saying, Look At These Idiots Taking The Blame for something we did. Then they will probly go out and do it again to see if they cant get some more innosent people to take their blame. This is the most stupidst thing that ever happened to me. Wouldnt they rather put away the people that did do it instead of an innosent man. What are they tired of the publick getting down their throughts about it so they get a innicent man and put him away so they can show the public that they are bad or something. What are they tired of looking for who did it so they pick up a innicent man and put him away so they can

close the books about it and get the publick off their backs about it.

So getting back to what has happend. The next day the judge came over and ask me if I had anything to say. And I told him that, cant they see that this was a dream and I lied about this. They are getting a uproar over nothing. God knows I didn't do it and this was just a dream after people comeing up to me saying I look like one of the guys and Mr. Smith questioning me caused me to have a dream about it. So then I came back to my cell. Then Mr. Smith and another officer came over. And I said, Now cant you see that this was a dream. And that I didnt do it. Then Mr. Smith said, if you think this was so much a dream, why is Carol telling the same story. I knew then Mr. Smith told him about my dream. I said, you probly got in his face and told him about my dream. His face turnd red as a beat. Then I said, you probly told him you did this and you did this until you told him about my dream. Cause I know Carol dont know nothing about my dream until you told him. I couldn't beleve that Carol didnt tell him were he was that night. Then he asked me what kind of guy I thought Carol was. I said, he is prity stupid, to listen to you and you tell him about my dream. Then I said, what did you do. Scair him and said you was going to do something to him if he didnt tell everything you told him to say. Then his face turned red again. Then he ask me if I ever told enyone about my dream. I told him, no. I never told no one about my dream cause it was a dream. I dont go around telling people about my dreams. Unless they are a prity neet dream then I tell someone about it.

Then he ask me how Carol acted when he got drunk or high. I told him Carol always gose to bed. Then he said, he acts like he dont know what's going on. Then I said, I bet he is a prity crazy guy to tell you everything you told him to say. Then I said I know you scaird him with something or you told him you would do something to him. Then I told him I know that you got in his face and told him about my dream. Cause he didnt know nothing about my dream. Then Mr. Smith's

face got red again. Then he grabbed me and all my buttens
came unsnapped then he grabbed my collers and jerked me
up and I fell against the wall. Then he said get him back in his
sell.

So then Mr. Baskens came over. Mr. Baskens said, Dont you
think this girls husbend would like to have a decent berrel. I
said, yes but I didn't do it. Than he said, will you show us were
shes at so we can see you innicent and put away Carol and
Odell. I said, no I dont now were she is at cause we didnt do
it. I also said, for anybody knows she might still be alive
somewere. Then the OBI agent said come on now show us
were she is at so then I thought that I could show them a place
and they would see that it was a dream. So I lied and said she
is in this ditch down by Sandy Creek. So then we went over to
the police station and got some more officers and we started
out their. So then when we got their I started thinking what if
I show them the ditch and they see shes not their and shoot
me and say I tryed to run from them. . . .

But the OBI agent said now you are going to take us
right to were shes at arnt you. I said, no cause she not their
cause it was a dream cant you see. Then the OBI agent got
mad and brought me back to jail. Then when we got back
the OBI agent ask me to come on now show us were she is at
and we started going up past the jail then I said, she might
be out by the store somewhere or she might be out near
Konowa or she might be still alive. Then I said cant you see
that this was a dream. I also said I am as innicent as you are
cant you see I didnt do it. Then he got mad and Mr Baskens
said, Im going to come up to the prison and make dam
shure you die. Then I said, if I do go to prison and they do
put me to deth they would be putting away a innicent man
just for a dream and telling a lie. Then the OBI agent backed
up to the jail. And then Mr. Baskens grabed me out. And
said get this SOB back were he belongs. Then I said, the
people that did this is probly siting back saying look at this
stupid eidiout, taking the blame for something we did. Then I
said, they will probly go do it again to see if they could put

some more innicent people away. So then I went back to
my sell.

So then the next day they had lineup and the day I found
out that Mr. Smith lied to me about what day it was when I
had my dream. Then after line up my lowyer came and talked
to me. He ask me if I did it and I told him no. Then he ask me
were I was that day I was so confused that I didnt know. Then
he said, if I did do it let him now and we would start working
on a temperany insanity case. I told him no that I didn't do it.
God knows I didnt do it then he ask me why did I say I did it
on film. That was the stupidest thing I ever did say. So then he
said you and Robert fixed the pipes. I was still confused. And
that is why I was confused cause Mr. Smith lieing to me about
what day I had my dream so then I came back to my sell.

Before I came back my lower said he would come back
tomarow to see me. So I came back to my sell and when I got
back it hit me. It seemed like the lord told my what I did that
day as soon as one of the trusties said it was Saturday April the
28 when she came up missing. I was trying to think back what
I did that Wensday. Then I rememberd what all I did that day.
And I was excited and I ask to see my lawyer. But the jailer
said that he had already left. So then the next day I was excited
to see my lawyer so I could tell him what I did but he didnt
come. So then I went to quart and that night Mr Smith and a
nother officer came over and said, if you still think this is so
much of a dream how come we found a peice of her jawbon
down their in the birnt down house. Then I said, I didn't do it.
Then he said, you and Odell and Carol cut her up and we
found your gass kan down their were you pored gass on her
and birnt her. Then I thought Carol must have told him that.
Then I said no that I didn't have nothing to do with it. Then
he said, you stood their and watched Odell cut her up and
put her in a hole in the flor. So I lied and said, yes that Odell
cut her up and I pored gass on her and we ran. Then I said I
dont know what Im saying this was just a dream and it wasnt
in my dream. So then I came back to my sell. Then when I

came back I heard word that they found peice of her jawbone down in the birnt down house, I about died. I ask the lord is this some kind of a sign for them to find out where she was at so they could find out who did it. I ask the lord did he have me to dream this dream and this lie so they could find out who did it. Then something hit me and I knew it wasnt a jaw-bone. And I was right it was a jawbone of a animel.

So then the next day I went back to quart and the judge told me what I was charged with then he ask me if I had any-thing to say and I told hem I cant see how come they cant see that this was only a dream. So then I came back and Mr Smith came and got me and took me over to the station for finger printing. Then when I got over there Mr Baskens was takeing my prients and he said, we looked pretty funny out their dig-ging around that birnt down house when a man and a dog come walking up and said that the house had been birnt down for a long time. I about laught. But I said, now cant you see that this was a dream. Then he told me to shut up that to talk about something else if I had anything to say. . . .

Then he took me back to a sell and I heard a voice say what are you in here for. I told him that I was in here for a dream. Then he said, that when they take you to prison and hook up that hose to your arm and then they shoot a neddle in the hose and it tubes down the hose and it gose in your blood streem and you die slow. Then I told him that it wasnt going to happen to me. Cause I am going to prove my innicence. Then I told him if it dose happen that they would be killing a innicent man for having a dream. Then he ask me what Odell looked like I told him that the guy in my dream had long black hair with black framed glases and a earring in his ear. Then he said did he have any tatoos. I told him no not in my dream he didnt. I new it was Odell but I didnt tell him that I knew who it was. Then I said, I get down on my nees every night and ask the lord to forgive me for bearing false wit-nesses. Then I told him that the reason why I told them about my dream they said I flunked the test and that I knew something. And I told then that I didn't have nothing to do with it. But they cep on at me so I remembered about my dream. Then I said lord please forgive me and get me out of this mess so they can find out who did this. Then Mr Smith came back and got me and then he had a cuple offesers to bring me back.

Then I came back and sit around and I was just getting ready to eat when the jaler came and got me and said, someone's hear to see you. Every time they come back to get me I would think they seen that it was a dream and let me out. Then I went up and it was Mr. Smith he told me that some of my finger prients was messed up. So then he took me back over to the station and he told me Carol was getting priented. And then he took me back to a sell then after a little bit a officer came back with Carol and put him in a sell next to me. When he was coming back he cept on telling the officer that I told you I was lying to you. So then he put him in the sell and left.

I ask Carol what he said. He said, I lied to them. I said about what. He said, I lied to them about Me Odell and Tommy doing it. Then I ask him why he lied for. He said, I lied to them cause they cept on at me about Me Odell and Tommy doing it. So I told them everything Mr. Smith told me to say. I ask him why did he tell them that in the first place for. He said, I was afraid that if I didnt tell them what thall wanted me to say that they would beat me up. Cause every time I would say something Mr. Smith was telling me And if I started to say something different that he would jump onto me and say no that you didnt do that you did this. Then he said I was afraid that they was going to beet me up or something. I ask him why didnt he tell them what he did that day. He said, I couldnt remember. Then he said, my God it's been a long time since she come up missing. . . .

Then I told him . . . don't talk to them anymore. If you got something to say tell it to your lawyer. He said, OK. Then he laughted and said, Tommy said that I was screwing a dead corps. I laughted and said, the reason why I said it was for them to see my statement was a lie. So Carol said, Tommy. I said, what. He said, I thought you was Odell. I said, no it's me. Then I said do you want to die for somebody elses doings. He said, no. Then I said, well then keep your mouth shut. And I don't know why you didnt denigh it in the first place then this wouldnt be happening. Cause they would have seen that it was just a dream I had . . . Then Carol said, I made that D.A. mad when I told him I didnt care if they put me to death over something I didnt do. He said, he got mad and stamped out of the room. I said why did you say that for he said to piss them off. I said I get down on my nees that the lord sees me you and Odell though and forgive me for bearing false witnesses. Then he said, I couldn't pick out Odell's picture and it was making them mad. I told him the reazen why you couldnt pick out Odell's picture cause you dont know him . . .

I ask Mr. Smith whitch one of the guys am I supose to look like. Then he said both. Then they brought me and Carol over here. I ask Carol if he was saved. He said, he was wanting to be. So then I ask the jailer if he would give Carol a Bible. He said he would. Then I wrote some scriptures for him to look up. And on it I put May the lord be with you. And tell the Gods truth. Then I put Stand tall and remember what happened that day. Then I gave them to the jailer. Then is when they found out Odell's inicence. The jailer Mr Scott told me. I told him that we were all innicent. See they found Odell inicent and they should see Carol's innicent and I am innicent. So cant they see that this is a uprore over nothing. Then the jailer said well see. But I cant let you out till they tell me to. I just knew that they was going to let us out. And seen that it was a dream and a lie I told them. So then the jailer came back and got me. I just knew that they was going to let me out. Then when I was walking up the hall, I could see Mr. Baskens and another officer and Mr Baskins had a sack in his hand smilling from ear to ear. And I knew that they seen I was innicent and he had my close in the sack and was going to let me out. Then we walked into the side room. Then I new something was going on. Then Mr Baskens said, suposen what I got

here in this sack. I told him I don't know. Then he opend it
and pulled out part of a scull . . .

With Christmas approaching, the two Indian foster boys that Bud
and Tricia had had in their home for several months were returned to
their natural parents; they would still come to visit from time to time.
They were the fifth and sixth foster kids Bud and Tricia had taken in
during the past two years; for their trouble they were paid $300 a
month for each child by the county welfare department. In return
they provided for the children food, shelter, and clothing, and an af-
fectionate family atmosphere that usually was what was needed most,
and sometimes genuine love, which could lead to emotional wrench-
ing on the inevitable day the children would have to leave.

The day after Thomas and Vernon left, the social worker telephoned Tricia: Could they take two more? Tricia said they could.

They were brother and sister. David was nearing two and a half, a
beautiful, blond child with, even at that age, a startlingly handsome
face—and a twisted foot that needed mending, that apparently had
been broken through the neglect, if not the actual abuse, of his parents. Lisa was more cute than beautiful, with a crooked smile that
could bring warmth into the coldest heart. She was fifteen months
old—and weighed only sixteen pounds. Her weight had been drop-
ping rapidly, the social worker told Tricia; she was losing strength. She
could not keep food down, would throw up everything she ate. The
diagnosis of the doctor was that she had a nervous stomach, probably
caused by not enough touching and fondling at home, by lack of love.
To put her in a hospital would be to see her wither and die, the doctor had said. The social worker felt that Bud and Tricia might be the
only people in town who could save her.

Bud and Tricia took the children in, and fell in love. The other
kids—Rhonda, Buddy, and Laura Sue—did not seem to mind shar-
ing the attention with the constant strangers in their midst. David
and Lisa were so cute that, more than any of the others, they seemed
like instant members of the real family. If love could help, then they
would have it.

For the first few days, nothing seemed to help with Lisa. She had a twinkle in her eyes, was clever for her age; that was apparent to anyone. But she kept giving back her food; she lost her newly acquired ability to walk; she lost yet another pound, was down to fourteen pounds now. Tricia called the social worker; the doctor's diagnosis was repeated; love was what she needed; in a hospital she would die.

One night Lisa seemed weaker than ever. She was throwing up, had not kept any food down in days. Even the twinkle in her eye was hard to find. Tricia held her, sat with Lisa on her lap, paced the floor with Lisa in her arms. All night long Tricia stayed up, holding the child, calming her, trying to give through the power of her will the love in her heart to the child. She was afraid Lisa would be dead by morning.

In the morning it was as if Lisa had weathered some internal storm. She seemed more her cute self again. Tricia had an intuition that perhaps some major crisis had passed.

She also had a revelation: perhaps it was not merely a nervous stomach; perhaps the child was allergic to milk. Tricia had heard of such cases. She eliminated milk from the child's diet, as a test. Her food began to stay down. In a few days she had gained half a pound back, then a pound. Little Lisa was clearly recovering; was even stumbling about the house with her funny stutter-step. She was, that year, their Christmas child.

While most of Ada prepared for the holiday, crowding the stores on Main Street, decorating their homes with Christmas lights, District Attorney Bill Peterson was busy preparing for the preliminary hearing in the Haraway case. The purpose of a hearing is to establish, to the satisfaction of the judge, that there is enough evidence against the defendants to bring them to trial. The burden of proof at this point is on the state—proof not of the defendant's guilt, but of the weight of the evidence. Such hearings usually take a few hours, in some cases a few minutes. This time, Peterson knew, it was going to take a lot longer. With no body found, with not a speck of physical evidence to prove that Denice Haraway was dead, the district attorney would have to marshall all his resources, all the witnesses he could conjure, to establish the corpus delicti.

Ultimately, he knew, unless they found the body, the case against

Ward and Fontenot would rest on the videotaped statements. But under the law in Oklahoma, as in most states, confessions cannot be introduced into evidence unless the state first proves the corpus delicti—proves, that is, that a crime has been committed, and that the defendants are somehow linked to that crime, with enough evidence that they may be brought to trial.

The Nettie Brown case had been crucial because it established the legal precedent that proof of Denice Haraway's murder could be circumstantial. The linking of the defendants to the crime would have to come from the witnesses at McAnally's and at J.P.s up the road, and from any other testimony he could unearth that might link the suspects to an old gray pickup, or to a lock-blade knife that might have been the murder weapon. So he conducted interviews.

At the offices of the two defense attorneys, Don Wyatt's out on Arlington and George Butner's in Wewoka, there was less to do at this point. They, too, had to research the legal precedents on no-body cases, on circumstantial evidence, on other points of law. But they did not have to prepare a defense; that would come later, at a trial, should the case ever go to trial. For the preliminary hearing, both attorneys were preparing to make their major stands on two points: that the state could not prove that a crime had even been committed, because it could not prove that Denice Haraway was dead; and that, even if she were, there was no evidence, independent of the taped statements, linking either suspect to the woman's disappearance.

Unless the state had evidence it had not yet made public . . .

If the judge, or any other judge down the line, would rule that the videotapes were not admissible, for whatever reason, both lawyers felt, the bulk of the state's case would disappear.

Wyatt was aided in his research by his junior partner, Mike Addicott, a tall, thin, moustached young attorney. Butner, without a staff the size of Wyatt's, was pretty much on his own.

A short, slender, dark-haired man who dressed neatly in three-piece suits, George Butner, like most of those involved in the case, had deep roots in this part of Oklahoma. His grandfather had moved to nearby Seminole County from Arkansas in 1888. The family was one of only three white families in the area at the time—amid the mostly

Indian settlements—and the town where they settled was soon named Butner, after them. A previous town of Butner, in North Carolina, had been named after their ancestors.

At the time of the Haraway case, George Butner had been an attorney for ten years. He and Barney Ward were the only two lawyers in the district who did mostly criminal law; such cases comprised about 60 percent of Butner's work. When he was asked by Judge Miller to represent Karl Fontenot as court-appointed attorney, Butner had just completed another murder case, in which he had done all the work himself, a case he had lost to Bill Peterson. He did not know much about the Haraway case when he accepted the appointment. Usually he did not have to follow cases in the newspapers; the cases came to him; and, not living in Ada, he had read even less about it.

He went to see his client at the city jail.

Karl told Butner he was innocent. But beyond that, he was of little help. He could not remember what he had been doing the night of April 28. He could not remember anyone who could testify to his whereabouts. He could give Butner the names of nearly everyone in the town he knew, in the hope that one of them might remember where he had been that night. But Butner did not have the staff—nor the money to hire investigators—to go on such a fishing expedition; there would have to be a starting point, and Fontenot could give him none.

The attorney felt that by holding the two young men in jail for twenty days before bringing charges, the police and the district attorney had handled the case "obnoxiously." From what Karl told him, he felt his client had been threatened at times during those twenty days, and perhaps before he made the taped statement as well. His best defense, he felt early on, would be to find some way to get the tapes declared inadmissible, so that the case would never go to trial.

Mercy's is a sandwich shop half a block from the courthouse, where Bill Peterson often ate lunch, along with judges, lawyers, courthouse workers, and other citizens. The name of the sandwich shop had nothing to do with the quality of justice in Ada, or anywhere else; the person who owned it and did most of the cooking was an Oriental woman named Mercy.

Every year, Mercy threw a Christmas party for her regular customers. So Bill Peterson went to escape from the pressures of his work—and was approached there by Norman Frame, Denice Haraway's faculty adviser, who liked especially to come to Mercy's on Wednesdays, when the daily special was Chinese. Frame asked the district attorney about the case; he had been notified to appear at the courthouse in January to testify as a witness to Denice Haraway's character; he would be glad to, he said, but he hoped it would not interfere with his teaching schedule.

Peterson assured him that, as a character witness, his testimony probably would not take very long; they would do what they could to work his appearance around his class schedule. Frame was pleased.

The district attorney was beginning to understand that, perhaps for a long time, there would be no getting away from the Haraway case.

A few days later, Christmas came to Ada; the lights blinked on the trees, the sound of singing filled the churches. Models of the infant Jesus slept in crèches; in gaily wrapped boxes slept Cabbage Patch kids. Gifts were exchanged at the Wyatts' and the Butners', the Petersons' and the Smiths'.

At the home of the Haraways there was a terrible vacancy; it was the first Christmas since the disappearance—since the murder, perhaps—of Denice. At the home of the Wolfs and the Wards the joy was darkly tempered; Tommy was in jail accused of murder, something they believed he didn't do, believed with all their hearts.

From his jail cell Tommy wrote a Christmas letter to Tricia. It moved her to tears. In it he said that this was the happiest Christmas he'd ever had, because he was in God's hands, because he had had time to think, and when this ordeal was over and he was released, he would make something of his life.

The Sunday before Christmas, Tricia and Bud and the kids and Miz Ward and as many of the others as could fit into the closetlike visiting room went to see Tommy, to show him their support; to offer him what Christmas cheer they could.

No one came to visit Karl Fontenot. No one had come to visit him since his arrest more than two months before.

Karl did get one present, however: a Christmas basket of fruit and candy.

It was from Detective Captain Dennis Smith.

7

TESTIMONY

The preliminary hearing in the case of Tommy Ward and Karl Fontenot began as scheduled in the Pontotoc County courthouse in downtown Ada on Monday, January 7. On the third floor of the courthouse there are two courtrooms: a small one to the left as you leave the elevator, normally used for hearings and small trials, and a larger one to the right. The larger courtroom was used for this hearing, to accommodate the large number of spectators. It contained four and a half rows of blond wood benches, each of which could seat about twelve people. For the first time that anyone could remember, spectators were frisked for weapons by sheriff's deputies as they entered the courtroom, lest anyone try to end the proceedings with a knife or a gun.

As in most courtrooms, many of the spectators were retired men and women who did not have to be at work that day and could find in the proceedings a form of free entertainment. Among the more concerned spectators were Tricia, Kay, and Miz Ward. Seated in the back row was a tall, lean man wearing high cowboy boots, blue jeans, a leather belt with his name carved in the back, a style of belt common in Ada, and the grounds for a strident joke:

Why does a cowboy wear his name on the back of his belt?
So he'll know who he is when he takes his head out of his ass.

As he entered the courtroom balancing a pile of lawbooks against his belly, District Attorney Peterson was aware that he would now be the central player in a highly unusual drama: the attempt to make a murder case in the absence of a body, in the absence of any physical proof of death. But in his own mind there was little doubt that Donna Denice Haraway was dead.

It was all a matter of personalities. His own father, for instance, was proof. His father had been a popular physician at the old Sugg Clinic across from the courthouse, now abandoned, and then at Valley View Hospital. For fifty years he served the people of the town as a doctor, and you could set your watch by his comings and goings. On the last day of his life—October 13, 1975—still practicing medicine at the age of seventy-two, he went out to cut down a tree on his property. He'd been talking about cutting down that particular tree; Bill had warned him not to do it himself, that he was too old for that sort of thing, that he should hire some eighteen-year-old kid to do it. But Dr. Peterson was stubborn, self-reliant; he went out on the property alone, with a chain saw, to do it himself. Later in the day a neighbor was passing the Peterson home; he noticed that the garage door was open; he had never in all the years they had been neighbors known the doctor to leave his garage door open when he was not putting in or taking out his car. The neighbor knew immediately that something had happened; feared immediately that Dr. Peterson was dead. At the hospital, the doctor was late for his rounds; he had never been late before without calling to say what time he would be in, or having someone call for him. Staff members at the hospital suspected immediately that he was dead.

He was found beneath the tree. It had fallen backwards, crushing him, instead of falling away. They could tell from the position of the body that he had seen it falling, had tried to scramble out of the way, but his feet had gotten tangled in the weeds. All he could do at the last instant of his life was to raise his hands in front of him, to try to ward off the crushing blow.

The point being—the district attorney had made the connection in his mind many times since Denice Haraway disappeared—that as soon as his father was seen to depart from his normal routine, people knew something was wrong; he was that kind of a man. Likewise, he felt, Denice Haraway had not just up and left on a whim. When people asked him about the possibility that she had faked her own disappearance, he replied, "Elephants could fly. But they don't."

His task now, as he entered the courtroom, was to convince Judge Miller of this under the rules of evidence. And also to convince him that there was sufficient evidence to bring Ward and Fontenot to trial. The district attorney had seen the tapes; he had little doubt that they were guilty. Dennis Smith and Mike Baskin thought of the two defendants as "trash"; the D.A., having been raised more genteelly, thought of them in different terms: "They are not the kind of guys you would invite home to dinner."

Peterson sat at the prosecution table, along with Dennis Smith. At the defense table to the left—farther from the judge's bench, closer to the jury box, should there ever be a trial in the case—sat the suspects and their attorneys: Don Wyatt and his associate, Mike Addicott, representing Tommy Ward; George Butner representing Karl Fontenot. The court reporter, Hugh Brasher, sat at his curious machine in the far corner, beyond the bench.

Judge Miller, tall, lean, moustached, twenty-nine years old, entered. All in the courtroom rose at the bailiff's direction, then sat as the judge did. Under Oklahoma law, Judge Miller would preside only at the preliminary hearing; should he rule that there was enough evidence for the case to go to trial, another judge, District Judge Ronald Jones, would preside.

Bill Peterson began his presentation with an elderly neighbor of the Wards, who said he had sometimes seen Tommy riding in an old gray pickup. Then came four witnesses who the D.A. knew were not his best: four young men whom he also would not invite home to dinner. They were part of Ada's running crowd—some of them had been in prison—who had run at times with Tommy Ward. A prudently logical man, Peterson believed that the best way to construct a case, be it for a judge or a jury, was in straightforward, chronological fashion. Since the evidence he hoped to elicit from these four predated the disappearance of Denice Haraway, he began with them.

The district attorney tried to establish through the four young men two things: one, that Ward had been in possession of a lockblade knife of the kind he had described in his tape as the murder weapon; and two, that he had normally worn his hair long, like the men in the composite drawings, but that immediately after April 28, 1984, he'd had it cut short. The four young men, under Peterson's questioning, testified vaguely to that effect. Under cross-examination, however, the defense elicited from the witnesses that an incident in which Ward had showed one of them a knife at a party had occurred in 1982, and that a witness who'd said Ward's hairstyle had changed right around April 28 had in fact not seen Ward from about four months before that date until four months after, and had no real knowledge as to when he'd had his hair cut short.

Peterson was not happy with the outcome, but he hadn't expected much more from this bunch; he would build his case slowly, methodically. He called two character witnesses for Denice Haraway: Norman Frame, her faculty adviser, and Donna Howard, with whom she'd been student teaching. Both testified about Denice's regular habits, to establish that she was not likely to have run off. Then he called Denice's younger sister, Janet Weldon. Ms. Weldon, too, testified about Denice's regular habits—about how happy she had been; about how she had talked to Denice on the phone less than two hours before she disappeared, and everything had sounded fine. Then came the following series of questions and answers:

BILL PETERSON: Do you recall giving Donna, as a gift, a blouse?

JANET WELDON: Yes, I do.

PETERSON: Okay. And would you describe that blouse to the Court, please?

WELDON: Well, it had a white-lace collar and it was light lavender and it had little blue flowers on it. And it was buttoned up the front. And it was pretty worn, because it was a shirt I had that I gave to her. It was pretty old. It was almost white.

PETERSON: When was the last time you saw that blouse on your sister?

WELDON: About a month before she disappeared.

PETERSON: Was it a—loose fitting around the sleeves, or was it tight?

WELDON: Tight elastic.

PETERSON: Short-sleeved or long-sleeved?

WELDON: Short-sleeved.

PETERSON: And since Donna's disappearance, have you done anything to locate this shirt?

WELDON: Yes.

PETERSON: What have you done?

WELDON: I looked through my clothes and I looked through hers, and it is not there.

PETERSON: When you say you looked through her clothes, what did you do, exactly?

WELDON: The day after she turned up missing and they weren't for sure what she had on, and no one could recall the shirt, and I thought of it. And I went through her clothes the next day, when I was putting some of her stuff away.

There were tears in Ms. Weldon's eyes as she testified.

Under cross-examination, the defense attorneys got Ms. Weldon to concede that it was possible she did not know everything there was to know about her sister's life, that it would have been possible for Denice Haraway to be involved in something without her sister knowing about it. The defense did not focus on the exchange about the blouse. The lawyers did not know its significance; they had not yet been permitted to see the confession tapes.

Sitting in the courtroom, watching, listening, Tricia Wolf glanced at the door to the courtroom each time it opened, each time someone was about to enter. Each time, her heart started to pound; each time, she thought the person walking in would be Denice Haraway, come to show herself, come to end these proceedings.

Kay Garrett, from time to time, saw someone bring in a note and hand it to Peterson or Smith. Each time, she thought perhaps Denice Haraway had telephoned from somewhere to say she was alive, and that's what was in the note.

Peterson called Karen Sue Wise to the stand. A slim, dark-haired woman, twenty-five, wearing glasses, Ms. Wise had been the clerk at J.P.'s Pak-to-Go, up the road from McAnally's, the night of the disappearance. It was she who had provided most of the information for the composite sketches, and was one of the key witnesses.

J.P.'s is three-tenths of a mile east of McAnally's on the road out of town. It is the last convenience store before the highway becomes truly rural. Beside it stands a pecan store that sells wholesale and retail, that also does some cracking. And which closes early. Out front are gas pumps; inside the door, the cash register and the counter are to the right; to the left is a magazine rack, aisles of snack foods and other convenience items; at the rear left, behind a glass partition, is a game room, with a single pool table in the center, electronic games against the walls; behind the clerk's counter is a doorway leading to a room that holds the wine, beer, and liquor.

On the night of April 28, 1984, Karen Wise had been working as a clerk at the store for less than a month. She was on the 3 P.M. to 11 P.M. shift. She testified that two men had entered the store at about 7 P.M. that evening, and stayed for an hour and a half. Most of the time they were shooting pool, she said. At one point one of the men had come to the front of the store and asked her for change to feed into the pool table. She said the men were acting "suspicious," that she became afraid. She said that a pickup was parked outside the store while they were there, that they left the store about 8:30, and that moments later the pickup drove off. Ms. Wise identified defendant Tommy Ward as one of the two men who had been in her store that night. She said she could not positively identify anyone present in the courtroom as being the other man. The pickup she described as "mostly red primer. There was gray primered spots."

Bill Peterson's next witness was Jack Paschall. Paschall was director of student teaching at East Central University; as such he had had several interviews with Denice Haraway; but he also worked occasionally at J.P.'s, helping the clerks during busy hours; he bought his beer there, knew the owners, lived nearby; his telephone was posted in the store in case a clerk needed help. Dark-eyed, dark-haired, intense, Paschall testified that he had entered J.P.'s about eight o'clock on the night of the twenty-eighth. He said he had seen two men there, and that Karen Wise had told him the men had been acting weird, watching her, and that she was afraid. Paschall remained in the store. About 8:30, he said, the two men left, got into an older-model primered Chevrolet pickup parked out front. He said it had a grayish or bluish tint, and that something was the matter with the tailgate—he couldn't remember what; the tailgate might have been dented, or might have been missing entirely. The men drove off in the pickup heading west toward town, Paschall said. (It was also the direction of McAnally's, perhaps thirty seconds down the highway.) Paschall said he was sure that the defendant Tommy Ward was one of the men who had been in the store. He said he could not identify anyone in the courtroom as the other man. On a scale of one to ten, Jack Paschall said, his certainty that one of the men had been Ward was a ten.

The hearing was adjourned until 9:15 the next morning. Bill Peterson was satisfied. These witnesses had held up; they had stuck to their identifications of Tommy Ward.

The suspects were handcuffed and taken from the courtroom by sheriff's deputies, down two floors on the elevator, out across the lawn, Ward back to the county jail, Fontenot across the street to the city jail. It had been their first lengthy stay outside their solitary cells since their arrests in October. On his bunk that night, Tommy Ward was shaking. He'd been shaking in the jail ever since his arrest—his hands, mostly, thin-fingered mechanic's hands. Even in his days of freedom, he used to shake some; it was one reason he had taken to drinking lots of beer and wine: to stop the shaking. But this night it was worse. Jim Allen's words were in his head, and they were making him tremble.

Jim Allen was a trustee in the jail, allowed to roam the corridors, sweep the floors. He could stop outside cells, talk to the other inmates. For many days now he had been talking through the bars to Tommy Ward, telling him what he ought to do.

"Tell them," Jim Allen kept saying. "Say it. All you'll get is seven to fifteen years. If you don't, they're gonna kill you. They're gonna put that needle in your arm."

Tommy Ward lay on his bunk and felt his hands shaking and thought about Jim Allen's words.

He didn't want to follow his advice.

He also didn't want to die.

The scene on Tuesday, the second day of the hearing, was much like on the first. The courtroom was crowded with spectators, among them Tricia and Kay and Miz Ward, local attorneys curious about how the case was going, and in the back row the tall man with dark hair and high cowboy boots and his name carved into his belt. Bill Peterson called a young man named Jim Moyer, a gas station attendant, to the stand. Moyer said he had been a customer in McAnally's about

7:30 P.M. on April 28 when two men drove up in a gray, late 1960s or early 1970s Chevrolet pickup. He said he had picked both Ward and Fontenot out of police lineups as the men he had seen. He said the men had been acting suspicious in the store, so that when he left he looked at the license plate of the truck. He went to his own car to write it down, but didn't have a pencil. Then another car drove into the parking lot, so he left.

Continuing to proceed in chronological fashion, Peterson called the three witnesses who had arrived at McAnally's shortly after 8:30 that night: Lenny Timmons, David Timmons, and their uncle, Gene Whelchel. All three described how a young man and a young woman had left the store together just as Lenny Timmons was entering. Whelchel said that when they discovered the clerk was missing, he realized the young woman they had seen leaving was Donna Denice Haraway. All three said the man leaving was of a similar type to Tommy Ward; none could positively identify Ward as the man they saw. Lenny Timmons, who had passed in the doorway within two feet of the couple leaving, was asked on cross-examination by Don Wyatt how certain he was that the man he saw was Ward, on a scale of one to ten.

"About a six," Timmons replied.

All three witnesses testified that they had seen no other person at the store or in the pickup. They said they had seen no weapon; that the girl seemed to be leaving voluntarily, and did not cry out for help. Whelchel said he'd thought they were young lovers.

They told about how, finding no clerk in the store, and seeing the cash drawer open and empty, they had called the police. They described the pickup they'd seen as "light-colored."

Monroe Atkeson, the store manager, and O. E. McAnally, the owner, both testified that Denice Haraway was a good employee, and had given no indication that she planned to leave. Sergeant Harvey Phillips, the first police officer on the scene, told of what he had found when he arrived: no clerk present, a purse with Denice Haraway's driver's license in it, car keys, her car parked beside the store. When Phillips completed his testimony, the judge adjourned the hearing until the following morning.

Several times during the proceedings there had been recesses: for lunch, and to allow the participants to stretch and use the restrooms. During one recess, the tall cowboy in the back row, the one with his name on his belt, approached Miz Ward. She knew him, knew that Tommy knew him.

"I know that Tommy didn't do it," the man said.

Miz Ward nodded, agreed, thanked him; she took his comment as a gesture of support.

During another recess, Jim Moyer approached Karen Wise in the corridor. Moyer was troubled; he had just finished testifying that Ward and Fontenot were the two men he had seen in McAnally's at 7:30 that night. But then, in the courtroom, he had noticed someone else: someone he felt looked a lot more like one of the men he had seen than Karl Fontenot did. He wanted to check his observation with Ms. Wise.

As he approached her, she seemed fearful, her eyes looking down the corridor. When he struck up a brief conversation, she stepped around a corner, so she could not be seen by someone. Moyer told her his feeling: that there was someone in the courtroom who looked a lot more like the second man than Karl Fontenot did. He didn't tell her which person he meant. He asked if she had noticed anyone like that.

Karen Wise told Moyer that she had. It was the tall guy in the back row, she said, with the long hair and the cowboy boots.

Jim Moyer nodded his agreement. He peered around the corner of the corridor. The cowboy was looking toward them. Moyer had the distinct feeling that Karen Wise was afraid of him.

When the hearing resumed Wednesday morning, Bill Peterson was prepared to spend the rest of the week, if necessary, putting twenty of Denice Haraway's relatives on the stand to testify that they had not seen her or heard from her since April 28. This would buttress the fact of her disappearance, and, by implication, he felt, the certainty of her death. To speed things up, the defense attorneys agreed to accept the testimony of the relatives contained in depositions already taken by the district attorney. Peterson spoke into the record what Steve Haraway would have said: that he and Denice had been planning for the future, that she had no reason to leave, that none of her personal belongings were missing from the apartment. One section of Peterson's summation of Steve Haraway's testimony mentioned the shirt that Denice's younger sister, Janet Weldon, had described in her testimony.

"Steve has looked through her personal belongings for a lavender-colored, almost white, shirt with ruffles around the collar and tight sleeves and light-blue flowers on the shirt. That is not in her personal belongings."

When the deposition testimony was completed, Judge Miller granted a continuance of the hearing until the following Monday. Then Tommy Ward told his attorney he wanted to make a statement. They huddled; Don Wyatt tried to talk him out of it; Tommy insisted. Spectators were sent from the courtroom. A tape recorder was turned on. Wyatt—not the district attorney—read Tommy his rights, warning him that anything he was about to say could be used against him in court.

Tommy said he understood. And there in front of Bill Peterson and Dennis Smith and Karl Fontenot and the attorneys, but without the press or the public present, he changed his story. He said that his mind had been clouded about the night of the disappearance, but that now it was clearing; now he remembered what had happened that night. He said he *had* gone into McAnally's that night, but not with Karl Fontenot. He said he had gone in with another fellow he knew, named Marty Ashley. He said Ashley knew Denice Haraway, and had begun talking with her. He said Ashley told Denice, "If you were *my* wife, you wouldn't have to work at all." And then Ashley kissed Denice Haraway on the cheek, Ward said, and asked her to run away with him. If she did, she would never have to work again.

Ashley returned to his pickup parked outside, Ward said. Denice asked Tommy if Ashley meant what he had said: that she would never have to work again. When Tommy said he guessed he meant it, Denice went with him out to the truck and they drove off.

So Tommy Ward stated, while the tape recorder turned. He said they dropped him off downtown, and were planning to drive to Tulsa, to stay with a friend of Ashley's named Jay Dicus. (Jay Dicus was the nephew of one of the town's most prominent merchants, who owned Dicus Supermarkets, three large markets in Ada.) Tommy said that was the last he ever saw of them.

When he was through, the recorder was turned off. The participants returned to their respective offices. Tommy Ward had dropped a bombshell.

Back in his cell, Tommy was shaking again, worse than ever. And his stomach was upset, real bad. His heart was pounding, louder and louder inside him, faster and faster. He thought he was having a heart attack.

He couldn't believe what he'd just done. It was so stupid, he realized once he got back to his cell. Because they would surely find out. He had thought when he made the statement that they would believe him; he would get seven to fifteen, like Jim Allen had been telling him.

"Just tell them you were there," Allen kept saying. "Tell them you were there, but you left before it happened. And you won't get the death penalty."

So he told them. He told them it was him there and Marty Ashley. It was Jim Allen who had suggested Ashley, Tommy would say later, because Ashley looked a lot like one of the drawings. So he had told them and thought they would believe it was the truth; only now back in his cell his stomach was messed up and his heart was beating so loud he thought he would die. Because he saw now that they would find out it was a lie. The police would check on it and find out it wasn't true.

His stomach got worse and worse. Tommy asked to see a doctor. The jailer, Ron Scott, had him fill out a medical request form. Scott then called for an emergency medical team to come to the jail. They checked Ward and decided to take him to the hospital for further examination.

He was taken to Valley View. His condition was diagnosed as a nervous stomach. He was given medication to calm his nerves, and he was returned to the jail.

Sheriff Bob Kaiser, reporting the hospital trip to the press, made it clear that Ward had not tried to commit suicide.

Dennis Smith went to see Marty Ashley, who denied being involved.

The police established, to their own satisfaction, that Ward's Ashley story wasn't true. Don Wyatt was furious at Tommy for lying again.

The story, as Tommy had told it, was absurd on the face of it, Wyatt felt. But he couldn't help wondering how thoroughly the police had checked to see if Ashley and Dicus might have been involved in some other way. The Dicus family had a lot of influence in Ada.

At his home in Tulsa that Saturday night, Tommy's brother Joel was awakened out of a deep sleep by the ringing of the telephone. As he picked up the receiver, he looked at his clock. It was two in the morning.

The voice on the phone was a man's. He did not say who he was. He warned Joel to stop helping defend Tommy Ward—or else! Then he clicked off.

Joel, a bachelor, hung up the phone, shaken. He wondered who it had been. Tulsa is 180 miles from Ada; few people there were following the case; hardly anyone there knew that Tommy Ward was his brother.

He decided the call had probably come from Ada.

He didn't get much sleep that night.

On Monday morning the courtroom was more crowded than ever. Word had filtered through the courthouse, through the town's legal community, out into the streets: Monday might be Tape Day. If the judge allowed the tapes to be shown, people would be able to see for themselves the full horror of the confessions.

The key legal question of the hearing would be whether the state had proved the corpus delicti. If the judge decided that it had not, then the confessions could not be used; then there could be no trial, unless additional evidence surfaced.

To bolster the state's contention that Denice Haraway was dead, Peterson put on the stand an OSBI criminal analyst, Lydia Kimball. Ms. Kimball testified that continuing, computerized checks with all fifty states had indicated that Denice Haraway had not applied for a driver's license anywhere under that name or her maiden name; nor had she been arrested or hospitalized; and that no unidentified body found anywhere in America was hers.

To link Ward and Fontenot to the alleged crime, Peterson called Mike Baskin. The detective testified about the police actions in the case, from the time of his arrival at McAnally's the night of the disappearance, through the arrest of the suspects and beyond.

Then Peterson tried to introduce the tapes. The defense attorneys objected, on the grounds that the corpus delicti had not been proved. Peterson cited legal precedents, among them the Nettie Brown and Rawlings cases, prompting the defense attorneys to protest angrily:

GEORGE BUTNER: I just want to reiterate on each of the cases that Mr. Peterson has submitted to you in regards to substantial evidence of the corpus delicti, in each of those cases there has been some evidence of a death, some evidence that there might have been blood. There's even been a medical examiner's report, there's been some evidence of a death, and you will find this in every case that's presented to you. And so, when Mr. Peterson argues substantial evidence as to the corpus delicti, judge, real corpus delicti is death in this case, and there has been no substantial evidence in regard thereto. There has been no blood, there's been no hair samples, no medical examiner's report, nothing. I believe if the court—if you will peruse all cases that the state presents to you, you will find that this is the connecting aspect in all and every one of them. And in this case, we do not have that. In fact, the closest we have is the fact that she walked out, of her own volition, without being dragged and that's the closest we have as to any actions or activities of her person. And I believe that the court will see that throughout these cases that's true: there is some evidence, and we have none.

BILL PETERSON: Your Honor, in Wilkins vs. State, 609 Pacific 2nd, 309—

DON WYATT: What year is that case?

PETERSON: 1980. It states, moreover, a jury may reasonably rely upon circumstantial evidence; to conclude otherwise would mean that a criminal could commit a secret murder, destroy the body of the victim, and escape punishment despite convincing circumstantial evidence against him or her.

WYATT: In each case, judge, the case stands for the proposition that the body is not essential; circumstantial evidence to prove a death occurred is sufficient. It's the same line of thinking in every case he's presented and you have no circumstantial evidence that a death occurred here.

PETERSON: But in conjunction with any confession given, the circumstantial evidence. We've got circumstantial evidence of a kidnapping, and we've got circumstantial evidence of a death. There has been no one who has seen or heard of this girl since April 28.

BUTNER: Amelia Earhart, too, but that doesn't make her dead.

The legal wrangling went on for hours. When it was done, Judge Miller ruled that the tapes could be admitted in evidence.

A recess was taken while a video monitor was set up in the courtroom. The spectators waited. Some had been there all day—it was almost 5 P.M. now—others were attorneys come to hear the arguments. The tall booted cowboy was in the back row once again. Tricia Wolf had not come today; she did not want to see the tapes. When Bud got off work at the feed mill at 4 P.M. he went over to the courthouse to see what was going on; he found a seat from which to watch the tapes, to report back to the family.

Tommy Ward's statement was played first. At the start of the tape, agent Rusty Featherstone could be heard reading Tommy his rights. The defense attorneys interrupted the tape, objected; no evidence had been introduced to show that Ward had been read his rights before the eight hours of questioning had begun, before the video machine had been turned on. The judge overruled the objection.

The thirty-one-minute tape was played in its entirety, showing Tommy Ward answering questions, telling how he and Karl Fontenot and Odell Titsworth had robbed and kidnapped and raped and killed Donna Denice Haraway.

Then Karl Fontenot's tape was played, after similar objections had been overruled. He, too, told of robbery, kidnapping, rape, and murder—and the burning of the body.

Many of the spectators wept as they watched.

The hearing was adjourned until morning.

In the corridors of the courthouse and out in the street, the defense attorneys talked to the news media. It was the first time they had seen the tapes. George Butner spoke of the "glaring inconsistencies" between the two tapes. "Not one shred of evidence has been produced to prove or disprove what is in the statements," he said. Mike Addicott said the defense would seek a change of venue for any trial, because of the emotional impact the crime had had on the local populace.

Some of the discrepancies between the two tapes were pointed out on radio and television newscasts that night, and in the Ada *News* the next day. It was the first indication the people of Ada had that the stories on the tapes were not identical.

Bud went home and reported to Tricia what was on the tapes. There was terrible stuff; but they had known that before. He focused on the inconsistencies; on how, several times on the tape, Tommy had called Odell Titsworth "Titsdale," until the police corrected him. To Bud this showed that the police had given him that name, that he didn't know Titsworth; and that if the police had planted that information, what else might they have planted? Because of the inconsistencies on the tapes, Tricia and Bud had new hope that the charges might be dropped.

The defense attorneys were gratified by the inconsistencies. They could be viewed as showing that Ward and Fontenot had not participated in the same event. The tapes were brutal and gory, however. And one passage on each tape bothered the attorneys the most; it had to do with the blouse Denice Haraway had been wearing. A portion of Ward's tape went like this:

Q. Can you tell me what her blouse looked like that she was wearing?

A. It was—it was white with little blue roses on it, I think, blue roses.

Q. . . . So it was a white blouse. Button-up or slip-on?

A. It's a button-up.

Q. Did it have buttons on the collar?

A. Uh-huh.

Q. Or would it be just a regular collar?

A. It had buttons on the collars and then it had little fringe deals around her collar and around the end of her arm, end of the sleeves.

Q. By little fringe, do you mean a lace kind of deal?
A. Yeah, uh-huh.

A portion of Karl Fontenot's tape went as follows:

Q. What kind of shirt did she have on? Was it a pullover type or button-up type, Karl?
A. Button-up.
Q. Did it have anything that you noticed about it, as far as any designs or—
A. Just the ruffles around the buttons and sleeves. The sleeves had elastic like in them.
Q. Was it a short-sleeved shirt?
A. Yes, it was short-sleeved.
Q. Did it have any lace around the collar?
A. Yes, it had ruffles around the collar like the front.

In the matching descriptions of the blouse, there was an ominous consistency that gave both Don Wyatt and George Butner a sinking feeling. Did these descriptions prove that Ward and Fontenot had both been there? That they were guilty after all?

Karen Wise was nervous. Since testifying at the hearing the week before, she'd gotten several disconcerting phone calls: quiet clicks, heavy breathing. Now, looking out the window of her second-floor apartment, she could see a man standing in the darkness of the alley below. Standing, watching.

The night was dark; the porch light cast a faint yellow glow into the alley; it let her see his outline, his shape, but not his face. He was tall, he was lean; he was wearing blue jeans; he was wearing cowboy boots; he was staring up at her window in the dark.

Her address was listed in the phone book: 223½ West Thirteenth. It was part of a rabbit warren of two-story frame buildings, once painted white, now graying, in need of a new coat; wooden stairways to the second-floor apartments crisscrossed the sides of the building and the rear.

Frightened, Karen moved away from the window; she kept out of sight; then she moved to another window and peered down. The man still was there, his hands jammed into his pockets, looking up at her.

The man walked down the alley; he came back and stared up at her. She moved away. She looked out another window. He was staring up at her. He walked down the alley a second time, again came back to stare at her windows. He walked the alley a third time, and again he came back.

Karen Wise called the police.

By the time a squad car arrived to check the alley, the man was gone.

The image wouldn't leave her mind: the tall, lean cowboy. She felt so vulnerable. She still worked at J.P.'s, where any stranger could walk in. Sometimes she wished she hadn't been working that April night, had never gotten involved. Other times she felt lucky. Instead of Denice Haraway, it could have been her.

She'd testified she was sure Tommy Ward had been in her store that night; she'd made no identification of Fontenot; now there was the cowboy in the alley; he looked a lot like the other man who'd been in her store that night.

In the daylight she went to the district attorney's office. She told him about the man in the alley. Bill Peterson told her she was being spooked. It was understandable, he said, involved in a murder case as she was. But it was nothing to worry about. It was probably somebody who was lost, who was looking for another apartment.

Karen Wise didn't think so—not in that lonely alley, not at that time of night, not the way he was looking up at her.

The hearing resumed on Tuesday. Bill Peterson called Odell Titsworth to the stand. He had a reputation as a fearsome thug, with his four felony convictions; he had black hair that fell in waves to his shoulders. But despite his record, there was a quiet gentleness about him; it was when he got drunk that he could turn violent.

Titsworth testified about all the reasons he could not have been involved in the disappearance, despite what Tommy Ward and Karl Fontenot had said on their tapes: he'd had a broken arm, broken by the police; he'd been nursing his broken arm that night at the home of his girlfriend and her mother. Peterson asked Titsworth to unbutton his sleeves and roll them up; there were tattoos from his wrists to his shoulders, on both arms. He said he had others: a tattoo of the grim reaper on his chest; a peacock on one leg; human figures on the other leg; a motorcycle on his back. He'd gotten them all in prison while serving time, he said.

Titsworth testified that while under arrest he asked the police to put him in a cell next to the suspects, so he could try to gather information from them; the police agreed. He said he was in the cell next to Ward for fifteen to twenty minutes. "He [Ward] said he was sorry he involved me and Fontenot, because he thought it came from a dream, and I was in his dream," Titsworth said.

He said he had never met either of the suspects before he was arrested in the case.

Peterson called Titsworth's girlfriend, Julia Wheeler, and her mother, Agnes Lumpmouth, to the stand. Both testified that Odell had been at home with them all that evening, in pain from a broken arm. The D.A. called Dennis Smith. The detective said Karl Fontenot had been unable to pick Titsworth from a photo lineup, and had said there were no tattoos or bandages on his arm the night of the crime.

On cross-examination, the defense attorneys kept trying to ascertain what information the police may have planted in the minds of the suspects before the taped statements were made. Smith was asked if in fact he was not the person who first mentioned Titsworth's name to the suspects. Smith said he didn't remember, that he might have mentioned it in the questioning of Ward.

The detective was asked whether he or anyone in his presence told Ward he had flunked a lie-detector test on October 18, before he taped his statement. Smith said he did not tell Ward that, and he did not remember anyone saying that in his presence. He was asked if he remembered a dream that Tommy Ward had had. "You asked, do I remember a dream that he had?" Smith said. "I don't know what he dreams. I wasn't there in the dream." Later he said, "Yes, I remember him telling me that he had a dream." But he said that had occurred days after the tape had been made.

About the town's response to the composite sketches, Smith said more than thirty people had called to suggest Ward, and that at least that many other names had been given as well. When he said the police had not taken the names of the people who were calling in, Mike Addicott asked, "How do you know that one person didn't make fifteen separate phone calls saying that looked like Tommy Ward?"

"I have no way of knowing," Smith replied.

After more than four days of testimony spread across two weeks, the hearing was not yet complete. But the judge and the attorneys had other cases coming up on their calendars. Judge Miller recessed the preliminary hearing until February 4.

The suspects were handcuffed and taken back to their cells, where they had been for almost three months. The attorneys for both sides left the courtroom, as did the spectators. Tricia was once more among them, now that the tapes had been played. Still among them, too, was the tall cowboy with the knee-high boots and his name carved into his belt.

Don Wyatt had an opening on his staff for a legal assistant. One of those who applied for the job that week was a pleasant, hard-working woman named Winifred Harrell. She'd been employed as a legal assistant for more than twenty years. For the first three years she had worked for Barney Ward, the blind attorney; she felt that was the best training she could possibly have had, having to do all of his reading for him. She then spent sixteen years with another local attorney, Lewis Watson. She had taken time off at the start of her second marriage, then had worked the past two years for still another attorney, Harold Hall. She was no longer happy there.

Don Wyatt was impressed with Winifred and her credentials. As he offered her the job, he felt he had to warn her. "If you take the job," he said, "you will be handling the Tommy Ward file."

Wyatt felt it was only fair to warn her.

Winifred, who lived on Kings Road, had stopped letting her little daughter walk home alone from the schoolbus after Denice Haraway disappeared. She had been following the case, the hearings, in the newspaper and on television; she was convinced that Tommy Ward was guilty; she was convinced that, should the case go to trial, a jury would convict him. But she took the job anyway. Handling the Ward file would involve doing research, keeping the lawyers apprised of when various motions had to be filed. She felt that she could do the job, despite her personal opinion of Ward's guilt.

Her opinion was shared by just about everyone she knew, on wealthy Kings Road and elsewhere—everyone except one old friend: Barney Ward. Her mentor, she knew, believed the suspects were innocent.

Don Wyatt didn't know what to believe. He was getting sick of Tommy Ward—of his lies, his phony stories, his making statements despite Wyatt's advice to keep his mouth shut. His confession tape had been proved to be full of lies; at Wyatt's request he had written a long account of what had happened the weekend of the disappearance—he said he had been at home that night—and during the early days of his arrest; across the front page of the narrative, which was 110 handwritten pages, Ward had written, "This statement is the truth nothing but the truth so help me God"; then he had turned around and made up the Marty Ashley story. In between he'd given other names to the police of young men who he said had been there. Filled with frustration, Wyatt went to the jail to talk to his client. He told him he had had enough of Tommy's lies. He said he believed Tommy had been involved, although he did not think he killed the girl. He said if the case went to trial, a jury would convict Tommy and sentence him to death. He said he believed Tommy was protecting the person who was with him; he wanted to know whom he was protecting and why. He said Tommy should tell the truth, name the real killer, and plead guilty; the most he would then get would be life imprisonment, which could mean parole in only five years.

Wyatt said the jury would convict because reputable witnesses placed Tommy near the store that night, and because of the brutal story on the tape. He focused on Tommy's description of the girl's blouse; it was so detailed, the lawyer said, that Tommy could not have dreamed it, or been brainwashed by the police, that he had to have seen it. And especially, he said, the jury would convict because Tommy had now told so many different stories that he was clearly lying most of the time—and why would he lie if he did not have something to hide?

Wyatt told Ward's family the same thing; he told them that to save Tommy's life they must convince him to tell the truth, to admit his complicity, and to name the real killer, and say why he had been protecting him: if there was another killer.

The family was horrified, confused. Tricia felt that maybe "they" had now gotten to the lawyer, had bought him off. Joel rejected this theory. He felt they must do as the lawyer said; and Tricia soon agreed: they must try to convince Tommy to tell the truth, whatever it was, so he would not be executed.

Saturday night in Tulsa, Joel was asleep. He was awakened by the ringing of the telephone. Sleepily he answered it, wondering who would be calling at this hour; it was nearly two in the morning.

The voice on the phone was a man's. He told Joel he had better stop helping to defend Tommy Ward—or else. Then the line clicked dead.

Joel remembered the voice. It was the same man who had called him two weeks ago, at the same time on a Saturday night, and had said the very same thing.

Joel didn't tell his mother, who was living with him, of the call; he didn't want to frighten her.

The next day, when Tricia went to visit Tommy, there were tears in her eyes as she sat on the stool in the small, dark room and looked at him through the narrow glass window. There were dark circles under his eyes; his skin was pale; he had lost a lot of weight, he looked emaciated; he was not being allowed any sunlight at the jail, or any exercise.

Tommy told Tricia they needed a new lawyer, someone who believed he was innocent; he told her what Wyatt had said. She told him she already knew, that Wyatt had said the same thing to her. The lawyer was right, she said; Tommy had to tell the truth, whatever it was, and place his faith in the Lord. If he was involved, she said, he should show the police where the body was, and get off with a life sentence; he could be paroled in five years.

Tommy insisted to Tricia that he was innocent. He said his dream had really been a dream. He said he kept telling this to the police, that when he told all the lies on the tape, it was because the police had insisted and because he thought they would let him go when they saw it was lies. About his description of the blouse, he said the police had given him that information; he said the police had been lying on the witness stand when they said they hadn't.

But why did you keep giving out different names of guys who had been there? Tricia asked. Tommy said he'd been giving them a name every time he thought of someone that he knew had a gray pickup; he hoped the police would question them and find out they had done it.

Tricia could only believe him: because, if he knew who had been there, why would he give out these other names? And because he was her baby brother; he was Tommy; she didn't think he could have done such a thing.

He told her something else, before the knock on the door indicated their ten minutes were up. He said the police had arrested a man that week and put him in a cell near Tommy's, a man who runs back and forth in his cell all day, shouting, "Pigs eat flesh and bones! Pigs eat flesh and bones!" Perhaps the man knows something about the Haraway case, Tommy said; why don't the police investigate him?

Tricia warned Tommy to be careful; the man might be a police plant, put there to work on his nerves.

Alone in his cell again, Tommy took up a pen and some lined loose-leaf paper. He wanted to explain to Don Wyatt how the two things had come about that had angered the lawyer the most: the description of the blouse, and the Marty Ashley story. After enumerating all the things in his taped statement that had been proven to be lies, he wrote:

> The only thing in my statement that they could hold
> against me was the blows. I told them in my dream that she
> had a dress on. Mr. Smith started at me and the OSBI agent
> about that one. They cept on at me saying she eather had a
> blows with Red stripes or one with Blue roses with ruffels. So I
> knew she couldnt of had both on so I said blows with roses
> and ruffels. But the way they was acting they was trying to get
> me to say the blows with Red stripes. Even after I said the one
> with Blue roses and ruffels. They cept saying are you shure it

wasnt the one with Red stripes. If people would only know
how they done me they would see why I lied.

And the other day when I lied was because Jim every day he
would come and tell me that even though you didn't do it you
giving that statement they are going to birn you. Then he
would say we need to think of a way that they can see that
your willing to take the 7 to 15 years at least they wont kill you
for something you didnt do. Then I would say I didnt have
nothing to do with it. And he would say do you think they
care rather you did it or not. All that matters to them is to sattisfy the public and get them off their backs. Then he cept on
comming back telling me that he shure hates seeing a innicent
man put to death over sombody else's doings but we need to
figure out a way that at least they wont put you to death. It got
me to thinking maby they are going to put me to death maby
they dont care rather they put me to death them knowing my
innicents. Maby they are going to pin this off on me to sattisfy
the publick. So thats why I made up the statement. I thought
well at least I could get 7 to 15 and at least I wont be put to
death over something I didnt do so I made up the statement. I
knew that they would see Marty Ashley innicent. . . .

God dont want me to try and do things myself. He wants
me to put him first and tell the truth that would be the way
out of this dont try to do it yourself you will only make things
worse. He says you lieing will only make things worse. Tell the
truth that is the only way you will get out. Thats your only
way of excaping. He says tell the truth and stick with it no
matter how bad things might seem, tell the truth. God knows I
didn't do it and he dont want me to lie and make things worse
he wants me to tell the truth and stick by it. And I will.

One day while the hearing was in recess, Tricia was at home when
she heard a knock on the front door. The kids were at school; Rhonda
was being taunted again by her classmates, because the case, during
the hearing, was being publicized again in the newspaper and on the
television news. The little foster kids, David and Lisa, were crawling
about the living room; Lisa, nurtured by Tricia and Bud for little more

than a month, was healthy now, was a pixieish little girl; David, with the face of a miniature Tab Hunter, demanded attention, had the habit of slamming his head into people's chests, hard, as if demanding love but also unconsciously venting aggression; it was a practice they were trying to break him of. Tricia went to the door and opened it; standing on the front porch was a woman named Vicki Jenkins.

Tricia knew Vicki from around town. Vicki's father worked with Bud at the mill; they would see each other in church sometimes, but they were not close. Vicki had never before come to the Wolf home. Surprised, Tricia invited her into the house.

Seated on one of the twin brown sofas in the living room, Vicki said she was upset: that there was something she needed to tell Tricia. She said she was a close friend of Karen Wise, who had testified against Tommy. She had been troubled ever since she heard of Karen's testimony, Vicki said, because Karen had told her before the hearing that she could *not* positively say it was Tommy Ward who had been at J.P.'s that night. She said Karen had told her that Karl Fontenot definitely was not one of the two, that although the other one "favored" Tommy Ward, she could not be sure it was him. Then the police had convinced Karen to make a positive identification, Vicki said.

Vicki also told Tricia that Karen had been getting threatening phone calls since she testified, and of the man Karen had seen lurking in the alley outside her house, who had frightened her so much that she had called the police.

Tricia thanked Vicki for the information. Her mind was in turmoil, was going ninety-to-nothin'. Who could this stranger in the alley be? Karen Wise had identified Tommy, but Tommy was in jail. Could the stranger be the real killer, who knew that Tommy was innocent? If Tommy had somehow gotten involved, could this be his accomplice, the one he was protecting? Was he threatening Karen so she would not identify him as well? But if he was the killer, why would he be hanging around Ada? Or was he still in Ada precisely because, in a town that small, if he left it would invite suspicion?

Tricia did not know what to make of it. She called Don Wyatt and told him what Vicki Jenkins had said.

When Bud got home from work, she told him of the visit. They also discussed the children. Rhonda was being hurt deeply by the taunting in school; her grades were suffering; thin already, she was losing weight. Bud's supervisor at the feed mill had suggested they send the kids to school in Allen, fifteen miles away; because their name is Wolf, the supervisor said, the kids in Allen would not know the relationship of Rhonda and Buddy and Laura Sue to Tommy Ward. But Bud was thinking that for the sake of the children, the whole family might have to move from Ada, despite their deep roots. One possibility, he told Tricia, was El Reno, a hundred miles away, west of Oklahoma City; Evergreen had another feed mill there; perhaps they would give him a job. He had to check, he said, to see if he would lose his seniority.

At the city jail, Karl Fontenot had adopted owl's hours. He slept all day and stayed awake all night, when the building was deserted except for the police dispatcher. In three months now he had not had a single visitor, except for a minister who had come at the beginning, whom Karl didn't know and didn't want and didn't count. Part of his nights he spent writing letters to his sisters in California, hoping they would answer; they never did. Unlike Tommy, Karl was introspective, was able to analyze himself to some extent: "I used to have a bar built around myself and wouldn't let anyone get close to me." He knew he was paying for that now in his aloneness. Living on the streets he had liked to fish and hunt and camp, and to draw; now, in the jail, he spent some of the long nights drawing. He fantasized sometimes about being a photographer "so I can see the world and travel." Always a quiet person, with little to say to anyone, he felt he was coping well with his time in the jail. Some nights, when it rained, he sat and listened to it all night long; he loved the smell of the rain.

It was the view of the detectives that Tommy Ward, reading the Bible for hours in his solitary cell, shaking, having nervous attacks, was at least showing remorse for what he had done, but that Karl Fontenot, less in touch with reality, was showing no remorse at all.

It was the feeling of Tricia and Bud and Miz Ward that Karl, having no family to turn to in Ada, no place to live except the streets, was enjoying his stay in jail, even though both he and Tommy were innocent, that he felt more secure inside than out, with a roof over his head, a place to sleep, meals guaranteed every day, for free. Periodically they heard through the grapevine that Karl was saying he might plead guilty, might say they had done it, even though they hadn't; they were afraid Karl would do that so he could live his life in prison.

The defense attorneys felt this was all some kind of game to Fontenot, that because he knew he was innocent, he was sure he would be freed one day, and meanwhile he would enjoy the game, that he didn't truly comprehend the trouble he was in.

In the county jail Tommy felt that his mind was clearing about that night in April, that he was starting to remember details. He told Tricia that was the night Willie Barnett had come by, and had started annoying the bird, Pretty Boy, and Tommy had made him leave the house. And then Jimmy had come by, he said, and they had gotten into an argument, because Jimmy said Tommy owed him $150, and Tommy said he didn't. That would prove he'd been home that night, Tommy said.

Tricia, excited and hopeful, relayed the information to the lawyers. Maybe now the district attorney would see that Tommy was innocent, she thought, and would drop the charges, and they could all get on with their lives, like before.

When the hearing in the Haraway case resumed on February 4, it was entering its fifth full day, a month after it had begun. Dennis Smith was on the stand. He conceded that the house in which Karl Fontenot had said they had burned Denice Haraway's body was burned down by the owner the year before; he conceded that soon after making the tape, Fontenot had claimed he was innocent, had said he had lied in the taped statement.

"I'd never been in jail or had a police record in my life and no one in my face telling me I killed a pretty woman that I'm going to get the death penalty so I told them the story hoping they would leave me alone. Which they did after I taped the statement. They said I had a choice to write it or tape it. I didn't even know what the word statement or confessing meant till they told me I confessed to it. So that's the reason I gave them a untrue statement so they would leave me alone," Fontenot would state later.

Smith, under questioning, discussed Fontenot's use of the word "abducting" in his statement; when Karl said he abducted her, he seemed to think it meant having sex with a dead person.

The detective was questioned about the incident in which he and Mike Baskin had brought a skull and bones to Tommy Ward's cell; Baskin had also been cross-examined about that. "We already had confessions. We wanted to get the body back for the family," Smith testified. "We knew we wouldn't have been able to use the body as evidence in court if we found it that way."

Soon after, the state rested its case.

The defense called only one witness: Karen Wise. The attorneys asked her about the information Tricia had relayed to them from Vicki Jenkins. Ms. Wise said she had been receiving strange phone calls since she testified at the hearing, and that she had been frightened by a prowler lurking below her apartment, a tall man in blue jeans and boots, walking up and down in the alley. Mike Addicott asked if she had not told a friend the prowler looked like one of the men at J.P.'s the night of the disappearance. Ms. Wise replied that the man resembled the one who had been with Tommy Ward that night.

The testimony concluded. Defense attorneys requested a continuation of the hearing until OSBI agent Gary Rogers could be subpoenaed to testify; Rogers had not been present at any of the sessions, though officially he was the officer who had brought the charges; he was away in Houston attending a law-enforcement training program. Judge Miller denied the request, in the interest of a speedy trial, he said, and because witnesses to all events connected to the case and attended by Rogers had already been questioned.

The defense attorneys then argued their central motion: that all of the charges should be dismissed for lack of evidence.

Judge Miller did not adjourn the hearing to ponder its climactic decision. He was ready with his ruling. There was tension in the courtroom. The district attorney, the defense attorneys, the suspects, the spectators—all sat motionless.

On the rape charge, the judge sustained the objection of the defense attorneys. He ruled that no evidence had been introduced, beyond the statements of the defendants, proving rape. The rape charge was dismissed. He overruled the defense objections on the other three counts. He ordered that Tommy Ward and Karl Fontenot be bound over for formal arraignment on charges of robbery with a dangerous weapon, of kidnapping, and of murder in the first degree.

Judge Miller set the formal arraignment for Ward for 9:45 A.M. Monday, March 4—a month in the future—and Fontenot's for March 5. At the arraignment they would be asked to plead to the charges against them.

Bill Peterson told the press after the hearing that he might appeal the dismissal of the rape charge.

Tricia and Bud and Miz Ward and the rest of Tommy's family were distraught; they did not understand the logic of the judge's ruling. "How can they bring charges of murder?" Tricia wanted to know once again. "They still ain't found her body. They still don't know for sure she's daid."

When Dennis Smith left the courthouse, he turned right, walked half a block, past the county jail, crossed Townsend Street, and entered City Hall. Police headquarters occupied the rear of the building and the basement; his office was downstairs. The entrance to City Hall was a double glass door. Scotch-taped inside the door on the left was a Xeroxed flyer, 8½ inches by 14 inches. Near the top of the flyer was the yearbook photograph of Donna Denice Haraway, and beside it her description; below it were the composite drawings of the two suspects Karen Wise had seen at J.P.'s. The flyer requested any information about the young woman's disappearance.

It had been pasted to the door for more than nine months. Smith made no move to take it down now.

In Tulsa on Saturday night, Joel Ward was awakened once again by a late-night call. It was the third such call in six weeks, on alternate Saturdays. The man's voice was the same as before; his message was more explicit this time. He didn't warn Joel to stop helping defend Tommy "or else." He warned that if he didn't stop helping Tommy, then the entire Ward family would be killed.

Joel hung up the phone, frightened. He thought of his mother, in her sixties, who once had had heart trouble, soft-spoken, unschooled, out of her depth in the world of courtrooms and lawyers, as were they all; of Tricia and the kids, Rhonda and Buddy and Laura Sue, so vulnerable in their school playgrounds or anywhere; of Kay, sweet and pretty now at eighteen; of all the others. He didn't know what to do about the threat.

He had been brought up to believe that in times of trouble you went to the police. He didn't dare do that now. He was afraid the caller *was* the police.

If there was any connection between the frightening calls to Karen Wise and to Joel Ward, no one was making it.

8

ANNIVERSARY

The Evergreen feed mill, towering as it does a block from the center of town, is the symbolic throbbing heart of Ada; the railroad track is its aorta. Carried in on the shuddering trains are corn, wheat, oats, and barley grown in near and distant countrysides; carried out by the trains in fifty-pound sacks are assorted feed mixtures for horses, cattle, pigs. With 120 employees during peak production, the mill is not the largest employer in town; Valley View Hospital employs more; so do Brockway, Solo Cup, Ideal Cement, and the J. P. Emco Company, maker of molded rubber parts for automobiles. But because of seasonal layoffs and hirings—production of feed is high in the autumn and winter, drops off in spring and summer when pastureland is abundant—more of the people of Ada have probably worked at the mill at some point in their lives than anywhere else.

When Tommy Ward's father died in 1979, Tommy quit school and got a job at the mill. He had two conflicting needs at the time. One was to work, to help support himself and his family; the other was to fill the emptiness caused by his father's death; he did this with drinking, dope, carousing. The needs were incompatible; he was fired after three weeks when he showed up for work drunk. During that brief stay at the mill, Tommy recommended his brother-in-law, Bud, for work. Bud was hired as a loader, hauling the fifty-pound sacks onto the trains. He quickly advanced to mixer, operating a computer that mixed the various feeds in the proper proportions. Highly thought of,

Bud was still at the mill six years later, supporting Tricia, the kids, and the foster kids.

Another who worked at the mill was a man named Donnie Meyers. Not long before Denice Haraway vanished, Donnie Meyers had disappeared, inside the mill, while on duty there; his work station was vacant. For six hours the mill was searched; Donnie could not be found. Then the feed that was being drawn out of a huge, sixty-foot-high tank stopped coming out. The foreman immediately said, "That's where he is! He's in that tank!" Workers climbed to the highest rafters of the mill and looked down into the tank. They saw a hardhat on top of the mound of grain. Donnie Meyers had fallen about forty feet, into eighteen feet of feed. He'd been sucked into the feed and had suffocated, his neck possibly broken in the fall. When they got him out, his face was black. At his funeral the casket was open. Some of his co-workers could recognize him only by a crooked finger that he had broken once.

Donnie Meyers had a sister who was a good friend of Tricia. The sister had worked for a few months, several years earlier, with Denice Haraway, at Love's Country Store on Mississippi. She told Tricia one day about how Denice, a nice girl, had been madly in love with a man from Texas back then; about how surprised she had been when she heard that Denice had married Steve Haraway instead of the Texas man. "Maybe he came back for her," she said. "Maybe he came back and they ran away together."

For months afterward, Tricia clung to this hope: that the boyfriend from Texas had come back, that Denice had run away with him. "I know I'm clutching at straws," Tricia would tell her friends. "But when your brother is in jail accused of murder, you clutch at straws."

What Tricia did not know was that the day after Denice disappeared, the police asked her mother, Pat Virgin, for a list of Denice's former boyfriends, who might have been jealous. The list was not long. Prominent on it was the man from Texas. The police asked the Texas Rangers to check him out; word came back that the man worked on oil rigs, that he had been working offshore the night Denice Haraway disappeared.

Tommy Ward was formally arraigned on the morning of March 4 on charges of robbery, kidnapping, and murder in the Haraway case.

At the same time, in the smaller courtroom at the opposite end of the hallway, another proceeding was taking place. A woman named Linda was seeking to regain custody of her two small children. Their names were David and Lisa; they were the foster kids in the home of Bud and Tricia Wolf.

In the larger courtroom, brought from the jail by sheriff's deputies in his prison-white coveralls, Ward saw a new face behind the bench. The long, lean, moustached face of Judge Miller was gone; his role, under state law, had been completed when he ruled that the suspects should go to trial on three counts. In its place was the round, pink, clean-shaven face of Judge Ronald Jones; as district judge, it would be his assignment to conduct the arraignment, to rule on subsequent motions, and to preside at the trial itself.

Accompanied by attorney Mike Addicott of Wyatt & Addicott, Tommy Ward pleaded not guilty to all three counts.

Tommy's family and the local press had expected that a trial date would then be set. But the defense attorneys had filed numerous motions in the case; Judge Jones set March 21 as the date on which these motions would be argued in court. Addicott told Ward's family that a trial was not likely to take place until mid-summer; Tommy would have to remain in jail at least that long.

At the same time, in the smaller courtroom, another judge ruled that the young mother of David and Lisa had not shown sufficient reason why her children should be returned to her; she was told she could apply again in mid-July. In the corridor between the two courtrooms, the young woman approached Tricia; she knew who she was, had been allowed to see the children periodically; had seen for herself how well they were doing.

"I want to get my children back," the woman told Tricia. "But if I can't get them back, I hope you'll keep them."

Tricia was deeply moved.

The next day, Karl Fontenot pleaded not guilty to the identical charges of robbery, kidnapping, and murder. His attorney, George Butner, was granted five days to file additional motions in the case. Judge Jones asked if Fontenot understood that consideration of the motions would delay his trial; Butner said that he did. The judge set March 26 as the date for arguing these motions.

One of the motions filed by Wyatt & Addicott was to get Tommy Ward to a state hospital for psychiatric evaluation; the lawyer felt that a change of scenery, after four and a half months in solitary confinement, would do Tommy good. When Tommy heard of this motion, he telephoned Tricia from the jail.

"Is he sending me there so they'll say I couldn't have done it?" he asked. "Or does he want them to think I'm crazy? Because if he does, I can act crazy, all right. I can make them think I'm crazy."

Tricia told him not to act crazy.

On Friday, March 15, Tommy Ward's sister Joice gave birth to a son in Tulsa; it was her fourth child. The same afternoon, his baby sister, Kay, eighteen, gave birth to her first child, also a boy, in Ada. In the space of an hour, Tommy Ward, in his jail cell, became an uncle twice.

His sister Melva, in California, was expecting her fourth child around June 1. And Tricia, who had miscarried in December, had learned the week before that she was pregnant again. She and Bud, despite their tight financial situation, despite their unavoidable preoccupation with the plight of Tommy, had decided they wanted one more child; they were surprised she had gotten pregnant so quickly. Tricia immediately got off her feet, went "down," as she called it, spent day after day sprawled on the living room sofa, resting, hoping that by remaining down during the early weeks of pregnancy she could overcome her history of miscarriages.

The night that Joice and Kay gave birth, Tricia had a dream. She dreamed that she was alone in a car parked near the old Ward house on Ashland Avenue, in which they all had grown up. She could not move the car, because a man was standing in front of it, pointing a gun at her; another man was in back of the car, also pointing a gun at her. One of the men was a neighbor, an old man, who had testified against Tommy at the preliminary hearing, saying he used to see Tommy riding around in a gray pickup; the other man was a leader of her church. In the dream the men had taken her children away from her.

"Why did you take my children?" Tricia asked. She was in a panic. "Why did you take my children? Why did you take my children?"

Her whimpering awakened Bud, asleep beside her. He propped himself up on an elbow and watched her twitching lips, and listened.

The next day, when Tricia related her dream, Bud told her what he had done.

"Why didn't you wake me up!" Tricia demanded.

Bud said, "Because I wanted to find out why they took your children."

The reason they had taken her children in the dream, Tricia said, was this: they had pointed guns at her, one from the front, one from the back, and said, "Because you killed Denice Haraway! Because you killed Denice Haraway!"

St. Patrick's Day fell on Sunday. It was Bud and Tricia's twelfth wedding anniversary. They made no special plans for the day. Tricia would remain beached on the sofa, trying to preserve the embryo growing inside her. It would be only the second Sunday she did not visit Tommy at the jail; the first had been the day of her miscarriage in December.

In the early afternoon, Bud went to the jail to visit. In the small visiting room Tommy seemed very nervous, his hands shaking while he talked and laughed. He said he had been praying a lot. He had started writing poetry to pass the time—religious poems, mostly. Some he had sent to Tricia. There were others, too, Tommy said, poems about the girls who had done him wrong.

He smiled when he said that.

The snaps of his white coveralls were open to the waist; Bud could see his smooth bare chest. He was wearing old cowboy boots, which he showed off proudly. The week before, his mother had brought him a new pair of tennis shoes, which is what he usually wore. But the jailers took away the laces, and he did not like the sneakers without laces; he had traded them to another inmate for the worn cowboy boots.

Mostly, Tommy told Bud, he just sits in his cell and twiddles his thumbs. And he demonstrated, twiddling his thumbs rapidly, first forward, then back.

"You're getting pretty good at that," Bud said.

Tommy laughed.

"The days are getting longer," he said. "Longer and longer every day."

He said he thought his trial date at last will be set on Thursday, after the lawyers argue the motions in the case.

When he returned to the house, Bud fixed lunch while Tricia remained on the sofa, beneath a light blanket. From time to time her muscles began to ache; carefully she swung her legs to the floor and walked three steps to an easy chair and sat there for a while. She thought back over the twelve years of her marriage: the three kids, eight foster kids in the last two years; she looked at Lisa, crawling about on the floor, smiling her chipmunk smile; Lisa was up to eighteen pounds, was doing fine.

She thought of Tommy.

Maxine had come by the day before to say happy anniversary, and had asked to see their wedding album. They had leafed through the dozen pages: the ceremony—how slim she was then—she and Bud stuffing their faces with wedding cake, a group shot of the groom and bride surrounded by all her brothers and sisters except Jimmy, who had been in the service. Tommy was in the center, neat in his blue suit; he was twelve then; he had been their ring bearer. Beside him was Kay, the flower girl, six years old; now she was eighteen, a mother for nearly twenty-four hours.

In mid-afternoon, Melva telephoned from California, to wish them a happy anniversary, and to find out how Tommy was doing. He was doing just fine, Tricia said. A few minutes later, as if the twins had a psychic connection, Melvin called from Virginia. She hadn't heard from either in weeks. Melvin was not calling to wish them a happy anniversary; he had forgotten about that. He was calling to say the aircraft carrier he was assigned to, the U.S.S. *Coral Sea*, was shipping out in the morning; he would be out of touch for three weeks. But he was hoping for an early discharge, he told Tricia; he thought he might be back in Ada by May 1. He had applied for it because of Tommy's situation.

"I'm gonna bring a bunch of big old Navy boys home," Melvin said, "and straighten things out."

When she handed the phone to one of the kids to hang up, Tricia recalled something Joel had said recently. "We were drifting apart," he'd said, "but Tommy has drawn us together."

And she recalled something Tommy had said: "When I got arrested, I thought all of you would hate me."

The two-story building at the corner of Fourteenth and Rennie is ocher brick with red brick trim. There was an eerie poignancy about it as it was washed by the late afternoon sun. The entrance on the corner was marked 200 East Fourteenth. It was the dental office of Dr. Jack Haraway, Denice's father-in-law, a member of the Rotary Club—"high society," in the eyes of Tricia Wolf. The door behind it, 202, led to a stairway and the apartment in which Steve and Denice had lived. The curtains were drawn, seemed always to be drawn these days. There was no sign of life.

Tricia had heard that shortly after the disappearance, Steve Haraway had gone off to Dallas or somewhere, and never had returned. Dorothy Hogue, the reporter for the Ada *News* who was covering the case, believed something different. "I never heard he left town," Ms. Hogue said. "I heard he just sits up there alone in that apartment, every day and every night. Just sits there, waitin' for her to come back."

The truth was somewhere in between. Steve Haraway had taken his final exams, had graduated from East Central. He had taken a job as a salesman with a dental pharmaceutical firm that was based in New Jersey. He still lived in the apartment, but five days a week he was out of town, traveling across Oklahoma, selling pharmaceuticals. On weekends he would return, visit with his family, visit with his friends. Some of the time he would sit alone in the apartment. Most of Denice's belongings still were there.

Alone in his cell, Tommy Ward, too, was thinking of a woman: of Lisa Lawson, the only girl he had loved.

As a teenager he had been shy with girls, had been teased by his friends because of it. He described his first relationships in the long essay he had written for Don Wyatt. He began the passage with a paragraph about his father:

> My dad was a good man. He wouldnt let me go some of the
> places I wanted to go. But it was for my owne safty. He would
> tell me about the good things and the bad things about the

world. I never got to come into town much. The only time I got to come into town was to go to church or to go to the store with him or mom. Sometimes I would sneak off and go over to one of my friends house across the highway. He always knew were to find me and he would punnish me for not telling where I was going. But I knew it was right for disobay-ing him.

So then time passed and I was learning more about the good and of the evel. And I alwase made shure I was doing good and staying in the house of the lord. Then people at school thought there was something wrong with me cause I never taken out a girl on a date. They would laugh and say he's almost 16 years old and never taken out a girl. I told them I didnt care what they thought. That when I meat a girl I want to make shure she is the right one for me. And at the time I didn't care to much about trying to find a girl. But there was a girl I thought was really nice to me and all. So one day I thought I would show them that I will go out with a girl. So I ask this girl if she would go out with me. She said, shure were will we go. I ask her if she would go to church with me. She started laughing at me. I ask her what was wrong. She thought I was crazy. She told me there was no lord or there was no God or no heven. We sit down and I talked to her about there was a lord and God and a heven. And I talked to her and tryed to get her to believe me. She still thought I was crazy. So then I didn't talk to her much after that day. I went to church and ask the lord to forgive her and that some day she would see that there is a lord and God and a heven.

A year passed after that without Tommy dating. His father became ill, had several operations, was sent home to die. Tommy wrote:

I quit school and got a job at Evergreen Feeds. Then I quit going to church and started running around with the wrong people. I didn't care about nothing. The truck drivers would come in and give me pills to take. I was working midnight to 8 oclock shift. Then I started smoking pot and staying out late and drinking and I didn't care about myself. Then one night my boss fired me. Cause I came to work drunk and I was late. But I didn't care. All I wanted to do was do all these bad things. I met a girl and all I thought about her was to go jump in bed with her. I didn't love her. Then she broke up with me. Then I started loosing my friends. And started running around with bad ones.

Then one day mom ask me to go to church with her so I did. I went up and ask the lord to forgive me for the foolish ways I been acting. I was loosing my friends and I lost my girl-friend and I ask the lord to forgive me. And he did. I started getting back my friends. And if anyone was in need of help I would help them out the best way I could.

Then time passed and I met lisa lawson. I was madley in love. I would do anything I could for her. She changed my life completly. I caird more about her than I ever cared about a girl. Then she was at me to get a job.

Tommy got a job with his brother Jimmy, in Odessa, Texas. He ran up large phone bills calling Lisa. He was fired and came back to Ada.

I was so happy to see lisa and be back with her. Then one day we broke up. I felt like the world had ended for me. She thought when I was in Texas that I was seeing another girl. Then a cupple weeks later we seen each other and we talked. Then I was happy to get her back. Then we started going to church with her grandpa and sometimes with my mom.

After a time, Lisa enrolled in Seminole Junior College, thirty miles away.

I would go up to the school with her and sit in the car all day till she got out of classes. Then one day she got a apt. So I moved in with her and went out looking for a job. I couldn't find one up there nowere. So then I came back to Ada and started looking for a job. lisa was mad at me for comming back to Ada. She thought that I came back to run around. So then she broke up with me.

Lisa began dating other people. Tommy kept trying to win her back. Lisa kept refusing.

One day when I was walking into town I seen lisa go by. I waved at her and she stoped. I started crying and I ask her to come back to me and she said no.

Tommy kept trying. He heard Lisa was dating a guy he knew named Ronnie Smith. He was very upset by this. He quarreled with Ronnie about her.

Then I apolijized for the way I was acting and told them I was sarry. That I still loved lisa and changed my ways and started back to church. Until I got the job in Norman. Cause I had to work 7 days a week. Then lisa assepted my polligy and I went back to Norman. Then this happened. I was writing a letter to her telling her that I was sorry for the ways I was act-ing. And I told her that I was leven it up to the lord if he ment for us to get back together he would see us back. Then I was writing to her about this. About Mr Smith questioniong me. And I told her that I was going to take a pollygraph test to prove my inincents. Then I wrote I will let you know what happens after I took the test. I didn't ever get to finnish the letter cause this happend.

That had been five months before. In jail he had tried to forget her. But now, with spring coming, though there were no seasons inside, he was thinking again of Lisa. He wrote her a letter, enclosed it in a note he sent to Tricia, asking her to see that Lisa got it.

The letter to Lisa wasn't sealed. Tricia read it. In the note, Tommy told Lisa how much he had been thinking of her of late, how his life had changed, how he was a different person now, how he had gotten a new outlook in jail. He wrote that when he got out he wanted to make something of himself. He was sure he was going to get out of this mess soon. He was hoping that when he got out, Lisa would want to share his life.

Tricia did not know what to do with the note. There was a problem with giving it to Lisa. Lisa had gotten married two months before. Her name now was Lisa Lawson Smith.

Tricia and Miz Ward had decided, when Lisa got married, not to tell Tommy.

On the first day of spring, the Ada Rotary Club held its annual fundraising pancake fry at the firehouse. The men and women of Ada began lining up at six in the morning to eat their breakfasts in the firehouse, and would continue to arrive until seven in the evening for their lunches, their dinners, their suppers. For three dollars each they ate and drank their fill of pancakes, bacon, sausage, coffee, three flavors of punch. The money raised would be used to support the Rotary Club's civic projects.

The members of the Rotary Club—businessmen and professional men of all descriptions—wore pink aprons and white paper caps. Though it was a Wednesday, a workday, they each were donating all or part of their day. Some stood behind large grills, mixing batter, pouring it onto the grills, turning the pancakes as they sputtered to the proper shade of golden brown. Others stood behind long tables that held warmers filled with bacon and sausage. Still others stood by large coffee urns, filling paper cups. Behind a table near the pancake makers, handing out packets of butter, dressed like the others in apron and paper cap, was Dr. Jack Haraway, the dentist.

"Surely you can use three of these," he said to a weather-beaten, wiry man moving past him, his plate laden with pancakes. The dentist held out his manicured hand. The man took the three packets of butter and moved on. There was no exchange of words between them. The man with the pancakes picked up a paper cup of coffee with his free hand and moved among the long tables that had been set up in the firehouse for the occasion—the fire trucks were parked on Twelfth Street, around the corner—until he found an empty seat. He sat and poured maple syrup onto his pancakes from one of the bottles that dotted the tables, and he began to eat.

The man was C. L. Wolf, Bud Wolf's father, Tricia's father-in-law;

an electrician by trade, a painter at Monday night art classes, a bowler on Wednesday nights, the proprietor of the small farm in Happyland that he was building with his wife, Maxine. C.L.—his full name was Charles Leo, as were Bud's and Buddy's, but nobody called any of them that—was fifty-seven, with gray hair and a quiet demeanor. He was not a member of the Rotary Club or of any civic group other than the Unity Baptist Church; a resident of Ada for thirty-five years, he was known only to his friends and business associates. But he was a vital cog in the life of the town, whose untouted skills enabled Ada to function.

C.L. worked at Luton Motors, a long, dark machine shop set behind a parking area on Twelfth Street. In a small industrial town such as Ada, motors were visibly at the core of life: they ran the pumps in the oil fields, the machines in the factories, the generators at the power plant. Hardly a day went by when a motor—or five motors, or ten motors—did not burn out somewhere in town. C. L. Wolf was the only man in town who could fix them. In the long, dark shop he would hoist the motors by himself onto his work table; small motors might weigh ten or fifteen pounds; larger ones might weigh 250 pounds. Opening the motor, he would rip out the tangled mass of blackened, burned-out wire that was its core. He would take strands of gleaming new copper wire and thread them piece by piece into the motor's heart, braiding them into the appropriate thicknesses. When the braiding was done, he would soak the motors in chemical solutions and varnishes, coating them, hardening the copper coils. Four or five hours of patient hand labor were required on every motor. Sometimes Solo Cup or Brockway or some other factory that operated around the clock wanted a burned-out motor repaired immediately. At those times, C.L. went home and wolfed down the supper that Maxine had prepared and then went back to the shop, telling her not to wait up; he worked alone through the night and waited for the motor to be picked up at six or eight in the morning; then he went home to get a few hours' sleep. In thirty-five years he had rewound about fifteen thousand of the town's motors.

C.L. was not the owner of the shop; he was one of four employees, but the only one who could rewind motors. After thirty-five years he was still receiving humble wages, no paid vacations, no paid holidays;

on those rare occasions when his work was caught up and there were no motors in the shop to rewind, he would be sent home, and would not be paid for his time until additional motors came in. The only fringe benefit known to exist at Luton Motors was that every year the boss bought several tickets to the annual Rotary Club pancake fry and gave them to his employees, so they could have a free pancake lunch.

So it was that C.L. came to the firehouse and filled his plate and took the three butters from Dr. Haraway and sat on a metal folding chair and began to eat. As he did, he recalled how he and Jack Haraway had grown up together in a town called Atoka, fifty miles south of Ada; how they had played football together. It was during the Second World War, and after graduation C.L. joined the Army Air Corps, went off to be a radio operator in the South Pacific. After the war, in 1950, he moved to Ada, because his parents had, and went to work for Luton Motors. At about the same time, Jack Haraway completed dental school and opened his office in Ada; eventually he acquired a large house east of town, and became active in church and civic affairs.

The two men, despite their boyhood together, had never become friends in Ada. When they passed on the street, they would nod. C.L. well knew who Jack Haraway was, but the dentist usually acted as if he could not quite place C.L.

As he drank his coffee, people passing among the tables said hello to him, and he said hello back. He knew a lot of the pancake eaters through the motor shop.

"Most everybody in town has motors," he said. "Even dentists have motors. On their drills, you know."

He did not recall Dr. Haraway ever sending him a motor to be fixed.

That same afternoon, the first day of spring, Bud Wolf, on vacation from the feed mill to allow Tricia to rest, needed to get out of the house for a time. He decided to take a brief hike: to go look at the site where, in his taped statement, Karl Fontenot said he and Tommy and Odell Titsworth had raped and killed Denice Haraway and burned her body.

Bud knew the area well. He and Tommy used to go hunting there often, years ago. They had been close then, when he and Tricia were newly married and Tommy was growing into his teens. Tommy had become for a time the brother that Bud never had. (He had one sister, who'd left Ada years ago.) Bud had become Tommy's idol; unlike Tommy's brothers, Bud didn't treat him as a runt.

It was a gray day, with intermittent drizzle. Bud drove his old green Pontiac to the edge of town and parked beside the power plant just outside the city limits, at the very spot where, on the tape, which Bud had seen at the preliminary hearing, Tommy had said they parked that night. As Bud got out of the car, his boots sank into mud made thick and soft by several days of rain. He opened a gate in a wooden fence, closed it behind him, began to follow a double path of tire tracks down a sloping meadow of wild grass and underbrush studded with thickets of trees.

As he slogged through the wet grass, Bud recalled pleasant days of hunting here with Tommy, hunting rabbits, squirrels, coons, doves. He came to Sandy Creek, swollen and muddy now, and recalled that one time as they walked along, Tommy, about twenty feet ahead of him, still a boy, had seen a cottonmouth water moccasin, about six feet long, an inch and a half across. Tommy had begun jumping up and down on the snake, yelling, "Shoot him, Bud! Shoot him!"

"Get away from him," Bud had yelled, but Tommy had kept jumping on the snake as it slithered toward the water, jumping up and down on it and yelling, "Shoot him, Bud!"

Finally the snake had slithered into the water and gotten away, and Tommy had wailed, "Why didn't you shoot him?"

"Because you were riding the thing," Bud replied, "because if I shot, I would have killed *you*."

Tricia had been there, too, hiding behind a tree far from the snake, and for months afterward they laughed at Tommy, and called him "the snake rider."

Another time, Bud remembered as he walked along, looking for the burned-out house, he had shot a snake, and he and Tommy had run to it and cut off its head; and as they did, a frog's leg began to move in the opening. There was a lump in the snake, and it moved toward the opening and crawled out: a frog that the snake had just eaten, a frog that was still alive, that Bud's shot seemed to have saved.

But after crawling a few feet away, the frog, too, died, its belly punctured by the same .22 shot that had killed the snake.

Recalling the times that he and Tommy had shared, Bud admitted to himself, or took upon himself, a burden of guilt: the feeling that if only he had stayed close to Tommy, his brother-in-law might not be in this mess. But Tommy had gotten in with a bad crowd, with drug users, and they had drifted apart.

Bud paused, looked around. It had been years since he'd been out this way. He couldn't find the house. Then he remembered that it was on a hill. Tricia used to say she would like to live in that house because it was high up with a view of the highway but was also isolated. He climbed over a barbed-wire fence and to the top of the hill behind it. There he found the remains of the house.

The spot held pleasant memories. In the days when the house was standing, abandoned, Bud used to station himself in front of it to shoot at doves. When he missed, and the doves wheeled about in the sky above the trees, Tommy, standing behind the house, would get a shot at them.

Now there was no house left, just a foot-high foundation, filled with rubble, fragments of burned wood, a broken old stove. A few inches above the ground, the foundation was sectioned into quarters by thin white string, placed there by the police when they searched it in October for evidence, for some proof that Karl's and Tommy's "confessions" were true. The string was still intact. On a tree about a hundred feet away, bright yellow ribbons fluttered: also placed there by the police, as a marker, five months earlier.

In his tape, Tommy had said Odell Titsworth carried Denice Haraway here from the power plant. According to a story in the Ada *News*, Denice Haraway weighed 110 pounds. Bud thought: I couldn't carry Rhonda this far. Heck, I couldn't carry Laura Sue this far.

He looked at the rubble in the corner of the house where, Karl had said, they burned the body. Police had gone over the area with a metal detector, looking for dental fillings. All they had found were rusty nails, which lay haphazardly now where the police had tossed them, outside the foundation of the house.

The place, with its curious strings, had the undeniable feel of a murder scene—except that the police had found no evidence here of a murder.

Bud looked farther through the rubble. Near the rear had been a room that had been tiled. A mound of broken tiles was all that remained. Atop the mound, washed clean by the rain that still was falling, was a curved fragment, about an inch and a half wide. Painted in the broken tile, against a soft white background, was a lovely pink rose.

The first pretrial hearing in the case of the State of Oklahoma versus Tommy Ward, following his March 4 arraignment, was held on March 21. His mother and his brother Joel drove down from Tulsa, leaving at four in the morning, to be present in the courtroom. Dorothy Hogue of the Ada *News* sat in the first row, taking notes. Alone at the prosecution table, District Attorney Peterson browsed through lawbooks, chewing on the end of a black pen. Attorneys Wyatt and Addicott arrived, carrying books and folders. The court reporter, Hugh Brasher, took his place beside the bench, and then Judge Ronald Jones arrived, also laden with lawbooks, and took his place. The spectator section was empty, because this would be a day for technical motions only. For the same reason, the defendant was not required in the courtroom; Tommy Ward this day would not get forty-three steps of fresh air.

The court convened at 9:45 A.M., fifteen minutes late. The hearing lasted two hours and five minutes. Little of substance was decided. Wyatt and Addicott, taking turns, argued their case on eleven motions they had filed with the court.

The major motions requested a separation of the trials of Tommy Ward and Karl Fontenot; a separate trial for Tommy Ward on each of the three counts remaining against him: armed robbery, kidnapping, and murder; a change of venue because of pretrial publicity; a request for state funds to pay for a psychologist or psychiatrist to examine the defendant; a request for examination at a state mental hospital; a motion to suppress certain statements made at the preliminary hearing, on the ground that on October 25 Don Wyatt had been prevented by the police from visiting his client in jail. On all of these the judge requested written briefs to be submitted to the court by April 1. He would then give the prosecution ten days, till April 11, to respond with its own written briefs.

Two other motions involved requests that the prospective jurors be questioned individually, out of earshot of the others, about their opinions on the death penalty; and that the jury be sequestered during the trial. The judge said he would rule on these motions at the time of the trial.

On only one motion did the judge issue a ruling that day. The defense had requested that he declare the death penalty unconstitutional, as cruel and unusual punishment. The judge noted that the United States Supreme Court had already decided that issue. Mike Addicott argued that the Supreme Court had been "flip-flopping" on the issue, and might change its mind again next year. The judge overruled the motion.

Only a few comments during the two-hour hearing seemed noteworthy: Regarding the tapes, the district attorney said, "We have confessions in which each defendant admits his guilt." To which the defense replied that the confessions had not been given "freely and voluntarily," that they had been "illegally obtained by coercion by the police, the investigators reciting to the defendants their beliefs about what happened and then asking the defendants, 'That's what happened, isn't it?' . . . It's clear from the inconsistencies [on the tapes] that these people weren't even there."

At one point Judge Jones asked if there would be a defense of insanity. "We don't know at this point," Don Wyatt replied. "Not at this moment."

When the defense said it would need transcripts of the preliminary hearing in order to argue some of its motions, the court reporter said, when asked by the judge, that the transcripts would not be ready until early May. The judge seemed upset by the delays in bringing the case to trial. He looked at the defense attorneys.

"We are not urging a speedy trial," Don Wyatt said.

The district attorney was hoping that physical evidence against the defendants—perhaps even Denice Haraway's body—would turn up in the months that now still lay before a trial. The defense, apparently unafraid of this, believed that the more time that passed between the disappearance of Denice Haraway and the trial of Tommy Ward, the more time there was for public passions to cool—as, indeed, they seemed to be doing—the better the chance that Tommy Ward and Karl Fontenot might be acquitted.

That night, on Ada's one local television station, KTEN, the anchorwoman reported on both the six and ten-thirty newscasts about a hearing "in the death"—not the disappearance—of a local convenience store clerk. The station showed film of Tommy Ward, in his prison whites, with his hands cuffed behind him, walking from the jail to the courthouse, then back again. Superimposed on the film was the word "today." The only problem with the showing of the film was that Tommy Ward had not been in the courtroom—had not left the jail—that day.

To the Ward family, the newscast was one more example of a determination by the media to help convict Tommy.

More likely, it was simply small-town journalistic incompetence: bad reporting; loose use of file film.

The impact, however, might be the same.

Don Wyatt still did not know what his defense of Tommy Ward would be. He felt that he would have to put Ward on the witness stand, in an attempt to refute the prosecution's taped confession. But he knew that because of the many lies that Tommy had been telling, the district attorney could easily rip apart his credibility.

Affidavits had not yet been taken from the witnesses who could give Tommy an alibi. Robert Cavins had been under pressure from the corrections department, for which he now worked, not to be certain in his testimony about which night that weekend he had found Tommy asleep at 11:20. Robert had been threatened with the loss of his job if he did not agree to be interviewed by the OSBI about his knowledge of the case, without an attorney being present. He had agreed to do so. An affidavit was needed, as well, from Willie Barnett about the time the family said Willie had spent with Tommy on the crucial night.

Wyatt decided that what was needed was a meeting of all prospective witnesses for the defense. Following the hearing on March 21, in a parking lot across the street from the courthouse, he told Joel and Miz Ward to pick a day on which all members of the family who had anything to say relevant to Tommy's defense could get together, along with any other witnesses they knew of, such as Willie Barnett, and he would meet with them.

Wyatt was feeling pinched by the poverty of the Ward family. The $3,000 retainer was almost gone. He wanted to hire an investigator to follow up on possible leads that Tommy and the family had mentioned. But he did not want to spend his own or the firm's money to do it. He wanted to win the case, but he was not in the charity business; he had sometimes done charity work in his younger days; but he felt he was too old for that now. He wanted more cash to use in Tommy's defense.

He got word of this to Tricia, who relayed it to Miz Ward and Joel. The afternoon of the hearing, while Tricia rested on the sofa, trying to preserve her pregnancy, Joel and Miz Ward went to a finance agency to try to mortgage the house and the land it stood on. They asked for $20,000.

There were legal problems, they were told. The house and the land had belonged to Jesse Ward, and when he died six years before, it had not been probated. Legal work was necessary before clear title could be established and a loan be given.

The lawyers were set to work on the problem. Joel and Miz Ward drove back to Tulsa to await developments.

On Ninth Street, the telephone was ringing. Bud answered it, frowned, cupped his hand over the receiver. He turned to Tricia.

"Do you want to talk to Lisa?" he asked.

Tricia was hesitant, afraid. She'd had no contact with Lisa Lawson for a long time. She was afraid the district attorney had talked to Lisa, had learned of Tommy's rage the night they had split up, was afraid he would put Lisa on the stand as a witness against Tommy, to testify to his violent temper, to suggest he might well have killed Denice Haraway. Reluctantly, Tricia took the phone.

The call was not what she had feared. Lisa Lawson Smith merely said she wanted to be friends; she said she believed Tommy was innocent, that he could never do such a thing, that even in his rage she knew he would never hurt her. She wished Tommy well.

Tricia debated about the note from Tommy to Lisa: whether to tell

Lisa about it, whether to give it to her. It was an odd coincidence, Lisa calling out of the blue, just a few days after Tommy's love note to her arrived. Tricia decided not to mention the note; there was no point. Lisa was a married woman now. Why stir up old feelings?

She did not know what to do with the note. She decided to give it to Miz Ward, for her to decide. The question was whether to tell Tommy, now, that Lisa was married, and have him face reality; or to let him, alone in his jail cell, hold on to his fantasy.

Sometimes Tricia thought that the best thing would be for Lisa to go down to the jail one Sunday and tell him the truth herself, shout it through the little glass window. Other times she thought that would be the worst thing.

Nearly eleven months had passed since the disappearance. The police no longer were actively searching for the body. But when officers or deputy sheriffs happened to be out in rural areas for any reason, they automatically poked around in the underbrush, on the slim chance they might find something. Dennis Smith did that; Mike Baskin did that; District Attorney Bill Peterson did that.

Smith was well aware of the topsy-turvy nature of the case, how it was the exact opposite of most murder cases. In most cases you find a body, he mused; then you reconstruct the crime; then you look for a suspect. In this case they got the suspects first; then they reconstructed the crime; they still didn't have the body. Without the body, he knew, "we're putting all our eggs in one basket." The basket was the confession tapes.

At the district attorney's office, seated behind his desk, with several volumes of transcripts of the Rawlings "no-body" case piled on the floor beside him, Bill Peterson that week discussed the Haraway case with a journalist visiting from out of state.

"There's lots of pressure in this case," he conceded, "but it's all self-imposed. No one is bringing pressure from the outside. I'm convinced they're guilty. I want to get a conviction because of the viciousness of the case. I want to get a conviction because of the criminal justice system. God will take care of what comes later. They violated not only the laws of man but the laws of God."

Regarding the failure to find a body, he said, "They could have chopped her up in little pieces and left her all over the county. The pieces wouldn't be there anymore. Animals would have gotten them." He said he did not know why they had confessed but refused to give up the body. But he was convinced Denice was dead, and that Ward and Fontenot had killed her.

Peterson conceded that he would have a big problem if the courts ruled the taped confessions inadmissible. He said he would still go to trial with other evidence—that Ward was the last to be seen with her alive—but that he would have difficulty getting a murder conviction without the tapes. But he did not expect them to be ruled inadmissible. They had been obtained without coercion, he said.

Peterson had learned during his five years in office never to take a jury for granted. But every time he went over the transcripts of the taped statements, he grew optimistic that he would get convictions of Ward and Fontenot.

"Ward says on the tape that while Denice was screaming, he told her to shut up or he would bite her tit off," Peterson said. "And he laughs. Later, when Karl is on top of her, he says he saw her guts spilling out, and told Karl he was fucking a corpse, and Karl said, 'That's the way I like 'em.' And he laughs again. When the jury sees that tape, those laughs are gonna convict them."

In the jail, while Don Wyatt and Mike Addicott and Winifred Harrell were compiling legal briefs on his behalf, Tommy wrote poems. Most were about faith and devotion, but a series of five poems chronicled his lingering feelings for Lisa Lawson. The first four dealt with broken love, in thinly disguised generalities. But the fifth poem seemed to indicate a broadening of understanding, a coming to grips with reality, a maturation. It went as follows, including his own insertion of Lisa's name:

Isn't it a shame to lose someone you love
Sometimes you feel that you'll never rize above
You wonder inside if you will ever forget
Then look for a way, but you cant see one yet
You cry and cry, it seems theres no end
Inside you feel you've lost more than a friend

These things I know, because I've been there too
May be your way out could be what I write to you
Once I had a girl, and I loved her so much. (Lisa)
I felt I couldn't live without having her tuch
I told her how I loved her, and how she made me feel
That with the love I had for her, I could climb any hill
Then I found she didn't love me, and it broke my heart
I felt I would die, and my world fell apart
Then it came to me in the mist of my tears
I looked at what would have happened if we shared our years.
First she didn't love me, and it cant be one side
You have to love each other or the relationship dies.
I thought of her feelings, and if she'd have lied
Oh, what a disaster, the visions just cannot hide
At first I told myself the problem was me
But love had me blind and I couldn't see.
The love that I had for her was so true.
Never would I hert her or make her feel blue.
Now how could she turn away somone so real
She must think thats the way for her all the guys feel.
I see her the one losing, now it's all plain to see
She will never find anyone to love her like me.

Across the street, in the city jail, Karl Fontenot continued to sleep during the day and to stay awake at night. He passed the long dark hours drawing pictures, reading romance magazines—he referred to magazines as "books"—and writing long letters to his family. In the letters he asked his sisters and brother to answer, to write back so he would know they loved him; he never received a reply. Five months had passed; he still had not had a single visitor.

At the city jail, visiting was permitted every weekday afternoon, five days a week. At the county jail, where Tommy was being held—with his family eager to see him—only the Sunday visits were allowed.

On Friday, March 29, George Butner argued a series of motions before Judge Jones on Karl's behalf, including one that the judge withdraw from the case. There were motions to examine the prosecution's evidence, motions that Karl's right to due process had been violated, motions that the defense be informed of any lenient treatment being given prosecution witnesses. Many of the motions were similar to those Don Wyatt had argued ten days earlier on behalf of Tommy Ward. On most of the motions the judge again asked for written briefs, and reserved decision.

As she lay on the sofa, feeling at times like a beached whale, Tricia had a lot of time to think. She tried to put herself in the shoes of Denice Haraway's family. She could feel their terrible pain, their loss. But there was one attitude she couldn't understand, try as she might. "They seem to want Tommy to be guilty," she said. "It's almost as if they want her to be dead."

On the last day of March, a Sunday, Tricia roused herself from being "down" and went to the jail with Bud to visit Tommy. They were surprised to see him wearing not prison whites but blue jeans and a brown pullover shirt with his cowboy boots: looking like a normal person. The inmate to whom he'd traded his tennis shoes for the worn boots had been sent to the state prison at McAlester, where prison garb is mandatory. He had given Tommy his jeans and shirt. The jailers had agreed to let Tommy wear them in the jail, though he would have to wear his white coveralls for trips across the lawn to the courthouse. Still, Tommy told Bud and Tricia, the clothing made him feel much better.

He also felt better, he said, because the trustees and some of the jailers had begun to come back to his cell and visit with him. They didn't used to do that, he said, because they had believed he had done this horrible crime. Now they were getting friendly, telling him they thought he didn't do it, because if he had, the body would have turned up by now.

Ada is located in Oklahoma Judicial District 22, which is composed of three counties: Pontotoc, Seminole, and Hughes. In each of the counties a different district judge presided over most of the cases that went to trial. In Seminole the judge was Gordon Melson, the former district attorney, who also served as the administrative judge for an eleven-county area. In Hughes County the judge was Gary Brown. In Pontotoc it was Ronald Jones. Round-faced, fastidious, with a thin smile that at times seemed painful, Judge Jones had been the judge in the Haraway case since the conclusion of the preliminary hearing. It had been the belief of everyone concerned that he would preside at the trial.

The prospect did not fill the hearts of the defense attorneys with hope. They knew that Jones was extremely conservative, that he supported the death penalty; they felt his rulings often leaned too far in favor of the prosecution; that was the reason George Butner had filed, among his many motions, one that the judge disqualify himself.

On April 9, with most of the motions still pending before him, Judge Jones stunned all of the participants by doing just that. He issued a half-page "Ruling on Motion to Disqualify," which concluded, "Having considered the request and motion of the defendant, Karl Allen Fontenot, I find that I have no bias or prejudice in this matter and that no grounds or reasons exist which require disqualification. However, this Trial Judge now requests that this case be assigned to another Trial Judge."

In other words, he was saying that while there was no legal reason for him to disqualify himself, he was doing so anyway. He declined to elaborate further to the press.

The defense attorneys shared a common speculation as to why the judge had withdrawn. They knew that although Judge Jones publicly supported the death penalty, he had never had to impose it personally; they believed that if this case led to a conviction, and to a recommendation by the jury of the death penalty, the judge, being a staunch Christian, might have a personal moral and religious problem with ordering a man to be put to death.

The district attorney implied that there might be a different reason. "If I told you why he withdrew, you'd laugh," Bill Peterson said. But he, too, declined to elaborate.

Whatever the reason, Don Wyatt and George Butner were jubilant. They had felt that with Judge Jones presiding, their clients were on an express train to disaster; that without him, they might have a chance. The judge's withdrawal, they felt, was the first thing that had gone their way since the case began.

The responsibility for assigning a new judge to the case fell on

Gordon Melson, the presiding administrative judge for the district. But the very next day, Judge Melson, too, excused himself from responsibility. He requested that the Oklahoma Supreme Court or its administrative arm assign a judge to take over the Haraway case. The judge said he was excusing himself "for a number of reasons." He, too, refused to elaborate.

Many of Denice Haraway's relatives lived in Seminole County, where Judge Melson presided. The belief on both sides was that the judge was friendly with members of her family, and had excused himself from appointing a trial judge to avoid any possibility of taint, of reversible error, should the case lead to a conviction.

The withdrawals by Judges Jones and Melson were filed quietly within the judicial system. It was eight days before their actions reached the ears of Dorothy Hogue, who broke the story in the *News* on April 18. During those eight days the state Supreme Court had not yet named a new judge in the case; all motions were on hold; the suspects remained in jail. On the day the story appeared in the newspaper, they had been in jail for exactly six months.

With no reasons given by either judge, the story was the talk of the town. The most widely expressed feeling in the streets and shops and factories was that, with the two suspects in jail for six months, and with still no body found, no definitive proof that Denice Haraway was dead—and with no sign of a trial on the horizon—the case was becoming a political hot potato that neither judge wanted to touch.

The delays in the case were slowly altering the public perception. The majority of the citizens were still convinced that Ward and Fontenot were guilty; if they weren't guilty, why had they made those tapes? If they hadn't done it, who had? But some people were beginning to speculate—as Tommy Ward was discovering even inside the jail—that if the authorities had enough evidence, the trial would have been held already. This reasoning led, for some people, to a further step: perhaps they weren't guilty after all.

Ken Shiplet is the owner of Shiplet's Tire and Appliance, on West Twelfth Street. He lives near the Reeves Packing Plant. During the first of the citizen searches in the fall, shortly after Ward, Fontenot, and Titsworth were arrested, he and his wife, Susan, joined in the search for Denice Haraway's body. They looked at a dump site not far from their house, where people had a habit of dumping all sorts of refuse next to a sign that says, "No Dumping." Susan spotted a burned jawbone. They approached a group of deputies and OSBI agents and gave them the bone. That was the one that turned out, days later, to be the jawbone of a possum. Shiplet also serves as a bail bondsman. In previous, unrelated cases he had arranged bail for Odell Titsworth. Now, six months after the police had cleared Titsworth, Ken Shiplet was not sure they hadn't let the wrong one go, that Ward and Fontenot might be innocent.

Darichele Alvarado worked backstage at the Ada *News*. As a child, she had gone to school with Tommy Ward. When she heard of his arrest in October, one striking image from their school days had come to her mind. She recalled a day in first grade, when they were having "show and tell," and Tommy had come to school, barefoot, carrying a chicken snake to show and tell about. Though the snake was coiled inside a glass jar, the girls in the class had screamed; the teacher had shouted, "Out, out!" and made Tommy take the snake out of the school. Darichele recalled Tommy as being a quiet, withdrawn boy; she felt now that for him to be guilty, he would have had to have changed an awful lot.

Teresa Perry is a young woman whose mother rented a house to Dottie Fontenot and the five little Fontenots when Karl was a child. She and Karl went to school together in nearby Byng. She recalled Karl as a slow learner who seemed a little strange, often giggling for no apparent reason. But in her recollection he had never been violent, was always kind, even to animals. She'd been shocked when he was arrested. As the months passed with no action in the case, Teresa became more and more convinced that Karl could not have committed this crime. Coming from a less affluent section of town, she felt, like many in the poorer sections, that the authorities were not above pinning the crime on an innocent person merely to close the case, and that Karl, being alone in the world and scared, with no one to help him, was a perfect person to pin it on.

On and off for the past four years, Teresa had worked at McAnally's, out on North Broadway, across town from where Denice Haraway had disappeared. The disappearance did not frighten her, did not induce her to quit. Something bad, she reasoned, could happen on your own front porch.

Steve Haraway's close friend, Gary May, was having a small problem with the logistics of the case. He'd known Denice, was certain she had not run away; he'd helped distribute the flyers after her disappearance. A native of Ada, he'd heard of "the Ward kid," but did not know him; he'd never heard of Fontenot. He'd assumed from the time of their arrest, from the time he'd heard they had confessed, that they were guilty; he did not really doubt that now. But there was something on the tapes that bothered him, in addition to everything the police had proved to be false. He couldn't understand why, if you were to kidnap someone from McAnally's on East Arlington, and wanted to rape her without being caught, you wouldn't drive from the store out east; there was nothing east of Ada but an unlighted highway, and dark, wooded areas on both sides, as you went out toward Deer Creek Estates, toward Homer, toward Love Lady, toward Happyland, and beyond. But according to the tapes, the suspects had driven west from McAnally's, along Arlington Boulevard, and then Mississippi, the busiest, best-lighted streets in town, at 8:30 on a Saturday night, when Arlington and Mississippi both would be crowded with traffic. And then, according to the tapes, the suspects had raped her and killed her about two blocks from Tommy Ward's house. To Gary, a college senior, those logistics didn't make sense. He did not believe Ward and Fontenot were innocent; confessing to something you didn't do didn't make sense either. But the alleged route made him wonder. The whole town, he knew, would be watching the trial, when they got around to a trial. If the suspects were convicted with no body found, he believed, the case would go down in the textbooks; but if they were freed, he felt, they probably would not live very long; someone who'd known Denice would kill them.

On Thursday afternoon, April 18, the same day that the account of the judges' withdrawal appeared in the newspaper, Don Wyatt and Tommy Ward's family got together for their meeting. It would be their first real discussion of what Tommy's defense might be.

Miz Ward drove down from Tulsa for the meeting, with Joice and her four kids; Robert had been unable to get off work; Joel had hurt his back the week before and had missed several days' work at his mechanic's job, so he, too, had to work this day. Tricia decided she could not attend the meeting; she had Joice's four kids to look after, and Laura Sue, who was already home from kindergarten, and David and Lisa; if the meeting lasted past three, Buddy and Rhonda would get home from school as well; she did not want to ask Maxine or anyone else to watch nine children.

While waiting to go to the lawyer's office, they discussed the length of Tommy's hair the night Denice Haraway disappeared. Kay had maintained for months that on Friday, April 20, a week before the disappearance, she had cut Tommy's hair short—above his eyebrows in front, up to his mid-ear on the sides and back—much shorter than the hair of the suspects in the composite drawings. She'd said she was certain it had been before the disappearance, because on that weekend she and her mother had gone to Lawton, and Tommy had been asking her to cut it before they went, and she had done so. Miz Ward had brought along a handwritten statement from Kay in which Kay said she would testify to that effect; Miz Ward would give it to the lawyer. Bud had recalled an incident he said took place that same weekend, April 21, 1984. He said Tommy had come over to borrow five dollars, because he had a date that night and no money. He recalled saying to Tommy, who was wearing a baseball cap, "What did you do to your hair?" and Tommy had swept off his baseball cap, and said, "Ta-da!" and made a bowing turn, showing the new short haircut Kay had given him the night before. Bud was certain of the date, he said, because it had been the day before Easter Sunday—which had been April 22. Miz Ward also had with her two Polaroid pictures of Tommy and Kay, in which Tommy had short hair; they had been taken just before Kay went to her high school prom. But that had been on May 11, two weeks after the disappearance—and therefore, Tricia realized, the pictures would be of little value.

On the way to Wyatt's office, they stopped at the house on Ashland to pick up Jimmy and his girlfriend, Nancy Howell, who were living there; they hoped also to find Willie Barnett and bring him to the meeting, but he was not at home. It was 1:30 in the afternoon when they gathered in Wyatt's plush office. Miz Ward, Joice, Jimmy, and Nancy Howell sat nervously in chairs around the perimeter of the office. Wyatt sat behind his large desk, would stand sometimes and come around and sit on the front of the desk to address them, then go back and sit in his chair. Out the windows behind him, beyond the sloping lawns, they could see the midday traffic passing on Arlington. On the wall across from the desk a grandfather clock tracked the passing minutes. They were attentive while Wyatt explained about the judge withdrawing from the case, about how all the motions would have to be argued again when a new judge was appointed. As he reached the major points he wanted to make, he spoke simply and carefully, like a teacher in front of a class; he knew that the complexities of the law were alien to the people in front of him.

He began by explaining about his need for a transcript of the preliminary hearing; this was essential, he said, so that at the trial he could confront witnesses who might be changing their story. He said the state, he, and Fontenot's attorney had agreed to split the cost three ways; depending on its length, the transcript would cost each party about $700 to $800. Miz Ward noted the amount. Then he turned to the next item.

"Now, we've got a young boy over there in the county jail who's told me, and Mike, and anyone else who would listen, different, conflicting stories. One day he'll give me a story about so many boys involved in this, that, and the other. This is the way it was. The next day he'll give me a different story. He's given us six or seven different versions of what actually occurred. All the way from 'I don't know anything about it' to 'I was there but somebody else did it.' I don't know what's true and what's not true. I do know that he's given some bits and pieces of factual information that, if true, could be proven, and if proven, might give him a defense. But I have no way to run out and find these people, track them down, interview them, check out these leads. Your lawyer doesn't do that."

"Yeah," Miz Ward murmured softly.

"I can arrange for that to be done. But if I arrange for that to be done, it costs you. Private investigators check these things out. If— if—Tommy is guilty—and I don't know that he is—if Tommy is guilty, I feel very strongly there was a third boy involved. All the facts that cannot be disputed would indicate there is another boy in addition to Tommy involved. Or in place of Tommy."

"Well, there was just two of the boys charged," Miz Ward said.

"True," Wyatt said, "but we've got a vehicle. Nobody ever answers the question of whose vehicle it was, or where is it."

"That's the big piece that's not fittin' in this puzzle," Nancy Howell said.

"My feeling is that that piece is a third party, another person," Wyatt said. "I don't know how to prove or disprove that. But I've got some vibes on some recent allegations made by Tommy, and various statements, that if I could get private investigators investigating, they may turn up something. Tommy at one time kind of spun the yarn about the boys that moved to Tulsa, and had a truck. I'm not so sure that's a yarn. The police checked it out, but you've got to realize that one of the boys involved was from a very prominent family. I'm not sure how close the police checked it. I would prefer to have a private investigator check it. Someone who doesn't know Dicus from Adam, and could care less; they just want to find out what the truth is. But there are lots of little bits and pieces that he's given us that need desperately to be researched and checked. Every stone needs to be turned over. We can't rely on Tommy telling us what happened, because Tommy either doesn't know, or refuses to tell. Or maybe he has told, and it's somewhere in one of the various stories he has told."

"I visited him Sunday," Miz Ward said. "He'd tell ya. I told him, 'Tommy, if you know where she is, even if she's dead, please tell me.' He said, 'Mama, I don't know.' "

"That's why we need an investigator," the lawyer said.

He went on to tell them that an investigator would cost money; he could not say how much—it would depend on the time he had to put in; and that they would have to raise the money. He had in mind an outfit in Oklahoma City called K-Mar, he said, which had done work for his firm before, at cheaper rates than another firm they had used.

"The point I'm getting at," he told the family, "is, the only money you have is tied up in your house. You can't afford to pay me the rest of the fee. You can't afford to pay for the transcripts, you can't afford to pay for an investigation . . . I'm not interested in the payment to me at this point. I'm interested in paying the expenses for the transcripts, for the investigators. What I'm saying is, don't send me up to defend him with my hands tied, without any help. Whether you can pay me or can't pay me is secondary right now. What I'm worried about is, let's get the case prepared. I don't need to sit here holding your house. If you can, use it to get the money so you can pay these expenses. All right? . . . I'm not in this for my health, either, but the main point right now is, I don't want to go try this case without being prepared. I can stand to try it without being paid a lot better than I can stand to try it without being prepared . . . I want to find that truck. I think if we can find that truck, we might have a defense."

Miz Ward said she thought Joel might be able to raise the money needed immediately for the transcript; for the rest, they would go to a bank or finance company and try again to borrow money against the house.

"Things are looking good," Wyatt told them, referring to the news that Judge Jones had withdrawn. He was hoping, he said, that a new judge, from another county, might grant a change of venue closer to his home, away from all the publicity in Ada. "That would be the best thing that could happen to us," he said.

"It's slow, I realize. But we've got to start getting ourselves ready . . . We've got to start preparing a defense. I thought I could do it with Tommy. I think we should just leave Tommy where he is and not worry about Tommy putting together his defense, because I don't think Tommy knows what is true and what is not true. Or if he does, he isn't going to tell. We will become confused listening to Tommy."

The others laughed softly.

"Yeah," Miz Ward agreed.

"The thing that gets me," Joice said, "I was at home, and Tommy was with *me* that night. 'Cause he took care of my kids. What gets me so confused . . ."

"Can you stand up in front of a jury," Wyatt interrupted loudly, "and say absolutely, positively, 'I know as a fact that on this night, at this time, Tommy was with me'?"

"Yes," Joice said, "because the next day I told Tommy that I was glad you was home with me, and he looked at me. He goes, 'I don't care what they say, they're going to get me anyway.' Them's his exact words. He goes, 'They're gonna get me anyway.' "

"The next day?" Wyatt asked.

"The next day. That's when they picked him up, the next day."

"No, that was Monday," Miz Ward corrected.

"On Monday," Joice said. "Because they was harassin' him anyway."

"Prior to her being missing?" Wyatt asked.

"Prior to her being missing," Joice said. "They was harassin' him and pickin' him up and everthing."

"He'd be walkin' down the street . . ." Miz Ward said.

"He'd be walkin' down the street," Joice said, "and they'd pick him up for nothin'."

They talked of Robert swearing that he and Tommy had fixed the plumbing under the house that night; Wyatt told Joice to have Robert get receipts from the place where he had bought the plumbing supplies.

"Willie!" Wyatt said. "Anybody know where Willie is?"

"We came by his house, and he had just left," Miz Ward said.

"The *elusive* Willie," Wyatt said.

"He's a real person," Joice assured him, laughing.

"If you were at home with Tommy during the night there," Wyatt asked, "did Willie come over?"

"Yeah, Willie was there . . . Tommy told him not to play with the bird."

"Will Willie remember that?"

"I think so," Joice said. "Willie talked to somebody else and told 'em he remembered Tommy telling him not to play with the bird. And Jimmy had come over to the house, too, while Willie was there. Both of them were there."

"And Tommy was there?" Wyatt asked.

"Tommy was definitely there," Jimmy said.

"Him and Tommy got in a fight," Joice said.

"We never got to throwing fists," Jimmy said. "We was just in a argument. That's why it brings my memory back to me."

The meeting went on a while longer, the lawyer urging them to bring in any factual material they could muster. When they left, Don Wyatt had in his mind for the first time the skeletal idea of a defense. First, he had alibi witnesses saying Tommy was with them at the time; but they were all family, except for Willie Barnett; Willie would be the key. Second, if they could find the truck, and tie it to someone other than Tommy . . .

His first move, after a new judge was named, would be to hire a private investigator, and see what he could discover.

Karl Fontenot's attorney, George Butner, had no such option. As a court-appointed attorney, he would receive a fee of $2,500 from the state for handling the murder case. There was no money granted for expenses with which to hire an investigator. The U.S. Supreme Court had ruled in the Gideon case, in 1963, that an indigent defendant is entitled to an attorney, even if he can't pay for one; that was by now an accepted part of American law. But that was as far as the ruling had gone. The state of Oklahoma had at its disposal in this case the investigative arms and personnel of the Ada police department, the Pontotoc County Sheriff's Department, the Highway Patrol, the OSBI, and the district attorney's own investigator; but the Supreme Court had never held that an indigent defendant was entitled to what a wealthy defendant could buy: the service of private investigators working to unearth exculpatory facts on his behalf. Butner could only sit back and see what Don Wyatt's investigator might find.

On Saturday, Joel came down from Tulsa to visit with Tricia and the family. He also had remembered something he wanted them to tell the lawyer. He'd remembered a night a few months before Denice Haraway disappeared. Tommy had ridden his motorcycle up to Tulsa. The bike had broken down, and Tommy stayed overnight at Joel's house. Before going to sleep they had watched TV. On the news was a story about a young woman who had been hit by a car while crossing a street; the car had dragged her for a quarter of a mile, killing her, mutilating her body. In the early morning hours, Tommy woke up on the living room sofa, screaming. Joel went in to see what was wrong. Tommy told him he'd had a terrible nightmare. It was so real, he said. In it, he was driving the car that killed the woman.

Joel asked the family to tell this dream to the lawyer. He hadn't wanted to tell it, to discuss the case at all, on the phone; he was convinced the police were tapping Tricia's phone.

Chris Ross, too, was having dreams.

Bill Peterson had two assistant district attorneys. Ross was one of them, had been for two years and three months.

Ross was twenty-eight years old; his hefty body was topped by a moon face and merry eyes that could lull the unwary; they masked a fierce intelligence, an instinct for the jugular, that would make him a strong prosecutor. The defense attorneys had moved for separate trials for Ward and Fontenot; the prosecution wanted to try them to-gether. If the judge—when one was appointed—granted a separation, the D.A. had decided, then he would try one case and Chris Ross the other. For several weeks now, Ross had been having trouble sleeping because of the anticipation. He would sleep for about forty-five min-utes and then wake up, his mind instantly alert and working on the case, so involved the instant he was awake that he was sure he had been dreaming about it, though he could not recall the dreams them-selves. The conflicting facts, the images, held his mind the way a trap held an animal; he wrestled, tried to free his mind, but could not. Af-ter long hours in the dark, weariness would finally lull him to sleep again; forty-five minutes later he would awaken, prosecuting the case in his head.

Like his boss, he was convinced that Ward and Fontenot had killed Denice Haraway, that they had done it alone, that they had rung the name Odell Titsworth into their stories merely as a scapegoat, that there had been no third person. Believing this, Ross in his sleep-stolen nights found himself thinking over and over about a single statement of Tommy Ward's, amid all the facts and fantasies and permutations of the case, amid all the bits and pieces from different witnesses that would have to be strung together into a coherent whole to convince a jury beyond a reasonable doubt. Over and over he played in his mind something Tommy had said on the tape. The exchange went like this:

Q: Did she have a bra on?
A: Yes.
Q: What did he [Titsworth] do with it?
A: He took it off later, after I was biting her on the tit.

Of all the vicious details recounted on the tapes, that was the im-age that kept coming back to Ross's mind as he waited in vain for sleep. Titsworth, in Ward's narrative, had at that point already raped her; why would he then be taking off her bra while Tommy bit her on the breast? The answer to that question seemed important some-how—but Ross didn't know what the answer was, or why it was im-portant. In fact, the question itself was absurd, he told himself, because Titsworth hadn't been there at all. Still, the image wouldn't go away, much as he tried to kick at it, as at a worrisome dog, and relax, and sleep.

Tricia stood outside the house in the late April sun, gazing somewhat wistfully up Ninth Street; it was a quiet street that dead-ended a block and a half away; there was little through traffic. Beside her on the patchy lawn was an overturned tricycle, other toys awaiting the return of the kids from school. She could have been any one of tens of millions of housewives across America, except that what she was wishing for, just then, was to see her brother, accused of a brutal murder, come walking down the street.

She recalled how, about three years before, Tommy and another fellow had left Ada to go motorcycling across the country; they had gone to California, then all the way east to the Carolinas, stopping in places to make some money by working in garages, or as dishwashers, or by picking tomatoes. Every so often Tommy would call, to let them know he was all right. One day after about a year, when they hadn't heard from him for a while, Tricia and the kids were standing in front of the house, right where she was standing now, when out of the quiet distance they saw Tommy come walking up the street. They'd had no idea that he was on his way home. The kids jumped up and down with glee, and ran to meet him, and climbed all over him. Tricia waited till he approached, and hugged her around.

Standing there now, remembering, Tricia was overcome by the memory; she wanted more than anything to see Tommy come walking down the street again.

Donald Powers lived in the tiny village of Chandler, in Lincoln County, about eighty miles due north of Ada, near the old Route 66. He had been a judge for twenty-eight years, but had retired two years before. Since then he had spent as much time as he could playing golf. But in Oklahoma it was not uncommon for a retired judge to be called back into service from time to time, to help out in a county where the court calendar had gotten backed up, where there was an overload of cases. So Judge Powers was not surprised when the chief justice of the state of Oklahoma called and asked if he would take on a murder case in Pontotoc County.

It was the Haraway case, the chief justice told him.

Donald Powers had never heard of it.

The retired judge said he would take the case if it fit in with his schedule. He was told that a trial date had not yet been set. Why then, yes, he would take it, Judge Powers said.

The chief justice thanked him, and said it was his. The attorneys in Ada were notified. They didn't know Judge Powers. Bill Peterson, asking around, learned that the judge was a conservative, a strict constructionist of the law who ran a tight courtroom; the D.A. wanted nothing more. Don Wyatt and George Butner were hoping for someone who had not been exposed to the fierce emotions surrounding the case; they, too, had gotten their wish.

Judge Powers got in touch with the Pontotoc County court; he requested a copy of the transcript of the preliminary hearing in the case, and of all pending motions. The transcript—five volumes, 1,090 pages—was not quite ready; the motions were sent to him. In the quiet of his home, eighty miles from Ada, the judge began to prepare.

Sunday, April 28, 1985. One year to the date of the disappearance. The anniversary was called to the attention of the town in a front-page story by Dorothy Hogue in the *News*.

UNSOLVED, VIOLENT
CRIMES HAUNT ADA

the headline said. The story summarized briefly the Haraway case, and the Debbie Carter case that preceded it. The last paragraph of the Haraway segment said:

Although authorities have searched many local areas, both before and after the arrest of Ward and Fontenot, no trace of Haraway has ever been found. However, Det. Dennis Smith said he is convinced the case is solved.

The day was no different for Miz Ward than any other Sunday; she drove down from Tulsa to visit her son. She picked up Jimmy, and they went over to the county jail; Bud and Tricia would be coming later.

As Tommy entered the small enclosure behind the narrow glass window, he had two sheets of paper with him. After a quick exchange of greetings, he said excitedly, "I wrote some more poems. You want to hear 'em?"

"Yeah," Miz Ward said.

Tommy read the poems. The first one began:

What makes life worth living
Is our giving and our forgiving
Giving our kindness
That leaves the joy behind us . . .

"That's pretty," Miz Ward said when he was finished reading. "Now, how you getting along?" Tommy hesitated. "You feel nervous?"

"Getting a little shaky and everything," Tommy said.

"Yeah."

"I'm ready to go home."

"I'll bet."

"Have they said anything about when they're going to set the trial and everything?"

They discussed the new judge being appointed, which Tommy had heard; and noted that he had set arguments on motions for May 16. Tommy had heard his trial might be in June. "I'll be glad to get out of this mess," he said. "Everything is okay, I guess. Slow. A lot of things start trying to go through my mind and everything, you know. I think it's old Satan working on me. Trying to break me down and everything. But I just keep grittin' my teeth and pushin' on. 'Cause I know the Lord is looking down on me and everything . . . It's just a matter of time and patience . . . Sometimes when I'm prayin', I wonder if the Lord can hear me, the way I am locked up in a little room and everything."

"He sure can," Miz Ward said. "He sure can."

"I remember one time I was layin' there and I heard this voice. It goes, 'Why are you worrying so much? You didn't do it and everything. So what's to worry about?' I mean, I jumped up and I ran to the door and I looked out the door and looked around, and there wasn't nobody there. I turned around, and boy, I got a rush all through my body, and everything. I said, why, it was the Lord, telling me He's watching over me, and not to worry. Ever since then, you know, I haven't been so worried about it and everything. When it starts to get me down, I know it's Satan. I just praise the Lord, and tell him [Satan] to leave me alone."

There was a knock on the door. Tommy's visiting time was up. He asked his mother if she had a pencil; there were some things he needed her to bring to the jail; he read off a list: hand cream, ink, pen, paper, erasers, a lighter, magazines, stamps, soap, a pencil sharpener.

He read the list twice more while Miz Ward wrote it down. Then he had to go back to his cell.

There had been no mention, on either side of the glass, of the significance of the date.

At the city jail across the street, there was no mention of it, either. It was a day like every other; no one came to visit Karl Fontenot.

Soon it was night. The clocks read 8:30; then they read 9. The Haraway case entered its second year.

9

INVESTIGATOR

For twenty years, from 1951 to 1971, Richard Kerner was in the Air Force. Thirteen of those twenty years he was with the military police; the other seven he was with the office of special investigations, doing criminal investigations within the military. For three years, from 1957 to 1959, he was on assignment to the Central Intelligence Agency.

When he left the Air Force, he spent ten years in private industry, with several different firms. He was not doing investigative work; he found the jobs unrewarding, both emotionally and financially. He lived in Yukon, a suburb of Oklahoma City, and in 1982 he set up shop there as a legal investigator, under the corporate name K-Mar Legal Investigations. He did not like the terms "private investigator" or "private eye," because they smacked of prying into tawdry divorce suits. Kerner handled criminal investigations and civil suits, but refused to get involved in divorces. In the spring of 1985 he was president of the Oklahoma Private Investigators Association. He was fifty-two years old, six feet one inch tall, weighed 230 pounds.

Kerner had been hired by Don Wyatt in the past, to do investigations in civil suits. In November of 1984, Wyatt called to ask if Kerner would take on some investigations in a murder case. The name of the suspect was Tommy Ward. Kerner said he would, but the attorney did not call him back with a definite assignment. Wyatt made a similar call to Kerner in January, while the preliminary hearing in the case was in recess; again, nothing definite was forthcoming. The case faded from the Oklahoma City newspapers. Kerner knew few of the details. He had all but forgotten about it. Then, in early May, Wyatt called again; he wanted the investigator to work on the case.

On May 9, Richard Kerner drove to Ada. He met in the attorney's spacious building—an opulent contrast to his own one-room office—with Wyatt and Wyatt's office manager, Bill Willett. For more than an hour and a half he listened as Wyatt talked about the case, about how Tommy Ward claimed his confession had only been a dream. It was Kerner's experience that suspects, in order to get the best possible defense, usually told their attorneys the truth; listening, Kerner felt that Don Wyatt genuinely believed his client was innocent.

Wyatt outlined several courses of action he wanted Kerner to pursue. The most significant were: (1.) researching the disappearance of other Oklahoma convenience store clerks—notably the one in Seminole—and noting any similarities with the Ada case; (2.) interviewing other potential "suspects/witnesses," particularly Marty Ashley and Jay Dicus, whom Ward had named in his kiss-and-run story; (3.) trying to locate the pickup truck described by the witnesses; (4.) locating and interviewing Mildred Gandy, who allegedly saw Denice Haraway at the Brook Trailer Park in Ada, in the company of two young men, two days after her disappearance; (5.) interviewing Karen Wise, the clerk at J.P.'s, about why she allegedly told Vicki Jenkins she was not sure about her identifications; (6.) interviewing Willie Barnett, who allegedly was visiting Ward around the time Denice Haraway disappeared. If possible, Kerner was to get recorded statements from those he interviewed: with their knowledge, if he felt they would cooperate; without their knowledge when that seemed more feasible. He was to submit a written report to the law firm by May 31.

Kerner drove back to Yukon, to his office in the Spring Creek Executive Suite on Vandament Street. There were thirteen offices in the suite, whose members shared a common secretarial service. Kerner's office was fourteen by sixteen feet, with a desk that faced a floor-to-ceiling one-way glass wall; Kerner could see out, but people outside could not see in; the view was of trees, a green lawn, a medical building across the way. Against one wall was another desk on which rested Kerner's computer. Here, in front of the keyboard and the console screen, his investigation would begin; Kerner inserted his DataTimes menu into the computer; with it, he could punch up newspaper stories that had appeared in the *Daily Oklahoman*, as well as in newspapers as far off as Dallas, Chicago, St. Louis. He punched in the code for the *Oklahoman*, and a series of key words. The computer printed a list of all headlines that had appeared in the *Oklahoman* in recent years dealing with the abduction of clerks from convenience stores; the list contained convenience store abductions in Chandler, Clinton, Seminole, Cushion, and Wewoka. He punched up the full stories that had appeared under the headlines and printed them; he carried the printouts to his desk and read them; each mention in a story that had a similarity to the Haraway disappearance he marked in red. By far the most similar, in almost every respect, was the disappearance of Patty Hamilton from the U-Totem store in Seminole.

A few days later, Kerner drove to the Oklahoma Department of Public Safety, in a one-story building in Oklahoma City. There he asked to see the complete driving records of Marty Ashley, Jay Dicus, and several others whose names had been mentioned at one time or other by Tommy Ward. He was permitted to inspect and copy the records, at a cost of $4.50 each; any citizen could do the same. From the driver records, he knew, he could acquire a lot of useful information: full names with their correct spellings, addresses, birth dates, social security numbers, the types of vehicles owned. Records of traffic citations could place an individual in a certain town on a certain date.

Marty Ashley's records showed an address in Paul's Valley, about thirty miles west of Ada. An extensive list of traffic citations placed Ashley in the Ada area from June 1980 to February 1983. Since then there were citations in other towns in central Oklahoma. He'd received three citations in 1984; none of the vehicles involved were pickup trucks. Other names Kerner checked, such as Jay Dicus, produced no records; the investigator decided they might be nicknames; he would need more information. Don Wyatt also had asked him to check out a pickup with a certain license tag; Joel Ward had seen the truck in a suburb of Tulsa, and felt it closely resembled the one described as leaving McAnally's, except that it had recently been painted yellow. The truck turned out to be registered to a name unfamiliar in the case; Kerner called Don Wyatt, who told him not to pursue that avenue for now.

But Kerner did set up a lunch appointment, for later in the month, with Dexter Davis, the assistant police chief of Seminole. He wanted to learn as much as he could about the Patty Hamilton case.

On May 16, the attorneys on both sides got their first look at Judge Donald Powers. As he took his place behind the bench in the third-floor courtroom, his black robes seemed to be the cloth he'd been born to wear. He had a large, squarish face, fair skin with a hint of ruddiness, wavy hair combed back that was so pure gray it was almost white. He looked like the Hollywood image of a distinguished judge.

The business before the court this day was routine. The defense attorneys had requested that Ward and Fontenot be tested as to their competency to stand trial; Judge Powers swiftly granted the motion. He ordered that they be committed to Eastern State Hospital, at Vinita, for a period of no more than sixty days. This would not be a determination of whether they were insane, merely of whether they understood the charges against them and would be able to assist their attorneys in preparing their defense.

The application filed on Ward's behalf by Don Wyatt claimed that Ward was unable to distinguish reality from the imaginary, that "continued use of powerful drugs over a long period of time" had rendered his powers of reasoning and comprehension useless, that he could be led and directed by other persons, that he could be manipulated without regard to the consequences, that he "lives in a dreamlike state," and that therefore he was not competent to undergo further proceedings.

The judge ordered that the two suspects be transported to Vinita at the earliest convenience of the sheriff's department. He said all proceedings in the case would be suspended until their return. He would use the time, he said, to read the five-volume transcript of the preliminary hearings, which had been delivered to all of the parties that day.

As the hearing concluded, Wyatt asked the judge to grant permission for Ward to have a haircut and a shave. His client had been denied a razor and a pair of scissors ever since his arrest, the attorney said. The judge responded that if that were not done at Vinita it should be handled upon their return, that the length of the defendants' hair at this time had nothing to do with the case.

When Bud got off work that day, a Thursday, he went to the jail and brought Tommy a carton of cigarettes, to last him through his first few days at Vinita. A jailer gathered his personal belongings—mostly letters he had been saving—into a paper sack, for the family to keep while he was gone. The following morning, Tommy and Karl were placed in a squad car and taken by sheriff's deputies on the five-hour drive to Vinita, north of Tulsa.

Looking out the window as they rode, Tommy was thrilled by the deep rich greenery of the countryside. He remembered snow on the ground the last time he'd been outside the jail; he'd expected now to see only a faint green haze of early spring; he had to remind himself it was the middle of May; the time that stood still in the jail went racing along outside.

Held in separate jails, Tommy and Karl had not seen each other in six months except during their court appearances. Now, with the trees, the hills, the ponds, the cattle and horses, the oil pumps of central Oklahoma passing outside the windows, they had a chance to talk. They gabbed on and off between silent times of looking at the scenery; they did not discuss the case.

After an hour, the road passed through McAlester, where the Oklahoma State Penitentiary is located. The deputies drove past the prison. The boys could see a wire-mesh gate at street level, and up a grassy slope behind it a high whitewashed wall, with gun towers on the top.

At the hospital at Vinita, the sheriff's deputies were instructed to wait until they were told they could leave. Inside the hospital, their forms processed, Tommy and Karl were asked a series of simple questions: Did they know what a judge was? Did they know what a jury was? Did they know what a lawyer was? They answered "yes" to each of the questions. Their answers were noted on a one-page form. They were given a few other simple tests. The evaluator, Dr. Sandra Petrick, noted for her files—but did not write on the form—of Fontenot: "At the time of his arrest, he did not understand the implications of a confession." Then they were taken out to the patrol car, where the deputies were waiting.

Take them back, the deputies were told; they are competent to stand trial.

The deputies shrugged, put them in the car, and began the long drive back. When they passed through McAlester, Karl said, "I want to go by that prison again, and see what it looks like on the outside. Before they put me inside."

"Why do you want to do that?" a deputy asked. "You starting to plan your escape?"

The suspects were back in the Ada jails by early evening. At Tommy's request, a deputy named Virginia telephoned Bud and Tricia, to let them know he was back already; so they would come to see him on Sunday. When they did, he told them about the trip; about Karl's remark about being put inside the prison. The comment had shaken Tommy, who was clinging to the hope that, sooner or later, they would be freed. It was a comment open to various interpretations. It frightened Tommy's family; it made the attorneys, when they were told of it, wonder. Did it mean that Karl was thinking about pleading guilty, whether or not he was guilty or innocent? Or did it show that he was more in touch with reality than Tommy, that he perceived better the serious, perhaps fatal nature of their circumstances, given the confession tapes they had made? All felt that to some degree it reflected the different life situations of the two friends: Tommy poor but deeply loved, with a loyal family, loyal friends; Karl abandoned by his family, no one to turn to, unvisited, living on the outside a homeless existence. Perhaps Karl *wanted* to be in jail.

Or had the statement been merely an idle comment, a passing attempt at humor?

The competency ruling put the case back in the news. The following day, at the Wal-Mart department store, a shopper placed her purchases on the checkout counter. As the clerk rang them up on the register, she commented, "Isn't it terrible about that Haraway case? Why are they holding those guys so long without any evidence?"

"They must have some evidence," the customer said.

"I don't know," the checkout clerk said. "My husband works at the jail, and he's gotten close to that Tommy Ward. He writes the most beautiful poems. The most beautiful poems. I haven't heard much about evidence."

The silent customer paid by check. The clerk routinely asked for her place of employment.

"I work at the district attorney's office," the customer said.

Ben Brewer is one of Ada's barbers. He is the proprietor of Ben's House of Hair, on Fourth Street. On Tuesday, May 21, he received a phone call from one of his regular customers, Bud Wolf. Bud wanted to know if Ben would go over to the county jail and cut his brother-in-law's hair.

Ben had been there a few times before to cut the hair of inmates; it was not his favorite thing to do, but he did it as a favor to customers. He told Bud he would do it, but that he needed a ride over there; Bud should come by and pick him up about 5:30, when he closed the shop.

During the afternoon, as he cut a customer's hair, Ben mentioned that he'd be going over to the jail after work to give a haircut. "I hope it ain't one of them Haraway guys," the customer said.

Ben had had stranger requests than going to the jail. He had, a few times, cut the hair of corpses. The most recent time had been a few months before.

"Picked him up by the ears," Ben recounted later. "They was real cold. Just sort of trimmed around the ears, because that's all you can see in an open casket. Sort of a fake haircut. Didn't charge 'em for it. Later the funeral home sent fifteen dollars. Told 'em I didn't want the family's money. They said no, the haircut was included in the price of the funeral."

At 5:30, Bud came by on schedule, and drove Ben to the jail. They entered the waiting room for visitors. A deputy locked the outer door behind them; the jailers brought Tommy into the room. Bud and Tommy hugged, arms tight, chests pressing hard against each other. It was the first time they could hug in six months.

Tommy wanted his hair cut real short, white-walled on the sides. Ben cut it the way he wanted. Bud watched as shocks of Tommy's long, straight hair fell to the floor. It was much darker than it used to be, Bud noticed, after six months untouched by sunlight.

As Tommy was being led back to his cell, one of the deputies grabbed a camera; he looked so different, the deputies felt, they needed a new picture of him.

Bud drove the barber back. As they rode through the streets, the barber told him, "I did that just for you, because you're a regular customer. If the jail had called me up, I would have said no. If that prisoner had called me up, I would have said no. I did it just as a favor to you." He paused. "Who was that, by the way?"

"I told you," Bud said. "That's my brother-in-law."

Ben asked, "Well, what'd he do?"

"He's one of the suspects in the Haraway case."

Ben fell silent for a moment. Then he said, "I don't judge. I just cut hair." He paused. "Somebody done it."

Bud said, "Yeah, somebody done it."

"Well, if those boys didn't do it," Ben said, "then they should let 'em outta there." The rest of his thought he didn't speak aloud. The rest of his thought was: if they did do it, they should kill 'em, long and slow.

Ben charged five dollars for the haircut, the usual; no extra charge for going to the jail.

The next day the barber received another call, this one from a policeman who was a regular customer. Ben was almost expecting it.

"I'd like you to do me a favor," the policeman said.

"What's that?"

"I'd like you to come over to the city jail and cut someone's hair."

Just as he anticipated, it was Karl Fontenot. The boy's black hair hung in waves to his shoulders. He seemed to Ben like a wiseguy teenager. As Ben worked with the scissors, and clumps of hair fell to the floor, Fontenot said, "You'd better save that hair. Pick it up and make a wig out of it."

"Why should I do that?" the barber asked.

"That hair's gonna be famous some day," Karl said.

Ben decided the hair wouldn't be famous. He didn't pick it up. He thought: if I did bend down and pick up that hair, and carry it out, and people found out about it, they would jump me and beat me up.

The day that Tommy Ward got his haircut, Richard Kerner drove east on Interstate 40 to Seminole, where he had lunch with the assistant chief of police, Dexter Davis, in a small downtown cafe. Amid the clatter of silverware on formica tabletops and the rancid smell of old grease on the grill, they discussed at length the details of the Patty Hamilton disappearance. Kerner knew, from the newspaper stories he'd punched up, the many similarities between the Hamilton and the Haraway cases: both disappeared from convenience stores, never heard from again, no bodies found. In both cases money was missing from the register, but in both cases it was possible the money had been taken by the next person who came along, after the abduction; it was possible robbery had not been a motive in either case. Davis told Kerner of vehicles the Seminole police had checked out in the Hamilton case, of a suspect from Enid, Oklahoma, who had been checked out and cleared by the OSBI. He said he was still investigating the Hamilton disappearance, that he thought the girl might still be alive, that there could well be a connection between the crimes in Seminole and Ada.

The next day, after numerous unsuccessful attempts, Kerner established telephone contact with Willie Barnett—"the elusive Willie," as Don Wyatt had called him. After a brief conversation, Willie hung up. Kerner called back immediately. A female voice said that Willie was not at home. After a bit more conversation with the woman, however, Willie got back on the line, and agreed to talk to the investigator. He said he did visit Tommy Ward at his house one evening, about 8:30 to 8:40 P.M., when Ward was stretched out on the couch, asleep. He had walked to Ward's house from his own, he said, and Tommy woke up and they talked for about ten minutes, and then he left. He said that Ward's "uncle" had been there at the time, and told him that Tommy had been on the couch because he was feeling sick. Willie said he had known Tommy for only about two months at the time. He told Kerner that this might have been the night the Haraway girl disappeared—but that he couldn't be sure. He said Ward's "uncle"—presumably he was referring to Tommy's oldest brother, Jimmy—had told him it was the same night, but that he himself could not recall positively whether it was or not.

To Kerner, pulling answers out of Willie felt like pulling teeth. To some questions Willie did not respond at all, and after a long silence Kerner had to ask if he was still on the line. Willie said that in the two months he'd known Tommy he'd never seen him in a pickup truck. Kerner repeatedly asked Willie to meet him somewhere, to talk. Willie refused. But he did, reluctantly, give Kerner his address, on West Twelfth Street. The investigator wrote it down, for a follow-up visit.

The next day, May 23, Kerner went to Ada. He drove out Country Club Road, past the Arlington Shopping Center, past a small industrial complex that housed Blue Bell jeans, Remington Arms, and others, and turned left at the entrance to the Brook Mobile Home Park. He was hoping to interview Mildred Gandy. She was the woman who allegedly had told Maxine Wolf the previous November that she had seen Denice Haraway alive at the trailer park, in the company of two young men, two days after she disappeared.

The Brook was a well-kept mobile home park, in which circular cul-de-sacs, five to ten mobile homes on each, opened off two long entry and exit roads. In some of the cul-de-sacs there were basketball backboards, and on some of the hoops, fresh cloth nets hung undamaged. A swimming pool, unused as Kerner passed, was enclosed with wire fencing. Clothes were hanging to dry on clotheslines beside some of the trailers. The investigator drove along the entry road until he spotted the park office toward the rear. In the office he found the manager, Mary K. Lavielle.

Kerner told Ms. Lavielle whom he was looking for. The manager said Mildred Gandy had lived at lot number 97 at the park, but that she had moved away two weeks ago; she had left a forwarding address and phone number in Choctaw, Oklahoma. When the investigator stated his mission, Ms. Lavielle pulled out a map of the trailer park. Together they checked the records of the trailers surrounding lot 97, which would have been visible from Mrs. Gandy's place; nothing of value was obtained, Kerner felt.

As they looked at the records together, the investigator felt that Ms. Lavielle was nervous. She kept asking questions about the case. Kerner had the feeling that there was something on her mind that she was hesitant to talk about; if not, he thought, she would have given him the information he wanted and then escorted him to the door. But her questions continued; she showed Kerner into an adjoining room, where they sat on chairs beside a bare table; the rest of the room was empty; Kerner had the feeling it might have once been a recreation room for the trailer park residents, with a Ping-Pong table or something.

The investigator became more and more convinced that Ms. Lavielle had something to say; he switched into his "keep the conversation going mode," to see what would happen. The manager told him how back in August of 1983, a fellow named Monty Moyer lived in the park, and that Steve Haraway had been planning to move in with him, but never had. (That was the month, Kerner would realize later, that Steve Haraway married Donna Denice Lyon.) Ms. Lavielle talked on and on, which is what Richard Kerner wanted. He'd been there about thirty-five minutes, he calculated, when Mary Lavielle finally blurted out what was on her mind. She said that at the time that Denice Haraway disappeared, she had been working at the Ada Finance Company, that she and three other persons had looked at the composite drawings in the newspaper, and that they had all agreed on who the two men were. They were not, she said, the two who were presently being held in jail!

Kerner was wearing a business suit, a white shirt, a tie, as he always did while working. One reason he always wore a suit, aside from neatness, was so that he could keep his microcassette tape recorder invisible but handy in the inside breast pocket. The recorder was not turned on; he only used it surreptitiously when he felt the person he was interviewing would not cooperate, would not record a statement voluntarily. His excitement began to build as Mary Lavielle responded to his questions; he could feel his heart thumping against the small leather case of the recorder.

"What were the names of the men who looked like the drawings?" Kerner wanted to know.

"One of them was named Randy Rogers," Ms. Lavielle said. "The other was named Sparcino."

Did she feel sure of that?

The drawings looked just like them, Ms. Lavielle said. And, she said, Janice Manuel, who had worked with her at the finance company, felt the same way. And so did Kendall Holland, who owns the Ada TV Rental. And so did Shirley Brecheem, the manager of Security Finance. The names tumbled out of Mary Lavielle, as if they had been bottled up for a long time. All four of them had agreed at the time, she said: Randy Rogers was the suspect with the blond, earlobe-length hair; the other was his friend, Sparcino, who had shoulder-length brown hair.

They felt sure of it, she said. They had notified the police of those identifications at the time.

And the police? Richard Kerner wanted to know—had the police come to talk to her about these identifications?

"No," Mary Lavielle said. None of them had ever been interviewed by the police.

Richard Kerner was intrigued. If what Lavielle was telling him was true—and he couldn't imagine why she would make it up—then he might be onto something big, a major break in the case, right at the start of his investigation. Four different people identifying the composite drawings as another set of suspects entirely! And the police not contacting them for further information! At best, he thought, that was shoddy police procedure. In his experience, the police did that routinely: they would visit with the people who phoned in identifications; show them the originals of the draw-ings, which were usually better than the newspaper reproductions; ask how they knew the people they were naming, why they thought it looked like them, what their habits were; get all the infor-mation they could; follow every lead, however slim. If Lavielle was correct, then that had not been done in this case. He could only won-der why.

But was Lavielle correct?

Kerner thanked her for her time. He drove out of the trailer park, went to the Security Finance Company on North Oak Street. There he interviewed the manager, Shirley Brecheem. Ms. Brecheem confirmed Mary Lavielle's story. She went a step further. She said the composite drawings were so like Rogers and Sparcino that they looked like pho-tographs of each of them. She said she recognized them because Rogers sometimes had come in to the company for loans, and Spar-cino was with him.

Kerner asked Ms. Brecheem if she would give him a recorded state-ment about what she was saying; Ms. Brecheem said she would.

Kerner took his recorder from his coat pocket, set it on the desk between them. Part of their ensuing conversation went like this:

KERNER: Okay, as I understand, you have had dealings with two men in making them loans and/or rejecting loans, and you identified the police composite drawings as being these two men. Is that correct?

BRECHEEM: That's right, I did.

KERNER: We're talking about a Randy A. Rogers and a Robert A. Sparcino, is that correct?

BRECHEEM: Yes, sir.

KERNER: In your own words could you tell me briefly what happened when you saw the composite drawings of the suspects on the television?

BRECHEEM: Well, I hollered at my husband and said, "I know these two guys. One of them has a loan and I turned the other one down."

KERNER: And then what happened?

BRECHEEM: Well, I called the police station and told them who I thought it was.

KERNER: Okay, did you call anybody else about . . .

BRECHEEM: I called the next morning and talked to some sergeant—gave the social security numbers, date of birth, areas where they were originally from.

KERNER: And this was immediate. You saw the drawing on TV, and you immediately said this is Randy Rogers and Robert Sparcino?

BRECHEEM: Yes. I mean to me they looked identical to the two . . .

KERNER: Shirley, you have seen pictures of Tommy Jesse Ward and Karl Fontenot on television and in the newspapers, and I have showed you a picture of both, and it's my understanding that the composite drawings still fit Rogers and Sparcino, better than they fit Ward and Fontenot.

BRECHEEM: Well, it looks most like them. It looks like a photograph taken of them.

KERNER: You're talking about the composite drawings?

BRECHEEM: Yes.

KERNER: Looks close enough . . .

BRECHEEM: Of Rogers and Sparcino, that it could have been someone taking a picture of them.

The conversation went on a bit longer. At the conclusion, Shirley Brecheem said, "I would of bet a hundred dollars that it was the two. I was that convinced, and I still am. It looks just like them."

Brecheem had said she had never been interviewed by the police about her identifications. Kerner had it all on tape now. He got copies from Ms. Brecheem of all the background information the loan company had on Rogers and Sparcino. He hurried to his next stop, the Ada Finance Company on North Constant. He interviewed the manager there, Janice Manuel. She told, with a tape recorder running in front of her, a story similar to Shirley Brecheem's. She didn't know Robert Sparcino, she said, but she felt at the time that one of the drawings looked just like Randy Rogers; she had called the police to tell them that; the police had never contacted her further.

Kerner moved on, to the Ada TV Rental on Main Street. Again getting permission to use the recorder, he interviewed the manager, Kendall Holland. Kerner showed Holland the composite drawings. The manager said one of them was a very good likeness of Randy Rogers. He said Rogers had worked for him some time prior to the disappearance of Denice Haraway; he said he had fired Rogers after about three days for poor work performance. He said he had never personally called the police about the resemblance, but that he'd had discussions about it with Jan Manuel at Ada Finance, and that when she called the police she'd most likely mentioned his identification as well. Like the other three, the description Holland gave of Randy Rogers fit the one under the composite drawing on the police flyer. He added that Rogers had "a wild crowd of friends."

The investigator returned to his car. His report on this first phase of the investigation was not due till the end of the month, but this was information he felt couldn't wait. As he drove out Arlington toward Don Wyatt's office, he could hardly believe what he had. The first four people he had talked to, all in one day, had all named the same person as the man in the composite drawing. They were all upstanding, responsible citizens, with no reason to be biased in the case. And they all said it wasn't Tommy Ward, it was Randy Rogers. The investigator was shocked, dumbfounded, that the Ada police or the OSBI had not talked to any of these people.

Kerner met with Don Wyatt behind the closed door of the lawyer's office; he told him what he had. Wyatt, often unperturbable, grew excited as Kerner continued with his narration. He did not play the three tapes for Wyatt, but told what was on them.

What about Mary Lavielle at the trailer park, Wyatt wanted to know. You didn't tape her? Kerner said he had not. Well, get on back there, Don Wyatt said; get her on tape as well.

Kerner returned to the trailer park. Mary Lavielle voluntarily repeated on tape what she had told him earlier. Now he had all four.

As he drove home to Yukon that evening, the investigator was exhilarated. His first real day in the field, and he believed he might have cracked the case.

For the next week the investigator spent much of his available time on the case. On May 24 and 25 he had long telephone conversations, from his office, with Mildred Gandy at her new residence in Choctaw. He summarized the conversations on paper for his written report to Don Wyatt:

After lengthy discussion, Gandy said it was about five weeks before the disappearance that she saw Donna Haraway standing in the doorway of a trailer on lot #95 at Brook Trailer Park. She seemed reasonably sure it was Haraway, and recalled the incident when Haraway's picture was observed on television and in the paper. On the day Gandy [had] seen Haraway, an older model Chevrolet pickup truck, dull gray in color, with large tires on the rear end, was departing this trailer at lot #95. She recalled that a sandy-blond-headed man lived in this trailer and drove the truck. The hair length was to the earlobe. Gandy said a lot of parties went on at this trailer with a younger crowd. She observed the truck pulling a small trailer with saw horses in it and was told by the park office that the occupants of this trailer were in the construction business. She did not know if the blond-haired person lived at the trailer or not. She believed the people in the trailer on lot #95 moved shortly after Haraway disappeared. Gandy recalled that during this period in March and April 1984 a Cherokee Paving Company owned some land near the trailer park and was dumping a lot of loose dirt on this land from the construction site of McDonald's in Ada. Gandy wondered about the missing girl being buried under this dirt, making a connection with her at the trailer . . . Gandy seemed sure the girl at the doorway of the trailer was indeed Haraway, but was shaky on the dates. At first she agreed it was after the disappearance, on either May 2 or 3, 1984, but later said she figured out the date to be in March 1984. This investigator has a feeling that Gandy believes that if she says she saw Haraway before the disappearance she will not get involved in a court appearance. It seems somewhat unlikely that Gandy would see Haraway weeks prior to the disappearance and then make a connection from a news photograph.

Kerner called Mary Lavielle and got the names of the people who had rented the trailer on lot #95 from August 1983 to August 1984; they indeed had been in the construction business; the names were unfamiliar to the case. His first attempts to track them down were unsuccessful.

On May 29 Kerner once again went to Ada. With his tape recorder ready to go in his pocket, he pulled off the highway in front of J.P.'s Pak-to-Go. He was hoping to interview Karen Wise about her positive identification of Tommy Ward as being in her store the night of the disappearance. But inside the store was another clerk. Karen Wise was not on duty; she had recently moved, and had no telephone. Kerner reached Wise's mother at Kerr Lab, where she worked; the mother agreed to help Kerner get in touch with Karen; she said she expected a call from Karen later in the day. Kerner called the mother back three times; he was told that Karen had not yet phoned.

Stymied there, Kerner went to interview Vicki Jenkins. She was the woman who had come to Tricia's house to tell her that Karen Wise had not been sure about her identification of Tommy. Vicki denied this to the investigator; she said Karen Wise had never said anything to her about being unsure of the identifications she had given to the police.

Kerner tried to reach Karen again, but couldn't; he left a message at J.P.'s for her to call him collect; he tried to reach Jack Paschall, the other witness at J.P.'s that night, but couldn't. He went to another place where Randy Rogers had worked for a time, got the names of people that Rogers used to run with. One of the names mentioned was Marty Ashley. A friend of both told Kerner the composite drawing favored Randy Rogers and did not look like Tommy Ward at all.

Continuing on his rounds that day, the investigator went to interview Jay Dicus; he learned that Dicus had moved to Denver, Colorado, just a few weeks earlier. The person he spoke with connected Dicus and Marty Ashley with Randy Rogers and Bob Sparcino, through a mutual friendship with a woman named Jackie Mantzke. The interview was being conducted at Dicus Cycle, a bike shop. In the midst of it, Jay Dicus's father returned to the shop; he gave Kerner his son's telephone number in Denver; he said Jay had left town merely because he was tired of Ada.

As the investigator left the shop, phone number in hand, a third generation of Dicuses approached him: Frank Dicus, Jay's grandfather. Frank Dicus told Kerner that someone he didn't want to name had said there were two burned-out houses west of town, and that the police had searched the wrong one, that Denice Haraway's body was probably in the other one. The grandfather didn't say who it was that had told him this; Kerner suspected it had been Jay. Frank said he just had to tell someone about this, that he could take the investigator to the building. Kerner told him he might return later to go inspect this second burned building.

For now, Kerner went to the courthouse to check the Pontotoc County records on all the names that were turning up. He discovered that an arrest warrant for burglary had been issued for Randy Rogers on July 27, 1983—and that he had apparently left town about that time. To the investigator, this did not necessarily mean that Rogers had not been involved; the highways that led out of Ada also led back. He also learned that Marty Ashley had been arrested four times in 1979 and 1980.

Kerner went to the law office, finished reading the 110-page statement that Tommy Ward had written for Don Wyatt shortly after his arrest; he jotted down other names mentioned by Ward as part of his running crowd. Then he called Jay Dicus in Denver. Dicus denied any knowledge of the pickup truck involved; he said he did not know Rogers or Sparcino; he admitted knowing Jackie Mantzke; he said it was his belief that Odell Titsworth had killed Denice Haraway and had moved the body since doing so, and had threatened Ward and Fontenot with death if they told on him.

The conversation went on for a long time. Kerner felt it produced little of value, since Odell Titsworth seemed to have been effectively eliminated by the police as a possible suspect; Dicus seemed to be only guessing.

The month of May was drawing to a close. Back in his office in Yukon, the trees in full bloom outside the one-way glass wall, Kerner compiled a written report for Don Wyatt on all that he had obtained; he summarized possible areas for further investigation; he attached an itemized bill for the work he had done to date; and he waited for further instructions.

On Memorial Day weekend, Melvin Ward was discharged from the Navy in Virginia. He returned home to Ada. He gave Tricia a home-coming gift of two hundred dollars. Tricia used most of the money to buy new shoes for all of the children, and for herself; Bud bought himself a used three-piece suit at the Salvation Army for $15, and a new tie for $4.95.

On Sunday, Melvin went to visit Tommy; he was the closest in age to Tommy of all the boys in the family; they had been the closest friends, hanging out together, one time—a chagrined memory—jumping up and down on the roof of a car until it caved in. He hadn't seen Tommy in more than a year, since long before the trouble began.

Rhonda went with Melvin to the jail. They entered the visiting room before Tommy was visible through the window. Melvin sat on the low stool, Rhonda sat on Melvin's lap; when Tommy entered, all he could see at first was Rhonda. He asked how she was doing; she said she was doing fine. Tommy leaned over to spit some tobacco; as his head was turned, Rhonda jumped off Melvin's lap; when Tommy faced the window again, there was Melvin, unexpectedly, a big gleaming grin on his face.

On opposite sides of the glass, the appearance of the brothers contrasted sharply—Tommy extremely thin from his seven months in the jail, darkness under his eyes from worry, his hands shaking, his hair darker than normal for lack of sunlight; Melvin fresh from the service in lean good shape, biceps bristling, belly firm, hair bright yellow, face tanned. They exchanged greetings, jokes, pleasantries. Then Melvin asked Tommy about the case.

"Why did you make that tape?" Melvin said.

"They question you for five hours," Tommy said. "They keep telling you you did it, you did it. After five, six hours you don't know what you're saying anymore. After five, six hours you'll say anything."

It crossed Melvin's mind to ask Tommy if he was holding something back; if he knew who did it, and was protecting someone else. But Melvin didn't ask the question; he didn't want Tommy to think he didn't have faith in him.

The next court hearing in the Ward-Fontenot case was scheduled for June 11. Winifred Harrell helped Don Wyatt prepare the motions, already argued once, before Judge Jones, that now would be argued again, before Judge Powers.

In recent weeks there had been changes at the law firm of Wyatt & Addicott. Don Wyatt had added to the firm a third partner, a tall, youngish former judge in the area, Leo Austin. New business cards were printed up: "Wyatt, Addicott & Austin." Judy Wood, the receptionist at the front desk, had to get used to this new, longer way of answering the phone in her smooth, pleasant voice. In less than a month, however, the firm's name changed again. Mike Addicott, who had helped with the Ward case, moved to Florida, where his wife's family lived; new cards had to be printed up, a new sign posted on the lawn: "Wyatt & Austin." Leo Austin began the tedious task of getting acquainted with the firm's many pending cases; most important, he had to read and absorb the five volumes of the preliminary hearing in the Tommy Ward case; when it went to trial, he would be at Don Wyatt's side.

Soon after, Wyatt hired another young lawyer, Bill Cathey, to help primarily with the industrial cases. Once more the cards, the signs, were changed, this time to "Wyatt, Austin & Associates."

Tommy Ward's family did not yet know about Richard Kerner's findings. Wyatt, visiting Tommy, told him that things were looking up, but did not elaborate.

In private, Wyatt was feeling good about the case for the first time. Over and over he read the investigator's report, to explore its details, its various implications: Rogers, Sparcino, named by all those witnesses; the police not contacting them; possible connections with Ashley. The leads would have to be followed up. He was beginning to see, for the first time, how he might be able to raise in the minds of a jury the critical seedling of reasonable doubt.

There was also the mention of the second burned-out house. Perhaps that was only gossip, perhaps not. It could be where the remains of Denice Haraway could really be found. Wyatt did not know if he wanted the investigator to check that out. His job was to defend Tommy Ward, not convict him; there was no telling what a second burned house might reveal.

The irises of May were barely clinging to life; the scent of lilacs perfumed Ada's mansions and shanties alike; June's roses peeped newborn from tight buds; the pecan trees were hung again with green husks. At the Unity Missionary Baptist Church, Buddy Wolf, soon to become eight years old, was baptized amid pride and joyful noise. And in the county courthouse, a date was set for the start of the trial of Tommy Ward and Karl Fontenot.

After all this time it sneaked up on the town, even on the principals, unawares. The spectator section in the courtroom was vacant; even Tricia was unaware that the boys would be in court this day, June 11.

They sat at the defense table, in their jailhouse coveralls, with their attorneys; Bill Peterson at the opposing table; Judge Donald Powers, with his court robes and his courtly manner, presiding.

The attorneys argued their motions; they had filed written briefs; the judge made his rulings, swift and sure. They had argued to sever the trials of the two defendants. Denied, Judge Powers said; the suspects would be tried together. A victory for the prosecution. They argued for a change of venue, because of the publicity about the case, because of the emotions it had aroused in the town. Denied for now, Judge Powers said; he would attempt to hold the trial in Ada; if it was determined at that time that an impartial jury could not be empaneled here, then he would move it elsewhere. They argued about the manner of jury selection, wanting the prospective jurors to be questioned individually, out of earshot of each other, particularly as to their views on capital punishment. Rulings on jury selection would be postponed until jury selection was about to begin, the judge said. The defense requested a copy of the October 12 interview tape, in which Tommy Ward repeatedly maintained his innocence; granted, the judge said.

More technicalities. Then, suddenly, it was done. The judge said he was ready to go to trial; there had been enough delays; the trial could start in eight days, on June 19, if that was the will of the defendants.

There was a moment of anguish, of mental throat clearing, at both tables. Eight days? Neither side was ready.

That was impossible, Bill Peterson told the judge; it would take a week merely to prepare the subpoenas for all the witnesses. (Thinking: some of these guys you don't just call up and say come on over; you have to track them down, hit them with the legal papers to make sure they will show.)

There was also the question of vacations; most people took their vacations in late June or in July or in August; key witnesses might be unavailable. Both sides joining in. The attorneys had conflicts in the next few weeks. Don Wyatt would be taking his vacation in July; Bill Peterson in August.

The judge listened patiently, or perhaps impatiently. The suspects had been in jail for nearly eight months; they had a constitutional right to a speedy trial. If there was going to be another long delay, he wanted to hear from the mouths of the suspects themselves, have it in the court record, which the court reporter was busily punching into his tapes, that this was agreeable. He told the two defendants that they should be aware of the advice of their attorneys, but if in spite of this they wanted an early trial date, now was the time to speak up. He particularly wanted Fontenot to speak, because his attorney had been appointed by the court.

"I am in no hurry," Tommy Ward said.

"It [a later court date] is fine with me," Karl Fontenot said.

That being the situation, the judge ordered that jury selection in the case would begin in this courtroom on the morning of Monday, September 9.

Bill Peterson was pleased; there would be plenty of time to prepare.

Don Wyatt and George Butner were pleased; there would be a lot more time for Richard Kerner to proceed with his own investigation.

The defendants seemed incapable of opinions. Three more months in jail before they would be freed, or three more months in jail before they would be convicted—you could look at it either way. Confinement, there being no choice in the matter, was becoming a way of life to Karl Fontenot; confinement, there being no choice in the matter, was becoming the Will of God to Tommy Ward.

September 9, then.

In the corridor outside the courtroom, Dorothy Hogue, who had been in the front row taking notes, was approached by Judge Ronald Jones, who had withdrawn from the case; Jones's office opened off the corridor. Ms. Hogue was excited; it was a big story.

"I wish you didn't have to print the trial date in the paper," Judge Jones said to the reporter.

"Why is that?" Ms. Hogue asked.

"Because half the town will schedule their elective surgery that day," the judge said.

At home that evening, Tricia and Bud heard the news for the first time on television: a trial date had been set. September 9. Tricia calculated in her mind. She was due the first week in November; she would be seven months pregnant during the trial.

The next day it was the front-page headline in the Ada *News*:

FONTENOT, WARD
TRIAL DATE SLATED

The town was buzzing once again.

10

THE SECOND SUMMER

Summer in Ada was hot, humid; afternoon temperatures climbed to 100 degrees, hovered there week after week; combined with the high humidity it made a simple outdoor stroll an act of discomfort. The air felt wet to the touch, but such clouds as rolled in seemed rarely to crack and let loose rain. The sun blazed on all alike, rich and poor, involved or unconcerned, except for the two suspects, Ward and Fontenot, tucked away in their cells, far from the light; and except perhaps on the victim, whose whereabouts, dead or alive, remained unknown. But the glare of the Haraway case did not blaze on all alike; to each of those involved it was refracted by the prisms of their individual backgrounds, their differing status in Ada society, their professional training or lack of it, their unavoidable prejudices, the depths of religion in their lives and in their souls.

To the family of Denice Haraway, to the police, to the district attorney, to most of the town's establishment, the prism refracted a simple spectrum of guilt. Denice was gone, and because they knew no power on earth could have induced her to leave her family, her husband, her career, willingly, or to put them through this torment without a phone call or a letter or some other possible sign, then she most certainly, however terrible the thought, was dead; and, if dead, then someone had killed her. Tommy Ward and Karl Fontenot were part of the despised running crowd, whose members were probably capable of any imaginable affront to society, to the sanctity of life; most important of all, they had confessed; they had put on videotape their

despicable tale of rape, torture, murder. Viewed through this re-
spectable prism, there was no reason why anyone, even under police
questioning, intense or not, would say they had done such things if
they had not; the fact that they had immediately repudiated the confessions was simply the normal attempt of criminals—of butchers—
to avoid paying the price for their crimes. They had rung in Odell
Titsworth to place the blame for the actual killing on someone else;
all the other statements on the tapes that had been proven false they
had simply made up to baffle the police, to confuse the issue, to con-
ceal what they had done with the body. And if, in spite of unofficial
talk of a life sentence in exchange for the body, they still held out, it
was because they had burned the body and thus had nothing to offer;
or because they had thrown it more than a year ago into the Canadian
River, or the North Canadian, and had no idea now where it might be,
where the denuded bones now rested. The spectrum of this crime
might contain shadows absent from most murder cases: the lack of a
body, the lack of a weapon, the lack of the vehicle; but these were, by
summer, merely disconcerting nuances in the black and white picture
of guilt. Tommy Ward, between May and October of 1984, had
changed his story to the police of what he had been doing the night
of the disappearance. Everything else had flowed from that, inex-
orably, and would culminate, they fervently hoped and mostly believed, in the conviction of Ward and Fontenot in the county
courthouse in September, and in a sentence of death. Only this would
satisfy the demands of justice; only this would put the case to rest.

To the family of Tommy Ward, to his mother and Tricia and Bud,
to all seven brothers and sisters, to many people at the lower, less-
educated, less-sophisticated end of Ada life, the light refracted differently. By now most of them were admitting to themselves that Denice
Haraway was probably dead; from everything they'd heard, she wasn't
the kind of person to run off. But how could the police be sure, without a body, so sure that they could bring murder charges? She was a
college girl, she was pretty, she'd only been married for eight
months . . . she might have seen something better come along; perhaps not, but how can they be so sure? And then the tapes: they were
fantasy, in this view. Titsworth had not been there, though that was
on the tapes; the house had not been burned down that night, though

that was on the tapes; where had the pickup gone? Where had the body gone? Hardly anything on the tapes checked out. "Disregard everything they confessed to," they seemed to hear the police, the district attorney, saying, "but believe they are guilty nonetheless." From this vantage point they wanted to know why they, or anyone, should. Some felt they themselves had been harassed by the police from time to time; they knew firsthand the fear that could lurk at the end of a nightstick, or in a cell. They knew of the unsolved Patty Hamilton disappearance in Seminole, of the unsolved Debbie Carter murder in Ada; they viewed Dr. Jack Haraway of the Rotary Club and the First Christian Church as "high society"; they sensed on the police and the OSBI a great pressure to solve this one; they believed that the police—most of them once poor and unnoticed like themselves, but now in positions of power—were capable of doing anything to get a conviction when they felt they needed one. And so, through this prism, Tommy Ward and Karl Fontenot were victims as much as Denice Haraway might be. Tommy had demonstrated his innocence by not leaving town, they felt, by repeatedly answering all police questions voluntarily, without being arrested, without even getting a lawyer; he had taken a polygraph voluntarily, to prove his innocence, and no evidence had been produced, beyond the unsupported word of the OSBI, that he had failed it. Uneducated, not very bright, Tommy could have been confused and manipulated by the police; weary after five hours of questioning, he had said on tape whatever they wanted him to say, merely to get them out of his face, believing that his lies would free him when they were exposed as lies. Karl Fontenot, in this view, totally incapable of violence, had been fed Tommy's "confession" by the police, had regurgitated most of it back for the same reasons. If Tommy had been smart enough to ask for a lawyer right away, neither boy would have spent a single day in jail, and the police might be doing what they ought to be doing: might be out there looking for the truth, for the real killer of Denice Haraway. If she was dead.

Those were the two opposing views of the case as summer began. There were no shades of gray. Dennis Smith, Bill Peterson, the Haraways, the Lyons saw on the hands of Ward and Fontenot the bright red of bloody violence. Tricia and Bud, Miz Ward, and the others saw just as clearly, around their necks, the dark purple of injustice.

The only middle position was held by those in the town who admitted that they didn't know. Among these were the two defense attorneys. George Butner did not know, in early summer, if his client, Karl Fontenot, was guilty or innocent. He suspected he was innocent; but the tapes certainly bothered him, especially the matching descriptions of the blouse. He did not want to bring himself to believe that the police, or the OSBI, had knowingly and willfully framed his client by feeding him Tommy's description of the blouse. And yet, the rest of the tapes, almost everything proven false . . . He didn't know what to believe. He certainly didn't know how he was going to prove that Karl was innocent. And in this case, it seemed likely, that's what his task would come down to: a task that obliterated a thousand years of the evolution of criminal law. In this case, in the face of the confession tapes, his client and Don Wyatt's would likely be considered guilty until proven innocent.

Wyatt, too, did not know what to make of the case. He believed that Karl Fontenot had had nothing to do with Denice Haraway's disappearance. About his own client, Tommy Ward, he was uncertain. He felt that if Tommy had been involved, one or more others had been as well: others who had been the masterminds, who had had the truck, who had disposed of the truck and the body. He sometimes felt that Tommy himself did not know if he had been involved. On a scale of one to ten, one being that Tommy was totally innocent, ten being that he was guilty, Don Wyatt's feeling in late spring was about a five. He simply didn't know.

Then he received the first of Richard Kerner's reports about Rogers, Sparcino . . . callers not questioned by the police. Ever so slightly, the needle on the guilt meter in his mind began to shift; ever so slightly it nudged toward innocent.

He called the private investigator to his office once again, and put him back to work on the case.

The house at 730 West Twelfth Street was an old frame building that had not been painted in many years; on a dirt plot beside it stood an abandoned car. This was the home address that Willie Barnett had given to Richard Kerner. The investigator at first suspected it would not be a real address; the first time he went there it seemed vacant.

But he came across a note from the family in the lawyer's office stating that Willie did live on Twelfth Street. On June 17 he went there again, parked in the street, walked up to the front door. The door, behind a screen door, was open. The screen door was latched.

Kerner knocked. A woman came to the door. When Kerner asked if he could talk to Willie, the woman yelled to the rear of the house. A man's voice asked who it was. But the man did not come to the door. Kerner said again he wanted to talk to Willie. The woman yelled that someone wanted to talk to him. The man yelled back. He did not want to be interviewed. For several minutes this continued: the investigator asking questions of the woman; the woman relaying the questions inside; Willie answering through the woman, without ever making himself visible. Kerner grew increasingly frustrated. He knew how crucial Willie Barnett might be to Tommy Ward's defense: he might be the only alibi witness who was not a member of the family. If the screen door had not been latched, Kerner felt, he could have got his foot in the door, as any good investigator would, talked his way inside, and confronted Willie, perhaps got him to talk. But the door remained latched. Kerner remained on the outside. Willie refused to come out.

Stymied, Kerner moved on to other areas he had been instructed by Wyatt to investigate. He traced the yellow truck that Joel Ward had seen in Broken Arrow, a suburb of Tulsa. Joel had thought it might be linked to Jay Dicus, and might recently have been painted yellow, over gray. Kerner inspected traffic records, conducted numerous interviews, made a visit to Broken Arrow. The investigation took many hours of many days; like many other trails Kerner would follow, it turned out to be irrelevant. He traced the truck to a man who spoke to him willingly, who said the truck had been yellow for four years. Other people he interviewed confirmed this. The truck and its owner were not involved in the case.

In late June and early July the investigator spent thirty-seven and a half hours checking that lead and others, mostly tracking down people in the running crowd who were mentioned in Tommy Ward's long essay to his lawyer, young men who Tommy said owned old pickup trucks. Sometimes it took five or six interviews to establish the whereabouts of the person he was looking for.

One young man he interviewed, Larry Jett (name changed), was at his job in a yard ornaments shop. Rows of plaster-of-Paris elephants, birds, Bambi-like fawns, roosters surrounded them as they talked. Jett conceded that he knew Tommy Ward, but claimed he had never owned a 1970s Chevy pickup, as Ward had told his lawyer. Jett volunteered that at the time of Denice Haraway's disappearance, he (Jett) had been living in Kansas with a roommate, Melvin Harden. The investigator noticed a quickness with which Jett mentioned where he'd been living at the time; Kerner hadn't asked. Jett mentioned the names of other people Ward ran with, who did own old pickups. Kerner noted the names as possible areas for further probing.

Wyatt had asked him to interview Marty Ashley, of Tommy's "kiss-and-run" story. The investigator talked to half a dozen people merely to find out where Ashley was now residing: in Paul's Valley, thirty miles west. He marked that down for a future visit.

Tricia, nearly five months pregnant, was at the kitchen stove, frying up a mess of catfish steaks; catfish was their favorite treat, and Bud had found them on sale at the Dicus Supermarket on Fourth Street. He stood beside her now, cooking vegetables. When the food was ready they sat with the three kids at the table in the dining room.

David and Lisa, the foster kids, were gone; Tricia, often weary, with her belly getting bigger and the days getting hotter, with all the kids out of school, had decided it was getting too hard to handle all five of them, that in July she might tell the social worker to find them another home. But before she had a chance to do that, David came down with measles; the doctor thought they might be German measles, which could endanger Tricia's unborn child; he told her to keep away from David. Bud spent a frantic time on the telephone with the social worker as she tried to locate someone to take in the kids immediately; she finally found a foster parent who lived only a block away. The woman took David and Lisa, and agreed to keep them even after David recovered; she would bring them by sometimes to visit Bud and Tricia and the kids.

The family ate the catfish and talked. The day before, at the jail, Tommy had told them Don Wyatt had visited, had said things were looking good; Bud and Tricia were not sure what he meant; the lawyer had not yet informed them of the investigator's findings.

After dinner, in the small living room, Laura Sue was idly turning the pages of a 1980 Ada school yearbook; it had pictures of all the grades in it, including a picture of Rhonda. Bud began to turn the pages with her; then he stopped. He was struck by a picture of one of the high school boys: it looked exactly like the composite drawing in the Haraway case that was supposed to be Tommy.

Ever since the drawings had appeared, Bud had had the feeling that he knew someone who looked like that, and it wasn't Tommy. Here was the boy. He read the name under the picture. They knew the family slightly; he was a good kid, a good student.

"I'm not saying he did it," Bud said. "But I think we should show this to Wyatt."

"What for?" Tricia asked.

"To show he's a lookalike. To show that an identification through a composite drawing is useless."

"He knows that," Tricia said. "Wyatt isn't the one who needs convincing."

On Thursday morning, June 20, Tommy Ward had an experience he had never had before. He was lying on the bunk in his cell. He was not sure if he was awake or dreaming; he seemed to be somewhere in between. Suddenly he had the strong sensation that his spirit was about to leave his body, that his spirit was about to go out and hover over the land, and find out who had committed the crime: who had done what to Denice Haraway. At first it was a good feeling, very powerful. Then he had another, frightening thought: "If my spirit leaves my body, I will be dead." With a willful effort he shook himself back to consciousness, so that his spirit would not depart.

Bill Peterson, in his office in the courthouse, was preparing for the trial, though it was still more than two months away; he'd been doing so on and off ever since the preliminary hearing. Now he was going through the transcript of the hearing, preparing his list of witnesses, noting the important testimony he would need from each one. He was planning to take a vacation with his wife in August; they would visit relatives in Florida. He would take his work along.

He was estimating that the jury selection, plus the prosecution case, would take two weeks; he did not know how long the defense would take. "I've heard they're saying they'll have as many witnesses as we will. I don't see how they can do that, but maybe they will."

He was not looking forward to such a long, pressurized ordeal; he had never tried a case that lasted more than a week.

Across town, in his offices on Arlington, Don Wyatt, too, was preparing for the case. He was elated by Richard Kerner's initial findings, and planned to keep him in the field most of the summer to see what he could turn up. He knew the police and the district attorney were aware of Kerner's activities; some of the people Kerner talked to had been visited soon after by the police, who wanted to know what he had asked them. That did not bother Wyatt. He wanted "to keep the pot boiling" all summer, if possible. Perhaps, he thought, if the police kept on the case, instead of sitting back waiting for the trial, *they* might turn up something that would clear Tommy Ward.

In his mind the defense was taking shape. He might call as many as fifty witnesses: all those who had called in to the police names other than Tommy's that fit the composite drawings, the people who had seen two possible suspects out at the trailer park, the alibi witnesses in the family, and Willie Barnett if possible. One idea he'd had pleased him immensely. He was going to subpoena from the college the skull and bones the detectives had taken to the jail to frighten Tommy. Every day of the trial he was going to enter the courtroom and set on the defense table a large paper bag. At the end of each day he would carry it out again; it would get the attention of the jury. At a dramatic moment during the defense, he would open the bag and whip out the skull and bones. If it startled the people sitting on the jury, he reasoned, they might understand how much more frightening it had been when shown to a young man locked in a cell; and yet it still had not obtained any additional information for the police.

In his mind, too, a powerful opening statement was forming, which he hoped Richard Kerner's investigations through the summer would justify. "Not only are we going to prove to you that Tommy

Ward did not commit this crime!" he envisioned himself telling the jury. "We are also going to tell you who did do it!"

Wyatt was thinking that he probably would have to put Ward on the stand. This was unusual in a criminal case, he knew, but he felt he might have to do it so Tommy could explain away the tapes. He had obtained permission from the judge to have a psychiatrist or psychologist examine Tommy at the jail, to explain "how anyone could be so stupid as to make up all those lies and think that was going to get them out of trouble." If that turned out to be strong testimony, he might not have to put Tommy on; he would thus avoid the likelihood that the D.A. could hang Tommy's lies around his neck. Wyatt knew that the tapes were deadly; but he saw some points in their favor: Odell Titsworth and all the other things on the tapes that had proved false.

For the first time, Wyatt was beginning to feel he could win the case. He was planning a vacation in July, to go hunting and fishing in the Northwest; then he would return to prepare the case. In a courtroom, preparation was everything, he believed. And he believed he could outprepare Bill Peterson.

In his cell in the county jail, Tommy Ward was becoming concerned about Karl Fontenot over in the city jail, about the "crazy things" Karl was saying. They'd had a chance to talk during the ride to the hospital at Vinita; they had talked again while in the courtroom together on June 11, the day the trial date had been set. Tommy voiced his concerns one Sunday during the visiting hour: "In court the other day," Tommy said, "he sits there, he says, 'Man,' he goes, 'I have a good mind to just go in there and plead guilty.' He goes, 'They're gonna convict us of it anyway.' I said, 'Bull!' I said, 'When you get your witnesses up . . .' He goes, 'Well, my lawyer ain't gonna do nothing about it!' I said, 'Bull! Your lawyer is fightin' for you just like he was a hired lawyer.'"

Tommy said he told Karl they would have Jannette Roberts as a witness. "He goes, 'I didn't think anybody would want to witness for me.' I says, 'Well,' I says, 'it's just you not caring about anybody. You don't care about nobody, so nobody's caring about you, you know.'" Tommy laughed. "He's gone plumb crazy. He was telling me about this girl that was one of the disc jockeys over there at the police department. He told her that if she didn't come up there and let him screw her through the bars, that he was gonna kill her just like he killed that girl. That's what he told her. I said, 'You saying things like that, they're gonna get up there and testify against you.' I said, I told him, 'First, I know you didn't have nothing to do with it.' I said, 'I still know you didn't have nothing to do with it.' His hair was short and he was working up there at Wendy's. But I told him, I said, 'Now I'm starting to doubt. The way you been acting, I'm starting to think you mighta had something to do with it.' He said, 'No, I didn't have nothing to do with it.' I said, 'Well, then keep your mouth shut then.' " Tommy laughed. "He's crazy."

Tommy spoke, too, of his own situation: "I don't know why they didn't drop it in the first place. They ain't got no evidence . . . I'm just wanting to laugh it off and laugh it off as much as I can, you know. I can't believe it that my own hometown is doing this to me. I've lived here; I was born and raised here all my life. There wouldn't be no rea-son I would want to go and do something like that, especially in my own hometown, you know . . . They say moneywise, is the reason why, 'cause I was short of money. Any time I needed any money, my mom would give it to me. And if mom didn't have it, my brothers and sisters would. And if they didn't have it, you'd see me on the side of the road picking up beer cans. I told the truth. I said, don't you think my mom, my brother, and them would rather give me this money than give it to them lawyers and everything, instead of having to go through this. That's when they started coming up with the drug deal, you know, saying I was all doped up on drugs and just don't remem-ber doing it. I said, Bull! I said, Man, I don't think there's any kind of dope in the world to get somebody to go out and do something like that and everything and not remember it."

There was a knock on the door of the visiting room; Tommy's time was up.

Five days later, on June 28, Karl Fontenot was led from his cell in the city jail across the street to a cell in the county jail. Initially the sus-pects had been placed in separate jails so that they could not commu-nicate, could not coordinate their stories. As the months passed, that simply became the way it was; no one thought of changing the arrangement. The reason the move was made now was vague, even to Dennis Smith; there was some hope that by putting them together, letting them talk about the case, some new clue would be overheard by a jailer or another inmate that might lead the police to the body; partly it was because Karl was not being prosecuted by the city; the county jail was where he belonged, and there was nothing more to be gained by keeping the suspects apart. As he was led across Townsend Street, Fontenot left behind in the city jail what was undoubtedly an Ada record: eight months and ten days in a cell without a visitor other than his lawyer, without a word of support from anyone he knew.

As he entered the county jail, Karl would not have quarreled with Tommy's assessment of him. He knew it was true that he did not trust anyone, did not let anyone get close to him. He was introspective enough to understand some of the reasons why: because all those whom a child learns to trust had deserted him: his mother frequently disappearing when he was little, because she was being abused by his father, then coming back because she had no place else to go; his father disappearing for good when Karl was twelve; his mother getting herself killed by a car when he was sixteen; his sisters and brothers turning him out into the street, saying he was old enough to take care of himself. If his life so far had taught him anything, it was to mistrust the very concept of trust. And his time in jail was only reinforcing that: not a call, a letter, a visit from his family in all those months.

At times, the outward shield he adopted against further wounds was the persona of a wiseguy, a smart aleck, an operator. Don Wyatt, for one, felt Karl had more "street smarts" than Tommy. Others, looking at Karl, saw a wounded puppy.

In a different jail now, with new inmates to talk to, Karl went around saying that he might plead guilty, might say he had been there and that Tommy had done it; that way, he figured, he'd get twenty years in jail, maybe, but they wouldn't kill him. Tommy heard this talk and got even more nervous than usual. Tommy trusted, perhaps to a fault; he trusted his family, he trusted that at the trial he and Karl would be found not guilty. Watching Karl "talking crazy," he thought, "When we are freed, they may have to put Karl in an institution."

After several days, Karl stopped talking about pleading guilty. He calmed down, in Tommy's view. They became friends again, began to chat, to play dominoes in the open area among the cells, which they were now allowed to frequent; the months of solitary confinement had, for no stated reason, ended.

Tommy told Karl that reading the Bible and trusting in the Lord was helping him to endure the time in jail. He began to read Biblical verses aloud to Karl. Not since his early childhood a churchgoer, Karl sat quietly and listened.

In the ensuing weeks Karl would begin to claim that he had been saved; that he had found God; that he, too, had put his faith in the Lord, and the Lord would see him through. Whether this was a genuine religious feeling, or a pose that Karl felt might be useful in winning sympathy, or some combination of the two, only Karl could know.

DONNA WAS KIDNAPPED, RAPED, AND CREMATED!

So screamed a headline in July from the magazine racks of Ada, from magazine racks across Oklahoma, across America. Printed in blue capital letters on a bright yellow background, it was the lead headline on the cover of a bimonthly magazine called *Startling Detective.*

Inside, beginning on page thirty-four, was a six-page spread on the Haraway case. The same headline ran across the bottom of the first two pages: DONNA WAS KIDNAPPED, RAPED, AND CREMATED! Above it, filling one of the pages, was a black-and-white photograph of Tommy Ward, in his prison coveralls, being led from the jail by two deputies. Facing it was the yearbook photograph of Denice Haraway. On the succeeding pages were the composite drawings, a picture of Karl Fontenot, a picture of Patty Hamilton, the girl who disappeared from Seminole. Above the story was a byline: "by Jack Heise."

A friend of Tommy's sister Kay saw the magazine and told Kay, who told Bud. Police officers heard about it and bought copies. So did the D.A.'s office, and the Haraways. By the time Don Wyatt heard of it, the newsstands of Ada were sold out; he got hold of a Xeroxed copy.

Dozens of other Xeroxed copies were passed from hand to hand through the town.

The article was a highly sensationalized account of the case. It treated most of the statements on the Ward and Fontenot tapes as if they were proven facts, while, out of respect for the laws of libel, always attributing the statements to the suspects. Narrating the events of April 28, 1984, the article was dotted with inaccurate statements, was padded with quotations and invented dialogue from Ada police officers, all of whom said they had never heard of the author, Jack Heise, had never talked to anyone from *Startling Detective*.

Describing the witnesses arriving at McAnally's, the article said, "They saw two men and a woman leaving." This was wrong; they had said they'd seen one man and a woman leaving.

One witness, the article said, thought "the young woman might have had too much to drink, particularly when she was pushed roughly into the cab of a pickup truck." The witnesses had said no such thing; the woman had appeared to be walking normally; she was not pushed into the truck.

The piece told how Sergeant Harvey Phillips was the first officer at the scene. It continued: " 'One of the guys had his arm around her and I thought maybe she was a bit tipsy,' the witness said. 'But she didn't call out or say anything. Possibly I could have stopped it.'

" 'And most likely would have gotten yourself shot,' Phillips said. 'She must have been a gutsy girl to go with them without calling out for help because she knew they had a gun.' "

All of this had been invented by the writer. No one had ever said anyone was tipsy; no one, in the entire case, had ever mentioned a gun.

On and on the story went, filled with inaccuracies; it described Detectives Smith, Baskin, and Danny Barrett arriving at the scene, along with Police Chief Richard Gray; of these, only Baskin had been there. It had lab technicians dusting for fingerprints; that never happened. It went at great length into the stories on the tapes, making the implicit assumption that the stories were true; it never mentioned that both suspects had repudiated the tapes. Changing the name of Odell Titsworth to "Mike Callender," for legal reasons, it did say he had been cleared by the police. Other statements on the tapes that had proved false—such as the body being burned in the house—were presented as true.

For obvious reasons—since no trial had yet been held—the final paragraph stated: "By law, until such time as they may be judged at a fair trial, Ward and Fontenot must be considered innocent of the charges that have been placed against them."

The magazine billed itself as the "World's Top Crime Magazine." It was published by Globe Communications Corp., which listed an address in New York State. It had been in business for seventy-five years.

When Bud and Tricia read the article, they felt sick. It clearly portrayed the boys as guilty, they felt; particularly the large picture of Tommy above the unattributed, unmodified headline. They wanted to know if they could sue. Don Wyatt felt the magazine had probably covered itself legally with its final disclaimer; in any case, they would have to await the outcome of the trial; if Tommy was found guilty, there would hardly be grounds for a lawsuit.

The Haraway family was embittered by the article as well; the garish treatment seemed a further violation, now of Denice's name. The references to the woman having been drunk or tipsy were especially libelous, they felt. Four different members of the family called the district attorney's office to ask if they could sue the magazine. Chris Ross told them that was not the province of the D.A.'s office, that they should consult a private attorney.

Both Peterson and Ross found the article highly offensive. Though it seemed to leave no doubt as to the guilt of the suspects—a feeling he shared—Dennis Smith nonetheless found it disgusting. Sergeant Phillips, in whose mouth many fictitious words had been put, went around for days wanting to punch the author, but no one knew the author; his name was not familiar in Ada.

Bud Wolf's first thought when he saw the article was of the letter received by the Ada *News* back in November, enclosing a twenty-dollar bill, asking for the clippings on the case; that crossed the mind of Dennis Smith as well. Dorothy Hogue, who had received the request, went through the drawers of her desk in the city room of the *News*; she found the envelope. It was from a Jack G. Heise, with an address in the state of Washington.

The article in *Startling Detective* thus cleared up at least that one small mystery in the case: the mystery of who had cared enough about it to send for clippings from half a continent away.

This was no consolation to the offended parties; Harvey Phillips still wanted to punch the author. The others would have been glad to join in.

The Haraway case had caught the attention of Jack Heise in the town of Bothell, Washington. In space 66 of the trailer park in which he lived, Heise pored through newspapers from across America, looking for good crime stories. When he found ones that interested him, he would clip the stories.

When the suspects were arrested and made their brutal taped confessions, Heise had clipped the write-ups in the *Daily Oklahoman* and the Tulsa *World*. Because the case was taking place in Ada, he pulled out a handy directory of every newspaper in the country, listed state by state, town by town, and he got the address of the Ada *News*, and sent for their clippings. Later he typed his article, using what facts he could from the news clippings, inventing what he needed. "Paraphrasing" was the way he thought of it, not "inventing." For this and countless similar articles he had done over the years, for various police and detective magazines, he received about $250 each.

Jack Heise found no shame in the practice. He'd been doing it for fifty years. When he was a reporter in Seattle, he had done it for extra income. Now he was retired. He was seventy-five years old. He banged out one such article a week; the money was enough to live on.

"You paraphrase the best you can," he said. "It's an okay living. Especially when your hair is gray and you have no teeth, and nobody cares anymore."

The grass on the campus of East Central University was still a bright green, not yet burned out by the summer heat. Students taking summer classes sprawled in the shade of the trees that dotted the lawns, studying, eating sandwiches. Richard Kerner strode up the central walkway, then bore half-right down another path, toward the education building. He had an appointment there with Jack Paschall, who'd been at J.P.'s with Karen Wise the night of the disappearance, who'd testified he was sure that Tommy Ward had been in the store that night.

Paschall told Kerner the same story he had told to the police, the same story he had told under oath at the preliminary hearing: how he had come to J.P.'s that night, how Karen Wise had told him she was nervous, that it was two guys shooting pool who were upsetting her; how the men had left soon after, in an old pickup truck, with either gray primer or red primer on it, with something unusual about the tailgate. Paschall said he did not know Tommy Ward, but he was sure he'd been one of the two in the store that night. He said again, as he had said before, that he did not recognize Karl Fontenot.

The same afternoon, July 11, Kerner drove thirty miles to Paul's Valley. There he placed a home at 307 East Bradley under surveillance; it was the home of Marty Ashley's mother. Kerner had been watching the house for less than an hour when a short, slight, blondish young man came out of the front door and walked toward several cars in the yard that seemed to be under repair. Kerner approached the young man and addressed him as Marty Ashley; Ashley said that's who he was.

Ashley agreed to answer the investigator's questions. They sat in Kerner's car and talked. Ashley said he had been questioned long ago by Ada detectives Dennis Smith and James Fox about Ward's story that he, Ashley, had run off with Denice Haraway; he said he had given the detectives a recorded statement saying that Ward's story was totally false. He said he had never in his life been in any kind of vehicle with Tommy Ward; he mentioned he had seen Ward riding in old pickups from time to time, and gave Kerner the names of several young men they might have belonged to. He denied knowing Randy Rogers or Bob Sparcino. Ashley told the investigator he was pretty much of a loner, that he had not run around very much with Jay Dicus or Tommy Ward or anyone else in Ada.

About Denice Haraway, Ashley said he had seen her working at McAnally's, but had not known her name till she disappeared. He said, smiling, that he wished she *had* run away with him, because she was a very attractive lady.

Kerner's gut feeling was that Ashley was telling the truth.

In mid-July, Tommy's sister Melva passed through Ada for a few days with her husband, William, and their four children. Melva was allowed to visit Tommy at the jail on a Thursday, because she had driven so far and would be gone by Sunday. She thus became the last of Tommy's seven brothers and sisters to see him in jail, to lend her moral support.

Her husband was in the Army, and was being transferred from California to a base in Europe; they had driven east from California, would be flown the rest of the way. Seeing them gave Tricia an idea. She had always known that, even if Tommy were acquitted, he could not return to Ada; he might be killed. He would need to leave the state, she felt; and now she thought: perhaps he should leave the country as well; once he was freed, he perhaps should go to Europe till things calmed down. He could stay close to Melva and William there.

Richard Kerner continued to investigate; the list of names he had checked grew longer: names Tommy had mentioned, now names Marty Ashley had mentioned. On August 1, looking into the contacts of Larry Jett, he went to Elmore City, a village of six hundred people fifty miles southwest of Ada, to a mobile home in which Jett's common-law sister-in-law lived. No one was at home in the trailer. But parked on the two-acre lot, about seventy yards away, Kerner saw an old pickup. It was painted with gray and red primer; the front was facing him. Slowly the investigator walked toward the truck. With each step his feeling grew stronger: that when he circled to the back of the truck, it would be missing its tailgate. Kerner walked to the back; the tailgate was gone.

Circling the pickup repeatedly, he photographed it from many angles. It fit perfectly Karen Wise and Jack Paschall's description of the truck at J.P.'s, he felt, except that it did not have larger tires on the rear.

The investigator wanted to climb into the cab; take scrapings from the seat, the dash; perhaps find hairs or something that could be linked to Denice Haraway. But he had no legal authority to do that. Instead he drove to Ada and showed the pictures to Don Wyatt.

The lawyer was instantly excited. This might be the truck, he felt. He told Kerner to find out everything he could about the history of this truck, and about everyone connected with it. If it seemed to tie in, Wyatt thought, he might try to buy the truck; have some lab go over it microscopically for fingerprints, for anything that might link it to the missing girl. It would be a longshot after a year and a half, but it might be worth a try.

Kerner wondered. The OSBI, "the badge-carriers," as he thought of the police, had laboratories at their disposal to conduct such tests. He did not know if, or where, they would find a private lab to do it.

Wyatt told Miz Ward he needed more money to pay the investigator. He said the bills were up around $2,000 now, but that they were well worth it: the investigator might have found the truck in which Denice Haraway was taken from McAnally's.

That same day, August 1, Wyatt and Kerner went to the jail to talk to Tommy. A new theory was brewing in the attorney's mind. The most damaging evidence against Ward, aside from the taped "confession," was the adamancy with which both Karen Wise and Jack Paschall insisted that Tommy had been in J.P.'s that night. Suppose they were right, Wyatt reasoned, suppose Tommy had been shooting pool in J.P.'s—but then had left, and had gone to a party, or home, or wherever. Suppose the incidents at J.P.'s and McAnally's were not related; suppose there had been different people, different trucks. It certainly was possible. The witnesses at McAnally's could not say for sure it was Tommy. Wyatt wanted to see what story Tommy was going to stick to.

At the jail they told Ward they had found the truck that might have been involved. They asked him if perhaps he *had* been at J.P.'s that night.

Tommy said no. He insisted that he had been at home all that evening. He told again how Willie Barnett had visited, how he had bothered the bird.

"Where did you go after you left J.P.'s?" Wyatt asked.

"I wasn't at J.P.'s," Tommy repeated. Frustrated, he said, "If you have the truck, why don't you find out who done it?"

"Let's hope we don't find *your* fingerprints in the truck," the attorney said.

"Don't worry, you won't," Tommy said.

In Richard Kerner's view, the session had not been productive. Don Wyatt felt Tommy had been more lucid than in the past, perhaps because there were no more drugs in his system. It seemed, at last, that this would be the story Tommy would stick to: that he had been at home all evening.

On the positive side, in Wyatt's view, that fit in with what the family said. On the negative side, it left the Wise and Paschall identifications unexplained.

Ward himself was extremely upset by the visit; he felt Wyatt had turned on him, was trying to convict him instead of trying to clear him. He felt they had been trying to mess with his head, to get him confused again. For three days he brooded incessantly about the meeting—so much so that when his mother and his sister Kay came to see him on Sunday, and he told them about it, he thought it had taken place the day before, instead of three days before. More than ever, the days in the jail were running together into endless night.

Kerner returned to Elmore City. He talked to the police there. He was told there were frequent drinking and drug parties at the trailer where the truck was parked, with some of the participants coming from the Ada area. The Elmore police agreed to keep an eye on the red and gray pickup, which had not been moved since Kerner's last visit; they said if someone was seen driving it they would arrest him for having an expired license tag, and would impound the truck.

The investigator continued with his interviews, his checks of driver records. He discovered that Marty Ashley once had four moving violations in a 1977 Chevrolet pickup. On August 13 he returned to Paul's Valley. At Don Wyatt's request, he took detailed photographs from all angles of an old Ford pickup he'd noticed among the cars being repaired in the yard. Kerner then went to Ada and showed both sets of pictures to Jack Paschall: those of the red-and-gray pickup in

Elmore City, and those of the truck Ashley had. Paschall said he could not rule out the Elmore City pickup, but that the Ashley truck looked more like the one he had seen.

Kerner asked Paschall again about his identification of Tommy Ward. The professor said he was 100 percent sure, but that this of course was subject to "human frailties."

The investigator went back to the yard ornaments shop, with its row after row of silent chickens, elephants, fawns; to Larry Jett, whose sister-in-law held title to the truck in Elmore City, where some of Ada's running crowd partied. He was struck during this second visit, as he had been during his first, by Larry Jett's slim stature, sandy-blond hair, facial features; he bore a strong resemblance, the investigator felt, to Tommy Ward.

Kerner asked again about Jett's owning an old Chevy pickup. Jett, who had previously denied this, now merely shrugged, and did not answer the question. He told Kerner that since the investigator's last visit, he had been cornered twice by Ada police, who wanted to know what Kerner had asked him. One of these times, he said, an officer had grabbed Kerner's business card from his hand and kept it. Jett said he did not know how the Ada police knew Kerner had been to see him.

Kerner asked where Jett had been on April 28, 1984; Jett repeated that he had been living in Kansas with Melvin Harden; Harden was also back in Ada now, he said, address unknown. He gave Kerner the names and addresses of several women who might know where Harden was.

Kerner went to Seminole, met again with assistant police chief Dexter Davis, showed him everything he had; Davis said none of these names or trucks had turned up in the investigation into the disappearance of Patty Hamilton.

The investigator met with Wyatt and gave him a written report of his findings thus far; Wyatt told him which areas to follow up. He needed the investigation completed by August 30, the lawyer said.

July's warmth had become August's heat. The cooler days topped out at 96 or 98 degrees. The warmer ones reached 102. The humidity was stifling. Merely to be outdoors was a chore.

A fierce lightning and thunderstorm struck Ada at three o'clock in the morning, on Wednesday, August 7. The crashing thunder awakened many people; it was as if the accumulated heat and humidity of weeks had suddenly cracked in an outburst of wild rage. Balls of thunder rolled, crackled, boomed upon the town. Lightning lit the sky over the farms, plummeted like avenging white swords into the town.

On the outskirts, the lightning struck nineteen different oil pumps; the rain flooded the fields. In town, the lightning struck the wood-frame home of Bud and Tricia Wolf and their children.

The thunder had awakened them first; the children left their beds, huddled together in fear. Bud and Tricia lay awake in their bed; Miz Ward, staying with them, was awakened in the back bedroom. In front of their eyes, flashing white current leaped in bits and pieces through the inside of the house, making a crackling noise, as if some fierce electronic ghost had entered.

The children screamed. The momentary ghost left. There was a smell of burning. The adults, shaken, tried to comfort Rhonda, Buddy, Laura Sue. The thunder moved farther away in the night sky. Bud tried the lights—some of them worked; some of them didn't. He checked every room, to make sure there wasn't a fire.

The storm passed. The night dragged on. Sleep was only fitful. In the morning, as always, the kids turned on the twelve-inch color television set; it didn't work. Bud looked behind it; the entry wires leading from the antenna on the roof had been scorched, seared. He checked the lights again; all those on the same circuit as the TV set didn't work. He went outside and looked up at the roof. The bolt of lightning clearly had hit the TV antenna and forked three ways. One part had come down through the antenna, had burned out the TV set; a second fork had left a long vertical burn scar on the catalpa tree that stands in front of the house, shading the front porch; the third fork had sheared shingles off the roof of the house next door.

No one had been hurt.

At Luton Motors, truck after truck arrived, bringing in the motors of oil pumps that had been burned out by the storm. C. L. Wolf had just ordered a thousand pounds of copper wire; he figured now it would be gone in three months. "That's what keeps our business athrivin'," he said. "These lightning storms."

Tricia, sitting in her living room, the large painting of Jesus that C.L. had painted hanging behind her, called their insurance company, to see if they could replace the TV and the Coleco electronic game attached to it, which had also been destroyed by the lightning. She was told their policy had a $250 deductible figure; they could get no insurance money, because the TV set was ten years old.

What with her maternity bills, and recent dental bills, money was very tight. They would not be able to replace the TV.

"The kids will have to go without for a while," Tricia said. Then, instantly finding a bright side, as with her abiding faith she always tried to do, she added, "Maybe they'll do better in school this year."

A friend said to Tricia, "What more do you need? I can't believe it! The house getting struck by lightning now!"

Tricia just shook her head.

"Do you think the Lord is testing you?" the friend asked.

Tricia said she didn't know.

On the third floor of the Pontotoc County Courthouse, behind a glass door marked "Court Clerk," midway between the large courtroom and the small courtroom, the names were filled in, in the blank spaces on the forms. They had been taken at random from the county voter rolls. There were 225 of them. When the forms were complete, they were stuffed into envelopes, sealed, and taken to the post office a few blocks away. From there, the next day, they went out across Ada, across Pontotoc County; were dropped by mailmen into the slots of vertical mailboxes affixed to the front of frame houses and brick houses, were shoved into the larger horizontal mailboxes that stood along dirt roads in rural areas. They were opened in the afternoon or evening by people who worked at the feed mill and at the cement plant, by teachers and by farmers, by executives and by construction workers, men and women, young and middle-aged and elderly, housewives, retired folks, handicapped people, city employees. The message was the same to all of them: they were to report to the county courthouse in Ada on the morning of September 9, 1985, for jury duty.

They received the notices with varying degrees of irritation and interest. Many would look on it as an inconvenience, to be avoided if possible; others would accept it as a civic duty, a part of what made America work.

To some the date meant nothing: September 9, a Monday like any other. Others immediately knew, or would be told by friends soon after: that was the day they would start choosing the jury for the Haraway case.

11

SCENARIOS

The district attorney's office was behind the first door to the left, inside the main entrance of the courthouse. The door was of reflecting glass that made it difficult to see if anyone was inside. Behind this door, beyond a reception area, in his private inner office, Bill Peterson spent much of the summer interviewing the witnesses he planned to call in the Haraway case.

Many had appeared at the preliminary hearing; with these he went over the testimony they had given, and asked if there were any questions he should ask them on the stand that he had not asked before, his reasoning being: "They were there, I wasn't; they have to tell me what they know." Other witnesses were new. He went over with them, too, what they knew, what he would ask them. Before he left for his vacation in early August, he compiled a list of seventy witnesses to be subpoenaed; more would be added later. The subpoenas were sent out by certified mail, or hand-delivered by members of the sheriff's department across the hall.

Under the law, the state was required to notify the defense of all witnesses it planned to call; the defense was not required to tell the state of its witnesses, except for any alibi witnesses: those who would testify that the defendants had been somewhere else at the time of the crime. When Don Wyatt looked at the state's list of witnesses, he immediately came up with a stratagem; he decided to have defense subpoenas served on all of the state's witnesses. This would enable him to keep them out of the spectator section of the courtroom, even after they had finished their testimony for the state. He had counted on the state's roster about twenty relatives of Denice Haraway; he did not want them sitting in the courtroom, crying, in front of the jury.

Combining the state and defense witnesses, Wyatt's legal assistant, Winifred Harrell, prepared more than 120 subpoenas. Some were sent out by certified mail; others were served by a private process server; the most difficult people to find were tracked down and served by Richard Kerner.

With a month to go before the trial, the atmosphere developing on both sides was as before a heavyweight championship fight: in one corner would be wealthy Bill Peterson, district attorney, upholder of the law; in the other corner would be rich Don Wyatt, defense attorney, defender of the poor. The trophy to be won would be, for Peterson, an end to the Haraway case, a conviction for his office and the police in a murder trial without a body, perhaps even the death penalty for the suspects: a triumph for justice. The trophy for Wyatt would be another victory for Ada's most publicized attorney, an accusation of overzealousness hurled in the face of the police and the OSBI, freedom for Ward and Fontenot: a triumph for justice. Whether a fair trial could be held in Ada, whether justice would be served, what indeed justice demanded in this case, were questions that still split the town.

Neither side was suffering from overconfidence. As Peterson took the case records with him to Florida, to go over them yet again, one of Don Wyatt's aides bought a large green-slate blackboard and carried it into the law office. A secretary asked what it was for. The aide said it was for the Ward case. Before long, an unseen hand had chalked a single word on the board. It said, "HELP!"

If help was to come for the defendants, its most likely source would be Richard Kerner. The dogged investigator was once more in Ada, interviewing dozens of people, tracking trails that led nowhere—much as the police had done, day after day, in the months after Donna Denice Haraway disappeared. By a circuitous route he finally obtained an address in Ada for Melvin Harden, the friend with whom Larry Jett had said he'd roomed in Kansas at the time of the disappearance. Kerner interviewed Harden at his home. The result of that interview he summarized in a written report for Don Wyatt:

"Harden explained that he had left Ada in the summer of 1983 with Randy Rogers and went to the state of Texas. He said that he got into trouble in Texas because of Randy Rogers and went to prison September 22, 1983, and was released in March of 1984, and returned to Ada. Harden was questioned concerning being Larry Jett's room-mate in the state of Kansas and stated that he had never been in the state of Kansas in his life."

When Harden said that, Kerner's mind had flashed back to the elephants, the chickens, the plaster-of-Paris fawns: to the yard ornaments among which Larry Jett had so quickly volunteered the information, unasked, that he had been living in Kansas at the time of the disappearance, with Melvin Harden.

"Harden had no idea why Jett would claim that they were room-mates up in the state of Kansas," Kerner's report continued. "Harden related that Larry Jett was acting strange and nervous after Donna Haraway disappeared and is still very nervous over the Haraway disappearance. Harden strongly believes that Jett knows something about the Haraway disappearance or is in some way involved in it."

Together, Kerner and Wyatt assessed the evolving situation. They reviewed the young men they felt were possible suspects, besides Tommy Ward and Karl Fontenot:

1. *Randy Rogers and Bob Sparcino*. At least four disinterested Ada citizens had said the composite drawings were of these two men. They apparently had left Ada about a year before the disappearance; Kerner had made extensive driver record checks, hoping to find that one of them had been ticketed in the Ada area after that, preferably in an old pickup. He had found no such evidence. That did not mean that they had not come back to Ada; but there was no proof that they had.

2. *Larry Jett*. He apparently had lied to Kerner about being in Kansas at the time of the disappearance. Melvin Harden had said Jett always acted nervous about the disappearance. A red-and-gray-primer pickup with no tailgate, parked in Elmore City, belonged to his sister-in-law, in an area where Elmore City police said young Adans liked to do drugs, to party. And he looked a lot like Tommy Ward.

3. *Marty Ashley and Jay Dicus.* Kerner's gut feeling was that they were not involved; but Ashley did have possession of a truck that Jack Paschall had said was similar to the one he had seen that night. Don Wyatt had obtained a snapshot of Ashley, in which he had a moustache; he drew a moustache on one of the composite drawings; Wyatt and Winifred felt the drawing now looked exactly like Ashley. And Jay Dicus had moved away to Denver.

The lawyer felt that any of these young men might have been involved. But he could not prove it about any of them. All Wyatt and Butner had to do to win acquittals for their clients was to raise reasonable doubt in the minds of the jurors. But in the face of the taped confessions, they knew, their best defense would be to prove that someone else had done it. And to name names.

Don Wyatt sent Richard Kerner back into the field.

It was Rodeo Week in Ada. A bandstand was erected on the grassy civic square beside the courthouse. Every day at noon hundreds of Ada citizens sat on metal folding chairs in the strong August sun or stood in the shade of the pecan trees to watch and listen to entertainment by those who would perform at Ken Lance's Sports Arena in the evening. The highlight was Red River, a country music group composed of eight young men about the ages of Tommy Ward and Karl Fontenot. They were Ada's most popular group. They seemed to have been influenced heavily by the group Alabama. They were very good. As their music thumped with a strong country beat across the square, cheerleaders from Ada High sold hot dogs and soft drinks from wooden booths along the sidewalk; high school boys tried to flirt with them. Off to the side, in the humid shade, stood Tony Pippen, the tall, slim, middle-aged gentleman who was the managing editor of the Ada *News.* Pippen had come to Ada to run the paper about a month before the disappearance of Denice Haraway. He had immersed himself in the civic life of the town, boosting in daily editorials its cultural life, its economic growth, the activities of the chamber of commerce, the local charities. An amiable gentleman in every respect, he avoided by nature the controversial or the divisive. At no time since the disappearance more than fifteen months earlier had anyone from the *News* attempted to interview any of Denice Haraway's family, not wanting to intrude on their privacy, their grief. Nor had anyone interviewed the family or friends of the suspects, perhaps not wanting to intrude on their grief, either; or perhaps not wanting to be controversial, not wanting to offend the police; or perhaps simply because no one had thought of it.

Ada's motels were jammed with rodeo cowboys from all over the west, come in pickups or beat-up jalopies to participate. Empty horse vans dotted the parking lots. While Red River played in courthouse square, the cowboys were ten miles away, in Fittstown, in a small arena surrounded by a low fence, undergoing time trials in calf-roping and other events; only the fastest would compete in the rodeo itself. Not far away, a few oil pumps grazed desultorily. Fittstown was the site of Fitts Field, the largest, most productive oil field in the region after it was discovered in the early 1930s. It had made a number of Adans rich, had built several Kings Road mansions, had pulled the economy of Ada out of the Depression by 1934, while much of the nation struggled in poverty for years after. But the field was mostly played out now. There had been new minibooms during the oil crises of 1973 and 1979, when the price of oil soared; then it had tapered off again. Most of the activity now involved flooding the wells with water to float the remaining oil closer to the surface, so it could be pumped out more cheaply. Oil was still important in Ada, but it no longer supported the town. The dreams of Ada no longer centered on bringing in wildcat wells.

Steve Haraway had given up the apartment that he and Denice had shared. He'd moved to Norman, where he had a lot of friends. He still came to Ada often to visit his folks.

Tommy Ward stopped writing letters and poems about Lisa Lawson. His family still had not told him she was married; they assumed he had heard it through the grapevine, with so many young men he knew going in and out of jail on minor charges. In August, Tricia got two letters from a stranger, Charlene (name changed). Charlene wrote that she had been in the jail several times on forgery charges since Tommy was arrested; they had gotten to know each other, she wrote Tricia; they planned to be married as soon as Tommy got out of this mess. Tricia kept the letters, but did not ask Tommy about them. He would be going on trial for his life in a few weeks; she did not think this was the time to be discussing marriage.

Tricia was becoming concerned once more about Rhonda. School would be starting soon, and the trial was set for soon after. Rhonda's teacher and her principal at Latta Elementary School had been very supportive, talking to Tricia on the phone at night, telling Rhonda all through the previous semester that she was not to blame just because her uncle was in trouble. But, as Miz Ward said, "Kids could be cruel."

Karl Fontenot had taken to drawing pictures in his cell: pictures of Indians, cars, birds. He was passing the time.

On Monday, August 19, a twenty-nine-year-old woman in Oklahoma City, Linda Thompson, attended an aerobics class. Then, with her two young children, one of them four and the other two, she went to a shopping mall. At or near the mall, all three were kidnapped.

Ms. Thompson and her children were taken to a house in the city. The next day a woman dropped the children off, safely, at a babysitter's. Ms. Thompson was not seen again. From the people at the house where they had stayed overnight, police got the names of her alleged kidnappers. A hunt for the woman and her kidnappers was begun, first in the city, then in the state, then, as days passed, nationwide.

The alleged kidnappers, both of whom had criminal records, were identified in front-page stories in the *Daily Oklahoman* as Dale Austin Shelton, twenty-eight, and Don Wilson "Bubba" Hawkins, twenty-six. Both were from Seminole.

The name of the town leaped out at Richard Kerner as he read the news account: Seminole. That was where Patty Hamilton had been kidnapped from a convenience store in 1983, and vanished. Kerner, as well as the Ada police and the OSBI, had long believed the Hamilton and Haraway cases could be related, because the circumstances had been so similar, and the towns only thirty miles apart. Now two tough dudes apparently had kidnapped a young woman in Oklahoma City; and they hailed from Seminole! Kerner began to file the clippings on the case. One of the clippings said Shelton had begun a prison term in April 1983 and was not released until June 1984. That would put him in jail at the time Denice Haraway disappeared—if the report was correct. But Kerner knew there were such things in jails as weekend passes. He would continue to follow the case.

On August 27, the investigator received a phone call from Ted Campbell, a police officer in Elmore City who had helped him during his visits there. Campbell told Kerner the Elmore City police had gotten involved in the search for Linda Thompson, because one of the suspects, Dale Shelton, during an earlier arrest, had given an Elmore City address. Campbell said he and other officers had gone to the address, a home in a rural area. In it, they found iron bars installed in one of the bedroom windows, and an assortment of "kinky" sex objects, such as dildos. The Elmore City police believed the two fleeing suspects might have used that home in the past few days.

Kerner thanked Officer Campbell for the information. As he hung up the phone on his desk, and gazed through the one-way glass wall, the name Elmore City was ringing in his head like a gong. He'd found a pickup that resembled the one in the Haraway case parked near a trailer in Elmore City. The police had told him drink-and-drug parties were held in Elmore City with some of Ada's running crowd attending. Now the two kidnap suspects in the Thompson case, who were from Seminole, had been linked to what looked like a sex-torture chamber—in Elmore City.

The investigator called Dexter Davis in Seminole. The assistant chief said he, too, was very interested in the Oklahoma City kidnapping by the men from Seminole. Kerner summarized for Don Wyatt what Davis told him: "Davis explained that there is a connection between Dale Austin Shelton, one of the two Seminole men, and the missing Seminole convenience store girl. This connection is that Shelton lived with his parents approximately one mile from the foster father of the missing convenience store girl in Seminole. On one occasion prior to the Seminole girl's disappearance, her foster father discovered someone had raped his mare in a barn on his property and after doing this inserted a piece of pipe crossways in the mare's vagina. Davis explained that Shelton's wallet was found there in the barn; but no charges were ever preferred against him in this incident."

Reading Kerner's report, Don Wyatt ran through the growing list in his mind:

Rogers and Sparcino.

Larry Jett.

Marty Ashley and Jay Dicus.

Now Shelton and Hawkins.

He was up to his ears in possible suspects, up to his ears in scenarios about what might have happened to Denice Haraway. But he couldn't prove any of it, couldn't prove any of these men had been involved. The trial was less than two weeks away, and the prosecutors still held the trump cards: Ward and Fontenot, on those gruesome, lie-filled tapes, saying they had done it.

Richard Kerner swung his car off Arlington Boulevard into a service station. He did not pull up to the pumps; he did not need gas. He parked not far from the office. He wanted to talk to Jim Moyer.

Routinely, Kerner wanted to interview all those who had placed Tommy Ward at or near McAnally's. He had spoken to Jack Paschall several times; Paschall had stuck to his identification of Ward, had not identified Fontenot. Karen Wise, whose testimony had been the same, continued to avoid him. Now he would see what Moyer had to say. Perhaps there would be some useful detail that the D.A. had not brought out at the preliminary hearing.

Moyer had testified that on the night of the disappearance he had stopped at McAnally's about 7:30 to buy a pack of cigarettes; two men had been inside along with the clerk, he had said, and they had been acting suspicious. He'd testified that at police lineups, he had picked out Tommy Ward and Karl Fontenot as the men.

Now, at the gas station, Moyer told Richard Kerner—who indicated that he was investigating the case—that he was upset. He had been calling Bill Peterson all summer, he said, but the secretaries at the D.A.'s office would not put the call through unless he told them what it was about. And he did not want to tell the secretaries, he said; he wanted to tell Peterson personally.

"What is it you want to tell Peterson?" Kerner asked.

"I want to take back my identification of Karl Fontenot."

"Why is that?"

Moyer told Kerner about the man in the back of the courtroom during the hearings: the man he thought looked much more familiar than Fontenot. He told how he had asked Karen Wise about him, and how Karen had said the same thing, and how she had seemed afraid of the man.

All this was news to the defense. Kerner, excited, cursed himself. He had expected a routine interview; he had not been prepared for this. He wished desperately he had gotten this conversation on tape—but his recorder was in his briefcase, in his car.

They continued talking. Traffic was heavy, noisy on Arlington in mid-afternoon. He asked Moyer more about the man in the back of the courtroom.

He had letters carved on his belt, Moyer said. A word. A name.

A name?

L-u-r-c-h (name changed).

Cars stopped for gas. Moyer had to fill the tanks. Kerner told him that he would wait in his car, that perhaps they could talk more there; it would be quieter. Cooler.

Moyer said okay.

Kerner went to his car. He opened his briefcase, took out his microcassette recorder, switched it on, placed it on the backseat. Over it he draped a towel. It was a good recorder; it would pick up well from there.

The investigator waited behind the wheel. When the customers left, Jim Moyer got in on the passenger side. Kerner switched on the air conditioner. The following conversation ensued:

RK: Hi, Jim. We will get a little cool air here agoing.

JM: Who are you with?

RK: I am a legal investigator working on the behalf of Tommy Ward, who is in jail for this crime, and for his attorney Don Wyatt. What is your full name? James—ah . . .

JM: Middle initial C.

RK: James C. Moyer Jr. Okay, on April 28, 1984, in that convenience store, these two guys walk in. Do you identify these guys later in a lineup or anything?

JM: Yeah.

RK: You identified one as Ward and the other as Fontenot, or did you identify the other one?

JM: I identified the other one, but didn't know the name at that time.

RK: Okay, since that time you have seen the tall guy elsewhere?

JM: Right, at the preliminary hearing. That's where I saw him.

RK: Okay, so you're—

JM: You see, that's nearly a year later.

RK: And the tall guy that's in the convenience store then is not the one that's in jail at the present time? Not Fontenot?

JM: Not when I saw him. I've been trying to get ahold of Peterson to let him know, but he's hard to get ahold of. I wanted to let him know.

RK: Okay.

JM: But, ah, I didn't see this other guy that much, but I remember when I was standing up at the counter he was walking the back aisles and I got kind of paranoid because I felt like I was being watched and I turned around and I remember he looked up at me . . .

RK: This tall guy you saw at the preliminary hearing had R-C-H on his belt? On a leather belt?

JM: I thought it said like L-U-R-C-H.

RK: Oh, Lurch. Okay.

JM: He knows Tommy. When they took Tommy down to go to the bathroom, he said something to him.

RK: Was he Indian-looking or what?

JM: Kind of, but not like full Indian.

RK: Not like full Indian?

JM: Maybe only a quarter or so.

RK: So, at least at the upcoming trial you are going to be saying then that the tall guy which is Karl Fontenot is not the one you saw in the store that night that the girl disappeared?

JM: Right.

RK: You saw this guy with Lurch on his belt at the preliminary and he spoke to Tommy and he was the tall guy?

JM: Yeah, he kept staring at Karen, and I noticed she was nervous, and without saying who or anything, I just asked her while we were waiting downstairs, I said, "Is there someone here who looks kind of more familiar?" And she said, "Yes," and said the same guy. And I didn't tell her who. But whenever he came in view, she kind of slid around the corner so he wouldn't be staring at her. I don't think he recognized me because I changed my hair quite a bit from straight to getting it permed and maybe no moustache and that night I had curly hair and a moustache.

RK: (*Laugh.*)

JM: It probably would be hard for someone to recognize me.

RK: Oh boy, looks like you are going to get busy here . . . (*Moyer opens the car door.*)

RK: But you're still sure on Tommy Ward as being with this guy in the store that night?

JM: Yeah, he walked up real close right in front of me.

RK: You didn't know Tommy before or anything?

JM: No. When I worked over here, there used to be some kid come in on a little bitty motorcycle. This kid was probably sixteen or eighteen years old, and he set up this tile thing. Well, that night I thought that's who it was walking in and I started to say hi to him. This guy that walked in, he had his head kind of down and looking real low, and I didn't say hi to him, but that's who he reminded me of at first—this other kid. That helped me remember him. He reminded me of someone else.

RK: Lurch on the belt may mean nothing, but he's what—six feet or what?

JM: Probably, with his boots on.

RK: He was taller than Fontenot?

JM: Taller than me.

RK: Slim build?

JM: Yeah, tall and slim.

RK: Did he have long hair?

JM: Yeah, about like . . . (*He gestures.*)

RK: Shoulder-length hair—shoulder-plus hair?

JM: That Wyatt guy got me all messed up that shoulder-length hair. When I talk about shoulder-length hair, I mean from the side.

RK: Well, this kind of changes things, because now one of the witnesses says Fontenot was not with Tommy Ward.

JM: Well, for all I know he could have been passed out in the truck. I didn't look in the pickup as I passed by. I was going to get a tag number.

RK: What color do you remember on your memory bands of that pickup's main color?

JM: Ah, a dark color like gray, or no, it could have been green with those crazy lights there. I think they had some yellow lights out front.

RK: Could it of been off-white or a dull off-white looks gray?

JM: No, it would have reflected that light out front.

RK: And this is all you know. You see them and you leave, but they made you suspicious, especially the tall guy messing around in the back?

JM: Well, he was watching me—if somebody came into a store and was looking for something—then, ah, they wouldn't just hit all the outside aisles, they would go up and down the aisles and that's what brought my attention to him.

RK: What age bracket do you think he might be in?

JM: Ah, twenty-two to twenty-four.

RK: Did they get in whether Ward had a long-sleeve or short-sleeve shirt on?

JM: Yeah, thinking back on it I think it was a white T-shirt.

RK: You don't remember the fact that he had tattoos on his arm. No one seems to remember Ward's tattoos?

JM: I don't remember any.

RK: You have no doubt on Tommy Ward being one of these two guys?

JM: No.

RK: And you are reasonably sure the guy at the preliminary with Lurch on his belt is the second man and he knows Tommy and spoke to him at the preliminary?

JM: Right.

RK: Did you hear what he said or anything?

JM: Ah, it probably had something to do with how the case was going. Was it rough or something like that?

RK: Okay, he had cowboy boots on—that's a clue.

JM: Some kind of boots. I don't know if they were cowboy.

RK: And just jeans and shirt, I suppose.

JM: For the preliminary he was wearing a long-sleeved shirt like with snaps on the sleeves, cowboy, western-style. I don't think his boots had pointed toes. I gotta go service some cars.

RK: Okay, thanks a lot, Jim.

JM: You got it?

RK: I think so, yeah.

JM: I might be helping the wrong people.

RK: Yeah, you wouldn't want to give me a recorded statement on this?

JM: Oh, I would rather not.

RK: You would rather not. Okay, but you are going to say the same things that you told me at the trial, right?

JM: Yeah, that's why I've been trying to get ahold of Bill Peterson. To let him know that I've changed my mind on this one guy.

RK: Peterson don't know it yet, huh?

JM: He's so busy, every time I call up they want to know who is calling and what is it about. "I'm not going to get him unless you tell me what it is."

RK: He's not going to be too happy that one of his witnesses backed out on one of the two guys in jail. But you have to tell the truth. Hell, whoever it helps or hurts, you can't—

JM: Well, I don't want the wrong person to get convicted.

RK: That's right.

JM: Whoever is responsible should have to pay, but I don't want to get the wrong person. That's what I want to do, just get everything all straight.

RK: As I recall, even on the times, yours was somewhere around seven-thirty—it could have been plus or minus?

JM: Well, whoever did it might have chickened out then and came back a second time.

RK: Came back?

JM: That's probably why they were shooting pool in the meantime at J.P.'s.

RK: Sure. You might have scared them off the first time. Okay, Jim,
     I appreciate it.
JM: Okay.

Moyer got out to help a customer. Kerner drove off east on Arlington through the waves of heat. He cut up the short, sharp ramp that
led to the parking lot behind Wyatt, Austin & Associates. He reached
into the backseat, under the towel, and checked the recorder. He had
gotten it all on tape.

The investigator went inside, told Don Wyatt what he had; Wyatt
smiled, shook his head, spit tobacco juice.

Now they had a fifth scenario to ponder: this Lurch, whoever he
was, and someone who looked like Tommy Ward.

The mansions fronting Kings Road were familiar to Winifred Harrell
as she drove her van to work each morning and home each evening.
There was the Delaney mansion, built in the 1930s by Gus Delaney
with oil money from the Fitts field; later sold by his widow, who now
was living out her years in a smaller house next door. There was the
house with an Olympic-sized swimming pool indoors, fed by an un-
derground spring. There was the house of the woman Winifred believed was the richest person in town: built not by oil money, but by
the profits from bingo parlors the woman ran in other parts of the
state. Most of the pioneer oil speculators and their spouses were dead;
many of the Kings Road mansions were owned now by the doctors
who had treated them in their last years.

As she drove the familiar route, the five volumes of the Ward-
Fontenot preliminary hearings on the seat beside her, Winifred was
tired. For the past two weeks she had been working almost around the
clock, taking the black-bound volumes home in the evenings, and on
Saturdays and Sundays as well. She was going through the testimony
of every witness, summarizing on paper for Don Wyatt the crux of
what each one had said, noting the pages on which he could find their
testimony. He would need this for his cross-examinations during the
trial.

Winifred had read, too, Richard Kerner's reports on his investigations to date; they had altered her opinion of the case. In the beginning she had been as convinced as all of her Kings Road neighbors that Ward and Fontenot were guilty, and would be convicted. For eight months, despite working professionally in Ward's defense, she had retained that personal opinion. Now, in the past two weeks, for the first time, she wasn't sure. These other possible suspects . . . these other trucks . . . these other scenarios. Now Winifred Harrell did not know what to believe.

Don Wyatt was not liked by most of the lawyers in Ada: perhaps because of his personality, which could be abrasive; perhaps because they were jealous of his earnings, his offices; most likely a combination of both. He was close to, and proud of, his wife, Jean, a psychiatric social worker. Beyond that his good friends were few. The closest was his office business manager, Bill Willett, a hearty, bluff, energetic man whose explosive laughter, upon his hearing a joke over the telephone, boomed through the entire building, which seemed to revolve around his central, unwalled desk. It was with Bill Willett that the lawyer often went hunting birds or shooting skeet, his favorite outdoor recreations. Beyond that, Wyatt was an indoor man, and a private man. He had a talent for painting when he found the time: a skillfully rendered scene of pheasants in flight hung behind the front desk of his receptionist, Judy Wood, and was the first thing visitors saw upon entering the building. He liked to read; needing only four or five hours of sleep each night, he stayed up in the dark hours devouring novels. His tastes were catholic: a small shelf above his desk, holding a handful of books, was divided between Stephen King and Philip Roth; he was one of the very few people in Ada to cherish a copy of *Portnoy's Complaint*. His own secret dream was to write a novel and get it published. He had written most of one once: five hundred pages, single-spaced. With uncharacteristic carelessness he had not made a duplicate. He had kept the manuscript in his office on Main Street, because he thought it would be safer there than in his home. Then the office building had burned down. Along with the countless legal files that had to be reconstructed, he lost his novel. In his mind now was an idea for another one, if he ever found the time: a novel about the corruption of justice in a small town.

Wyatt was proud: proud of his large civil practice, the fifth or sixth biggest in the state; and proud of some dramatic victories in criminal cases. In one of his first cases, in 1977, he defended a woman who was accused of murdering her lover; she had run him over several times with her car; the prosecution was seeking the death penalty. Wyatt demonstrated that his client was a "battered wife"; she was found guilty of manslaughter in the second degree, and got a two-year sentence. He handled a triple-homicide case involving an auto accident, and got the defendants off on a misdemeanor. He defended a woman who was accused of shooting her husband five times; the man was wheeled into the courtroom in a wheelchair, a quadriplegic as a result of the shooting. Wyatt demonstrated that the man was a drug user, and a wife-beater; he won an acquittal. The wife had said the husband was coming after her with a gun when she shot him; the husband said he was in bed, preparing to sleep. But he'd had his pants on, his keys in his pocket, when he was shot; the jury believed the wife.

These and other cases, he believed, had created a kind of aura in the town, the aura that "Wyatt wins." He was hoping it might intimidate the district attorney's office, even in the Ward case.

Some people viewed Wyatt as a bully; some of those close to him thought his forceful manner was a cover for insecurity. Whatever his inner feelings, he clearly could adopt a bullying stance when it suited his purposes. Such was the mood Tricia found him in when she went to his office on Tuesday, September 3. He had called and said he wanted to see her and members of the family. Tricia rounded up her mother and Kay and went down there, and found the lawyer angry with them. He was angry about money.

They had given him $5,000 to date, Wyatt told them (most of it from Joel); much of this had gone to the private investigator; some for the transcript; some to a psychiatrist who examined Tommy in the jail. There was only $500 for his own fee. He wanted something settled about the house; he was not going into the courtroom next Monday to defend Tommy unless they settled first about the house.

This was pure bluff and bluster. Once Wyatt took the case, his fee was his own problem; the court would not have let him withdraw because he wasn't being paid. He had told that to Tricia at the beginning; she remembered it now. But she didn't want him angry like that.

Miz Ward said she'd had an offer of $15,000 for the house and the property on which it stood; Wyatt said that would not be settled by Monday. He wanted her to sign over the deed to him, now, though the original agreement gave them until October 25 before he was entitled to the house. Miz Ward smiled blandly, not seeming to understand. Tricia told her to go ahead and sign the deed, pointing out that Miz Ward did not want the house anyway, that she preferred living in Tulsa now.

Miz Ward agreed. She signed over to the lawyer the house she'd moved into in 1938, the day Jesse planted the pecan tree. When that was done, Wyatt's attitude changed. Suddenly he was their friend again. He told them about Richard Kerner's findings. They were encouraged; they felt that after all these months, Wyatt was finally working full speed on the case.

He told them about the trial procedure. He said they should dress well. He said those who were not witnesses should be in the courtroom as much as possible, showing support for Tommy. Miz Ward should hug him whenever possible, he said. Miz Ward said she had done that anyway, at the preliminary hearing, and an officer told her he was about to shoot her when she first moved toward Tommy. After that she had always asked permission. Wyatt told her, "Don't ask permission. Just ignore them and go hug him. That carries weight with the jury. So does support by the family in the courtroom."

He told them he wanted as many family members as possible present during the jury selection, so they could tell him, or write notes to him, about any prospective jurors who'd had fights with the family, who might have grudges against family members; so he could reject them as jurors; and, in the same way, to point out to him any people they knew had good feelings about the family, so he could try to keep them on.

He also mentioned a woman who had called his office to say she had information that would "definitely" exonerate Tommy. She was coming to see him on Wednesday.

Buoyed by this, and by the investigator's findings, Tricia, Kay, and Miz Ward left the attorney's office feeling optimistic. His anger at not being paid was forgiven; he was working hard for Tommy.

When they got home, Tricia fixed on an idea that wouldn't go away. The woman who had called, who had said she could definitely exonerate Tommy: who better could prove he was innocent than Denice Haraway! Perhaps it was Denice Haraway herself who had called! Or if not her, then someone who knew her, someone who had seen her alive!

That night, obsessed with the possibility, the hope, Tricia could hardly sleep. Her mind was going ninety-to-nothin'.

On Wednesday afternoon, she called Wyatt, to find out. He told her that yes, the woman had shown up. But if she had any real information, he said, she had become frightened and had not told him. What she did have to say, the lawyer told Tricia, "didn't amount to a hill of beans."

The Indians of Oklahoma once lived in harmony with the wealth of the land, as did Indians across America. Now, most of them lived close to the poverty level, victims of culture shock, poor education, racial prejudice—as were Indians across America.

Days before the trial was to begin, a poor Indian woman was stabbed to death amid a cluster of mobile homes at the southern edge of Ada. The police detained her husband briefly, then released him. Apparently there were no witnesses, or none that would talk to the police. The killing was the subject of a brief item in the Ada *News* the next day; then it disappeared from public view, quickly forgotten.

Maxine and C. L. Wolf wondered aloud why this Indian woman's life seemed to mean nothing to the authorities, while they were still pursuing the Haraway case after a year and a half, in the absence of a body.

They wondered aloud, but they felt they knew the answer: the dark-skinned and the poor did not count for much, in Ada or anywhere else.

Don Wyatt told Miz Ward he wanted Tommy to have a clean, pressed suit to wear, every day of the trial. She was relieved to discover that Bud's suits fit Tommy; he could wear those. Then she was called by a deputy at the jail, and was told to bring over a suit for Karl; he could not be tried in his prison garb; that would be prejudicial.

Miz Ward did not know why it was her responsibility to supply

Karl; she knew him, but not well; she had not even been to visit him. But by her quiet, retiring nature, and her general bewilderment at the way the world worked, she was not one to question authority. She went to the Salvation Army store a few blocks from Tricia's house and picked out a rust-colored, three-piece suit, in good condition, marked "$15." She was able to buy it for ten dollars—more than she could afford—along with a shirt. The Saturday before the trial she brought them to the jail.

Only later did she learn that the deputy thought Miz Ward was in possession of Karl's clothing.

Don Wyatt held a Sunday meeting at his office with George Butner, Fontenot's attorney. Butner had been unable to obtain money from the state to hire a private investigator; Wyatt filled him in on Richard Kerner's latest scenarios. In mounting the defense, they agreed, Butner would have to follow Wyatt's lead. Wyatt had told Tricia and Miz Ward he thought they had a fifty-fifty chance of getting the boys off. Butner was not that optimistic. He did not see how they would get around the tapes.

At the jail, waiting, Karl Fontenot used an evocative phrase to a visiting journalist. He said he felt "lost in the case."

Bill Peterson went to church with his family, then went home, his mind, too, going ninety-to-nothin', as not he but Tricia would have said. The sun was blazing outside, the temperature on September 8 still in the nineties. Dennis Smith and Gary Rogers and Mike Baskin and Chris Ross waited. Steve Haraway, in from Norman for the duration of the trial, was at the home of his parents, east of Ada. He, and they, waited. Judge Donald Powers, at his home in Chandler, packed a suitcase; he would drive the eighty miles to Ada in the morning, would stay at the Raintree Motel on Mississippi, a Best Western motel.

In the evening, many of the people of Ada went to church, as was the Baptist practice. Some drove to Wintersmith Park, and walked around the lake in the humid air, watching the ducks and geese glide on the surface. Students from East Central played touch football. On Main Street, Sunday traffic was light, as usual. One of the films showing at the McSwain Twin was a James Bond picture: *A View to a Kill*.

Atop the highest turret of the feed mill a red light flashed, flashed, as it did every night.

Bud and Tricia had fifteen people staying in their cluttered three-bedroom house: themselves and the three children; Miz Ward; Melvin; Joice and her four kids, down from Tulsa; Kay and Billy and their infant son, also down from Tulsa. Joel and Robert would be arriving Sunday night. Mattresses were strewn on the floor everywhere; and babies; and children. But unexpectedly amid the chaos, there was an evening of quiet. Joice's husband, Robert, when he arrived from Tulsa, took one look around the jammed house and took Joice and their four kids to the Indian Hills Motel, on Broadway, to give Tricia some peace. For a few hours, Bud, Tricia, their own three children, and Miz Ward were alone there. The calm seemed almost unnatural amid the clutter.

Tricia shooed the kids to their room, went in to put them to sleep. Bud and Miz Ward sat in the living room. Most times the TV set would have been on; the TV was always on, whether anyone was watching it or not. But now the tube was dark, silent, its innards burned out by the lightning. In retrospect, even that lightning storm seemed to have a meaning: the broken set would spare them from seeing the nightly reports of the trial on the news.

Tricia looked down at the scrubbed faces of the kids. She was feeling better about Rhonda. She had talked to Rhonda's teacher about the coming ordeal; the teacher had warned the sixth-grade class: no one was to say a word to Rhonda about her uncle, about the trial; if they did, they would be punished severely. Thus far, all the kids had been obeying.

In the living room, beneath the large painting of Jesus, Bud and Miz Ward talked quietly about the case. Bud said a large part of him still believed Denice Haraway was alive; that she had run off, taken a new identity, was living somewhere far away, in Pennsylvania, or West Virginia, or California. Not that she would willfully let someone be tried for her murder, he said. But that she was unaware of what was going on in Ada. He raised what he said was a "weird" question: what would happen if Tommy was convicted, and then, just as the gavel rang out, Denice Haraway walked into the courtroom? He wondered what the legal situation would be then.

Miz Ward agreed with Bud. She said she, too, still felt Denice Haraway was alive; that she had run away with someone, for some reason.

The kids were safely asleep. Tricia returned to the living room. She sat down heavily, tiredly, easing the weight of her large belly. She was due November 5; she was hoping the emotions of the trial would not be too much of a strain on the infant inside her.

Only a few days earlier, when the woman with "information" had called Don Wyatt, Tricia had hoped it was Denice Haraway. But now she said no, that after all she had heard about the Haraway girl, she didn't think she would run away like that; the greater part of her now felt Denice Haraway was dead.

12

TRIAL BY JURY

At 6:07 in the still-dark morning of September 9, the first train whistle of the day wailed across Ada—at first, from a distance, mournfully; and then, as the train drew closer, maniacally. It was heard by many of those involved in the Haraway case as they lay in their beds, awakened early by adrenaline rush.

Detective Captain Dennis Smith was out and about soon after, with his wife, tossing the day's copies of the *Daily Oklahoman* onto the lawns of subscribers. Many of those involved in the trial due to begin that morning were startled as they unfolded the paper and read the front-page headline sprawled across four columns:

CUSTOMERS FIND

BODY OF CLERK

Their astonishment was only momentary, however. The headline had nothing to do with the Haraway case. It referred to the robbery-murder of a male convenience store clerk in Oklahoma City the night before.

At 8 A.M., District Attorney Bill Peterson was already in his office, alone, behind a locked door. Even at that early hour the air was warm and moist; the heat wave was continuing, and the courthouse air conditioning had not yet taken effect. The district attorney removed the jacket of his suit. He sat in the large swivel chair behind his desk, leaned back, gazed abstractedly at the walls, on his face a look of contemplation. His hand idly toyed with the wide end of the striped tie that rested on his belly.

Across the street from the courthouse was the office of the local gas company; beside it, a large dirt parking lot. Slowly the lot began to fill with cars, station wagons, pickups, as the people who had been called for jury duty this day arrived from their homes in Ada, or from the smaller towns of Pontotoc County: Roff, Stonewall, Tupelo, Francis, Byng . . . They walked across Thirteenth Street, alone or in clusters, entered the courthouse through the double glass doors, passed the D.A.'s office on the left, the sheriff's office on the right; passed vending machines displaying wrapped candy bars, bags of chips, passed soft drink machines, to the stairs; found their way by prior knowledge, or by asking, or by following the stream of people, to the third floor. There, outside the larger courtroom, a rectangular table had been set up; behind it sat court clerks. A single line formed at the table, crossed the third-floor hall, wound down the stairs as the prospective jurors gave their names to the clerks, who had to find them on a list that was seven legal sheets long. Signatures were then scrawled beside typed names, typed numbers. As each prospective juror signed in, he or she was given a temporary badge, and shown the way into the courtroom, through a small outer office to the left of the central doors. The main doors were locked, would be kept locked throughout the trial, for tighter security. The prospective jurors were not searched, but several sheriff's deputies stood in the corridor, others near the entrance, watching.

Slowly the entire spectator section in the courtroom was filled with prospective jurors, including the front row, normally reserved for the press, when there was any press. Additional chairs were carried in by bailiffs and placed along the side walls. When all were seated, there were eighty-three prospective jurors, from whom twelve, and two alternates, would be chosen.

The district attorney placed a box of books on the prosecution table. The defense team—Don Wyatt, Leo Austin, George Butner—huddled in a rear office they would use during the trial. Judge Ronald Jones, the presiding judge of the county—the one who had withdrawn from the case—entered the courtroom, and spoke to the assembled citizens about doing their public duty. Originally there had been a panel of 225 people who had been called for jury duty this day, he told them. More than 70 had been excused because they were physically unable to serve; some had been excused because they were convicted felons, others for other reasons. Now it was down to the people in front of him. He told them that those chosen as jurors would receive $12.50 a day. The jury would not be sequestered, he said—at least not at the start of the trial. He stated their goal in a single sentence: "We are seeking the truth as it is found to be established by competent evidence."

Then he left the courtroom.

On the lawn between the courthouse and the jail, two stories below, there were, somewhat unexpectedly, no spectators gathered, no gawkers, and no lines of deputies to keep them away. The door to the jail opened from the inside. Tommy Ward and Karl Fontenot were escorted out into the morning air. Ward was wearing a dark blue suit, a light blue dress shirt, a tie, all courtesy of his brother-in-law, Bud; Fontenot was wearing the rust-colored corduroy suit and the pale striped shirt that Miz Ward had bought at the Salvation Army; and a tie. Both were wearing handcuffs. Four uniformed sheriff's deputies walked with them the forty-three steps from jail to courthouse, a deputy on each side of each suspect, holding lightly to their upper arms. The sun shone brightly. The pecan tree beneath which they passed was in leafy bloom.

In the first-floor corridor the small retinue waited for the elevator. On the third floor, in the small outer office, out of sight of the prospective jurors, the handcuffs were removed. A moment later, at 9:52 A.M., Tommy Ward and Karl Fontenot walked into the crowded courtroom, to go on trial for their lives.

They sat at the defense table, facing the front, their backs to the prospective jurors. Don Wyatt, Leo Austin, George Butner joined them at the table. At the prosecution table to the right sat Bill Peterson, Chris Ross, Gary Rogers. From a rear entryway that led to the judge's chambers, the court reporter, a well-groomed young woman named Dawn DeVoe, entered, took her place at her machine at the far side of the bench. A moment later all in the courtroom stood at the bailiff's command as Judge Donald Powers entered and climbed to the bench, looking courtly in his black robe, with his wavy white hair, his rimless eyeglasses that were round at the bottom, flat on top.

"You may be seated," the judge said.

All sat.

The trial in the Haraway case was under way, thirty-nine days short of a year after the suspects were arrested, sixteen months and twelve days after Donna Denice Haraway disappeared without a trace.

DAY ONE

In brief opening remarks, the judge explained to the panel the procedure to be used in selecting the jury: each side would be allowed nine peremptory challenges, with which they could dismiss jurors without stating a reason; the number of dismissals for cause would be unlimited.

The court clerk, seated to the judge's left, reached into a box, pulling out tags. One by one she read out a number, a name. One by one the people whose names were called edged their way out from among the crowded benches, walked through the low swinging half door held open by the bailiff, took their places in the jury box, across the courtroom from the judge, to the left of the defendants. A few of those called winced as they heard their names, their faces clearly showing that they did not want to serve. Some strode forward purposefully, with an aura of grim satisfaction. Most tried to remain expressionless. As the jury box filled, the attorneys on both sides watched intently. It was an axiom of trial law: often the case is decided by who winds up in the jury box.

When all twelve of the brown swivel chairs were filled, Judge Powers told them of the case: the State of Oklahoma versus Thomas Jesse Ward and Karl Allen Fontenot; the defendants accused of robbing, kidnapping, and murdering Donna Denice Haraway. He then asked if any of them had read of or heard of the case.

All twelve raised their hands.

The judge told them to think about whether, based on what they had read or heard, they had formed an opinion. He said they had formed an opinion if, in their minds, they knew, "I'm not starting out even right now."

There was laughter in much of the courtroom.

The judge said he would read a list of names: of the principals in the case, the attorneys, and all the witnesses that would be called by the state. They were to think about whether they knew any of these people, had had any dealings with any of them. He would not name the defense witnesses, he said, because the defense, under the law, did not have to make that public. He read the list. Then, one by one, beginning with the first seat in the jury box, he questioned the panel about whether they knew any of the names he had read, about whether they had formed an opinion in the case that they could not set aside.

Panelist one was excused, for having an opinion; so were panelists two and three; panelist four was excused because a nephew was married to Melva Ward.

Number five said that although he had heard of the case, he knew nothing about it. "I don't take the local paper or watch the local station," he said. "I have a satellite."

There was laughter again. He was allowed to remain, for now.

Panelist six had an opinion. Number seven knew Betty Haraway, Steve Haraway's mother. Number eight knew some of the witnesses.

On and on it went, through the morning. There was a recess for lunch. Then it continued through the long afternoon. As each panelist was dismissed for cause, the clerk reached into her box, pulled out another number, another name. Another member of the panel moved from the thinning crowd in the spectator section into the jury box: often to leave soon after, excused for cause, for having an opinion. But as the day wore on, more and more said they did not have an opinion; or that if they did, they could set it aside, and weigh only the evidence in the case as it would be presented in the courtroom.

One woman said that Tricia Wolf, Tommy Ward's sister, shopped in the store where she worked. Don Wyatt stood and said the woman would be called as a witness; she was excused. Another said she thought she had gone to grade school with Tommy Ward, but she had no opinion; she was allowed to remain, for the time being.

A man named Keith Hildreth said he was the personnel manager at the Evergreen feed mill, and that he knew Tommy Ward's brother-in-law Bud Wolf. The judge asked whether, because of this acquaintance, if Bud Wolf were called as a witness, the juror would give more or less credence to what Bud Wolf said than to the word of other witnesses.

"I would give his word more credence," Hildreth said.

He was excused for cause. The judge explained to the others that if he asked that question of them, he wanted to know if they would give more or less credence to a witness—but they should not say if it was more or less.

Laughter punctuated the growing weariness.

More were called; more were dismissed. Evening was approaching. The judge recessed the case till 9 A.M. He warned the panelists, on their honor, not to read or watch news reports of the proceedings; not to discuss the case with anyone, not even their spouses.

The remaining panelists filed out, quietly.

That night, many of the participants relaxed in front of their television sets. It was the start of *Monday Night Football,* and the Dallas Cowboys were playing; Ada, only 180 miles from Dallas, was Cowboy country. A few attended a benefit concert for Valley View Hospital given by country singer Hoyt Axton, whose brother, John, lived in Ada; the singer was a frequent visitor.

In the morning they were back.

DAY TWO

The questioning of the panel resumed.

Tommy Ward was wearing Bud's three-piece beige suit. Karl Fontenot was wearing the dark blue suit that Tommy had worn the day before.

A panelist said Dennis Smith was investigating a crime in which her husband had been victimized; she was excused. Another had pending business with the D.A.'s office; she was excused. A third was close to Odell Titsworth's family; she was excused.

There were seats available now in the spectator section; the press, allowed to stand the day before, reclaimed the front row. There were seven news reporters present: Dorothy Hogue of the Ada *News*, others from the local TV and radio stations, from the *Daily Oklahoman* and the Tulsa *World*; by happenstance, all seven were female.

Miz Ward, Melvin, Joel, Kay, Joice sat behind them. During a recess, Joel told Don Wyatt that one woman on the panel, Mary Floyd, stern-looking, gray-haired, used to be a teacher at Latta Elementary School, and that she had disliked Tommy when he was little. Wyatt pondered the information; he was hoping to keep Mary Floyd on the jury. Her daughter was going to be a witness for the defense. He told the family this; they left it up to him.

After the recess the defense attorneys used a number of their peremptory challenges; Wyatt let Mary Floyd remain.

He had, in his mind, no profile of the jurors he wanted; he went by his gut reactions. His belief about the jury was, "When it's right, you'll know it."

At the prosecution table, Bill Peterson would be satisfied with "upstanding citizens, with a stake in society."

The questioning continued. Every panelist was asked, by the judge or by Peterson, whether, if there should be a conviction in the case, they would have any problem imposing the death penalty, which the jury would have to decide. Of more than sixty-five panelists questioned, only one, a slight, gray-haired woman, said she would have a problem.

"No matter how strong the case?" the judge asked.

"I don't believe in taking lives," the woman said.

She was excused for cause.

Later, Judge Powers would marvel that out of all those questioned, only one was opposed to the death penalty. Twenty years ago, he mused, there would have been twenty times that many, even in Ada.

The Feed Store Restaurant was on Broadway, half a block from the courthouse. It had a large menu. The specialty was baked potatoes with an assortment of toppings. Wooden booths lined both walls; several rows of tables filled the center. A number of the people still on the panel went to lunch there. One of them was a tall, slim, attractive young woman named Shelley Johnson. She was married, had two children, ages five and two and a half; her mother-in-law was taking care of them.

Mrs. Johnson, like many of the others, had been upset when she got her jury notice; she was nervous about being questioned. Now she felt both sides had gone easy on her. Coming to the courthouse the day before, she had not wanted to be selected; now she was hoping to remain; they had gotten her interested.

She had not expected to stay on the panel even this long, because she was so close in age, even in appearance, to Denice Haraway.

"When I got home last night, my husband had the kids fed and dinner ready," Mrs. Johnson said. "All I had to do was fix breakfast this morning. I could get into that."

The court session resumed. With seats now available, Tricia was present for the first time. She had just returned from a doctor's appointment, and was happy; she had not gained any weight since her last visit.

The questioning of panelists continued. Bill Peterson waived the state's sixth peremptory challenge: the state was prepared to accept the panel now in the jury box, he said.

The defense continued to remove people. Wyatt, Austin, Butner huddled together, going over the names, agreeing on whom to eliminate with their sixth, seventh, eighth challenges.

The state continued to pass.

The defense had one challenge left. The attorneys felt it was as good a jury as they were likely to get, without being able to read their minds. But they had to use up their last challenge, in order to protect their court record. Should they lose the case, and want to appeal on the grounds that a change of venue should have been granted, that an unbiased jury could not be found in Ada, then they had to use up all their challenges.

The attorneys looked from one face to the other in the jury box; they conferred; they looked again; finally they shrugged, agreeing.

They dismissed panelist number five: Shelley Johnson.

The young woman flushed deeply; stood; left the jury box.

"She was making eye contact with the district attorney, but not with anyone at our table," Don Wyatt said later. "We had to choose someone. Who knows?"

Shelley Johnson, disappointed, went home to fix dinner. In her place a short, dark woman named Janet Williams was called. She answered to the satisfaction of both sides the routine questions: she had formed no opinion in the case; she knew none of the witnesses; none of her family was in jail.

There was no reason to excuse her for cause. At 4:12 P.M., Judge Powers asked those remaining in the jury box to raise their right hands, and he swore in the jury in the Haraway case, a day earlier than either side had expected.

In the spectator section, about fifteen panelists remained uncalled of the eighty-three that had appeared the day before. Two alternates were called, to sit with the jury, to vote only if a regular juror became incapacitated. The defense was permitted one peremptory challenge for each alternate seat; the attorneys liked both people who were called, but had to dismiss them both, to protect their record. Two more were called, seated, sworn in.

The jury was complete. It was composed of eight women and four men. Both alternates were men. The panel included school teachers, housewives, retired people, a worker at the cement plant.

The judge admonished them, as he would every night, not to discuss the case, not to read of it in the papers or watch the TV news. Then he sent them home. The presentation of evidence would begin in the morning.

As they left, several of the younger women smiled at one another, as if they had made new friends; as if they had passed some inspection, some test.

The library at Wyatt, Austin & Associates was lined with sets of lawbooks bound in deep blue, green, beige, and maroon. Filling most of the room was a conference table surrounded by leather chairs. That night, the members of Tommy Ward's family were called into the library, one at a time, to prepare the testimony they would give.

Seated around the table were Wyatt, Austin, Winifred Harrell, Austin's attractive young wife, Shawna, and the newest member of the firm, Bill Cathey. With each witness, Wyatt played himself, asking the questions he would ask at the trial. Leo Austin, tall, serious, played the district attorney, cross-examining the witnesses, giving them a taste of what they could expect in court.

For the most part, the lawyers felt the rehearsal was a disaster.

Kay was called first. She would testify as to how she had cut Tommy's hair short, above his ears, the week before Denice Haraway disappeared, a week before she and Miz Ward went to Lawton to visit Melva. Young and pretty, she made a good appearance, was open and unhesitating in her replies; she did well. Joel was called next; his testimony would be peripheral; he did all right, once he got the hang of it. Then came Joice, the key alibi witness; and then her husband, Robert. Their story was basically the same, but it differed in many little details—enough that Bill Peterson might destroy them. With each new question and answer, the attorneys grew increasingly exasperated; repeatedly they had to warn the family not to volunteer information, to answer only the question that was asked.

Joice said she, Robert, and Tommy had been at a party at the Canadian River the night before the disappearance; that the next morning Tommy was hungover and feeling sick, and stayed in the house all day, and that she did the same. She said Robert left for work about 2:30. In the evening, she said, Willie Barnett dropped by, and started annoying the bird, and Tommy sent him home; then Jimmy came over, and he and Tommy quarreled about some money Jimmy said Tommy owed him; then he left. She went to bed about eleven, she said; Tommy had never left the house. About one in the morning, she said, she got up to use the bathroom, and there was no water. Robert came up and told her they had shut it off because a pipe was leaking under the house, and he and Tommy were fixing it. She went back to sleep.

Robert, questioned next, said he got home from his job as an ambulance driver at 11:20 that night, and found Tommy asleep on the sofa. He watched television, then heard water running. He checked all the faucets, then went outside; water was puddling from a leak under the house. He did not know how to turn the water off; he woke up Tommy, and Tommy turned it off. Together they spent several hours fixing the pipe, he said.

Most of the discrepancies between the two stories concerned the party the previous night. Wyatt told Robert he would be a strong witness if he and Joice got their memories together, but a disaster if they did not.

Miz Ward was next. She was shy, diffident, mumbling her answers stoically. That was not what the lawyers wanted; they wanted tears. "You know what you sound like?" Leo Austin chided her. "Your attitude is like, 'Well, I've got eight. If I lose one, I'll still have seven.' You've got to show some emotion up there. Your boy is innocent and they want to kill him!"

Miz Ward mumbled that she would try.

The rehearsals had started at 6:30; now it was past 10:30. There was exasperation in the room. Finally they called in Tricia, in her eighth month, who had been waiting for four hours; Bud was home with the kids.

Tricia was nervous. But her sunny personality, her strong voice, changed the mood; it was as if a dark shade had been thrown up, letting in the light.

Her only testimony would be about the phone call she received from Tommy from the jail the morning after his arrest, in which he had told her, right then, that he had told the police a dream, and they had made him say it was real.

"What else did he tell you?" Wyatt asked.

"He said the police had called him all sorts of names."

"What names?"

"Oh, you know . . . names."

"What names?" Wyatt insisted.

Tricia flushed. She looked down at her hands, folded on her belly; then looked at Wyatt. "I can't say them," she said.

"You'll have to say them," Austin said. "We want you to say them."

Tricia thought a moment. "Can I use initials?"

"Go ahead," Wyatt said.

Tricia flushed again. "S.o.b. He told me they kept calling him an s.o.b."

"Good," Wyatt said. "Now say the words. What names did he say they called him?"

Tricia shook her head. "I can't. I don't even know if I can say them initials in the courtroom."

They let it go, for now. Perhaps her obvious sincerity, her inability even to repeat a swearword, would impress the jury. Wyatt, sizing her up as the matriarch of the family, told her how badly most of the others had done. He told her that Joice and Robert had better get their stories together: not to lie, but to get their memories straight, and if they didn't remember things, to just say they didn't remember. "They better become good, strong witnesses," he said, "or else they will inject a lethal poison into Tommy."

Leo Austin, playing Bill Peterson, had asked each of them, "Wouldn't you lie to save your brother?" All of them said, "No." Wyatt told them that *he* might lie to save *his* brother's life. "A better answer," he suggested, "might be: 'I would, or I might'—however they felt—'but I don't have to, because he didn't do it! I'm telling the truth.' "

Now Wyatt said to Tricia, "I believe Tommy is innocent. It will be a grave injustice if they convict that boy. But they will, unless we have good witnesses. We can't perform miracles for you. It has to come from the witness stand."

Tricia asked if there would be time to do this again one night, after she talked to the others. Wyatt said it depended; if the state ended in two or three days, there would not be time; if the state's case went into the following week, then perhaps they could.

It was after eleven when they piled into their cars and went home. The lawyers were shaken. They knew these people had not been to college, did not understand the law, had never been in a situation such as this before. Still . . .

Only Winifred Harrell, driving her van home to Kings Road, felt good. She had never met the family before; their names had been abstractions on subpoenas, voices on the telephone. But she had been impressed, this evening, with Joel; she had been even more impressed with Tricia. No one growing up in that family, Winifred felt, could do what Tommy had said on the tape that he had done. She had begun by believing without doubt that he was guilty; Richard Kerner's scenarios had raised doubts. Now her conversion was complete. She was convinced that Tommy Ward was innocent.

DAY THREE

The spectator section in the courtroom filled slowly. The Ward family occupied most of one row: Miz Ward, Tricia, Kay, Melvin, Robert, Joel. For a time, Dr. Jack Haraway, Steve's father, was sitting beside Joel Ward; neither seemed to know who the other was. With the dentist was his wife, Betty, their daughter, Cinda.

Ward and Fontenot entered with their attorneys—Ward in blue, Fontenot in rust. Tommy hugged Miz Ward, who was wearing a full pink dress. Mrs. Haraway watched, expressionless. Dr. Haraway turned his head. All the other Wards hugged Tommy, patted him on the back.

The attorneys for both sides left the courtroom, disappeared into the judge's chambers. Ward and Fontenot were alone in the front part of the courtroom. No guards were visible.

"If they try to escape," a girl reporter for a local radio station said, "I'll take my shoes off and run after them, and kill them myself."

Ten minutes passed, twenty, thirty. A copper-colored water pitcher on the judge's bench reflected the recessed ceiling lights in an abstract pattern. The press, the spectators, began to wonder: was a plea bargain being worked out?

"They'd have to pass it along to the defendants," said Bill Willett, Don Wyatt's aide, who was standing in the doorway.

Would Wyatt take it, if one was being offered?

"Last night was scary," Willett said. "And the investigator's material is so convoluted . . ."

Nearly an hour passed before the attorneys returned, before Judge Powers took the bench. There had been no talk of a plea bargain by either side. What had occurred amounted to two small victories for the defense.

In the first, Wyatt had learned that state witnesses planned to say Tommy Ward had threatened them, or talked of robbery, on other occasions. Wyatt was convinced these incidents had been invented. His legal arguments were that any such testimony was irrelevant to the charges before the court. Judge Powers agreed; those witnesses would not be allowed to testify.

In the second, Bill Peterson was angry. The D.A. said he had learned that one of the jurors had lied to the court the previous afternoon. He was referring to the last juror seated, Janet Williams. Mrs. Williams had lied, he said, when she told the court she had no family members in jail; in fact, her husband was in jail right now, the D.A. said. He wanted Mrs. Williams dismissed from the jury.

The judge had Mrs. Williams brought from the jury room to his chambers. Mrs. Williams said she did not have a husband—that she had been divorced, in another county.

Peterson, nonplussed, still wanted her dismissed from the jury. Judge Powers ruled that Mrs. Williams had told no lies; that she had no family in jail; he said he thought she would make a fine juror.

The defense attorneys were gleeful. They had a woman on the jury who might be expected to be sympathetic to the plight of the defendants, who might be open to an argument of police coercion; and the D.A. had just attacked her truthfulness.

Peterson was glum as he returned to the prosecution table.

The witness rule was invoked: all those in the courtroom who had been subpoenaed to testify in the trial had to leave. Slowly, all of the Wards except Melvin filed out. For the rest of the trial, Melvin, who had been away in the Navy at the time of the alleged crime, would be the family's eyes and ears in the courtroom, reporting each evening what had transpired that day.

At 10:20 A.M., the district attorney moved to a lectern and read the formal charges: of robbery, kidnapping, and murder in the first degree. In brief opening remarks, he said that the state would prove the defendants were guilty on all three counts. And he summarized the evidence that would be introduced.

George Butner, in his opening statement, said the defense would show that the suspects had been pressured by the police into making false confessions; that outside of these forced confessions, there was no evidence whatever in the case.

Don Wyatt reserved his opening remarks until the defense's turn to present its case.

Then the first witness was called.

His name was Wayne Girdner. He had not testified at the preliminary hearing. An insurance man in Tulsa, he had written the insurance on Joel Ward's modern pickup truck. He testified that a few years back, Joel had come to him with a gray-primered pickup, a 1968 to 1973 model. The implication was that this could have been the truck used in the abduction of Denice Haraway, and that Tommy Ward could have had access to it.

On cross-examination, it was established that Girdner had never insured this truck, had no application forms or any other written documentation that Joel had brought him such a truck.

The second witness, a tall, slim, elderly man named J. T. Mc-

Connell, was a neighbor of the Wards on Ashland Avenue. He repeated his testimony from the hearing, saying he had often seen Tommy Ward riding up and down the street in an old gray pickup.

Under cross-examination, he said he'd seen Odell Titsworth in the pickup, driving it. And it could have been a late 1950s model, not an early 1970s one, as he had said at the preliminary.

Sticking to his plan of sequential presentation, the D.A. then called three members of Ada's running crowd, who testified that Tommy Ward had long hair at the time of Denice Haraway's disappearance, and that he once owned a knife. Under cross-examination, their memories became hazy about the dates, just as they had at the preliminary. The defense suggested one witness had been let out of a prison term early in return for his testimony in this case.

During the lunch break, from 12:10 to 1:30, three lady jurors ate at the Feed Store. So did Dennis Smith, Mike Baskin, Gary Rogers, and Bill Peterson, at a table out of their earshot, about thirty feet away.

The jurors were not discussing the case; the judge had warned them not to. Their talk touched on the religious.

"Nobody's perfect," one juror said. "There's only one perfect person."

"And He created us," the second juror said. "And look at the mess we're in."

In the afternoon, the testimony began to focus on Denice Haraway. Her faculty adviser at ECU, Norman Frame, testified about what a mature, interested student she had been. Her student-teaching mentor, Donna Howard, talked about how Denice was planning for the future, about how she had taken home workbooks that weekend.

Of each of these, the defense asked only one question: Did Denice Haraway smoke? Norman Frame said he didn't know. Mrs. Howard said she had never seen Denice smoke.

A recess. Steve Haraway stood in the corridor, tall, slim, wearing a Navy blue blazer, dark pants, a white shirt, a dotted tie. "Just my luck. I'm next and they recess," he said.

Don Wyatt hailed a journalist. "Have they thrown anything at the wall yet that stuck?" he asked. He obviously felt that they hadn't, that the defense was doing well.

Bill Peterson, passing nearby, heard the loud question and frowned.

Steve Haraway took the stand looking calm, composed. He gave his name, and then further identified himself: "I was married to Denice Haraway."

He told of their plans for the future; of their normal activities that day; of being called to the store that night, after his wife was discovered missing.

He said he had not seen or heard from her since.

Nothing was missing from their apartment that night, he said—no luggage, nothing. Only the clothes she had been wearing. She always wore jeans and tennis shoes to work, he said, and always took a gray zippered sweatshirt, because it was cold in the walk-in cooler. He did not know what blouse she wore that day, he said, because he was away at work when she left for her job at McAnally's.

He had talked to her on the phone about 7:30 that night, he said. Nothing had seemed wrong.

The purse found at McAnally's was entered into evidence. "That was my wife's," Steve said.

Under cross-examination, he said his wife did not smoke.

Soon after, Denice Haraway's sister, Janet Weldon, took the stand. She spoke of making plans with Denice to go shopping the following week, of speaking to her on the phone between 6:30 and 7, and nothing being wrong.

Much of her testimony centered on the blouse Denice allegedly had been wearing when she disappeared. Janet said she had gone through Denice's clothing within a few days; the blouse with the little blue flowers was missing; she was familiar with the blouse because it had been hers; she had given it to Denice when she, Janet, had begun to put on weight. She said she was contacted by the police about a week after October 18—a week after the arrests—and that she had told them then about the blouse. She said she had not told the police which blouse was missing earlier because she had not gone through all of Denice's clothing, and could not be sure it was missing, or that it was the only one missing.

"Would you lie?" Don Wyatt asked on cross-examination.

"No, I wouldn't."

"Would you shade your opinion?"

"No, I wouldn't."

George Butner was harsher. He reviewed Ms. Weldon's testimony that she had gone through Denice's closet shortly after she disappeared, but did not tell the police about the blouse she thought she'd been wearing until six months later, until after the arrests. As Butner repeated this, he looked incredulous, for the benefit of the jury.

Court was recessed until 9 A.M. Bill Peterson looked at Butner with hateful eyes for this questioning of Denice Haraway's sister.

Earlier that day, as the opening arguments were being made before the jury, Richard Kerner was knocking on the door of a trailer in Del City, adjacent to Oklahoma City. It was the residence of Jannette Blood Roberts. He had come to serve her with a subpoena for the defense.

Kerner had been serving many subpoenas; he'd been unable to find an address for Mrs. Roberts until today. He did not know what she had to do with the case.

When he explained who he was, Jannette led him into the living room. Kerner began to chat, as he liked to do with potential witnesses, just to see where it might lead. Jannette told him that Karl was living with her and her husband and family at the time of the crime; that Tommy stayed over a lot; that Tommy was living with them when he was arrested.

Kerner had noticed a pickup parked outside. It was nothing like the one described at the scene of the crime. Yes, sometimes she had let Tommy and Karl borrow it, she said.

Then why would they need some old gray one? Kerner asked.

"They wouldn't," Mrs. Roberts said. "And besides that, they both had short hair at the time."

"Short hair?" Kerner asked. "Are you sure?"

"Karl went to work for Wendy's, and they made him cut his hair. And Tommy was looking for a job, so he'd cut his hair, too."

God damn, Kerner thought, excited. And said, "I wish you had pictures of them, or something."

Suddenly, Jannette Roberts, too, grew excited. "I do have pictures! We took pictures on Easter!"

She hurried down a narrow hallway in the trailer, knelt on the floor. Against the wall just inside the bedroom was an old oak trunk that was one of her favorite possessions, in which she kept her other favorite possessions: her wedding dress, pictures she had not put in her photo albums; she was an inveterate picture-taker with her Polaroid camera. For several minutes Kerner stood in the hallway, watching, as Jannette's hands rummaged through the trunk. Finally she came up with a bunch of snapshots. They went back into the living room and looked at them.

"Holy shit!" the investigator said.

"What?" Jannette asked.

"Wait till they see these!"

One of the Polaroid snapshots showed Jannette, wearing a housecoat and pajamas and slippers, seated in the foreground on a sofa. Visible in the dark background, seated at the other end of the sofa, was Tommy Ward. His hair was short, above his ears. Written in blue ballpoint ink in the white bottom margin of the picture was a date: "4–22–84." That was six days before Denice Haraway disappeared.

They'll argue that the picture was dated recently, Kerner thought; was taken some other time. But he had just seen Jannette take them from the trunk with the dates already on them; she had not known he was coming; and it was he who had brought up the subject of pictures; she had not volunteered them.

He looked at another one: a picture of a little girl posing cutely beside a large Easter basket.

"Who's that?" Kerner asked.

"My daughter."

The picture had the same date written on it. In the corner of the picture, Jannette's foot was visible; she was wearing the same robe, pajamas, slippers, as in the picture with Tommy in it. And the Easter basket was not unwrapped.

Another set of pictures showed Karl Fontenot standing around at a party. His hair, too, was short. Those pictures were hand-dated "4–16–84"—twelve days before Denice Haraway disappeared.

Kerner gave Mrs. Roberts her subpoena; she let him take the photographs.

Late in the afternoon the investigator drove to Ada, the pictures in his briefcase; he was due at Wyatt's office anyway, for a meeting.

The state's case, having gone through a dress rehearsal at the preliminary hearing, was already largely worked out: a logical progression toward the playing of the tapes. There was little improvising to do at this point. The defense, however, was still only in rough outline. In Wyatt's mind, it went like this:

1. Establish that the police had coerced the confessions.
2. Present the alibi witnesses, and perhaps Tommy himself.
3. Present Richard Kerner's various scenarios, to further establish reasonable doubt; to suggest alternatives to the guilt of Ward and Fontenot.

The details still had to be pondered. The lawyers bought fast-food snacks after court, and went to Wyatt's office to kick things around. First they reviewed how the first day of testimony had gone. George Butner said he thought the D.A. had erred in not starting off with testimony about the disappearance. "He should have had Steve Haraway shed a tear or two," Butner said. "If only we could put a bomb under those tapes, we'd have no problem."

Wyatt, Butner, Austin sat around the conference table in the library. On the green-slate blackboard were the names of all the possible suspects they could raise; and the words "Elmore City"; and the names of all the people who had given Kerner taped statements saying the composite drawings were others besides Ward and Fontenot. There were a lot of names; Wyatt was thinking they had to call all of them, lay out all the scenarios; Butner wanted to streamline the presentation as much as possible, so as not to confuse the jury.

As they talked, Richard Kerner arrived. He entered the library, opened his briefcase, wordlessly handed the batch of snapshots to Don Wyatt. The lawyer looked at them, one by one. Then he looked up at Kerner.

"Where the hell did you get these?"

"Jannette Blood Roberts," Kerner said with satisfaction.

"Where did *she* get them?"

"She took them herself. Except for the ones she's in, of course."

Wyatt spread the pictures out on the table for the others to see. The one with Ward in the background they had to pick up, look at closely, to make out; but there he was.

"Is there a date on those?" Butner asked.

"Easter Sunday," Kerner said. "A week before the disappearance."

"That's hand-written," Butner said. "Is there a developing date or something?"

They examined the pictures. They were Polaroids, therefore undated. Wyatt turned them over, looked at the back.

"Doesn't every roll of film have a different number?"

He looked carefully. The pictures of Karl, hand-dated April 16, had one number. Those of Tommy, dated April 22, had another number. But the one with Tommy, and the one of the little girl with the Easter basket, had the same number; they had been taken with the same roll of film.

"The basket is still wrapped," Kerner said. "What kid doesn't open their Easter basket on Easter Sunday?"

Don Wyatt shook his head, as if he could hardly believe this new evidence.

"She's under subpoena?" he asked.

"As of today," Kerner said.

The mood in the room became jocular as they looked at the pictures again and again. Finally they put them away, turned to the scenarios on the blackboard. For several hours they debated which witnesses to call, in what order, the easiest way to get in testimony about Rogers and Sparcino, Larry Jett, Shelton and Hawkins, Elmore City. By late in the evening they came to agree with Butner. They would not call all those people who had identified the composite drawings; instead they would simply put Kerner himself on the stand, and let him lay out the scenarios.

"How you going to get that admitted?" asked Leo Austin, a former judge. "Everything somebody told Richard is hearsay."

They debated that for a while. Butner had an idea: "What if Richard says, 'Then my investigation led me here. Then my investigation led me there'?"

"I don't know," Austin said. "The judge might allow it that way. But

Peterson will be jumping all over him, screaming 'hearsay.' I'd say it's chancy—but it might work."

By the time they agreed on strategy the dark wood conference table was a messy litter of empty cans of New Coke, Cherry Coke, Diet Slice. It was late in the evening. In another part of the building, Odell Titsworth was waiting to be interviewed about the testimony he would give for the defense; so, too, was his mother. As Marie Titsworth waited, she vacuumed all the offices.

With the trial on, the case was back on the front page of the newspaper, was the lead item on the KTEN newscasts each night, was once more the talk of the town. Over a breakfast of sausage and eggs, biscuits and gravy, coffee, two middle-aged men were discussing it at the Village Restaurant Thursday morning.

"They're making a big deal they don't got that body. If they was to get rid of the body, they wouldn't bury it. They knew that area out by Reeves Packing Plant. They just cut her up in little pieces and put her in plastic bags and threw her in that acid pit. You know, they make dog food out of that. Somebody's bought her and fed her to their dogs already."

"It's terrible sometimes. You know people did it, but the legal system, sometimes you can't get into evidence what you know, and they get off."

"But if they get off, somebody'll probably take care of them anyway."

"It really bothers me, what's happenin' to the world the last ten years. The Antichrist is here, and people don't even know it. Ya know, anybody who doesn't believe that Jesus Christ is the living Son of the living God *is* the Antichrist. Even the Jews."

DAY FOUR

Steve Haraway's testimony had been completed. But because the defense had subpoenaed him as well, he could not sit in the courtroom. His mother and father and sister would watch the proceedings each day, would tell him at night what each witness had said, just as Melvin was doing for the Wards. But sitting, waiting at his father's house, was frustrating. On Thursday he went hunting coyotes.

In the courtroom, Pat Virgin of Purcell took the stand. She was

Denice Haraway's mother. She was shown Denice's driver's license, which had a picture on it. "That's my daughter," she said. She was fighting back tears as she sat on the witness chair, in a turquoise suit. "She was a very beautiful girl. Slim . . . She was in very good health as far as I knew . . . She seemed very happy."

On the defense table, as she testified, was a large brown paper sack, with bulges inside. The sack bore the marking "Dicus Discount Supermarkets."

Mrs. Virgin stepped down. Soon after, a man named Richard Holkum took the stand. Now with the Alcohol Commission, he had been, at the time of the disappearance, an Ada city policeman. Holkum testified that at 7:45 P.M. on the night of April 28, 1984, he had stopped by McAnally's, which was on his way home. He was off duty, in civilian clothes. Denice Haraway was the clerk at the time, he said, alive and well. She was wearing blue jeans, tennis shoes, a gray sweatshirt with a hood, and a light pastel blouse, lavender or blue, with a print or design on it.

"Okay," Bill Peterson said. "And did you relay this information to the police?"

"Yes, sir," Holkum said.

"Okay. Did you—was it anything that they already didn't know?"

"At that time," Holkum said, "I don't know if they had the information already or not."

There was little cross-examination. The defense attorneys were thrilled with Holkum's testimony; they had not known of his existence. They had tried hard to get Janet Weldon to say she had told the police about the blue-flowered blouse soon after the disappearance; she had insisted she had not. Now an Ada police officer had admitted he'd seen the blouse. This would buttress their planned arguments that the police had fed the suspects the information on the tapes—including the critical, detailed description of the blouse.

It appeared to some that the district attorney had made the first blunder of the trial in calling Richard Holkum to the stand. Bill Peterson didn't think so. He did not know if the defense attorneys knew of Holkum's stop at McAnally's; he could not risk their suddenly calling him to the stand later. That would look as if the prosecution had been trying to withhold evidence.

Karen Sue Wise, the clerk at J.P.'s, who had supplied most of the details for the composite drawings, was called next. She told of the two young men shooting pool in her store that night, acting weird. She identified Tommy Ward positively as one of them. She said she could not remember what the other one looked like. The truck outside she described as "mixed red primer and gray primer." Asked why she remembered Ward, she said, "His eyes. He was staring at me, watching me. It scared me real bad."

Ms. Wise was questioned and cross-examined at length. Don Wyatt showed her a composite drawing—the one he had drawn a moustache on. Then he showed her a photograph of Marty Ashley. He asked if this man had been in her store that night. She agreed that the pictures were similar. But she said, "I know him, and that is not the man."

"She knows Ashley!" Wyatt whispered excitedly to George Butner. But later Ms. Wise amplified. She said she had gone to school with him, knew his appearance, but did not know his name.

She admitted seeing a man in the back of the courtroom during the preliminary hearing who looked familiar. "I recognized a familiar face," she said. "I guess I was just scared."

Cross-examined by Butner, she said the cowboy she had seen loitering one night outside her apartment "resembled" the man in her store on April 28. Butner placed his hands on Karl Fontenot's shoulders as he sat at the defense table. "Was Karl in your establishment on April 28, 1984?" he asked.

Ms. Wise replied, "I don't know."

Bill Peterson, on redirect examination, referred to the man outside her apartment who had frightened her. "Was that the person in J.P.'s that night?" he asked.

Ms. Wise said, "I don't know."

As they broke for lunch, Tommy Ward felt things were going well. "I guess the Lord is starting to answer my prayers," he said.

Bill Peterson was also feeling good. He asked a journalist, "Any stuff sticking today?"

Peterson called Jack Paschall, the ECU professor and part-time employee at J.P.'s, who had joined Karen Wise at the store that night. A dark, intense man with sideburns and a moustache, Paschall again identified Tommy Ward as one of the men in the store that night. He recalled attending a lineup on November 8, picking out number 6—which was Ward—and saying to Gary Rogers, "If it's not him, it's his twin brother"; then adding, "No, it's just him."

He had never identified the other man, he said, and still could not do so. But of Tommy Ward, "I'm sure within the limits of human frailty."

Cross-examined, he told of two conversations with Richard Kerner, in which he had been shown photographs of two different trucks. He said he could not rule out either, that some of the details he recalled about the truck could be wrong.

Wyatt showed him a Polaroid picture the police had taken of Ward when they first questioned him on Tuesday, May 1, three days after the disappearance; his hair was very short. Wyatt noted that the disappearance had occurred on a Saturday night, and that Ada's barbershops were closed on Sundays and Mondays. He asked if Paschall would stick to his identification of Tommy Ward even if it was proved that his hair had been short on April 28. Paschall said he would stick to his identification, even then.

On redirect, Assistant D.A. Chris Ross observed that Ada's barbershops are open on Tuesdays.

The next witness was Jim Moyer, the gas station attendant who said he had stopped by McAnally's for cigarettes about 7:30 P.M. and had seen two men acting suspicious there. He said he was sure one of them had been Ward; he was not sure about Fontenot. He recalled on cross-examination the man in the back of the courtroom at the preliminary hearing, who looked like the man in the store with Ward.

Wyatt asked if Moyer recalled telling Richard Kerner, "I may be wrong. I may be helping the wrong side here." And he introduced the tape recording, which had been made without Moyer's knowledge; this was the first he knew of its existence. Judge Powers allowed the tape to be played for the jury. They heard Kerner ask, "You are reasonably sure the guy at the preliminary with 'Lurch' on his belt is the second man and he knows Tommy and spoke to him at the preliminary?" And they heard Moyer answer, "Right."

"I wasn't sure about Fontenot," Moyer said after the tape had concluded. He told of trying to reach the D.A. all summer to tell him this, without success. He said that during the preliminary hearing in the winter he had told a detective about "Lurch," but that no one ever came to ask him more about it.

Of the truck he had seen outside, he said he'd seen no one else in it, and that there was nothing unusual about it—it had a tailgate.

The next witnesses, Lenny Timmons and David Timmons, told in detail about driving up to McAnally's and finding the clerk missing. They repeated that they had seen nothing unusual about the couple leaving. Lenny Timmons repeated about Ward that on a scale of one to ten, his certainty was a six. "It may or may not be the man," he said. About the woman, he said, "Nothing was apparent to me that she was being forced."

"Everything looked normal?" Wyatt asked.

"Yes."

David Timmons said the man had his arm around the woman's waist. He said when the pickup left, it went east, away from town. He, too, saw "nothing unusual" about the couple leaving.

All through the testimony the jurors watched the witnesses, and listened—except for one elderly man, juror number nine, who sometimes looked at the ceiling; and one young man, juror number one, who stared intently, with narrowed eyes, at Ward and Fontenot.

It was 6:15 when the judge recessed the proceedings until morning.

DAY FIVE

Gene Whelchel led off. He echoed the testimony of his nephews, the Timmons brothers, about how they had found the clerk missing from McAnally's. He said he did not at first realize that the woman leaving was the clerk; but that later, when he looked at the driver's license, he realized it was she.

Sergeant Harvey Phillips, the first officer on the scene, testified to what he found there. When he was through, Don Wyatt approached the lectern with a magazine in his hand. There was a hint of scorn in his voice as he asked, "Are you the same Harvey Wayne Phillips that was quoted in *Startling Detective* magazine?"

The officer said he had never talked to anyone from that magazine.

Wyatt for a moment looked puzzled, almost stunned. He had not known the author of the article had made up all those quotes. He hesitated, turned, walked back to the defense table. "*Startling Detective!*" he muttered under his breath, with disgust. He tossed the magazine onto the table and took his seat.

Two new witnesses, Arthur and Mary Scroggins, an elderly couple, testified. Arthur Scroggins said he was driving west on Richardson Loop, in the area of the Holiday Inn, on the night in question when, about nine o'clock, a gray-primer pickup passed them, going west, at a high rate of speed. Mary Scroggins said that as the truck sped by she noticed three people in the pickup, and that one had blond hair. She did not know if they were male or female, she said.

The manager and the owner of McAnally's testified about Denice Haraway's fine work habits, her reliability.

Then the courtroom was cleared. Bill Peterson was preparing to introduce the tape of Tommy Ward being questioned on October 12. But there was a place on the tape where Dennis Smith asked Ward if he would take a polygraph examination; and any reference in court to a lie-detector test could lead to a mistrial. Judge Powers wanted to view the tape alone before deciding what to do.

A video screen was set up in the courtroom. With the jurors already gone, the judge cleared out the spectators and the press.

In the corridor, a lady reporter from a radio station looked over her notes, to phone in a report. She had developed her own shorthand; she did not like the defense attorneys, did not use their names in her notes. Instead she referred to them as "HD 1" and "HD 2." "HD" stood for "Hot Dog."

Detective Captain Dennis Smith was not permitted in the courtroom, because he would be a witness. He spent much of the time standing in the corridor, finding out during recesses what was happening inside. Now, with the judge busy viewing the tape, Smith went to the Feed Store for some iced tea. He knew the tape was more than ninety minutes long; he'd been there.

As he sipped his tea, a lawyer not involved in the case came in. He razzed the detective about the lady on the jury whose ex-husband was in jail. "The most important thing in any case is who you got in that box," the lawyer said.

Smith was thinking not of the jury box, but of the bag on the defense table. He was wondering what was in it, for Don Wyatt to bring it in and let it sit there every day. He was pretty sure he could guess—the bones and the skull they had brought to Tommy Ward's cell. He was not overly concerned. He was hoping the incident might even prove useful with the jury—by showing that the police had done everything they could to recover the body for the family.

The lawyer, sitting at another table, came over again. He told the detective of a T-shirt he had seen, that he hoped to get. The T-shirt said, "Innocent Until Proven Broke."

The October 12 tape was the one in which, for almost two hours, Tommy Ward declared his innocence to Detectives Smith and Baskin, while Smith was holding in front of him a large picture of Denice Haraway. After viewing the tape, Judge Powers decided to admit it as evidence, with the reference to the lie-detector test excised. The defense attorneys were joking happily as they emerged from the courtroom and crowded into the elevator.

"We're on a roll!" George Butner said.

"We sure are," Wyatt agreed. "That's the best evidence we've got!"

So why was Peterson entering it?

"That's what the judge said," Don Wyatt noted. "The judge said, 'Why do you want to enter this?' Peterson said, 'I want to enter it.' Heck, we're not objecting!"

The district attorney was sticking to his formula of laying out all the evidence. If he did not enter this tape, he reasoned, the defense undoubtedly would. And he wanted the confession tapes to be the ones the jury saw last.

The afternoon session began with Jimmy C. Lyon, a tall, heavyset, balding man, a truck driver. Asked his relation to Donna Denice Haraway, he said, "I'm her daddy."

He said he had not seen or heard from her since April 28, 1984.

Her brother, Ronald Lyon, wiped a tear from under his eyeglasses as he said the same thing.

One by one after that, Bill Peterson called twenty-one witnesses, each of whom spent less than a minute in the witness chair. They were friends of Denice Haraway, cousins, aunts, uncles, great-aunts, second cousins. The D.A. asked each the same question: Had they seen or heard from Denice since April 28, 1984. Each of them answered, "No," and stepped down.

Most of the witnesses were expressionless as they answered. The jurors were impassive as they watched.

The next witness, Lydia Kimball, an OSBI criminal intelligence analyst, testified about the extensive checking she had done in the past sixteen months to locate Denice Haraway, dead or alive: driver records in all fifty states, hospital records, prison records, all unidentified bodies in the country for the past two years. All had been unsuccessful.

"Then you have no proof that she is dead or alive," Wyatt observed on cross-examination. "Are you still looking for her right up till today in all fifty states?"

"Yes, I am," Ms. Kimball said.

Bill Peterson asked if she was still looking for Denice Haraway's remains as well.

"Yes," she said.

Between witnesses, Tommy Ward looked at the spectator section. He smiled at a blond woman seated halfway back. The woman mouthed with her lips three words to him, "I love you."

Tommy smiled.

The woman was Charlene, who had met Tommy in jail, who had written to Tricia saying she and Tommy planned to marry after the trial.

The state's forty-ninth witness was Detective Mike Baskin. He recounted his actions as the first detective to arrive at McAnally's. He described his search for Denice Haraway that night, and the county-wide search held the next day. Then he arrived at May 1, 1984—the day that Tommy Ward was first questioned. The attorneys for both sides approached the bench, as if on some prearranged schedule. After a brief conference, the judge again ordered the jury taken from the courtroom. The critical moment of the trial, in terms of the law, was at hand. The defense would now move that no statements made by the defendants could be used, because the state had not proved the corpus delicti—that a crime had been committed, and that the defendants had had something to do with it.

Leo Austin, the former judge, Wyatt's partner, approached the lectern. He made his argument facing Judge Powers, the jury box empty behind him. He was well aware of its importance. If the judge ruled that the corpus delicti had not been proved, he would have to dismiss the charges. And the boys could never be tried again, even if physical evidence were found against them—because that would be double jeopardy.

Austin cited relevant portions of the law involving corpus delicti. "The way I read that, your honor," he said, "is that the state has to prove before the confessions and admissions can be entered, can be considered by this court and by this jury, that the state must prove that a death has occurred, and that that death was caused by the conduct of another person. The court has heard the evidence. There's only a few witnesses that can testify as to any conduct on behalf of these defendants. We have before us evidence as to the conduct and so forth of Ms. Haraway. We have before us two witnesses—Timmons witnesses—who are not positive in their identifications of these defendants, especially defendant Fontenot, only defendant Ward. On the basis of a zero to ten, Lenny Timmons gave us a six. The other witnesses—Ms. Wise, Moyer—have not connected the defendants with this store but with another store. They agree it's on the same night, but I ask the court, is that sufficient to show that these defendants were involved with this crime?

"Even assuming for one moment that the state has presented evidence beyond a reasonable doubt to show that there was the death of a person in this case, I ask the court to search the evidence—even circumstantial evidence—and find where there is any evidence showing that these two individuals were involved in the conduct—the cause of death—of Ms. Haraway, even assuming that there was a death. The instruction is clear, your honor. It says, 'Such proof must consist of evidence which is wholly independent of any confession or admission made by the defendants.'

"Your honor, we talked to the jury in this case, and told them that they were going to have to search their souls. This is the kind of case where we feel strongly that the state has not proven a corpus delicti. They have not proven the death. There is no body. I realize that they can show it circumstantially, but they have not proven it beyond a reasonable doubt. Even assuming for one moment that they have proved that, I ask the court to search the record and find that these two individuals caused the death. It says, 'And the fact that her death was caused by the conduct of another person.' I respond to the argument of the state."

Austin left the lectern. George Butner adopted his argument on behalf of Karl Fontenot.

"Court's going to overrule the motion," Judge Powers said immediately. "I think there is sufficient circumstantial evidence by which the jury can find the corpus delicti, and I will overrule the objection at this time."

Bill Peterson, at the prosecution table, nodded. It was as if a weight had been lifted from his chest. A feeling of serenity flooded through him. The tapes would be admitted as evidence—all of them. He felt confident now that he would win.

Judge Powers would say, after the trial, that the ruling had been, in his own mind, "a close call." But if he had, indeed, agonized over the issue, he had made up his mind before Austin presented his arguments. Austin said later that day, "Before I started, the judge said, 'Let's get the corpus delicti argument out of the way.' That sort of takes the enthusiasm out of your presentation."

The jury was returned to the courtroom. Mike Baskin resumed the stand. He said he had read Tommy Ward his Miranda warnings before questioning him on May 1. Asked if Ward had understood his rights, Baskin said, "I can't remember the exact reply, but it would have had to be affirmative or there would have been no interview."

He said Ward on May 1 had short hair that was sticking up in the back, with gaps. "It didn't look like too good of a haircut." He said Ward had small scratches on his right hand.

The questioning leaped to October 12, to the interview with Ward in the basement of Norman police headquarters. Baskin told how Ward had given a different story that night from the one he had on May 1 about what he'd been doing the night of the disappearance. He said that the ensuing questioning was not intense, that Ward had not been threatened in any way.

It was late Friday afternoon. There would be no time to show the tape that day. The trial was recessed till Monday. The attorneys from both sides, along with Dennis Smith, went into the district attorney's office, to edit the tape; to excise the part in which Ward was asked to take a polygraph and agreed to do so. Judge Powers drove home to Chandler, to his wife and his own bed, for the weekend.

The county fair was in town at the old rodeo grounds. There were rides, food booths, exhibits. An intermittent drizzle was falling, but Bud and Tricia wanted to get out of the house that night to get their minds off the trial. They took Rhonda, Buddy, and Laura Sue to the fairgrounds, to walk around.

Melvin and Miz Ward stayed home in the house on Ninth Street. In early evening, the telephone rang. Melvin answered it. The woman calling identified herself as Peggy Lurch.

She said she was the wife of Jason Lurch. She said that police investigators had come to their house that day; they had told her husband they wanted him in court Monday morning. Peggy was a friend of Joice, she said; she thought the family should know what was going on. Jason might call later, she said.

When Melvin hung up, he told Miz Ward; she called Don Wyatt at home. Wyatt asked her what she knew about Lurch. She said that Jason knew Tommy. At the preliminary hearing, she said, he had come up to her during a recess and told her, "I know Tommy didn't do it."

"What did you think he meant by that?" the lawyer asked.

"I just thought he was being nice," Miz Ward said. "He knew Tommy, and he knew he wouldn't do something like that."

Wyatt kept his own thoughts to himself: perhaps Lurch knew Tommy didn't do it, because he knew who did; perhaps because he, Lurch, had done it! Wise and Moyer thought they had seen him that night . . .

"Tell him I'd like to meet with him in my office," Wyatt said. "Sunday. At three o'clock."

When Bud and Tricia got home from the fair with the kids, they were told about the call. Soon after, the phone rang. Bud answered. It was Jason Lurch.

Lurch agreed to come to the Wolf house at 2 P.M. Sunday, and to go with them from there to the lawyer's office.

But on Sunday, Jason Lurch didn't show.

13

"MYSTERY MAN"

Steve Haraway went to Norman for the weekend, to spend time with his friends. Karl Fontenot spent Saturday night making picture frames out of empty cigarette packs. Tommy Ward joked about the case with a friend, who was in jail briefly for driving without a valid license.

"When I get out of this mess," Tommy said, "I'm gonna get me a police escort out of this town. When I get rich, I'm gonna buy me a brand-new pickup—and I'm gonna paint it gray primer."

On Sunday, after church, Bud and Tricia waited at home for Jason Lurch. Two o'clock passed, and two-thirty, and three. Lurch did not appear. They went to Wyatt's office without him.

Bud went over the testimony he would swear to about Tommy's having short hair at the time. He said that on Saturday, April 21, late in the afternoon, Tommy had come by the house to borrow five dollars, because he had a date that night and was broke. He was wearing a baseball cap and looked different; no hair was falling from beneath it.

"What happened to your hair?" Bud recalled saying. Tommy, he said, swept off his baseball cap with a flourish, and said, "Ta-da," and did a full, bowing turn, showing off his new short haircut.

The attorneys were much impressed with Bud; he was gentle, soft-spoken, a solid citizen; he'd held the same job at the feed mill for six years; before that he had worked as a bookkeeper for the city of Ada.

He was a leader of his church. They could not ask for a better witness. Except that he was Tommy's brother-in-law.

Bud told them he was convinced that Tommy was innocent.

Richard Kerner arrived at the law office, bringing Jannette Roberts; the lawyers went over her testimony about the Polaroid pictures of Tommy and Karl with short hair. Then Wyatt turned to Kerner.

"Find Jason Lurch," he said. "Give him a subpoena. See if you can get him down here to talk to us."

Wyatt told the investigator to explain to Lurch the lawyer's current theory: that Lurch had done nothing wrong; that he had been in J.P.'s the night of the disappearance, shooting pool with someone who looked like Tommy Ward, someone with a red-and-gray-primer pickup; that the pickup at McAnally's—described as grayish-green—was different; that the two incidents were not related. Tell Lurch he had nothing to fear from the defense, Wyatt said.

But Wyatt feared that the district attorney had already gotten to Lurch, and that to remain uninvolved in the case, he would deny being at J.P.'s that evening.

They had no idea of Lurch's whereabouts. The investigator set out to find him.

Wyatt and Austin met the same afternoon with the psychiatrist from Oklahoma City who had interviewed Ward in his cell, had given him a battery of standard tests. They were hoping he would say that Tommy, psychologically, was incapable of committing such a crime.

The doctor told them that on the basis of his tests, he felt Tommy was below normal in intelligence; that he had a lot of insecurities, neurotic problems, bundled up inside him; that he could easily be programmable by the police. But he could not say for sure that that was what happened. He could not rule out that Ward might have done it. He thought, in fact, that he might have, he said.

The lawyers were disappointed. They felt the young, bearded shrink was making sure he would not be asked to testify.

They decided that he wouldn't.

When he left the office that evening, Wyatt's mind turned again to the man in the back of the courtroom. The "mystery man," the *Daily Oklahoman* had called him, after the playing of the Jim Moyer tape.

No lawyer likes an unknown quantity at a trial. "I'm afraid of Lurch," Wyatt said.

DAY SIX

A video screen was already set up in the middle of the courtroom, facing the jury box, as the jurors took their places in the morning. A smaller video screen was placed on the judge's·bench. The spectator section was full.

The overhead lights were turned off. There were no windows in the courtroom. The only light was from the corridor, coming in through the small glass panels in the doors.

The videos were switched on. In near darkness, the jurors watched the screen facing them. The spectators and the press could see the screens at oblique angles.

The image of Tommy Ward appeared on the screens. He was seated, wearing a light-colored athletic shirt, blue jeans, sneakers. His questioners in this October 12 tape, Detectives Dennis Smith and Mike Baskin, were not visible. Only their voices could be heard; they spoke softly most of the time. When, for about half of the hour-and-forty-five-minute tape, Smith held a picture of Denice Haraway up in front of Ward, the back of the picture appeared on the screen as a dark rectangle.

The jurors saw Ward being told his rights, and saying he did not want a lawyer. They saw him tell a different story of what he'd been doing the night of the crime than he had told the detectives on May 1. They heard him say that the first time he was questioned, he had been confused about the dates. They then saw him deny repeatedly, for more than an hour and a half, that he'd had anything to do with the disappearance, or that he knew anything about it.

They did not see any reference to a polygraph.

When the tape ended, there was a short recess; afterward, Mike Baskin resumed the witness chair. Under questioning by the assistant D.A., Chris Ross, Baskin admitted letting on during the interrogation that he knew more about the crime than he did; this was standard procedure, he said. Ross asked about the incident of bringing the skull and bones from the college to the jail; he knew that if he did not bring it up, the defense would. Baskin said they had done this to try to learn the location of the body.

As they walked down the stairs for the lunch recess, Ross and Baskin, who looked somewhat alike, were joking.

"Well, Baskin, did I minimize your damage?" Ross asked.

"No," Baskin said, "you've thrown me to the wolves."

In the corridor, Melvin Ward was standing by himself, smoking a cigarette, looking shaken. He had left the courtroom while the tape was on, because, he said, he could not bear to watch this "police badgering" of his brother.

In the afternoon, Don Wyatt cross-examined Baskin. He asked if he had lied to Ward on the tape when he said there were witnesses. "Part of it was lies," the detective said. Wyatt pressed the point further, saying a claim that the police had a statement given by a witness under oath was "an absolute, bald-faced lie." Baskin said he would call it "a poor choice of words."

Wyatt walked to the defense table. He opened the paper sack that had been carried into and out of the courtroom for four days. He pulled out a skull and some bones.

"Wasn't this the same mind games," he asked, "as when you brought this into the cell at night?"

If the jurors were startled by the skull and bones being produced in court, as Wyatt had hoped, there was no indication of it. They continued to watch impassively.

Baskin conceded that bringing the skull to the jail was not proper police procedure; he said the district attorney had chewed him out about the incident several times. "I agree that probably I shouldn't have done it, and it was a mistake," he said.

George Butner focused his cross-examination on the notion that all of the major statements in Tommy Ward's subsequent confession had been planted in Tommy's mind by the police during the October 12 questioning: the ideas that there had been two men, a pickup, a kidnapping, rape, murder, that Denice had screamed, had cried, had run away, had slipped and fallen. Punching his fist into his hand, he enumerated how each of these facts or actions had been contained in the police questions on this tape, as when the detectives asked: Do you think she screamed? Do you think she tried to run away?

Butner asked how the police could not have known what blouse Denice had been wearing until after the confession tapes were made, since Ada policeman Richard Holkum had seen her that night. Baskin replied that communication in the Ada P.D. was not well coordinated.

The detective conceded that fingerprints were never taken at the scene. He said a cigarette found burning in an ashtray at McAnally's had been discarded before he arrived. Don Wyatt suggested that since Denice Haraway did not smoke, the cigarette might have been the perpetrator's; and that through saliva tests, they might now know the blood type of the perpetrator—if such tests had been done on the cigarette. Wyatt noted that the man leaving with the girl had opened the glass door, according to the eyewitnesses, and that glass is the very best surface from which to take fingerprints.

The next witness was Jim Allen, who had been an inmate in the county jail in December of 1984. He was a trustee, a cook, and could wander around inside. He said Tommy Ward had told him in the jail that Ward and Marty Ashley had abducted and raped and killed Denice Haraway, and that Ashley had dumped her body into the Canadian River. He said he and several detectives had gone out in that area to look for the body, but had found nothing.

It was 4:20 P.M. Detective Captain Dennis Smith took the stand, the fifty-first witness for the state. He was wearing a beige suit, a yellow button-down shirt, a striped tie. Under direct examination, he reviewed his involvement in the case, from the night of the disappearance to the present moment. Of the October 12 questioning, he said he had attempted to bluff Ward, in order to elicit information. He said this was a common procedure, "to try to get at the truth."

Of the skull incident, he said that when, around October 25, he pulled the bones out of a sack in front of Karl Fontenot, "Karl stepped back and asked if Tommy had given a confession, and you found her at the river."

The questioning moved to the January 9 story by Ward that Denice Haraway had run away with Marty Ashley. An audiotape of the statement was played for the jury. Late in the tape, Ward said he hadn't known what Denice Haraway looked like, and that Jim Allen got hold of a picture, to show him. At the defense table, Don Wyatt whispered to Butner, "That's it!" And he wrote in large capital letters on a pad: "ALLEN PLANTED THE STORY."

Also on the tape, the jury heard Wyatt ask Ward: "You never told Karl before today about your dream?" And Tommy said, "No."

Richard Kerner's gray 1985 Mercury Marquee glided smoothly along State Road 99, heading south, away from Ada. He was going to find Jason Lurch.

On Sunday he had located Lurch's grandmother in an outlying town; she did not know where Lurch was living. On Monday he sought out other relatives, in decrepit houses in town. Early in the afternoon, in exchange for half a pack of cigarettes, someone told him Lurch was working as a cowboy, breaking horses, in a village twenty-five miles south of Ada. "Go to the store, and down a road, and there's the place where Jason is at," he was told.

Kerner followed the directions. He found the lone store in the village, drove a short distance down a dirt road to a house. Three men in their twenties were standing in the open space in front of it, talking. Flat land, parched by the drought, spread in every direction.

Kerner got out of his car and approached them; all three were dressed like cowboys.

"I'm looking for Jason Lurch," he said. "You know where I can find him?"

The men looked from one to the other. None of them spoke.

Kerner chose the tallest of the three and addressed him. "You Lurch?"

At first there was no response. Then the man said, "Yeah. What do you want?"

The other two edged away. They moved between the investigator and his car. They positioned themselves, blocking the way to the driver-side door.

The sun beat down on the flat land. Kerner did not know if he was in trouble or not. He could feel the extra weight he had let accumulate around his middle in recent years; he was aware that he was fifty-two, a grandfather. He thought: years ago I could have taken on three guys, but not now.

"I'm a legal investigator, working for Tommy Ward's attorney, Don Wyatt," he said. "The attorney would like to talk to you."

"What about?" Lurch said.

Kerner told him what about. Lurch said he did not think he wanted to talk to the lawyer.

Kerner persisted. He told Lurch how he might be able to help out his old buddy, Tommy, who was in a jam. He wasn't committing himself to anything, Kerner told him. Why not just come see what Don Wyatt had to say?

After half an hour, Lurch wavered. He said he had no transportation. Kerner said he would drive him to Ada, and bring him back afterward.

Lurch agreed.

They climbed into Kerner's car and, mostly in silence, rode north.

When court adjourned for the evening, Wyatt, Austin, Butner, and Willett stood talking in the parking lot across the street. Leo Austin was extremely dismayed by Ward's Ashley tape; he felt several of the jurors, hearing these lies, had already made up their minds that Ward was guilty. Butner also seemed down, even though things appeared to be going well for his client; there had been no evidence yet against Fontenot.

"What's going on at your office tonight?" Butner asked.

"We're gonna talk to Lurch," Wyatt said.

"You think he'll show?"

"He's there now."

Butner, who had dinner plans elsewhere, said, "I've got to see Mr. Lurch."

They drove to Wyatt's office. Jason Lurch was waiting in the conference room, with Richard Kerner.

Lurch was a tall, thin man with long dark hair that he was wearing in a ponytail, falling from under a cap. He had on blue jeans, a red T-shirt, cowboy boots that reached to his knees, that had scuffed, rounded toes. Lurch sat in a chair, Wyatt in another; the others were on a sofa across the room. Wyatt explained why they wanted to talk to him. At times Lurch grinned, showing a lot of teeth. There was something that seemed eerie, even evil, about the grin, the others would agree later. Kerner thought: he's the kind of guy who would stab you in the back for a nickel.

Lurch admitted to being in the courtroom every day of the preliminary hearing. "I've known Tommy about ten years," he said. "I wanted to see what kind of evidence they had against him."

He confirmed that he had said to Miz Ward that he knew Tommy didn't do it. "I don't know who did it," he said now. "I just know Tommy didn't."

Wyatt leaned forward in his chair. "I want to make this clear," he said. "We don't believe you had anything to do with it, either. We've come to believe that the incidents at J.P.'s and at McAnally's were two separate incidents; that perhaps you had been at J.P.'s, and were remembered by Karen Wise, who recognized you at the preliminary. We don't think you were involved. But if we could show that you were at J.P.'s that night, with someone else, and then left, that would help Tommy prove his innocence."

Lurch told them that in April 1984 he was working at an auto repair shop in Ada; that he worked for the shop most of the day, was trusted by the owner, and had his own key; sometimes he would stay after closing, paint cars and trucks, to make extra money for himself.

The attorneys remained expressionless as the information registered: Lurch could easily have painted a truck without suspicion.

Lurch said he had a nephew, about twenty years old, who lived a block and a half from J.P.'s. "Lots of times we'd stop in there for a pack of cigarettes or a soda pop," he said. "We were in there a whole lot. That girl"—he meant Karen Wise—"was always in there."

"Is it possible you went in there the evening of April 28, 1984?" Wyatt asked.

"Yeah, it's possible," Lurch said. "I coulda been workin', and gone over there to get some pop and stuff."

Butner asked him to describe his nephew. "He's shorter than me," Lurch said. "A kind of slight build. He's got sort of sandy blond hair, parted in the middle. About shoulder length."

It was the exact description under the composite drawing that was supposed to be Tommy Ward. When asked, Lurch said he did not think his nephew looked like Tommy Ward.

The nephew, Ricky Brewer (name changed), worked for one of the

Ada factories. He hadn't seen him for a while, Lurch said. He said Ricky did have a pickup at the time. It was yellow, he said, and shiny, not primered, and had large wheels front and back. The tailgate was off at the time, he said, because it had gotten dented.

"You ever been in McAnally's?" Wyatt asked.

"No, never," Lurch said. "We always stopped by J.P.'s."

The mood in the room was lightening. Wyatt seemed convinced that his theory was true: that there had been two different sets of people seen, two different trucks; that Karen Wise and Jack Paschall had seen Jason Lurch and perhaps his nephew; that it was mistaken identity. Despondent when court adjourned half an hour earlier, the lawyers now felt exhilarated.

"We want you to testify," Wyatt said. "You've been subpoenaed. You're under court order, so it's not really a question of whether you want to."

"An investigator from the D.A.'s office come out and talked to me Friday," Lurch said. "He read me my rights first. He asked me about Ricky's truck. That's why I didn't show up Sunday. He made it sound like maybe I was a suspect."

"Did he give you a subpoena?" Butner asked.

"No."

They asked if he had ever been convicted of a felony. Lurch said no. Wyatt emphasized how important his testimony could be to Tommy Ward. "You understand that Ward's on trial for his life here? Your testimony could save a man's life, who we believe is innocent."

Lurch said he understood. "I'll be there," he said; though he would need transportation. They said Richard Kerner would pick him up.

Wyatt told Lurch he could be held as a material witness; he could be held in jail until it was time for him to testify. "We don't want to do that," Wyatt said. "We're not threatening you. I just want you to understand how important it is that you show up." If he did not show up, Wyatt pointed out, he could be arrested.

Lurch did not have a telephone where he lived. He said he checked in at the store nearby every few hours. They told him to call in to Wyatt's office the following afternoon, and each morning and afternoon after that, till they knew when they would be calling him as a witness. They would arrange for Kerner to pick him up.

Lurch said he would do that.

The attorneys seemed reluctant to let him go; he was that important to their case.

George Butner remembered something else. He remembered that Jim Moyer, the other person who had recognized Lurch at the preliminaries, had placed him at McAnally's, an hour before the disappearance. Lurch repeated that he did not go to McAnally's: except perhaps in the afternoon sometimes, when his wife would stop by there for food; he never went in the evening, or with anyone else, he said.

There seemed no way around that just now.

"When you appear in court, could you dress just the way you are now?" Wyatt asked.

"I always dress this way," Lurch said.

"Could you let your hair down, so it hangs to your shoulders?"

"I could do that," Lurch murmured, as if reluctant.

Lurch had a small stubble goatee; he said sometimes he had it, sometimes he didn't. Wyatt asked if he would shave it before coming to court. Lurch hesitated, then nodded he would.

Lurch and Richard Kerner left. There was little conversation in the car as the investigator drove him home. The mood, however, seemed friendly.

Butner went to his dinner near Wewoka. Wyatt, Austin, and Willett discussed the day's events. Despite Lurch, Leo Austin was still pessimistic.

"Some of those jurors are ready to cut Tommy's balls off right now," he said. "And they haven't even seen the bad tape yet. The best we can hope for is a hung jury. And then bail out of the case. And hope the family doesn't have enough money to retain us again."

"I wouldn't belly up to the bar with this one again," Wyatt said.

The lawyer was still convinced, however, that Tommy Ward was innocent. And he still had faith in his own ability: that somehow he would pull the case out of the fire, would win an acquittal.

Richard Kerner, arriving back at his Ada motel late after taking Lurch home, was disappointed. He dined on crackers from a vending machine. He wasn't very hungry.

Until this evening, Kerner had been convinced that Tommy Ward was innocent. But now he didn't know. Why, he wondered, would Lurch come to every day of the hearings, if he had not been involved? That showed an inordinate interest in the case. Perhaps, Kerner thought, Ward was letting Fontenot take the second rap because Lurch was bigger, and tougher; because Lurch had threatened him. Perhaps, he thought, the culprits were Jason Lurch and Tommy Ward.

DAY SEVEN

In the morning Dennis Smith resumed the stand. Wyatt asked him why he had held a picture of Denice Haraway in front of Tommy Ward during so much of the questioning on October 12. "In order for him to know who we were talking about," the detective said. He described the October 18 questioning as a "low-key type of interrogation."

Wyatt suggested that Odell Titsworth had been held in jail long after the police knew he was not involved, so he could be used to threaten the other two.

George Butner hammered again at the idea that all of the key elements in the confession tape had been planted in Ward's mind on October 12. And he focused on Officer Holkum's testimony, suggesting that Holkum had given the detectives a detailed description of what Denice Haraway had been wearing within a day or two after her disappearance. Smith said, "Apparently we didn't" pay attention to what Holkum had seen that night; he said no detectives had interrogated Holkum until after October 18. Pressed, he admitted that this had not been good police procedure.

The detective was followed to the stand by Marty Ashley. Bill Peterson asked if he had raped and killed Denice Haraway.

"No, sir," Ashley replied.

Peterson asked if Ashley had kissed her and driven away with her.

"No, sir," Ashley said.

Watching, Dorothy Hogue of the Ada *News* thought: he looks a lot more like the composite than Fontenot does.

But that, she knew, did not mean he'd been involved.

In the afternoon, the state called Gordon Calhoun, a college student from Whittier, California, a sometime worker at Disneyland. At the time of the disappearance, Calhoun had been living in Ada, next door to Jannette Roberts. He was clean-cut and earnest-looking. He testified that on the night in question, he'd had a party at his apartment, but that Ward and Fontenot had not been there.

Calhoun said that in May, he and Fontenot "talked about the Haraway case. Karl mentioned he knew who did it. I didn't believe him. I had no reason to believe him."

He said Fontenot was the type of person who always said things that were not to be believed.

On cross-examination, Wyatt handed him Jannette Roberts's Polaroid pictures. Calhoun was in one of them, with Fontenot, that was dated 4-16-84. He conceded that he was present in the picture.

Wyatt asked him to describe Karl's hair in the picture, for the benefit of the jury.

"It is above his ears."

"It's above the collar, is it not?"

"Yes."

Wyatt handed him the composite sketch that supposedly was Fontenot. "It does not compare," Calhoun said. "Not with the long hair."

Wyatt handed him the picture showing Jannette's daughter, Jessica, and the Easter basket, hand-dated 4-22-84; and the one, dated the same, that appeared to show Jannette and Tommy. Wyatt asked him who the man on the couch was. Calhoun studied the snapshot closely. "It looks like Tommy Ward," he said.

"Tommy's hair was well up over his ears, wasn't it?" the lawyer asked. "Cut short, wasn't it?"

"Yes."

"If the dates are correct," Wyatt said, "state's exhibits one and two [the composite sketches] could not be Karl Allen Fontenot and Tommy Ward?"

"No."

"Am I right?"

"You're right."

Calhoun looked around the courtroom uncertainly. The pictures had been a surprise to him and to the prosecutors.

Wyatt asked if the other picture did not contain "an unopened Easter basket," and "a little kid standing next to it, kind of anticipating."

"Yes," Calhoun said.

On redirect, Peterson, examining the pictures, emphasized that the dates were handwritten, and that Calhoun did not know by whom. Calhoun stated that on April 28 he had seen Karl, and that he had long hair.

Wyatt asked him to turn over the pictures of Tommy, and of the child with the Easter basket, and to read off the last three digits of the code numbers.

Each was 554.

"They appear to have come from the same roll of film, don't they?" Wyatt asked.

"Yes."

The two pictures of Fontenot, hand-dated six days earlier, both bore the code 212—different from the Easter pictures.

"If the dates are correct," George Butner asked, "these photographs are better evidence than your testimony, is that correct?"

"I suppose," Calhoun said.

It was 4:55 P.M. There was a brief recess. Tommy Ward, who had been praying to Jesus for deliverance, could not help wondering if his life was going to be saved by an Easter basket.

Others in the courtroom were wondering the same thing. The corridors were astir with conversation about this unexpected evidence. Gordon Calhoun was down in the district attorney's office on the first floor.

When the recess ended, the state recalled Calhoun. Peterson showed him the pictures again. Calhoun said the clothes he was wearing in the picture of himself and Fontenot were the clothes he had worn on a fishing trip to Blue River on Memorial Day. He said the pictures were not taken on April 16, 1984, as they were dated.

The silence in the courtroom seemed almost to stir with relief.

The clothes were cutoff jeans and a T-shirt. Questioned by Wyatt, Calhoun said he wore a T-shirt almost every day, but that he wore the cutoff jeans only about once a month. Wyatt asked if he could have worn the jeans in April. Calhoun insisted the pictures had been taken on Memorial Day.

He admitted that he had talked to Bill Peterson for two or three minutes during the recess.

Like most of the witnesses, Calhoun was excused subject to possible recall. In his case it meant he could not yet go home to California.

The day's testimony ended with Leonard Keith Martin, who'd been in the city jail in October 1984. As a trustee, he'd been sweeping the floor outside the cells, he said, when he heard Fontenot say: "I knew we'd get caught. I knew we'd get caught."

Asked whom Karl was talking to, Martin said, "To nobody. There was nobody else there."

Gordon Calhoun had seemed, to some observers, to be among the most believable witnesses to take the stand. He was neat and intelligent. He'd lived in Ada, attending ECU, for only a short time, and had no roots in the town. Now he lived out west. He appeared to have no personal stake in the outcome of the trial. He was the kind of witness a jury was likely to believe.

The state had called him to discredit one of Tommy Ward's early stories—that he had been at a party at Calhoun's apartment that night. Bill Peterson was being thorough, as was his custom. Don Wyatt had jumped at the opportunity to have the Polaroid pictures entered into evidence and verified during the testimony of a strong state's witness.

Calhoun's testimony had appeared, at first, to be a major breakthrough for the defense—until after the recess, when he said the Fontenot pictures had been taken Memorial Day, and therefore were falsely dated. That clearly had been devastating to the defense. One picture did have the wrapped Easter basket—but would the jury accept that mute testimony, in light of the doubt Calhoun had cast on the others? That the same roll of film was used did not prove conclusively the pictures had been taken the same day.

The attorneys, hurrying to Wyatt's office, tried to put these thoughts from their minds. Waiting for them, they knew, were pictures Richard Kerner had taken that day—pictures that had gotten Wyatt excited, that made him think they might have solved the case—with suspects other than Ward and Fontenot.

Their attention returned to Calhoun's testimony, however, when, at 6 P.M., moments after they arrived at the office, Calhoun showed up there as well.

The young man looked upset, confused. He told Wyatt that his conscience was bothering him. He said he was afraid that during Peterson's redirect examination, he may have left the impression with the jury that he was sure the "April 16" photos were taken Memorial Day. He was not positive about that, he said, and did not want to leave the wrong impression. He was on no side, he said; he just wanted to tell the truth.

Wyatt's spirits soared; he was impressed with the young man's concern. He told him they had two options. They could bring that out when they called him to testify for the defense; or he could go talk to the judge in the morning, and explain his position, and ask the judge if he could go right back on the stand to clarify it. Wyatt told him to do whichever he wanted; he did not know if the judge would go along with the second option.

Calhoun left, to decide what to do.

Wyatt, Butner, Bill Willett, and Bill Cathey went into the library. Wyatt spread before them the new pictures Kerner had taken. The investigator had tracked down and photographed the truck Jason Lurch had mentioned the night before—the truck his nephew, Ricky Brewer, had owned at the time of the disappearance. In the pictures was a pickup, pale gray or beige. It was shiny, not rough—but it had patches of red primer all over it, larger wheels on the back, and had no tailgate. It seemed to the attorneys to fit the description of the truck seen at J.P.'s by Wise and Paschall—even more than the others Kerner had photographed.

Kerner had talked to the nephew as well. He was very cooperative. He was married, had children, worked the night shift at a factory. But he was also about five-eight, slim, with sandy-brown hair, shoulder length, parted in the middle—just like the composite sketch. The attorneys were joyful, began joking. They felt these pictures, combined with Jason Lurch's testimony, would convince the jury it was they who had been seen at J.P.'s that night.

And perhaps—since Jim Moyer placed Lurch at McAnally's—it was possible that these two were the killers.

George Butner was elated. For the first time since he took the case he felt there was a chance of getting Ward and Fontenot off. But with two other sets of truck photos already introduced by the defense, he felt they needed to get an identification of this truck from Wise or Paschall.

The attorneys agreed that Paschall probably would say it might be the truck and it might not be—as he had done with the other truck pictures. They decided Karen Wise was their best bet. But they did not know how to reach her; she had been avoiding Kerner.

They decided to call Sue Mayhue, the woman in the D.A.'s office who kept track of witnesses, to ask her for Wise's phone number. But they knew this would tip off the D.A., who might tell Ms. Wise not to talk to them.

"Ask for three numbers," Bill Cathy suggested, grinning.

They liked that idea. Bill Willett made a list of several witnesses whose numbers they would ask for, to confuse the opposition, to send them scurrying. He called the D.A.'s office. Chris Ross answered. Ms. Mayhue had already left. Willett looked up her home phone number, and called her there. The line was busy. He called again a few minutes later. There was no answer. The attorneys were convinced that Ross had called her and told her not to be available.

Still, the lawyers were in a boisterous mood.

Talking further, they decided to jettison the Elmore City scenario, to focus in on Lurch and his nephew as the likeliest suspects. Wyatt got an idea. Xeroxed diagrams of the longer scenario had already been prepared for their own use. They could "accidentally" let one slip to the floor during a recess in the morning, let the D.A. find it and be thrown off the track.

Between Gordon Calhoun's conscience and Richard Kerner's photos, they felt things were going their way. Their new optimism was irrepressible; they laughed and joked for the first time in weeks.

But they knew that the confession tapes would be played the next day, and that they were disastrous to the defense.

"Tomorrow I'm going to wear my flak jacket," George Butner said.

Wyatt sent word to Tricia that night: he did not know if Tommy would get off; but they should have plans ready to spirit him out of town, directly from the courthouse, in case he did.

DAY EIGHT

By now the cast of characters was as in a long-running show, and the audience was diminishing. Dr. Haraway, Betty Haraway, and their daughter, Cinda, sat in the second row, as they did every day; Melvin Ward sat in the third row, the press up front. The rest of the spectator section, filled to capacity the first few days, had thinned to about two-thirds. But this afternoon would be box-office. Word had spread through the courthouse, and this afternoon the benches would be packed, the spectators hip to hip in discomfort; this afternoon they would show the tapes.

The morning began with a former inmate at the city jail, Terry McCartney Holland, on the stand. Mrs. Holland told of a conversation she'd had in the jail with Fontenot shortly after his arrest. She said he first told her that he, Tommy, and Odell Titsworth had done it. He was excited when he said that, she said; he told her the same story that was on the tapes; and he gave her three guesses as to where they had put the body: in the river, in the concrete bunker, in the burned-out house. She added that he later told her other versions, in which he was not involved, just Tommy and Odell. On cross-examination, she said she felt Karl got a kick out of telling these stories; he would be wide-eyed as he told the stories, walking all over his cell; he enjoyed the notoriety, she said. Karl told "tall stories" about everything, she said. He told her what a great guy his buddy Tommy Ward was—"a great-looking guy, well-built, stocky." She expected, from Karl, to meet "a great god" in Tommy Ward, she said. She heard so many different stories from Karl that after a while she didn't believe any of them. He scared her at first—then she realized he was "just a blowhard," she said; but Karl did think a lot of Tommy; it was sort of "hero worship."

Bill Peterson and Chris Ross then began the ironic part of their task: to prove false much of the information on the taped confessions. If they didn't do it, the defense would, with much greater impact on the jury.

They called Forrest Simpson, the man who owned the burned-out house. He told how it had been a useless eyesore, how he had salvaged what he could, and burned the rest to the ground, in June of 1983—ten months before Denice Haraway disappeared.

They called Michelle Wheeler, Odell Titsworth's girlfriend. She told how Odell's arm had been broken in a scuffle with the police two nights before the disappearance, how it had been in a cast for weeks afterward. She said Odell had tattoos on both arms from his knuckles to his shoulders, as well as on his back, his chest, his thighs, his legs. She said he was in severe pain from the broken arm on April 28, and did not leave the house.

They called Michelle's mother, Agnes Lumpmouth, whose home Michelle and Odell were staying in. She, too, said Odell was in great pain, so great that he had to sleep sitting up, and that he did not leave the house that night.

They called Dr. Jack B. Howard, the orthopedic surgeon who treated Titsworth's arm for a spiral fracture. "If it were my arm, it would hurt like the dickens," he said.

Now it was the afternoon of the eighth day. Courthouse workers, other attorneys packed the spectator section along with the regulars. The state was approaching the climax of its case.

Rusty Featherstone, a deputy inspector of the OSBI, took the stand. He was a stocky gentleman with a neatly trimmed, ruddy beard. He wore a dark blue three-piece suit, a striped tie, glasses. His manner suggested a self-assured scientist more than a cop, though he had been an OSBI agent for four years, a police officer before that.

Featherstone was the OSBI's polygraph expert. It was he who had questioned Tommy Ward on October 18 for several hours with lie-detector apparatus attached to Ward's body. But in the ensuing questioning, by law, the fact that a polygraph exam had been given could not be mentioned in court. Both sides questioned him, and Feather-stone answered, as if the questioning had been no different from any of the other interviews. Though the agent had told Ward he had failed the polygraph, no evidence to support this, or to undermine it, would be presented in court, or anywhere else.

Featherstone said that Ward had appeared in his office, voluntar-ily, at 10:30 in the morning of October 18, dressed casually in jeans and a short-sleeved shirt. He said Gary Rogers introduced them, and left. At 11:05 he read Ward his rights, Featherstone said. He asked routine questions about Ward's medical history, he said, and then asked what Ward had done on April 28. Ward said he had worked on the plumbing at his house until 9 P.M., then went to Jan-nette Roberts's place, and then to a party at a neighbor's, Gordon Cal-houn. He met Fontenot at the party, and they stayed there till 4 A.M., then left.

The questioning went on for some time, Featherstone said. Then he told Ward that he had the impression Ward was carrying some kind of burden he had to get rid of.

Tommy said he'd had nothing to do with the abduction, Feather-stone said, but that he said he'd had a dream in which he was in-volved. In the dream, the agent quoted Ward as saying, he and Karl had left with the girl, went out to a power station. Titsworth threat-ened to rape the girl. Ward threatened to leave, and he did.

The agent said that soon after, Tommy said he only wished it was a dream, that it had really occurred.

"Mr. Ward seemed to me still not to be relieving himself of what was troubling him—his burden," Featherstone testified. Then, he said, Ward admitted he had stayed for the sexual assault, and de-scribed it in detail.

At that point, Gary Rogers and Dennis Smith entered the room, the agent said. He said it was about two in the afternoon when Ward first said he had been involved. Though he had shown up voluntarily, from that point on Ward was not free to leave.

Bill Peterson prepared to enter the Tommy Ward confession tape into evidence. Wyatt objected. The jury was sent out of the court-room while Judge Powers listened to the arguments. The objections were overruled.

The two video monitors were once again set up in the courtroom. Downstairs, Bud and Tricia were waiting, nervously, in case their turn to testify would come. They knew the tapes were about to roll.

"This is the day we've been hoping for eleven months wouldn't happen," Tricia said.

14

THE TAPES—TOMMY

Tommy Ward's confession tape was admitted into evidence as state exhibit 30. The jury was brought back in. The tension in the courtroom hung like the humidity outside, thick and moist. The lights were dimmed. The tape began to roll. The image of Ward, seated, wearing jeans, tennis sneakers, a yellow and black T-shirt, appeared on the screens, one facing the jury, the other facing the judge. There was not a sound in the courtroom except for the voices coming from the video set.

What follows is the official, unedited transcript of the tape, as it was seen and heard by the jury:

STATEMENT OF TOMMY WARD
QUESTIONS BY AGENT RUSTY FEATHERSTONE:

Q. Okay, Tommy, I've got a few things I need to say first. The date today is October 18, 1984. We are at the headquarters office of the Oklahoma State Bureau of Investigation, located in Oklahoma City. We are currently in my office. I am Deputy Inspector Rusty Featherstone, as you know.

Present also in the room is Special Agent Gary Rogers of the OSBI out of the Ada office; Captain Dennis Smith of the Ada Police Department, detective division; and Agent Dee Cordray of the OSBI here in headquarters in Oklahoma City.

The time currently as is shown on our clock, also, in military time is 1858 hours, or 6:58 P.M. Okay?

Now, we've been at this for some time, talking about an investigation into the disappearance of Donna Denice Haraway from a convenience store in Ada, is that correct?

A. That's correct.

Q. Okay. Now, during the course of our conversation prior to this, have you been given the opportunity to go to the rest room at any time?

A. Yeah.

Q. Okay. Have you been allowed to have anything to drink or to smoke or to eat?

A. Yes.

Q. Okay. With that in mind, I want to remind you that earlier, we also discussed your rights. In other words, your rights as far as the right to having an attorney present while you're being interviewed in this investigation. Do you recall me advising you of your rights earlier—?

A. Yes, sir.

Q. —the Miranda warning?

A. Yeah.

Q. Okay. I'm going to reread those rights to you to help refresh your memory even further, okay?

A. Okay.

Q. My name is Rusty Featherstone, an agent to the Oklahoma State Bureau of Investigation. I wish to advise you that you have an absolute right to remain silent; that anything you say can and will be used against you in a court of law; that you have a right to talk to an attorney before and have an attorney present with you during questioning; that if you cannot afford to hire an attorney, one will be appointed to represent you without charge before any questioning, if you so desire. If you do decide to answer any questions, you may stop at any time you wish. Do you understand all of that?

A. Yeah.

Q. Okay. The next part is a paragraph entitled "Waiver." And in this waiver it states: "I fully understand the statement advising me of my rights, and I'm willing to answer questions. I do not want an attorney, and understand that I may refuse to answer questions any time during the questioning. No promise has been made to me, nor have any threats been made against me." Is that correct?

A. That's correct.

Q. Okay. You're doing this strictly through your own wanting to be voluntary.

A. Uh-huh.

Q. Nobody has coerced you or threatened you in any way.

A. (*Witness indicating affirmatively.*)

Q. You're doing this strictly because you want to tell the truth, is that correct?

A. That's correct.

Q. Okay. And earlier, when I read this form to you, I gave you the opportunity to look it over and to sign it if you agreed with it, is that correct?

A. That's correct.

Q. And did you do so?

A. Yes.

Q. Did you sign it? Okay. All right. What I'd like to do at this point is have you think back to the date we've been talking about, April 28, 1983, [*sic*] involving the investigation of the missing of Donna Denice Haraway from McAnally's—I'm sorry, 1984, 1984—from McAnally's convenience store at 2727 Arlington in Ada, Oklahoma. Okay? And I know we've already talked about it a little bit, but what I'd like for you to do at this point is just start on that afternoon. I think we might as well start with the party that you were attending.

A. Uh-huh.

Q. And then what happened, who you left with; and just in your own words at your own speed, I want you to go step by step through everything that happened to the rest of that evening involving this girl, okay?

A. Okay.

Q. Just go ahead and begin. Feel free to drink your Coke or have a cigarette as you talk—

A. Okay.

Q. —whatever makes you feel more comfortable.

A. Okay. All right. On—do I start with the date?

Q. That's fine.

A. All right. On—what—the 28th of April—

Q. Uh-huh.

A. April—me and—

Q. Do you recall the day of the week?

A. It was a Saturday.

Q. Saturday? Okay, that's fine. Go ahead.

A. Okay. I was at a keg party and I ran into a couple of guys that I hadn't seen in a long time. And one of them's name was Titsdale, and he asked me if I wanted to go riding around with them and go get high and drink some beer. And I told him sure. And so we went riding around, and went out by—

Q. Tommy, excuse me. Before you get into your story, now, you said Titsdale, now—

A. —Titsworth.

Q. Okay. What's his first name?

A. I can't recall it.

Q. Is it Odell?

A. Odell Titsworth.

Q. All right. And who was the other person besides Odell Titsworth?

A. Karl Fontenot.

Q. Karl Fontenot?

A. Uh-huh.

Q. Okay. Now, I'm going to ask you, if you would, to speak up while you're telling your story so we can hear.

A. Okay. And so they asked me to go riding around and get high and do some drinking with them. And so we went riding around and we went out by the Evangelistic Temple. And we was sitting out at the Evangelistic Temple where we got high and drank. After we got through drinking and all, Titsworth, he was asking me about going to—if I knew where a place was where we could get some money. And I told him about McAnally's, that a while back I heard that there was a robbery out there and that there was a large sum of money taken from out there. I said, "If you want to rob any place, that would be the place to rob." And so we started going out there, and we got out there and we went in. And Titsworth started throwing stuff around and she come out from behind the counter and he grabbed her and pushed her over to me. And I grabbed her and—put her arm around behind my back—I mean, behind her back. And I started to walk out the door with her. And Titsworth, he grabbed money out of the register. And we went out to the pickup.

Q. Okay, Tommy. Let me slow you down just a little bit, okay?

A. Okay.

Q. Let me back up and ask you one thing. Now, you say "her," okay?

A. Uh-huh.

Q. Who are we talking about when you say "her"?

A. Haraway.

Q. Haraway?

A. Uh-huh.

Q. Okay. Did you know her prior to this particular day?

A. Yes, I've seen her—my ex-girlfriend used to work out there.

Q. At the same store?

A. Yeah.

Q. Okay. And this is the McAnally's I referred to earlier, at 2727 Arlington in Ada?

A. Yes, sir.

Q. Okay.

A. And so I walked out with her, and we went out to the pickup. And Titsdale was—grabbed her from me, and they walked around. And I got in the pickup and Karl Fontenot got in the back of the pickup. And she was sitting in the middle. And Titsworth, he was driving. So we left there and went out around Richardson Loop to the power plant by Reeves' Packing Plant.

Q. Okay. Tommy, why did you take this girl with you?

A. Just because we didn't want her to identify us.

Q. Was this discussed prior to going into the store?

A. Yes.

Q. By who?

A. By Titsworth.

Q. What was said?

A. He said that we'd go in and get the money and leave, and I didn't have any idea that we was going to take her with us until he said that she could identify us. And I didn't think that they was going to do any harm to her, you know. But—

Q. What did he say he was going to do with her?

A. He told me that he was going to kill her after we got out to the power plant.

Q. This is while you were in the store?

A. No, when we was out at the power plant.

Q. Okay. But anyway, you took her from the store, apparently, because you thought she could be a witness?

A. Uh-huh.

QUESTIONS BY AGENT GARY ROGERS:

Q. Did she ever say anything at the store?

A. No.

Q. Did she say anything when you—who told her it was a robbery?

A. Titsworth.

Q. Okay. Who was the first person in the store?

A. Titsworth.

Q. Did he have any kind of weapon?

A. Yes, he had a knife.

Q. What kind of knife was it?

A. It was a lock-blade he carried on his side.

Q. About how long was the blade?

A. It was about this long (*indicating*), about six inches long.

Q. About a six-inch blade, lock-blade pocket knife?

A. Uh-huh.

Q. So he went in first and started throwing stuff around, is that correct?

A. Uh-huh, yes, sir.

Q. And you went in behind him?

A. Yes, sir.

Q. And at that point she came out around the counter to keep him from—what kind of stuff was he throwing around in the store?

A. It was the potato chips and stuff that was on the aisle, the side aisle right when you go in the door.

Q. Okay, so she came out around the counter.

A. —to draw her attention away from the counter, you know, around to where he was at.

Q. He grabbed her—

A. Uh-huh.

Q. —shoved her to you.

A. Uh-huh.

Q. You twisted her arm up behind her back and—

A. Yes, sir.

Q. Did she [start] saying anything then?

A. No, she was—well, she was asking what's going on and she was scared and everything. And Titsdale, he told me that we was going to take her with us. And so I stood there in the door with her until he got the money out of the cash register. And I started walking out the door with her and then that's when he come up beside me and grabbed her. And we went on out to the pickup and he put her in the pickup.

Q. All right. Where was the pickup parked when you got there?

A. It was out by the gas pumps.

Q. Between the gas pumps and the front door?

A. Uh-huh.

Q. Which way was it facing?

A. It was facing toward the east.

Q. Toward the east. All right. When you all got in the pickup and Fontenot got in the back of the pickup, you took out east on Arlington?

A. No, we went back west on Arlington.

Q. You just cut through the median there—

A. Yeah.

Q. —and then turned back west on Arlington?

A. Uh-huh.

Q. Where did you go from there?

A. Out to the power plant.

Q. I mean, what route did you take?

A. Richardson Loop.

Q. Okay. So in other words, you went down Arlington, west on Arlington to Mississippi?

A. Mississippi.

Q. Then back north on Mississippi to Richardson Loop?

A. Uh-huh.

Q. Then back west past the Holiday Inn and Wal-Mart—

A. Uh-huh.

Q. —on the Richardson Loop.

A. Uh-huh.

Q. Around the bypass and you dropped off on Reeves Road?

A. On Reeves Road.

Q. Okay. And then what happened?

A. Then turned back up right to the power plant.

Q. You went up to the power plant—

A. And went to the power plant and stopped up there. And I got out—

QUESTIONS BY AGENT FEATHERSTONE:

Q. Why did you go out there, Tommy?

A. Huh?

Q. Why did you go to the power plant?

A. I don't know. It's—Titsdale was driving and we pulled over up there.

Q. Whose idea was it to go out there?

A. I guess it was his, you know, we went on out there.

Q. He knew how to find his way out there?

A. Yeah.

Q. Okay. Was there any discussion in the pickup on the way out there, anybody talking?

A. No, not much, because he had the stereo up loud and all, and he—she was asking him what was going on, and he kept on telling her to keep her mouth shut.

Q. Okay.

QUESTIONS BY AGENT ROGERS:

   Q. Was she hit any time in the pickup?

   A. Yes, he slapped her a couple of times.

   Q. Who is he?

   A. Titsworth.

   Q. Titsworth?

   A. Uh-huh.

   Q. Where was he hitting her at?

   A. On the side of the face. And then we got out to the power plant and got out, and I told him that it was a crazy deal, you know, in doing this, and that I didn't want to have any part to do with it. And so he got her out of the pickup. And then they walked around to the back of the pickup with Karl Fontenot and put the tailgate down and Titsworth started taking her clothing off. And—

   Q. What did he take off first?

   A. He dropped her britches down and blouse—

   Q. What kind of britches was she wearing?

   A. Blue jeans.

   Q. All right. Did she have underwear on?

   A. Yes.

   Q. Did he take them completely off of her?

   A. Yes.

   Q. What did he do with them?

   A. He laid them on the side—on the ground beside the pickup. Just left them laying on the ground beside the pickup.

   Q. Left them on the ground by the pickup?

   A. Uh-huh.

   Q. Then what happened, what did he start to do?

   A. And then he started to rape her. And—

   Q. Did—you said something earlier—

   A. —she started to struggle.

   Q. You said something earlier about taking her blouse?

   A. Uh-huh, he undone her blouse right here (*indicating*). Her blouse was still on her until—

   Q. Did she have a bra on?

   A. Yes.

Q. What did he do with it?

A. He took it off later, after I was biting her on the tit.

Q. Okay. So you're saying that Titsworth took her pants and her jeans off.

A. Uh-huh.

Q. Undone her blouse.

A. Uh-huh.

Q. And then he proceeded to do what?

A. He proceeded to rape her.

Q. He started to rape her.

A. Uh-huh.

Q. What did she do?

A. She was screaming and everything, and he was telling her to keep her mouth shut. And he started slapping around on her. And then he pulled his knife out and cut her on the side a little bit, and told her that if she kept on struggling, that he was going to kill her.

Q. Okay. Where were you standing?

A. I was standing behind her and—

Q. What were you doing?

A. I was holding her head down. I was holding her by her hair of her head and I was sitting in the back of the pickup.

Q. Where was Fontenot?

A. He was standing beside the pickup, laughing.

Q. He was standing beside the pickup, laughing?

A. Uh-huh.

Q. Was he holding her in any way?

A. No, he wasn't holding her. He was just watching. And then after Titsworth got through, he told me that it was my turn. And I told him that I didn't want sloppy seconds. And he handed me the knife and everything, and I started teasing around with her and all and that I was going to rape her and, you know, just to show, you know, that Titsworth and Karl— that, you know, that I could do it and—but I was so drunk, that when I did try to rape her, that I couldn't rape her.

Q. Okay. So you pulled your jeans down and your shorts down?

A. Uh-huh.

Q. And you tried to have intercourse with her?

A. Yes, sir.

Q. But you couldn't achieve an erection, is that what you're saying?

A. Yes, sir.

Q. And so how long did you attempt to have sexual intercourse with her?

A. I tried about two minutes, and she started struggling. And she got away from me and took off running east, kind of going back toward town. And I took off running after her and caught up with her.

Q. How far did she get?

A. About thirty-five, forty foot. She didn't get too far.

Q. Did you have your britches completely down, or how did you do this?

A. No, I just had them down about halfway down my legs. And—

Q. When she took off running, what did you do, pull your britches up?

A. I pulled them back up and took off running back after her.

Q. Did she run—?

A. And I caught up with her and knocked her down on the ground and then started biting her on the tit. And then she—

Q. Did you tell her anything when you were biting her on the breast? Did you tell her something?

A. I told her that I was wanting to make love to her, that—

Q. Did you tell her something about if she didn't quit struggling, you was going to do something?

A. I said if she didn't quit struggling and everything, that I was going to bite her tit off.

Q. And then what happened?

A. And then Karl and Titsworth come up and started grabbing her and I got off of her. And then they walked back up to the pickup with her. And then that's when Karl started to (*inaudible*). And then—

Q. When he started doing what?

A. He started to make love to her.

Q. He started having intercourse with her?

A. Intercourse with her.

Q. Karl Fontenot?

A. Yeah.

Q. What was she doing then?

A. She was still struggling and everything. And then Titsworth, he was holding her while Karl was hitting her. And then—

Q. What were you doing?

A. He was holding her. I went back over and I was standing by the pickup and telling them that it's crazy and everything, and that I was going to the house. And then I went down to the house and I stayed at my house for about fifteen or twenty minutes. And then I was kind of worried about, what if they just left her up there, laying on the ground. And so I walked back up there and they were still there. And—

QUESTIONS BY AGENT FEATHERSTONE:

Q. Why were you worried that they were going to leave her up there?

A. Oh, I just was afraid that they was going to leave her there.

Q. Because she could identify you?

A. Uh-huh. Or if they did kill her and everything and left her body there.

Q. Tommy, you said earlier that you knew this girl. At the time that you were attempting to rape her, were you angry with her?

A. Yes, I was upset because she was laughing about my ex-girlfriend and me breaking up.

Q. (*By Agent Rogers*) Did you hold her responsible for breaking you and your girlfriend up?

A. No, I was just—I was thinking about it.

Q. When you went to tackle her, when she broke and ran, what happened to the knife? Did you have the knife before she broke and ran?

A. Yeah, and she—I just dropped it and Titsdale picked it back up because I—

Q. (*By Agent Rogers*) Titsdale or Titsworth?

A. Titsworth, excuse me.

Q. Okay. Did you touch her with that knife?

A. Yes, sir.

Q. What did you do?

A. I cut her a little bit on the side and across her arm.

Q. Was this while—

A. Just some scratches.

Q. —you were trying to get an erection?

A. Yes.

Q. Before she broke and ran?

A. Uh-huh. And then—

Q. Then when she ran, you had to pull your pants up and that's when you dropped the knife?

A. Yeah, and Titsworth picked it up. And I went and caught up with her and got her down on the ground and started struggling with her.

Q. That's when you bit her.

QUESTIONS BY AGENT ROGERS:

Q. Did you hit her?

A. Huh?

Q. Did you hit her, when you were biting her, did you hit her?

A. Not with my fist; I slapped her. I was slapping her, and then—

Q. Where were you slapping her at?

A. On her face. And then I started biting her on the tit. And then I was holding her down, and then that's when Titsworth and Karl come up and started pulling me off of her. And then Titsworth kept on calling her a bitch and everything, and grabbed her up and he started walking back toward the pickup with her.

Q. Once you got her back up to the pickup?

A. Uh-huh. And then that's when Karl started on her.

Q. He started raping her?

A. Uh-huh.

Q. Was she still alive then?

A. Yes, sir.

Q. How do you know she was still alive?

A. She was still moving around, crying and everything.

Q. Okay. And then, you say, Titsworth was holding her down?

A. Uh-huh.

Q. Was her head in the bed of the pickup, and her legs hanging off the tailgate, is that the way she was?

A. Yeah. And then Karl started with her and then—

QUESTIONS BY AGENT FEATHERSTONE:

Q. Who had the knife at that point?

A. Titsworth.

Q. What was he doing with it?

A. He was cutting on her side—on her side and on her—that's where he—when he cut her on the side of the throat.

Q. He was cutting her while Karl was raping her?

A. Uh-huh.

Q. Why was he cutting her?

A. I don't know. He just kept on calling her a bitch and kept on telling her that she shouldn't have tried to run.

QUESTIONS BY AGENT ROGERS:

Q. Was he hitting her or anything?

A. Uh-huh, he was slapping her with the back of his hand and stuff. And Karl told him to quit. And he goes, "Wait until I get through." And then that's when I went down to the house.

Q. All right. How long were you gone? How come you went down to your house?

A. Because I told him I wasn't going to take any more of it, you know, that I didn't want to rape her or anything.

Q. How long were you down at your house?

A. I was down there about twenty minutes.

Q. And then what did you do?

A. I walked back up there because I was afraid that they might have killed her and just dumped her out right there, you know.

Q. When you got down to your house, did you notice if you had any blood or anything on you?

A. No, I didn't notice that.

Q. All right. And then you went back up—you stayed at the house about twenty minutes, and then you went back up to the pickup where they were at. What was going on when you got back up to the pickup?

A. Karl was still raping her, and she had tremendous cuts all over her.

Q. All right. Where were all the cuts that you can remember at?

A. Mostly in the stomach, around in the stomach, and on her legs. She had a couple of cuts on her legs.

Q. Did Karl have his clothes off?

A. Yeah.

Q. All of them?

A. Uh-huh. And then I knew that she was dead because she was white.

Q. Was she moving?

A. No.

Q. Breathing?

A. I didn't see any breathing or anything.

Q. What was Titsworth doing?

A. He was sitting—well, he was standing right beside the pickup and leaning over the side of the bed of the pickup laughing at him, and saying, "You're raping a corpse."

Q. He—

A. And then that's when he stopped.

Q. Was he still trying to hold her down?

A. Uh-huh.

Q. Titsworth?

A. No, Karl.

Q. He was just leaning over the bed of the pickup?

A. Yeah.

Q. And he told him what?

A. He was telling him that he was raping a corpse.

Q. And did Fontenot say anything after he told him that?

A. No, he jumped up off of her and said that—he said that he liked it better that way.

Q. Fontenot said he liked it better that way—

A. Uh-huh.

Q. —when they were dead?

A. Uh-huh.

Q. And then what happened?

A. And then he told me that we had to get rid of her and all, and asked me a good place to get rid of her. And I told him about a house and about this ditch down by the Sandy River.

Q. Okay. Now, where was this house and this ditch you were talking about located from where you all were at, at that point in time?

A. The house was west of us—

Q. About—

A. —about a quarter of a mile.

Q. About a quarter of a mile west?

A. Yeah. And the ditch down—I can't think of what they—I called it.

Q. Concrete bunkers?

A. Yeah, it was a concrete bunker. And I told them where that was at. And he asked me to come back—come down there and show them where it was at. And I told them that I had to get back to the house because I was afraid, and that I didn't want to have anything else to do with it. And so I started to go back down to the house and I helped them put it—put her up on Titsdale's shoulder, and then Karl got around the front and was carrying her legs, and they started walking off down toward the woods. And I went on home.

QUESTIONS BY AGENT FEATHERSTONE:

Q. Where were her clothes at this point?

A. They put them back on her.

Q. All of them?

A. Uh-huh. And then, when they was walking off toward the woods and everything, I went back to the house. And then I didn't see them for the next couple of days.

Q. Did you notice anything about your own appearance when you got back to the house?

A. No, I—

QUESTIONS BY AGENT ROGERS:

Q. Was there anything unusual? Did you have anything on you?

A. I had some blood on my arms from her, and I washed it off.

Q. How did you get the blood on your arm?

A. It was from when I was trying to rape her. And then when I found out that I couldn't rape her, and all, that's when she was struggling and got away from me.

Q. Okay. So what you're saying, the last time you saw them was after you helped put the main portion of her upper body on Titsworth's shoulders—

A. Uh-huh.

Q. —and Fontenot came around in front of him and picked up her legs and they were walking west from where the pickup was at, down toward the road that leads down to the house?

A. Yeah, down toward the—

Q. To the Sandy Creek?

A. Sandy Creek, down there.

Q. Okay. So—

A. And so I don't know which way they took her. And then a couple of days after I seen them and all, he—Karl told me that they took her down to that bunker down there by Sandy, threw her off in it.

Q. What else did they tell you?

A. He told me that if I said anything about it and all that he'd come after me and kill me.

Q. Now, who told you that?

A. Titsworth.

Q. How much money was taken?

A. I don't know.

Q. Did you receive any of the money?

A. No.

Q. Do you know if Karl Fontenot got any of the money?

A. No, I don't know if he did or not, but I know I didn't because I was broke and the next day I had to bum some money off my mother to go get some cigarettes.

Q. Did you see Titsworth with any of the money?

A. Yes, I seen him when he was putting it into his billfold, when we was at the store.

Q. You mean he took time out during this armed robbery to take his billfold out and put the money in it out of the cash register?

A. Uh-huh, he had his billfold out and put the money—the bills in his—

QUESTIONS BY AGENT FEATHERSTONE:

Q. Did he put all the money in his billfold?

A. Yeah, the bills.

Q. How much money would you estimate—was there a lot of money or a little bitty stack of money or could you—

A. No, it was a small stack. Not too awful much. But I know it wasn't—it was more than a hundred dollars, I knew that, you know. I knew that just by looking at, you know, the stack and everything, I knew that there was (*inaudible*) money.

Q. Did he take anything else away from the store that you're aware of?

A. No, that was it, just the money—

Q. Any beer, cigarettes, any of her personal possessions?

A. No.

Q. How long would you estimate you all were inside the store?

A. About two minutes.

Q. Did anybody drive up during any of this time that you all were in the store?

A. I seen one car. It was pulled up by the ice box out there and telephone.

Q. Did anybody get out?

A. No. They just pulled up when we was getting ready to leave.

QUESTIONS BY DENNIS SMITH:

Q. Tommy, how far do you live from the power plant where Denice Haraway was killed?

A. I live about—I'll estimate about two blocks. It ain't too far at all.

Q. Okay. Are you familiar—

A. Across the highway.

Q. —with the area, then?

A. Yes, sir.

Q. The house and the bunkers where she was left?

A. Uh-huh.

Q. Why are you familiar with that area?

A. I've lived there all my life and I used to go hunting down there a lot.

Q. Did Denice Haraway, did she ask you all, did she beg you all not to hurt her or—

A. Yes.

Q. —what did she say when all this was happening?

A. She was asking *her* to—if we'd let her go and she wouldn't say anything. And Titsworth, he wouldn't let her go.

Q. What did he say to her?

A. He said that he was going to rape her. And that's when he started to rape her.

Q. Where was the first place that she was cut with the knife?

A. In her side, down the side—is where Titsworth cut her. When he started to rape her, he goes, "If you don't cooperate with me and everything," he says, "I'll cut you deeper."

Q. So it wasn't—the first cut wasn't really that deep?

A. No.

QUESTIONS BY AGENT ROGERS:

Q. All right. When you came back up from your house and you saw the body laying in the back of the pickup, tell us about the cuts that you observed then.

A. She had tremendous cuts all over her body, all in her sides and on her legs.

Q. Were they deep cuts?

A. And on the side of her neck. Yeah, the ones in her stomach was.

Q. How could you tell they were deep cuts?

A. I could see her ribs and her insides and her intestines.

Q. Was there much blood?

A. Yes, there was quite a bit of blood.

Q. And was Fontenot raping her, did she have those cuts on her at that time when he was having sexual intercourse with her?

A. Yes, sir. And then he took the knife, after he got through raping her and everything, after Karl did, and then took and stabbed her again.

Q. Where did he stab her at?

A. He stabbed her in—just right up above the deep cut, and made another deep cut, and that's when I could see her ribs. And he goes, "I'll make sure the bitch is dead."

QUESTIONS BY AGENT FEATHERSTONE:

Q. Tommy, were there any other knives out there, other than the one that Titsworth had?

A. No.

Q. Were there any other weapons that you know of of any type, like guns or clubs?

A. No, just the knife.

Q. Do you believe that she died due to any other reason other than the stab wounds?

A. No, that's what she died of, the stab wounds.

Q. Can you tell me what her blouse looked like that she was wearing?

A. It was—it was white with little blue roses on it, I think, blue roses.

QUESTIONS BY AGENT ROGERS:

Q. It had roses on it?

A. Uh-huh.

Q. You'll have to speak up just a little bit—

A. I believe that's what it was, little roses.

Q. So it was a white blouse. Button-up or slip-on?

A. It's button-up.

Q. Did it have buttons on the collar?

A. Uh-huh.

Q. Or would it be just a regular collar?

A. It had buttons on the collars and then it had little fringe deals around her collar and around the end of her arm, end of the sleeves.

Q. By little fringe, do you mean a lace kind of deal?

A. Yeah, uh-huh.

Q. So it had lace on the sleeves, and lace on the collar?

A. Collar.

Q. And it was a floral-type pattern, flowers on her shirt.

A. Yeah.

Q. And what kind of britches did she have on?

A. She had blue jeans.

Q. How about the type of shoes she had on?

A. I don't know. I didn't recognize the shoes—

Q. Do you know if they took anything off the body?

A. No, I don't, not besides her clothes.

Q. Did you—

A. And I don't remember seeing her with a ring or watch or anything, any kind of jewelry or anything on.

QUESTIONS BY AGENT FEATHERSTONE:

Q. Tommy, I think you said earlier you know her personally, is that correct?

A. Yes, sir.

Q. There's no doubt in your mind who that girl was that night, is that correct?

A. Yes, sir, uh-huh.

Q. Okay. Did she recognize you at any time during the night?

A. Yes, she recognized me when I had her down on the ground and everything.

Q. What did she say? How do you know she knew who you were?

A. She told me to leave her alone, that—and she called me by my name. She goes, "Tommy, I didn't think you'd ever do anything like this." And that's when it stunned me, and I went home.

QUESTIONS BY DENNIS SMITH:

Q. How many times did you cut her with the knife, Tommy?

A. Twice, once on her side and once on her arm. They was just little scratches. I wasn't meaning, you know, to do any harm to her.

Q. Was the knife sharp?

A. No, it was a pretty dull knife.

Q. (GR) How long did you try to have sexual intercourse with her?

A. About five minutes, and then I couldn't. And so she started struggling around and she got away from me. And when she got away from me, I dropped the knife and ran after her because I wasn't wanting to hurt her.

Q. Was anyone holding her while you were trying to have sex with her?

A. No, because I was—I had her down by myself—

Q. Where did you have her at?

A. Titsworth, he had her—his hand on her shoulder, but, you know, she wasn't struggling all that much because she knew that I wasn't wanting to.

Q. Were you on the ground, or were you in the back of the pickup?

A. We was in the back of the pickup, on the tailgate.

QUESTIONS BY AGENT ROGERS:

Q. You said earlier that you noticed when you came back up a large amount of blood. Where all was she bleeding from?

A. Mostly in her side from where the deep cut was.

Q. And where else?

A. On the side of her neck, right here (*indicating*).

Q. Any other areas?

A. On her legs and between her legs.

Q. So in her vaginal area, she was bleeding there, too?

A. Uh-huh.

Q. Was that from the cuts on her legs or—

A. No, I thought it was from him raping her. I don't know if he stabbed her or not there. I knew she was bleeding.

Q. (DS) What county did that happen in, Tommy?

A. Pontotoc.

Q. Once again, Tommy, I want to reiterate. Have any of the people present here or anybody during the course of any part of your interview today, promised you anything?

A. No.

Q. Have we threatened you in any way?

A. No.

Q. Did we try to coerce you in any way?

A. No.

Q. You are giving this statement of your own free will?

A. Yes, sir.

Q. Is there anything else that you'd like to add to this tape recording, prior to us shutting it off?

A. I knew I wouldn't have done it if I wasn't drunk, because I thought it was just a dream. And I know me, and I know I wouldn't do anything like that at all. It wasn't me.

Q. (DS) Tommy, how much education do you have?

A. Up to eleventh grade.

Q. (DS) Can you read and write?

A. Some. I have problems with a lot of words. I can't read or can't write them.

Q. Are you currently working now?

A. Yes, sir, every day.

Q. What are you doing?

A. I work for All-Siding.

Q. For All-Siding?

A. Uh-huh, in Oklahoma City.

Q. How long have you worked for them?

A. I've worked there about two weeks now.

Q. Steady?

A. Uh-huh.

Q. Have you had any problems on the job?

A. No, sir.

Q. What does your job require you to do?

A. Put siding on the side of people's houses.

Q. All right. What does that entail, what do you have to do to do it?

A. You've got to—well, like, you know, when we go pick up the materials and—

Q. Yeah.

A. —we go pick up materials at Forrest, and we take it out to people's house. And then we have to cut patterns and everything for the sides of the house and we cover the gables. And some of the houses we cover the whole house.

Q. Take measurements?

A. Yeah.

Q. All that?

A. Uh-huh.

Q. Are you a pretty good hand with them?

A. Yes, sir.

Q. Do you enjoy your job?

A. Yes, sir, I do. Before that I was working for Winningham Siding. I worked for him for about six months.

Q. And did you basically do the same job for Winningham Siding that you do for All-Siding?

A. Yes, sir. Besides they got—they're metal for the window frames and for the facer metal that goes around the facer. And they bend it theirselves at All-Siding, and they didn't at Winningham.

Q. So they've got equipment that—

A. Uh-huh.

Q. Can you operate this equipment?

A. No, I don't operate it or anything. The guys at the shop do. And when we was working for Winningham, when we had to bend it ourselves, Mike, the guy I was working for, he bent it.

Q. So you know how to do that stuff?

A. Yeah, uh-huh.

AGENT ROGERS: Can anybody think of anything else?

QUESTIONS BY AGENT FEATHERSTONE:

Q. Tommy, the only thing I want to make clear at this point, Agent Rogers mentioned that this was being taped. You are aware this is being videotaped, there's a camera directly in front of you in plain sight, is that correct?

A. Yes, sir.

Q. Okay. And there's also a tape recorder taking an audiotape of this same conversation, is that correct?

A. Yes, sir.

Q. Okay. Have you said anything here on this tape that was against your will?

A. No.

Q. Okay. Are you confused about any of this today, or do you understand what's going on?

A. Yes, I understand what's going on.

Q. Okay. You understand how serious this investigation is?

A. Yes, I do.

AGENT FEATHERSTONE: Okay. We'll end the tape at this time. I've got 7:29 P.M., and we'll conclude the tape now.

Still present in the room: Deputy Inspector Rusty Featherstone, Special Agent Gary Rogers, Captain Dennis Smith, and Agent Dee Cordray, as well as Tommy Ward.

When the tape ended, the lights were turned back on. Cinda Haraway, in the second row, had tears in her eyes. So did several gray-haired women spectators. Most sat impassive; as did the jury. The silence of a cemetery filled the room.

Judge Powers ordered a brief recess while the video equipment was taken down.

At 3:10 P.M., Agent Rusty Featherstone resumed the witness chair, for cross-examination. Don Wyatt pointed out that Ward on the tape described three people at McAnally's, whereas the eyewitnesses had seen only one, that Ward told of bags of chips being tossed around, whereas the eyewitnesses had seen no mess.

Wyatt asked why no tape machine had been turned on from 2 P.M., when Ward supposedly first said he was involved, until 6:58 P.M., five hours later. Featherstone indicated the procedure was to wait till the suspect was prepared to make a full statement.

He said Ward told of his dream between 1:30 and 2, and that Featherstone then told Gary Rogers the details of Tommy's "dream." He said he did not recall if he had discussed the details of the dream with Dennis Smith. He conceded that from 10:30 to 1:30 Ward had been questioned without a break, and had denied any involvement, until the agent told Tommy he needed to unburden himself, and Tommy told of his dream. At that time, he said, the questioning by himself and Gary Rogers had changed from "inquisitory" to "accusatory."

"You never accused him of lying?" George Butner asked.

"No," the agent said.

15

THE TAPES—KARL

Gary Rogers took the stand, an OSBI agent for nine years, the official formally in charge of the investigation, slim, dapper, as always. He told how, during the questioning of Ward, he made three phone calls to Ada, giving Mike Baskin three different areas to search for the body: the power plant region, the burned-out house, the concrete bunker. He said that after the tape was made, Ward was placed under arrest and returned to Ada. Rogers went to the burned-out house; Ada police, working with floodlights in the night, were digging through the rubble, sifting the dirt with screens.

He was asked about some of the names the defense had mentioned during various cross-examinations. He said the name Randy Rogers had come up in early May; that not a great deal was known about Bob Sparcino. He was asked why he thought Jason Lurch might have attended all of the preliminary hearing. He said Lurch's father-in-law was raised near where the Wards lived; he assumed they were friends.

The questioning turned to Fontenot. Rogers told how Karl was arrested in Hominy on October 19, and taken to the Ada police station. He was brought to Rogers's office about 1:30 P.M. The agent said he advised Fontenot of his rights, and then questioned him, in the presence of Detective Captain Smith.

George Butner approached the bench. He spoke to the judge. The jury was sent from the court. Butner argued against the introduction of Fontenot's taped statement.

"Overruled," Judge Powers said.

The jury returned. Rogers said he and Smith had questioned Fontenot from 1:30 to 3:15 before the video machine was turned on. He said that for the first fifteen minutes Karl denied any involvement in the disappearance of Denice Haraway; then he began to confess.

It was 4:55 P.M. Once more the lights in the courtroom went dark. Once more an image came on the two screens, this time of Karl Fontenot. Again there was absolute silence in the courtroom as the voices spoke from the tape.

What follows is the complete transcript of the Fontenot tape, as it was seen and heard by the jury:

(Q indicates questions by Gary Rogers; Q* indicates questions by Dennis Smith.)

Q. This tape is being made on October the 19th, 1984. The tape is starting at 3:15 P.M. The tape is being made at the Oklahoma State Bureau of Investigation office in Ada, Oklahoma. The people present, Special Agent Gary Rogers of the Oklahoma State Bureau of Investigation, Ada Police Department Detective Captain Dennis Smith, and Karl Fontenot.

The purpose of this tape is a statement being given by Karl Fontenot regarding the Donna Denice Haraway case.

All right, Karl, to start out with, I want to advise you of your Miranda warning. You have the right to remain silent; anything you say can and will be used against you in a court of law; you have the right to talk to a lawyer and have him present while you are being questioned; if you cannot afford to hire a lawyer, one will be appointed to represent you before any questioning if you wish one; if you do decide to make a statement, you may stop at any time. Do you understand each of these rights I've explained to you?

A. Yes, I do.

Q. All right. Having these rights in mind, do you wish to talk to us now?

A. Yes.

Q. Okay. To start out with, Karl, are you giving this statement of your own accord, freely and voluntarily?

A. Yes.

Q. Okay. Let's start from the beginning, and just go back to the date of April the 28th, 1984, in the late afternoon or early evening hours when you and Tommy Ward and Odell Titsworth were at a party. And just start from the beginning and tell me in your own words what happened.

A. Okay. After the party, got in Odell's truck. Went out from north of town. As we was going to McAnally's, we stopped there at the apartments and decided to smoke some pot and get high and everything, and we drank some. Then when we got—we planned it out before we got there. And then, when we got there, Odell set it up for us and everything. He took her out of the store, brought her to the truck.

Q.* Where were you all at then, Karl?

A. Right there by the gas pumps.

Q.* Okay. You and—

A. Me and Tommy was standing beside the gas—on the other side of the gas pumps by the passenger door.

Q.* Okay. Were you between the pickup and the—

A. And the gas pumps, right. And then after that, Odell forced her around to the other side—or Odell forced her into our side. She got in; then me and Tommy got in. And after that, we drove away from there. Drove down, went out behind the plant—

Q.* Which plant are you talking about, now?

A. The one out—right off the bypass.

Q. The power plant?

A. Yes.

Q. Just off the bypass on Reeves Road?

A. Off the bypass, yeah. We got there. We parked there. Odell ripped her clothes off of her, holding her down while I raped her.

Q.* Who raped her first?

A. Odell. Well, Odell raped her first.

Q.* Okay. Whenever you got to the power plant, Karl, who got out of the pickup first?

A. Odell.

Q.* All right. And you and Tommy Ward—

A. Me and Tommy got out after that.

Q.* Where was Denice Haraway at that time?

A. At the time that me and Tommy got out?

Q.* Yes.

A. She was with us.

Q.* Okay. So you all got her out of the truck with you?

A. Yes. As we was getting out of the truck, she got out, too.

Q.* Did she get out, too, or did you all—

A. We forced her out.

Q.* Forced her out of the pickup? Whose pickup were you in?

A. Odell's.

Q.* Odell Titsworth's?

A. That I know of.

Q.* Okay.

A. It was his.

Q.* What kind of pickup was that?

A. It was a Chevrolet, standard.

Q.* Was it a new pickup or a—

A. It was old.

Q.* Old pickup?

A. It was used.

Q.* All right. So all of you got out of the pickup.

A. Yeah.

Q.* You and Tommy had a hold of Donna Denice Haraway.

A. While Odell—

Q.* Okay. Did Odell come around and get her or—

A. He come around to the other side.

Q.* Of the pickup?

A. Yes, and met me and Tommy right there with her. And then he put her in the back of the truck, slung her in the back of the truck.

Q.* How did he—

A. First I let the tailgate down.

Q.* How did he get her or did he—

A. Grabbed by around the arms.

Q.* Okay. Did he pick her up or—

A. He more or less made her—we forced her around the truck.

I let the tailgate down on the truck, on Odell's truck. He put her in the back of the truck.

Q.* What was she saying all this time?

A. She was screaming, you know, trying to get away from us.

Q.* Was she scared?

A. She was scared.

Q.* What was she saying?

A. She was hollering for help. And then there wasn't nobody around for her to help.

Q.* Okay. Was she begging you all not to hurt her?

A. Yes, she was more or less begging us. And then we wasn't going for what she was saying.

Q.* What was she saying?

A. She was telling us not to rape her, not to do anything to hurt her.

Q.* Or what?

A. Or we would regret it.

Q.* Okay. What did you all say to her?

A. We told her just to be calm with us and we'd be calm with her.

Q.* Did anyone have a weapon on them?

A. Odell.

Q.* What kind of weapon did he have?

A. He had a pocket knife.

Q.* What kind of pocket knife was it?

A. I would say a Buck or a case.

Q.* Lock-blade type?

A. It was lock-blade, one-blade knife.

Q.* Show me about how long the knife was with it open.

A. With it open? About like that (*indicating*). The blade was about five inches.

Q.* Okay.

A. The handle was about four.

Q.* All right. Did it appear to be a sharp knife or a dull knife?

A. It was sharp.

Q. Did he carry it on a scabbard on his belt?

A. Yes.

Q. Is that how he carried it? Did he—

A. Yes, he carried it on his belt in a black case. And then when he got his knife out and everything, he had his knife out and—

Q.* Why did he get his knife out?

A. To punish her if she tried to get away.

Q.* How was he going to punish her with it?

A. I suppose, cut her.

Q.* Did he ever stick the knife up to her and—

A. Yes, he put the knife—

Q.* —tell her that he was going to hurt her?

A. —up to her.

Q.* What did he say?

A. He told her that if she didn't cooperate with us, that he would hurt her.

Q.* Okay. Did she cooperate then, or was she still screaming?

A. She wasn't screaming as much. She was moving around, trying to fight.

Q.* Okay. So did you all—

A. Me and—

Q.* Did Odell ask you all to help him, or—

A. No. Me and Tommy holded her down, and Odell raped her.

Q.* Where did you hold her down at?

A. I holded her right arm, and Tommy was about in the middle of her.

Q.* Okay. Where was Denice Haraway at?

A. She was laying in the back of the truck, her head up towards the front.

Q.* All right. Was her legs completely in the truck?

A. They was completely in the truck with the tailgate open.

Q.* All right. And what was Odell Titsworth doing?

A. He was raping her while me and Tommy was holding her.

Q.* Did he take his clothes off?

A. He started taking his off first and then started tearing hers off. He started with her shirt and tore her shirt off, tore her bra off. Then he pulled her britches off and everything. He left her shoes on and stuff. And then he raped her.

Q. What kind of shirt did she have on? Was it a pullover type or button-up type, Karl?

A. Button-up.

Q. Did it have anything that you noticed about it, as far as any designs or—

A. Just the ruffles around the buttons and sleeves. The sleeves had elastic like in them.

Q. Was it a short-sleeved shirt?

A. Yes, it was short-sleeved.

Q. Did it have any lace around the collar?

A. Yes, it had ruffles around the collar like the front.

Q.* Okay. So Odell Titsworth crawled up inside the pickup.

A. Yes.

Q.* And lay on top of her and raped her.

A. While me and Tommy was holding her down.

Q.* Was she protesting that?

A. She was telling him not to.

Q.* What was—

A. She was more or less telling him to stop.

Q.* Was she—

A. That we wouldn't get away with it.

Q.* Was she begging him not to do it?

A. Yes, she was more or less begging him.

Q.* Was she crying?

A. Uh-huh.

Q.* Was she hysterical at the time or—

A. She was moving around a lot, trying to fight her way away from him.

Q.* Was she scared?

A. Yes.

Q.* All right. So how long did Odell Titsworth rape her?

A. Ten, fifteen minutes, in between each one of us.

Q.* All right. Did he ever hit her while he was raping her?

A. No.

Q. Did he ever cut her?

A. No, not that I know of.

Q. Where did he have the knife when he was raping her?

A. Towards her neck.

Q. So he was holding the knife on her neck. Can you show me how with your finger how he was holding it?

A. He was holding it more or less at an angle.

Q. Was it up against her skin?

A. No, it wasn't all the way up against her skin.

Q. Okay.

A. He was threatening to cut her if she didn't cooperate with him.

Q.* Did he say, "I'm going to cut you," or did he say, "I'm going to kill you"?

A. He said he was going to hurt her.

Q.* Okay. And then when he got through, what did Odell say, then?

A. He didn't say anything. It was my turn. I said—he said—first he said, "Who's next? Then I said, "I guess I'll be next."

Q.* Okay.

A. And then I got up there.

Q.* Who was holding—

A. Tommy was standing on this side, and Odell was still over here with the knife holding her. He grabbed the knife back and, you know, had it in his hand, was holding it on her, and I raped her. And after that, Tommy, you know—

Q.* Was she still conscious then?

A. Yes, she was still *unconscious.*

Q.* Was she still struggling?

A. Not as much.

Q.* Well, I wonder why not?

A. Well, because he'd already raped her. She knew she'd already been raped once.

Q.* So the second time really didn't matter that much to her?

A. No, not—I wouldn't say it *didn't.* And then—

Q.* Was she crying or—

A. She was crying and screaming.

Q.* All right. So how long did you rape her?

A. About twenty minutes; fifteen, twenty minutes amongst all of us.

Q.* Okay. So the raping took about twenty minutes between all three of you?

A. Yeah, about twenty minutes.

Q.* All right.

A. Pretty close to a little bit after an hour.

Q. Do you have any idea what time of the day or night this was?

A. It was almost dark.

Q. So during that time of the year, say, 8:30, 9:00, something like that, or was it later or earlier?

A. It was later.

Q. What kind of light did you have out there, could you—

A. At the scene?

Q. Yes.

A. The dome-light's the only light that we had.

Q. Dome-light?

A. Only—

Q. Okay.

A. Yes.

Q. The dome-light inside the pickup?

A. And they had one on—

Q. The back of the cab?

A. Yeah.

Q. Was there any lights on at the power plant?

A. Yeah, there was a lot of lights on, floodlights.

Q. Could you see pretty well?

A. Yes, yes, we could see well enough to know what we was do-ing.

Q. Okay. Then what happened?

A. Then after that, Tommy—and after that, me and Odell stood there and holded her while Tommy raped her.

Q.* Okay. Did both of you get back in the pickup to hold her?

A. Yes.

Q.* All right. And—

A. I was on this side in between her legs, about middle-ways her legs, and Odell was up here by her neck with the knife.

Q.* Okay. Was she still conscious then?

A. Yes.

Q.* Still crying?

A. She was crying, more or less.

Q.* Still upset?

A. Yeah, she knew what was happening to her.

Q.* Was she saying anything?

A. She was hollering for help and telling us to stop, that we wouldn't get away with it.

Q.* Was she saying, "Please stop," or—

A. She was just hollering stop.

Q.* Okay.

A. That we would never get away with it.

Q.* Okay.

A. And then, after that—

Q.* Did she tell you all that she was going to tell on you or—

A. She didn't refer to that. She said—well, she did say that if he didn't—that if we didn't kill her, that she would go back to ya'll, get us turned in. So that gave Odell an idea to kill her. And then he told—we planned it out amongst the three of us.

Q.* Okay. Let me—let's back up just a moment. Okay. Karl, you said that Odell Titsworth and you were holding Denice Haraway in the back of the pickup.

A. Yes.

Q.* And Karl was taking his turn at raping her.

A. Tommy was.

Q.* Or—excuse me, Tommy Ward.

A. Uh-huh.

Q.* Okay. So he crawled in the pickup with Denice Haraway?

A. Yes.

Q.* And he raped her.

A. He raped her while me and Odell was holding her.

Q.* All right. Did—so after that happened, then after Tommy Ward got through, did you all let go of—

A. No.

Q.* —Denice Haraway or—

A. Odell was still holding her by himself. I'd let go and Tommy had got off of her.

Q.* Okay.

A. Odell had her under control after that.

Q.* What do you mean, had her under control?

A. Well, she was more or less giving up.

Q.* Okay.

A. At the end. And then he was holding her at the time, and we all got in the truck. After that all of us got in the truck. And then we went to go get a siphon hose and everything, me and Tommy and all of us, was to go get it.

Q.* With Denice Haraway?

A. Yes.

Q.* And you all drove her to get a siphon?

A. We drove the truck. And then—

Q.* Where did you drive to?

A. It was on the country road over there by the power plant. It was a dirt road that me and Tommy had had a siphon hose there.

Q.* Where you had it hid out there?

A. From a long time ago, yes. And then—

Q.* How come you had it hid out there?

A. Because we would siphon gas out of his mom's car.

Q.* All right.

A. We siphoned gas all the time out of his mom's—

Q.* Okay. Did you find a can or something?

A. Yes. We got back out there. We drove back out to the house out behind the plant. Found a gas can around the house. He carried her over his shoulder, and she was struggling. He was carrying her. Me and Tommy was behind him. He went up to the fence, put her over the fence. Me and Tommy went over the fence and watched her while he got over the fence.

Q.* Was she conscious?

A. No, she wasn't very lively, you know.

Q.* How come?

A. Because we'd all three raped her.

Q.* Had anyone cut her with the knife?

A. At one—I seen blood on her side is all I seen.

Q.* On her right side?

A. Yeah.

Q.* How did she get that?

A. I—undoubtedly, Odell, because he was the only one that had the knife at the time. Me or Tommy never handled the knife.

Q.* Okay. So did you see him stab her with the knife?

A. No, I noticed the blood as we was going towards the fence. And then he—when he threw her over, me and Tommy got over and watched her while he—

Q.* Was she still alive then?

A. Yes.

Q.* All right.

A. Me and Tommy watched her while he got over, and he carried her on to the house. Me and Tommy, after we got her all to the house, me and Tommy went looking for a can. We found a can, we got the hose, and we got gas out of the truck.

Q.* What was Odell doing?

A. He was with her.

Q.* Inside the house?

A. Yes. And we went and got the gas can and come back, got some gas—

Q.* What was the intentions of getting the gas?

A. To burn her.

Q.* Burn—

A. Burn the flesh.

Q. Burn her flesh?

A. Yes.

Q.* Denice Haraway?

A. Yes. Then after that, me and Tommy had siphoned the gas, went over there. He had already had her down on the floor and everything when we got there. And then he started stabbing her and everything.

Q.* Stabbing Denice Haraway?

A. Yeah. And then he put her off in the rotten place in the floor—

Q.* Where was that?

A. —or where the floor was missing.

Q.* Rotted out or missing?

A. Well, somebody had tore it up and then some of it was rotted. He placed her down in there. We put the gas on her. And after that, it was early that morning, I guess, somewhere around in the morning time, we burned her. And then we come back and burned the house.

Q. Okay. Now, what portion of the house was this in, Karl?

A. It was in one of the bedrooms.

Q. Was—as you—and I don't know the particular layout of the house at this time, but did you go through the front-door portion of the house?

A. Yes.

Q. Does it have a living area to it?

A. It had a living room, yes.

Q. All right, now, was the bedrooms one on the right side and one on the left side—

A. One on the—yes.

Q. —as you walk in?

A. We went to the right side.

Q. You went to the right bedroom?

A. Right bedroom.

Q. All right, now. Was the hole that was torn in the floor, was it up against one of the bedroom walls, or was it right in the center of the bedroom, the hole in the floor, or where?

A. It wasn't completely in the center. It was closer to the wall than it was the center of the floor.

Q. All right. As you're facing the bedroom from the living room, which wall was the hole closest to?

A. Over here (*indicating*).

Q. The wall on the right?

A. Yes, and then—

Q. So it's close to the outside wall?

A. Yes.

Q. It would be an outside wall.

A. The front of the house.

Q. Okay.

A. Yes. And after that, we come back that next—or that morning, and burned the house down.

Q.* Okay. You said you poured gasoline on her.

A. Yes.

Q.* And then what did you do after you poured the gas on her?

A. We lit the house. We lit the gas and burned the house and her.

Q. Did the whole house catch on fire or just part of it?

A. It just more or less built itself up; flames built up.

Q.* So what you're saying is, he carried her down there.

A. Yes.

Q.* You and Tommy went to get gas.

A. Went to get the can.

Q.* And you came back, went inside the room, and he—

A. He'd already had the gas on her and everything.

Q.* Well—

A. He had rolled her off in the hole.

Q.* All right.

A. You know, he'd stabbed her and killed her, I guess, you know, she was dead because he'd rolled her off.

Q.* When you said just a moment ago that he stood over her or was on his knees or something, what was he doing?

A. He was more or less squatting down.

Q.* All right. Did he have something in his hand?

A. He had his knife.

Q.* Was it open?

A. Yes, it was open.

Q.* Well, what was he doing?

A. He was attempting to stab her, and—

Q.* Did you see him stab her?

A. He was stabbing her.

Q.* How did he do it?

A. He had the knife in his hand like this (*indicating*).

Q.* All right.

A. And he was stabbing.

Q.* Hard?

A. Yes.

Q.* How hard? Show me how hard.

A. Hard enough to get the full blade in (*indicating*) like that.

Q.* Was he coming down hard with the knife?

A. No, he wasn't coming down real hard because the knife was sharp.

Q.* Show me on your body where the knife was going into her body?

A. It was on the front, around her chest.

Q.* Was she making any noise then?

A. She was hollering.

Q.* What was she hollering?

A. She wasn't hollering anything; she was just hollering. She was just—

Q.* Screaming?

A. Screaming, then she give up. And then after that, she died. And then we put the gas on her and burned her.

Q.* Okay. Who put her in the hole in the floor?

A. Odell.

Q.* All right. And then who put the gas on her?

A. Me and Tommy.

Q.* Okay. Who lit the match to start it?

A. Odell.

Q.* Were you all out of the house when you started the fire, or—

A. He'd put his knife up and we'd went outside and lit it.

Q. Did you lay a trail or something? Did you light a trail and burn it, or did you stand over the hole and throw the match in?

A. Just tossed it over.

Q. Okay.

A. It ignited.

Q.* Where did you spread the gas to, all around the house or inside it or where?

A. We spread it all around her and on her.

Q.* Okay.

A. And then the house just burned up on the inside.

Q. Let me get something straight, now. Did you all burn the house twice? Did you all come back a second time and set the house on fire again, or initially when you set her on fire, that got the whole house on fire? I'm not straight about that point.

A. It got her on fire and the house, too.

Q. Okay. So you all did not go back down and set the house on fire again after that—

A. Not that morning, huh-uh.

Q. Did you all, in fact, go back again—

A. Yes.

Q. —and set the house on fire again?

A. We went back to see if everything was gone, and the house was burned and there wasn't no remains.

Q. Okay. So you all only had to do it one time?

A. One time.

Q. Did you all carry any—you didn't see any remains left or anything?

A. No, there wasn't nothing.

Q.* You mentioned earlier that you saw pieces of burned flesh.

A. Well, it looked like ash, you know, from the wood.

Q. But you all didn't carry anything away from the scene there—

A. No.

Q. —as far as any body parts or anything?

A. Didn't carry anything. We all—me, Tommy, Odell got in the truck and then we left. We got out at Tommy's house, and from there Odell left.

Q. Okay. Did—or have you, to this point in time, been back out to that location?

A. No, I haven't. I'd been living in Norman. Me and Tommy moved to Norman from there.

Q. Okay. How long after this, the incident, did you all move to Norman?

A. It was months.

Q. Okay. So about a month or so?

A. It was a couple of months, around there. Two or three months. We moved back. Then after we moved there, I moved with Robert and them.

Q. Okay.

A. And Tommy stayed there at Jannette and thems.

Q. How much, if any, of the money from the robbery did you get?

A. He more or less kept the money himself.

Q. Now, who is he?

A. Odell.

Q. So are you telling me that you didn't receive any of the money at all?

A. No, I didn't. Neither did Tommy. He more or less kept the money himself and told us what the money was going to be used for and we agreed.

Q. What was the money going to be used for?

A. Gas to get away in the truck.

Q. To get away to where?

A. For him to get away in the truck. He was going to get away in the truck, and he drove it to his mom's house from there.

Q. Well, did that kind of bother you, I mean—how much money—did he ever tell you how much money you got out of the deal?

A. Close to a hundred and fifty or maybe a little over. It was around in there.

Q. Did that bother you because you all didn't get any money?

A. No, because we had already agreed and made our plans out how it was going to be used. And then from there, I don't know where he's at. From there, me and Tommy stayed together.

Q. Have you heard Odell talk about doing anything like this before?

A. I didn't know Odell very much.

Q. You didn't?

A. Tommy knew Odell more than I did. See, Tommy had brought Odell around me. And I met Odell. That was the first day I'd ever met him and then I ain't seen him since.

Q.* Did—I'm a little bit confused, I think, about the burning part. All right. After Odell Titsworth took her in the house—

A. Uh-huh.

Q.* —took Denice Haraway in the house, then you and Tommy left and went to get some gas?

A. Right.

Q.* All right. You came back, brought the gas in the house, Odell—Denice Haraway was on the floor.

A. Yes, in the hole. She was in the hole on the floor. She was on the floor right there beside the hole.

Q.* All right. Then he—

A. Then he'd rolled her—he'd stabbed her and then rolled her off.

Q.* Did he stab her in your presence?

A. While I was there.

Q.* Okay.

A. Me and Tommy was standing on this side of the hole.

Q.* Okay. And then he stabbed her how many times?

A. Four or five times, maybe.

Q.* Okay. And—

A. You know, after he'd stabbed a couple of times, I didn't look, you know.

Q.* Okay. So at that point, that was when she died?

A. That's when she died. And he put her off in the hole.

Q.* How big a hole in the floor was it? Two foot wide or three foot, maybe, or—

A. Around four.

Q.* Four foot wide?

A. Around four.

Q.* How long was it?

A. It wasn't too long.

Q.* So you—

A. I wouldn't—I ain't measured—I can't guess no measurements.

Q.* Did she have her clothes on at that time or—

A. No, she didn't.

Q.* Where were her clothes?

A. They were back at the truck.

Q.* Okay. What did you all do with the clothes?

A. Took them up there. Me and Tommy went and got them and brought them back to the house, put them in the hole with her and burned them.

Q. All right. Did you put her shoes in the hole with her?

A. Yes, all of her belongings, everything.

Q. All right.

Q. You say she was wearing—

A. Even her—

Q. —tennis shoes?

A. Soft, they were soft shoes, soft-soled shoes.

Q.* All right. And after he put her in the hole, who spread the gasoline, then?

A. Odell. He poured all the gas on her and everything. And we threw the match on her and walked out.

Q. Karl, let me ask you this: at any point in time, did you stab her?

A. No, I did not, nor did Tommy. Odell done all the stabbing right there on the left side of the hole.

Q.* Did you all try to stop him from stabbing her?

A. No.

Q.* Did you say anything to him or—

A. No, I just turned—me and Tommy turned away, didn't watch.

Q. What was the purpose of taking her with you from the store?

A. To keep from her coming to ya'll and letting ya'll know.

Q.* I mean, was that the plan, though, whenever you went there?

A. Yes.

Q.* Okay.

A. We had it all planned out, you know, to—

Q.* What were you planning on doing with her after you got her?

A. Raping her.

Q. Raping her and then killing her and getting rid of her?

A. Yes.

Q. Have you seen Odell since that night?

A. That night he let me and Tommy out at his house. I haven't seen him.

Q. You never did get back with him?

A. No, never did see him again, associate with him, haven't seen him. Till this day, I wouldn't know where he was at.

Q.* What does Odell Titsworth look like?

A. Kind of tall, slim.

Q. Tall compared to you? That would be, what, five-eight, five-nine, five-ten?

A. Around five-ten, five-eleven.

Q. About how much would he weigh?

A. One forty, one fifty, somewhere—

Q. What color is his hair?

A. Black.

Q. How does he wear it?

A. Well, it was more or less messed up when he was with us. But it—

Q. Is it collar-length, shoulder-length, is it long?

A. It was a little below his ears.

Q. Okay.

A. About an inch below his ears.

Q. Did he have a moustache, beard, or anything?

A. Not that I know of.

Q. All right. Does he have any scars, marks, or tattoos that you're aware of?

A. I didn't see any of that.

Q. And how long did you say you've known Odell?

A. That day. That day Tommy and me was at that party. He'd met—I'd met him just then.

Q. You hadn't ever seen him before?

A. Never did know him.

Q.* I think earlier, Karl, you said that you'd known him a year, a year and a half, or something like that.

A. Huh-uh. I'd known him that day.

Q.* How long have you known Tommy?

A. Four or five years, maybe—maybe six. And Tommy had brought Odell around the house and I'd met him.

Q. But prior to that day?

A. Yes.

Q. Okay, now, you're kind of confusing me a little bit. First you say that you had only met him that day, and then you said prior to the date of the incident Tommy had brought him around the house.

A. Yes, Tommy did have him around.

Q. Okay.

A. I'd met him for—I don't know how long it was. It wasn't—it was less than a year.

Q. Okay. But it just was—

A. Way before a year was up.

Q. Was it just a casual or passing acquaintance? Or what you're trying to tell me—

A. It was just meeting him and then him going.

Q. Okay. So it wasn't a close—

A. No relation—no.

Q. —relationship, it was just kind of in passing. He would be with somebody you would know, like Tommy.

A. Yeah.

Q. And you'd see him to recognize him.

A. See him with somebody else—

Q. Okay.

A. —that he knew, yeah.

Q. And then basically what you're telling me, Karl, is that the first time that you really got to know Odell Titsworth was the night of the incident of April the 28th, 1983? [sic].

A. Yes.

Q. Or '84, excuse me.

A. That's the most time that I've known him.

Q. Okay.

A. Right then.

Q.* So you're not really good friends with Odell Titsworth?

A. No.

Q.* You're better friends of—

A. More or less.

Q.* —Tommy Ward's?

A. Me and Tommy was friends. That was it.

Q.* Do you all have any other friends other than each other or—

A. Well, our kin.

Q. What kind of work—

A. Tommy's sister and them, I know them.

Q. What kind of work have you been doing?

A. I'd been doing fence work in Hominy.

Q. What, building fence?

A. Yes.

Q. Barbed-wire type fence?

A. Yes.

Q. What, for a rancher or a farmer or something?

A. Company.

Q. For a company?

A. Yes.

Q. What kind of education do you have? How far in high school—

A. I went to the twelfth grade.

Q. Did you graduate?

A. My mom—she died in—right before graduation, and then I'd quit.

Q.* So you quit. Where did you go to school at?

A. In Latta. It was the Latta High School. The last school I went to.

Q. Do you read and write the English language pretty well?

A. Yeah, just had trouble with history and that was about all.

Q. It's my understanding you were in the National Guard, is that correct?

A. Yes, I was in the National Guard.

Q. How long were you in the National Guard?

A. I done three months.

Q. You did?

A. And then they discharged me because of my back.

Q. What's the matter with your back?

A. They said it was messed up too bad to be doing the training. So they gave me a trainee discharge.

Q. What unit were you in?

A. It was in—the company was Alpha.

Q. Alpha Company? What town? Was it here in Ada, or where?

A. In—my training took place in Fort Benning, Georgia.

Q.* Okay. You went to Fort Benning, Georgia, for your—

A. Uh-huh.

Q.* —boot camp or—

A. Basic and AIT.

Q.* —basic?

A. Yeah.

Q.* And that was for—you were there for three weeks and—

A. Three months.

Q.* Three months.

A. And then right at the end, right before graduation, they discharged me.

Q. Okay. So you were in the infantry—

A. Yes.

Q. —unit in the National Guard?

A. Yes.

Q. And was it at Allen, is that where you—

A. Yes.

Q. —attended your drills?

A. That's—yes. Well, I never did attend any drills—

Q. You didn't?

A. —because I was discharged before—

Q. Okay. So you—

A. —I got back.

Q. —went through your active-duty status prior to going to trying to—

A. I went to the last day, the last day of training.

AGENT ROGERS: Dennis, can you think of anything else right now?

Q.* Yes. Is there any statement that you'd like to make regarding this incident that happened?

A. Well, I'll probably never do it again.

Q.* Okay.

A. Or at least I'll never get into any trouble like this again, you know, because I've learned my lesson.

Q.* Okay.

Q. Karl, during the period of time that we've interviewed you today, once again I'd like to ask you, have we threatened you or—

A. No.

Q. —promised you anything?

A. (*Witness indicating negatively.*)

Q. You're making this of your own free will, this statement?

A. It was on my own free will to get this recorded.

Q. Have you been allowed to smoke, drink, drink Cokes—

A. Yes.

Q. —anything that you wanted?

A. Yes, I was served right during the meeting.

AGENT ROGERS: Dennis, can you think of anything else? Okay. This statement is going to be ending at 3:50 P.M., same date, same people present.

The lights came up in the courtroom. The video screens were moved into a corner. The defense attorneys questioned Gary Rogers.

Wyatt established that no body had been found where the tapes indicated it would be, or anywhere else; that Odell Titsworth had not been involved; that the house had been burned down long before, and did not even exist as a house the night of the disappearance; that the eyewitness accounts of the Timmons brothers, about what they had observed at McAnally's, differed from the accounts on both tapes. He noted that Fontenot said on the tape it was "almost dark" during the kidnapping, whereas at 8:30 P.M., when the disappearance actually occurred, it had long since been dark.

"You have no proof, aside from these statements, that she was kidnapped, raped, and murdered. All you can prove, aside from these statements, is that she is gone."

"That is correct," Rogers said.

Butner asked if the OSBI or the Ada police or anyone else had been able to find any physical evidence to back up the stories on these tapes.

"Not that I know of," Rogers said.

"Do you ever discover physical evidence of a dream?" Butner asked.

"I don't follow," Rogers said.

Butner repeated the question.

"It depends on what kind of dream," Rogers said.

The entire courtroom erupted in laughter. When it subsided, Rogers said, "I guess not."

Wyatt asked if the agent was telling the jury that Randy Rogers, Bob Sparcino, and Jason Lurch had no connection to this case.

"Not that we know of," the agent said.

The next, and final, witness for the state—the sixty-seventh—was a psychologist from East Central University, Frederick Patrizi. The professor said he had long been interested in the dream process, had taught courses about dreams. He had been shown the two tapes last spring, he said, and the Ward tape again in August.

"Do you have an opinion whether the Ward video was a dream?" the D.A. asked.

"It's my opinion it was not a dream," the professor said.

He said the tapes were too logical; that a dream typically jumps around, has gaps; that typically, in a dream, people change. The tapes had no dreamlike quality, he said, "with the possible exception that they were rather bizarre."

On cross-examination, Wyatt established that the professor had never interviewed the suspects, and that he had seen the tapes in the presence of Mike Baskin, Gary Rogers, and Dennis Smith.

The professor was excused. The large, round clock above the spectator section read 6:25. Bill Peterson stood beside the prosecution table. His voice boomed loud in the quiet courtroom.

"The State of Oklahoma rests, your honor," he said.

Wyatt and Butner approached the bench. They moved that the state had not proved the corpus delicti on any of these charges; and that therefore the case should be dismissed.

"Overruled," Judge Powers said.

16

DEFENSE

George Butner was feeling good after the playing of the tapes. He did not know why. Perhaps because the worst was over; now the defense would get its turn.

Some of Tommy Ward's family went to Wyatt's office, for the second run-through of their testimony, which Tricia had requested. Tricia still could not bring herself to say swearwords, to say more than "s.o.b." The attorneys felt she would be effective on the stand.

Don Wyatt went home, to ponder the opening remarks he would make the next morning. Bill Cathey grilled Joice Cavins on her testimony. She was a nervous person, frenetic, given to outbursts; she was not the best kind of witness. But she was Tommy's alibi; they probably would have to put her on the stand. During the preparation, Joice stumbled over some of her answers, got confused. She broke down, crying.

"I don't want to kill Tommy!" she sobbed.

Chris Ross couldn't sleep that night. This was the assistant D.A.'s first murder trial, and he was all keyed up. The state had rested. He should have been able to relax, but he needed to work on his closing argument. Because the defense had two attorneys, the state would get two closing arguments as well. What Ross said would be the last words heard by the jurors before they began to deliberate.

For months he had been reviewing the tapes in his mind, over and over. How to make sense of them, with Titsworth not being there. Had there been a different third person? That did not fit in with the eyewitness evidence.

When he went to bed, he lay awake, the facts of the case dancing in his brain; he tried to figure out what to emphasize in his statement. He thought again, as he had many times, of Tommy's saying on the tape that Odell took Denice's bra off while Tommy was biting her breast. That had never made sense to him. It was close quarters; Tommy, biting her, must have pulled the bra off himself. That had led Ross to decide, some time earlier, that everything Tommy had done he had merely attributed to Odell. But that was elementary, he felt; he needed something more.

Hour after hour he lay in bed, waiting for sleep to come. At 3 A.M., still restless, he got up, filled the bathtub with hot water, and eased himself into it, hoping the warmth would be relaxing. Over and over the tapes ran in his brain, like some true-life horror film. Then, suddenly, in the tub, in a kind of synaptic leap, an illumination, it clicked into place. Suddenly, to Ross, the tapes made sense, psychologically— if his memory was correct. He needed to check his memory against the transcript.

He went back to bed. He could hardly wait till morning. Excited, he got to the courthouse early. He told Bill Peterson that as the defense began its case, he would like to be excused from the courtroom for a while. He spent the next few hours at his desk, going through the transcript of Tommy Ward's statement, line by line. When he was finished, he decided he was right.

He was uncertain, at first, whether to use his theory in his closing argument; it might be too complex for the jurors to follow. But he decided, fairly soon, that he would.

As Ross pored through the transcript, Gordon Calhoun and Jannette Roberts met in Wyatt's office, a meeting arranged by the attorney. Jannette told Gordon he was correct in that she had taken pictures at Blue River on Memorial Day. But those were different pictures, she said—and he was wearing the same thing.

Gordon said he would have to see the pictures to be sure. Jannette did not have her photo album with her. She said she would drive up to Oklahoma City to get it. They agreed to meet again at eight o'clock the next morning, to look at the Blue River pictures together.

DAY NINE

George Butner was not feeling well. He'd been bothered much of the night by an upset stomach; he thought it might have been caused by some pork he had eaten the day before. His stomach was still queasy when he arrived in court. He informed the judge of this in chambers; if he had to bolt suddenly from the courtroom, he wanted the judge to know, it would not be a sign of disrespect.

The judge asked if he wanted the session postponed. Butner said no, he would continue for as long as he could.

The defense of Tommy Ward and Karl Fontenot began with an opening statement by Don Wyatt. The attorney summarized briefly what the defense would try to show. Referring to his private investigator, he said, "He's going to bring you some revelations about who, in his opinion, is involved in this."

It was not quite the dramatic claim Wyatt had fantasized about months before, but it would have to do.

The first witness called by the defense was Dr. Clyde Butler, a biology professor at East Central. He said that when the detectives came to borrow the skull and bones, they told him the bones would be used to compare with ones found at search sites, to determine if the bones found were human. They did not tell him the bones would be brought to the jail, he said.

The professor was a witness because Wyatt wanted to suggest shoddy police tactics; he was the first witness because Wyatt wanted the jury to see that professors from the college were willing to testify for the defense as well as for the prosecution.

There was no cross-examination.

The next two witnesses, father and son, were Joel Ward's closest friends in Tulsa. One was an engineer. Both testified that Joel had never owned or been in possession of a gray-primered pickup; if he had, they would have known about it, they said.

Joel Ward was next. He testified about all the vehicles he had ever owned or possessed; none had been a gray-primered pickup, he said. He said the incident testified to by the insurance man had never happened. He did not know why the man had made it up, he said.

There was other testimony Wyatt would have liked to elicit from Joel. He would have liked the jury to hear about a dream Tommy had had at Joel's house, after seeing a news report about a woman who had been killed and mutilated in a car accident. In his dream, Tommy had caused the accident. Wyatt felt that the dream was psychologically significant; it showed a tendency in Tommy's inner makeup to have such dreams, in which he was the guilty one when in fact he was not. The attorneys had debated at length about whether to have Joel tell of it. They were afraid the district attorney would claim that such testimony related to Tommy's character, and that the judge might agree. Testimony involving character—involving things not directly related to the case at hand—was prohibited, unless the defense opened up that area. But if they did, Peterson could then bring in witnesses to tell about Tommy's getting drunk at times, about his smoking dope—neither of which would help with the jury. The D.A. could also bring in witnesses, prohibited till now, who claimed Tommy had threatened them at other times.

The attorneys had decided they would do without the dream. Joel Ward was excused.

Marie Titsworth was called. She told how the police had confiscated her daughter's pickup from in front of Don Wyatt's house, while she was cleaning there, and had returned it about a week later, covered with fingerprint dust.

Then her son, Odell, took the stand. Titsworth, twenty-six, was something of the town bogeyman, because of his four felony convictions and the publicity that surrounded them. He was known to Wyatt, and to Dennis Smith, as a soft-spoken, gentle person—who became violent when he got drunk. He had moved to Oregon in January, after testifying at the preliminary hearing; he'd been flown in for the trial by the state, in case Bill Peterson wanted to call him. But Peterson felt he had already proved through Titsworth's girlfriend, her mother, and the surgeon that Odell had not been involved. He saw no point in putting on the stand a fellow who hated cops, and whose mother worked for the defense attorney.

Wyatt called him instead. Titsworth, his black hair rolling in waves to his shoulders, told of his arrest the previous October, of his questioning by Detectives Smith and Baskin in a basement room of the police station. "I told them I didn't know nothing about it," he said. "I didn't know what they were talking about."

Titsworth said he was interrogated four different times while being held, that Baskin repeatedly called him a "sorry son-of-a-bitch." He said the questioning was much more intense than during any of his prior arrests. "They were hollering," he said, "trying to get me to say I done it. That I killed her and raped her, and Tommy and Karl was with me." He said that after one bout of severe questioning, back in his cell, he wondered if perhaps he had gone crazy and done something like that, and didn't remember it—till he remembered his arm was broken at the time.

Titsworth said that several days after the last questioning, Captain Smith told him. "It was just a dream Tommy Ward had. It was just a dream."

He said he was kept in solitary confinement, that he was taken to the cells of Ward and Fontenot and told by Baskin to act real tough, as if he was threatening them. "They were scared," Titsworth said.

He said later he was placed in cells next to Ward's and Fontenot's, to see what he could find out. They both told him they hadn't done it, Titsworth said. He said Ward apologized to him, and told him it had only been a dream.

"Even in your investigation of this matter, Mr. Titsworth, you learned it was a dream?" George Butner asked.

"Yes."

Titsworth said he had moved to Oregon because of his being linked to this case. "I was threatened by a lot of people around here. And it would be impossible to get a job in Oklahoma."

Court was recessed for lunch. The members of Tommy Ward's family dined on stuffed potatoes at the Feed Store. When they returned, the youngest sister, Kay Garrett, took the stand. Eighteen years old, a new mother, in the pretty bloom of youth, wearing a ruffled purple blouse, Kay testified that she had cut Tommy's hair very short between 3 and 4 P.M. on April 20, eight days before the disappearance. She said she knew it was that Friday because the following week she and her mother had gone to Lawton to visit her sister Melva, and Tommy had been pestering her to cut it before that trip. She produced a small appointment calendar from her purse, on which the trip to Lawton on the twenty-eighth was marked.

On cross-examination, Chris Ross, back in the courtroom, noted that the haircut was not marked on the calendar. Pointing out that she'd said she'd given Tommy a bad, gapped-up haircut, Ross asked why Tommy would let her cut his hair if she gapped it up.

Kay blushed, smiled shyly. "I guess he trusted me," she said. The warm laughter that erupted in the courtroom, even among some of the jurors, was the first hint since the trial began of any sympathy for the defense.

Bud Wolf was called next: Tricia's husband, Tommy's brother-in-law, his hunting partner near the abandoned house in the days, years earlier, when the house was still there. Led by Wyatt, Bud, wearing a three-piece suit, gave a soft-spoken recitation of his solid-citizen work record; of his activities at the Unity Missionary Baptist Church, where he served at times as treasurer and taught a boys' Bible class. Bud swore, under oath, that on April 21, 1984—the day after Kay had said she cut Tommy's hair—he saw Tommy with very short hair. He told of the incident of Tommy coming to the house to borrow money, taking off his baseball cap, saying "Ta-da!" and turning around to show off the scalping.

On cross-examination, Chris Ross, who knew Bud from foster-parent class, asked why he was certain this had happened on April 21.

"Because it was the day before communion at our church."

"Isn't communion every Sunday?" Ross asked.

"No," Bud said, "at our church we have communion only twice a year. On Easter Sunday, and again in October."

Ross smiled, shook his head slightly, resumed his seat; his bemused expression seemed to say: you learn something every day.

There was a brief recess. People congregated in the corridors. Don Wyatt told Bud, Kay, and Joel that they had done great on the witness stand. They were vastly relieved.

At the other end of the hallway, Theresa Shumard, a local news stringer who was covering the trial for the *Daily Oklahoman*, chatted with Gary Rogers and Dorothy Hogue. Mrs. Shumard, pregnant, almost as large as Tricia, said angrily, "As soon as they put the family on the stand, that proves he's guilty! If they need the family to speak up for him, that proves it!"

George Butner's stomach was still bothering him. The defense attorneys huddled in a rear office. They went over the witnesses they still planned to call. It was now mid-afternoon on Thursday. At the rate they were going, they would finish on Friday. The judge would probably sequester the jury once testimony was completed and they were ready to deliberate. That meant the jurors would be locked up in a motel, away from their families, for the weekend. They would be like caged animals, eager to get out; they would be angry, perhaps at the defense. An early recess today would allow them to continue the defense into Monday.

George Butner felt his stomach getting worse.

Court resumed. Wyatt called Dr. Bruce Weems, a physics instructor at East Central for eleven years. End the day with another professor, for the jury's benefit, Wyatt figured. Dr. Weems, consulting a book of astronomy charts, testified that on April 28, 1984, sunset had occurred in Ada at 6:43 P.M.

The significance was that on Fontenot's tape he said they had kidnapped Denice when it was "almost dark." By 8:30 P.M. it would have been long dark.

On cross-examination, Bill Peterson noted that at sunset the sky is not yet dark. Weems agreed, to the extent that "twilight lasts for several minutes after it's set."

The professor was excused. It was 3:30. George Butner approached the bench. He told the judge that he was sorry, but that his stomach had gotten worse. He did not think he would be able to continue.

Judge Powers was understanding. He announced to the court that Mr. Butner was not feeling well—because of something he ate, perhaps—and therefore they were going to recess for the day. Mr. Butner's wife was a nurse, the judge said, so he would be in good hands, and hopefully would be ready to resume at nine the next morning.

Butner thanked the judge for his sympathy.

While the case was progressing in court, Richard Kerner was continuing his investigation. Jannette Roberts had told him that Karl had gotten a haircut in April before going to apply for a job at Wendy's; that at the interview, he'd been told his hair needed to be shorter still, and he had gotten a second haircut. Kerner hoped to prove this was true through the employment records at Wendy's.

Kerner ascertained that Karl's first check from Wendy's was received on May 20. But his first employment application could not be located. The investigator tracked down and interviewed four former managers of Wendy's, which apparently had rapid turnover. All four remembered Fontenot. But none could recall the exact date he was interviewed and had his hair cut short. "It was believed," Kerner reported to Wyatt, "that Captain Dennis Smith received the Wendy's application and employment paperwork on Fontenot a long time ago."

Thursday morning, as the defense began in the courtroom, Kerner went to the gas station where Jim Moyer worked. He wanted to show him the pictures of the truck Jason Lurch's nephew used to drive. Kerner did not think Moyer would even talk to him, after it had come out in court that he had secretly recorded their previous conversation.

Moyer looked at the pictures closely. He said one detail was the same. He was studying a second detail when a car drove up. Moyer had to go and pump gas. When he returned to Kerner, the interruption had apparently given him time for second thoughts. He looked at the pictures again, and said he did not want to say if it looked like the truck he had seen at McAnally's or not. He didn't say it was not the truck; he just said he did not want to say. To the investigator, this seemed to indicate that it might well be the right truck, that Moyer just did not want to get involved again. Otherwise, Kerner reasoned, he could simply have said it wasn't the truck, and be done with it.

Frustrated, Kerner showed the pictures to Jack Paschall. As expected, Paschall said it might be the truck he had seen at J.P.'s and it might not be.

The investigator still could not find Karen Wise.

He hung about Wyatt's office that morning; he could not return to Yukon, because he did not know when he would be needed to testify. While the attorneys were in court, Jason Lurch called in. He talked to Kerner. Lurch said he had been going through his records, and that he had been wrong about what he'd said the other night. He was not living and working in Ada in April of '84, he said. He was living in Oklahoma City; he did not move into the Brook Mobile Home Park in Ada until July. And therefore he would not have been at J.P.'s that night.

Lurch asked the investigator to come on out to his house, to look at his records, his rent receipts.

Kerner was instantly suspicious. Lurch was a scary guy. This could be some kind of trap. The investigator did not care to be alone with Jason Lurch again on his desolate home turf. Especially now that he was changing his story. In Kerner's view, rent receipts from Oklahoma City would prove nothing; the city was only a ninety-mile drive from Ada; he could have come down any time. He was still suspicious of Lurch for attending all five scattered days of the hearing.

He could not come out today, the investigator told Lurch; Lurch should bring the rent receipts with him when he came to testify.

Informed of this conversation, that Lurch was changing his story, Don Wyatt was not surprised. He instructed Kerner to pick up Lurch the next morning and bring him into town. He told the investigator to wire his car; to tape their conversation without Lurch's knowledge. He told Kerner to go over Lurch's story while the tape was running— to get Lurch to recall what he had told them the other night: that he might have been with his nephew at J.P.'s.

Kerner was not thrilled with the assignment. He made that clear. But he agreed to do it.

Winifred Harrell offered him the use of her revolver. Kerner declined. "I don't like guns," he said.

He had carried a pistol for twenty years in the military; he chose not to do so in civilian life.

In all his experience, Kerner had never been still investigating a case while the trial was on—let alone while the defense was already on. He had never heard of a case where the D.A.'s investigator was reading someone else his rights five days into a trial. He'd been involved in many bizarre cases, but none like this; this one, he felt, defied description.

At 8 the next morning, Gordon Calhoun and Jannette Roberts met again in Wyatt's office, as planned. Jannette had her photo album with her. In it were pictures of Calhoun, hand-dated "Memorial Day, 1984." In them he was wearing a T-shirt and cutoff jeans—the same outfit he was wearing in those dated April 16.

The handwriting on the Memorial Day pictures looked faded, unlike those dated April. "I wrote these outdoors, with a scratchy pen. By Blue River," Jannette said.

Calhoun studied the pictures. He told Wyatt he could not say for sure when any of the pictures had been taken. He went to the courthouse and told Bill Peterson the same thing.

Since he could not be sure, both sides agreed to release Calhoun from recall, so he could go home to California, where his college semester had begun.

If, as he had feared, Calhoun had given the jury the impression that he was sure the Fontenot pictures were dated falsely, that impression would be allowed to remain.

Richard Kerner, dressed in a dark suit, white shirt, and a tie, bent into his car. His microcassette recorder was in his breast pocket. It was a good recorder—but one of its special features might, this morning, get him into big trouble.

The recorder used thirty-minute tapes. When the tape came to the end, the recorder issued a warning—a buzzing sound. If he was secretly taping Jason Lurch, and the buzzer went off, things might get sticky in a hurry.

He was supposed to pick up Lurch at the village store at 8 A.M. He drove out the highway, pulled up beside the store. Lurch wasn't there. He went inside, drank a cup of coffee, waited. Lurch didn't show.

He looked at his watch. It was 8:15. He did not want to walk the lonely road to Lurch's house; the cowboy made him nervous. He stalled, wrestled with his willpower. Finally he left the store and walked in the crisp morning air the few hundred yards down the road.

There were no other houses nearby, just a decrepit schoolhouse. Lurch's place, set fifteen feet down an incline, was a graying white-frame, ratty-looking. With trepidation, Kerner knocked on the door.

Lurch was in the kitchen, drinking coffee. Kerner waited just inside the house till the cowboy was ready, keeping the door open behind him. They got into the car. As he eased himself behind the wheel, the investigator reached inside his jacket, as if for a cigarette, and depressed the button that set the tape turning.

Kerner got the conversation going: about the rent receipts; Lurch, it turned out, had none. About where Lurch had been living at the time; Oklahoma City, Lurch said. Kerner tried to edge the talk to what Lurch had told the lawyers on Monday night. But the transition was difficult; he could not get Lurch to repeat that first story.

The tape was running silently. The hum of the car engine covered any minute whirring sound. The flat pastureland passed outside the windows.

Kerner tried again. More minutes passed. The investigator could hear in his mind the buzzer going off at the end of the tape. It would sound like Big Ben. With each passing mile he felt more frustrated. He could not get Lurch to repeat what he had told the lawyers: that he had been living at the Brook Trailer Park at the time; that he might have been at J.P.'s with his nephew that night.

It had not escaped Kerner's notice that the Brook was where Mildred Gandy had, at one time, said she saw Denice Haraway, two days after the disappearance. It might be true even though she'd taken it back and wouldn't testify.

Jason Lurch sat quietly. Kerner looked at his watch. Seventeen minutes had run out of the thirty on the tape running silently in his pocket.

He tried again for another minute, without success. Then he reached into his jacket, inconspicuously, as Lurch watched the landscape, the ranches, go by on the outskirts of Ada; and he switched off the recorder.

He swung the Mercury into the parking lot behind the law office. Wyatt's Charger was not there; he would already be in court.

Kerner had a Polaroid camera with him. He asked Lurch if he could take his picture. The cowboy said okay. Kerner clicked the shutter, with the red brick of the law office as background.

He escorted Lurch inside, left him there in the company of the receptionist and several women assistants. When Kerner left, there were no men in the building except Jason Lurch. The ladies did not appreciate this. Ever so slowly, they began to grow frightened.

Kerner had work to do. He drove down Arlington to Country Club Road, turned right, and drove out to the Brook Trailer Park. With the help of the manager, he checked rent records from 1984. The records showed that Lurch had not moved into the trailer park until July— just as he now maintained.

Kerner was not impressed. He himself had been commuting between Oklahoma City and Ada for days now: a ninety-minute drive.

The investigator drove to the courthouse, the Polaroid of Lurch in his pocket. He could be called to testify at any time.

DAY TEN

Tricia dropped the kids off at school, then went to the courthouse. She sat in a wooden chair in the corridor, wearing a maternity blouse and skirt, waiting her turn to testify. If she hadn't been called by midafternoon, Maxine would get the kids from school.

Twenty feet away, in the courtroom, Ward and Fontenot sat at the defense table, waiting for the judge to enter. "My heart is up in my throat again," Tommy said.

The first witness was Jannette Blood Roberts, thirty-nine, attractive in a world-weary way, as if she had seen it all. Jannette conceded that she had had drug problems in the past; she said that was all behind her now.

Wyatt showed her the Polaroids of Karl and Tommy. She said they had been taken on April 16 and on April 22, 1984—just as they were marked. She said she herself had dated them at the time. She smiled at the picture of her daughter next to the huge Easter basket; it was the first big Easter basket Jessica ever had.

She had no doubt about the dates, she said; the composite drawings could not be Tommy and Karl, she said, because they both had short hair at the time. Questioned by Butner, she said she had found the pictures in a trunk in her home, in the presence of Richard Kerner, and when she pulled them out they were already dated. She said that prior to that moment she had never talked to Don Wyatt, about pictures or anything else.

On cross-examination, Chris Ross hit hard at her record of two felony convictions. She said she had forged a prescription for diet pills, and had done six years at a state prison. After that, she said, she had become assistant manager of Taco Tico, a fast-food Mexican place, and was trying to turn her life around.

The cross-examination was tough. Mrs. Roberts seemed loose and natural in her replies. When Ross asked if five adults and three children really were living in her small apartment at the time, as she had testified, she shot back, "You bet. I'm very poor."

She had been shown the composite drawings on October 12, when Detectives Smith and Baskin came to see her. "I never thought it looked like them from the beginning," she said.

When Tommy came home from work on October 12, she said, she and her husband, Mike, had urged Tommy to talk to the police. They'd thought: "What could it hurt?"

Morning recess. Butner felt that Jannette had done very well on the stand. But he was getting worried about presenting the Lurch scenario, now that the trailer park records showed Lurch did not move there till July. Perhaps, Butner thought, trying to show too much would be a mistake. They did not have to offer the jury an alternate suspect.

They had the testimony about the haircuts, he reasoned, and the pictures of Tommy and Karl with short hair; Kerner would back up Jannette about the pictures already being dated when she fished them out of the trunk. They would have the alibi witnesses. Why not leave it at that? Reasonable doubt . . .

Winifred Harrell came to the courthouse, to watch a bit of the trial. She was upset. She had heard, through the town grapevine, that two of the jurors had been indicating they would hold out for a conviction "till hell freezes over."

One of the two was Mary Floyd, the retired schoolteacher, whom the family had wanted off the jury because she did not like Tommy as a kid. She'd been kept on because her daughter was going to be a defense witness, was going to say that the composite drawings were Randy Rogers and Bob Sparcino. But that line of defense had been dropped—and they had been left with Mrs. Floyd anyway.

Court resumed. Nancy Howell took the stand. She was the girlfriend of Jimmy Ward, Tommy's eldest brother. She said she and Jimmy had gone to the Ward house on Ashland Avenue about sunset of the night in question, and that Tommy had been there. Tommy and Jimmy had stood in the driveway and quarreled, she said, about money; Jimmy claimed Tommy owed him $150 as part of a car swap they had made; Tommy claimed the swap was even-up.

Ms. Howell produced a large wall calendar to indicate why she remembered the date: Jimmy had a weekend pass from a V.A. hospital. On cross-examination, Chris Ross noted that April 28 had many more notations than any other day; he implied that this calendar had been prepared just for the trial.

Jimmy Ward was called. A veteran of Vietnam, he had been in and out of the Veterans Administration hospital in Oklahoma City. He said he had prescriptions for tranquilizers and antidepressants; his hands fidgeted as he talked.

He told the same story as Nancy Howell, about finding Tommy at home that evening and quarreling about money.

Dorothy Hogue leaned toward a colleague. "Wyatt is hanging his client!" she said. "He's showing that Ward was angry that night, and that he needed money!"

The impact of the testimony was supposed to be that Ward was at home, and therefore not shooting pool at J.P.'s. And not out kidnapping anyone.

Court adjourned for lunch. O. E. McAnally, the owner of McAnally's, slim, white-haired, sat on a bench in a corridor. He reminisced about what a fine young lady, a fine employee, Denice Haraway had been. He had no doubt that the suspects were guilty.

He spoke of his recent decision to rid his stores of girlie magazines. "Maybe these young guys look at those pictures," he said, "and it gets them stirred up to do something like that."

Of Tommy Ward's four sisters, Melva was the most sophisticated and worldly; Tricia the most open and warm; Kay the most gentle and pretty. Joice was the family cutup, raucous and emotional.

Once, as a teenager, Joice wrote on the wall of an Ada underpass: "For a good time, call Melva Ward." And she added the correct phone number. Melva got obscene phone calls for weeks; she was angry at Joice for months.

Of all the sisters, Joice was the one most prone to shout, to cry, to lash out, to lose control. Now Don Wyatt had to play with fire, as Bill Willett had said; he had to put her on the stand. She was the alibi.

Taking the witness chair after lunch, Joice testified that she had been at home all day on April 28, 1984. She said Tommy had been hungover in the morning, from a party the night before. About 3 in the afternoon Tommy left the house, she said, to walk into town; he returned about 6:30 P.M., she said, and did not leave again that night. She said Jimmy, and Nancy Howell, had come over, and Tommy and Jimmy had quarreled. Then Willie Barnett came over, and Tommy asked him to leave because he was bothering the bird. She told of the plumbing breaking down late that night, and Tommy and her husband, Robert, fixing it.

Is it possible, Wyatt asked, that Tommy was at McAnally's about 8 P.M. or thereabouts?

"No," Joice said, "he was at home with me."

On cross-examination, Chris Ross asked if it was not true that Joice was attending classes on Saturdays at that time, to qualify for an

Emergency Medical Technician certificate. Joice said she had not attended the class that day.

When she was excused from the stand, the relief of the defense attorneys was almost audible. Joice appeared to have done well. She had not come unglued, as she herself had feared she might.

Then it was Richard Kerner's turn.

Under Wyatt's guidance, the private investigator recited his credentials: thirteen years in the Air Force Military Police; seven years attached to the Office of Special Investigations; ten years in private industry; then three years as a private investigator; a graduate of the FBI Academy; current president of the Oklahoma Private Investigators' Association. He had not wanted to mention that for three of his years in the Air Force, he had been an investigator assigned to the CIA. He could not talk about that, he'd told the lawyer. Wyatt got him to mention it, for the record, to impress the jury.

Kerner told of his investigations in this case: of the people he'd found who believed the composite drawings were exact images of Randy Rogers and Bob Sparcino; of the truck he had photographed at Elmore City. He was not permitted to mention the house with the bars on the bedroom window there; it was deemed irrelevant to this trial.

He told of conversations with law officers about whether the suspects in the Linda Thompson kidnapping in Oklahoma City in August, Don Hawkins and Dale Shelton, might have been involved in the Haraway case.

And he told of his suspicions of Jason Lurch, the "mystery man" in the back of the courtroom, who had looked familiar to Jim Moyer and Karen Wise. He had taken a picture of Lurch this very morning, he said, and he produced it from his pocket. He told of the truck he had found that had belonged to Lurch's nephew, Ricky Brewer. More than twenty pictures he'd taken of that truck, from every possible angle, were introduced by Wyatt.

Kerner said he had interviewed Brewer; he described him. Wyatt showed him one of the composite sketches, asked if it looked like Ricky Brewer.

"It's a very good likeness," Kerner said.

Chris Ross began the cross-examination; he had displayed during the trial an instinct for the jugular; Bill Peterson was allowing his assistant to do much of the hard-nosed questioning.

Reviewing Kerner's credentials, Ross brought out that his ten years in private industry had not been as an investigator, that he had held several different jobs; that one of them had been—there was derision in Ross's voice—with Shaklee Products.

He asked what Kerner had done in the CIA.

I can't talk about that, Kerner said.

You mean, Ross asked, you are going to drop the name CIA and then not tell us what you did?

That was correct, Kerner said; he was forbidden by law to discuss it, even if the judge ordered him to.

Ross did not ask the judge to order him to.

The assistant D.A. read a list of about twenty-five names—most of the names that had been called in after the composite sketches were first published. He asked if Kerner had investigated these people, as the Ada police had done.

"I did not have access to that knowledge," Kerner said.

He conceded that he did not know where Jason Lurch was living in 1984, that he had gotten no confessions in this case, that he had found no physical evidence linking any truck to this case.

"Can you say," Ross asked, pacing in front of the witness stand, "that Jason Lurch was in McAnally's on April 28?"

"No."

"Can you tell us who did it?"

"No, I cannot."

Then Kerner added, "I believe Mr. Lurch and Mr. Brewer are the most likely suspects of all I investigated."

Kerner said Jim Moyer had told him he believed it was Lurch he had seen in McAnally's that night.

"He also said it was Mr. Ward," Ross said. "You are going to substitute Mr. Brewer for Mr. Ward?"

"Yes," Kerner said.

"And they were also the ones at J.P.'s?"

"That would be my opinion."

The jury watched intently as the fencing continued. Kerner crossed his legs, appeared relaxed—as if to indicate he had been through this sort of thing before.

Ross asked if he had obtained any confessions from these men.

"No," Kerner said.

Ross sat down. Wyatt stood for redirect questioning.

"I have found no evidence," Kerner said, "linking Tommy Ward and Karl Fontenot to the missing girl."

Lurch, he said, had told him inconsistent stories: first that he'd been living in Ada at the time, then in Oklahoma City.

"You are not telling us, are you," Wyatt asked, "that Lurch and Brewer did it?"

"No, I'm not," Kerner said.

The attorney brought up, indirectly, the matter of Officer Holkum and the blouse, to suggest again that the police knew of the blouse before the arrests, and spoon-fed the information to the defendants.

"Would you assume," Wyatt asked, hypothetically, "as agent in charge, that others working for you would bring all relevant information to your attention?"

"Yes," Kerner said.

Chris Ross asked whether, if Karen Wise knew Lurch and Brewer, that would clear them. Kerner didn't think it necessarily would.

Wyatt countered by asking why, if Karen Wise knew Lurch, she would be afraid of him in court and would hide around the corner.

Kerner was excused. It was late Friday afternoon. Judge Powers told the jurors he would permit them to return to their homes for the weekend. But because the testimony might soon be concluded, he might sequester them on Monday night, so they should come prepared. Because their deliberations might take several days, the judge said, they might want to bring several pairs of underthings.

There was laughter in the court at the mention of underwear.

Richard Kerner was supposed to drive Jason Lurch home. Considering his testimony in court, he did not think that was a good idea. Bill Willett, a large man himself, did so instead. The ladies in the office were happy to see Lurch go.

There was no problem during the ride home. Lurch was as yet unaware of what had been said in court: that suspicion had been pointed, by the defense, at him.

Some in Wyatt's office were concerned about an unasked question: Wyatt had neglected to have Kerner testify about how, when Jannette Roberts found the haircut Polaroids in her trunk, they were already dated. Wyatt noted that Jannette had already testified to that. Some aides felt the jury would be more inclined to believe her if they'd heard Kerner say the same thing.

The investigator went home for the weekend, to catch up on other work. He said he would try to find out, over the telephone, if Lurch might have been living somewhere else in Ada, other than the trailer park, in April of '84. He told the lawyers he would be back in Ada Monday morning.

Judge Powers went home to Chandler for the weekend. Butner went to Wewoka, to be a spotter for the high school football team; the other attorneys on both sides retired to their homes, to relax, to try for a time to forget the case.

The next day, Saturday, September 21, Tommy Ward celebrated his twenty-fifth birthday, in the Pontotoc County jail.

Miz Ward had asked the jailers earlier in the week if she could bring a birthday cake: only if it was large enough to serve all the inmates and all the jailers—twenty-five people, she was told. On Saturday, Tricia and Bud went to the Cake Box bakery on Main Street and bought a large chocolate cake. It had white icing—and four small blue roses in the corner.

The little blue roses on the cake, and in the description of the blouse on Tommy's tape, was coincidental.

The cake said, "Happy Birthday Tommy."

They also bought three two-liter bottles of Sprite, and napkins and paper cups, and took them to the jail. Bud carried the heavy soft drinks. Tricia, between the large cake and her big belly, could barely fit through the door.

They were not permitted to see Tommy, because it was not a Sunday. A deputy took the food inside. The inmates and the staff wolfed down the cake and drank the soda pop. No one sang "Happy Birthday."

Saturday was cloudy, with intermittent drizzle; the heat wave had broken at last. About 3 in the afternoon, Bud and Tricia wanted to get out of the house. They packed the kids into the car, the trunk filled with fishing rods, and they drove to Wintersmith Park. There, for the next hour, they stood or sat on a small jetty that jutted into the lake, and they fished. The park was deserted; they had it almost all to themselves, except for the silent ducks and geese that glided through the dark water.

They did not catch any fish.

At exactly the same time, restless on this rainy Saturday, Mike Baskin and two other detectives drove to Sandy Creek. They were not going fishing. They were looking for Denice Haraway's body, one more time.

They parked near Reeves Road, got out, walked along the creek, poking in the brush, searching.

At the edge of the creek they came upon a pair of blue tennis shoes. There was a stain on one toe that looked like blood. Excited, Baskin picked it up. He studied it closely. He decided, disappointed, that the stain was mulberry juice, from a tree hanging over the creek. He tossed the sneakers down, and moved on.

Early Sunday afternoon, Tricia, Bud, the kids, and Joice went to the jail, to wish Tommy a happy birthday. He was wearing, for the visit, a new black T-shirt—a birthday gift from Charlene, the woman who was hoping to marry him. On the way home, hopeful of an acquittal, Tricia said, "Maybe this is the last time we'll have to go there."

Karl Fontenot also had a visitor that weekend—a winsome young lady, married, in her twenties. She did not know Karl, but her mother had known Karl's mother. Hearing that Karl had not had a single personal visitor in eleven months, the woman came to see him. She brought him a Bible and a checkers set.

Karl was exhilarated by the visit. He spent the night reading his new Bible.

He felt the trial was going well. He was especially happy about the Polaroid pictures showing both of them with short haircuts. Karl had taken the one that had Tommy and Jannette in it. He felt proud of that.

His new friend also brought him some magazines to read. The stories he liked best were those about people in jail.

Detective Captain Smith did not speak with Detective Baskin that weekend. But at three o'clock Sunday, Smith had the same urge Baskin had had the day before. He wanted one more crack at finding Denice Haraway's body, before the case went to the jury.

Smith, his wife, and another couple they were with climbed into the family Datsun. The captain chose a place he had not personally searched before: the portion of Sandy Creek near Reeves Road.

As they prowled along the creek, they came upon the same pair of tennis shoes Baskin had found the day before. There was darkness on one toe. Smith's friend thought it was blood. Dennis's heart leaped. He took the shoe, examined it.

Slowly his pulse quieted. He decided the dark spot was only tar.

DAY ELEVEN

Don Wyatt learned over the weekend that Jason Lurch and his wife had, for a time in 1984, lived at the Brook Trailer Park in the trailer of an elderly man, a Mr. Potter; ostensibly, for a fee from the state, they were taking care of him. If the trailer was in the old man's name, Lurch could have been living there without it showing on the trailer park records.

The first witness he called Monday morning was Pat Rockley, a social worker with the Oklahoma State Human Services Department. Ms. Rockley testified that the Lurches were supposed to be providing care for Mr. Potter, but that in fact they were stealing his welfare checks. She said she had recommended to Chris Ross that he prosecute the Lurches for their treatment of Mr. Potter, but that charges were never brought. Her investigation had begun in March of 1985, she said, and the Lurches had been associated with

Mr. Potter for two years. Jason Lurch, she said, was in and out of the Brook.

During his cross-examination, Chris Ross said he had not brought charges because the only complainant against the Lurches would have been Mr. Potter, and he was not competent. Asked if she knew where Jason Lurch was living on April 28, 1984, the social worker said she did not.

The witness stepped down. The defense attorneys huddled at their table, conferring. In the corridor outside, Tricia sat; she'd been told she would be the last witness called by the defense, to leave a good impression with the jury, and that today would be the day. Eleven blocks from the courthouse, on Broadway, Richard Kerner was talking to a clerk at the Indian Hills Motel.

The conference at the defense table went on for several minutes. The clock on the wall read 9:30 when Don Wyatt stood and faced the judge. "On behalf of defendant Ward," he said, "we will rest."

There was a stirring in the courtroom. The end had come unexpectedly soon.

Judge Powers summoned the defense counsels to the bench for a private conference; Bill Peterson, Chris Ross, Gary Rogers remained at the prosecution table.

Richard Kerner parked his car across the street and hurried into the courthouse, up the two flights of stairs. He had new information, he told Bill Willett: Lurch may have been living in Ada at the time of the disappearance, at the Indian Hills Motel. The old room records were not available at the motel, he said, but he would track them down.

Kerner was told the defense had just rested. He was extremely upset. How could they have rested, he wanted to know, without putting Jason Lurch on the stand?

Don Wyatt had evolved a different strategy. If he called Lurch as a witness, he reasoned, Lurch would deny living in Ada at the time, would deny being in J.P.'s with his nephew that night. And that would be the end of it. Wyatt could not badger his own witness. He was hoping that because Kerner had named Lurch from the stand as his prime suspect, and because the social worker had just painted a picture of

Lurch as a sleazy guy who would steal a sick old man's welfare checks, the district attorney would feel compelled to put Lurch on in the rebuttal period to follow, to say he had not been in Ada at the time. Then, Wyatt reasoned, on cross-examination, where attorneys have a lot more freedom, he could attack Lurch. He could bring out what Lurch had told the lawyers in their first meeting: that he had lived in Ada at the time, that he had painted trucks, that he and his nephew might well have been in J.P.'s that night.

He could only hope that Peterson would take the bait.

The attorneys returned to their seats. The clock said 9:57. George Butner stood and addressed the judge. "Defendant Fontenot," he said, "for the purposes of this hearing, rests."

In the corridor, Tricia was surprised. After all the rehearsals, she would not need to testify. It was fine with her. The attorneys knew best.

The rebuttal phase of the trial began. The state called David Stark, the director of emergency services at Valley View Hospital, in an attempt to impeach Ward's alibi witness. Stark said he knew Joice Cavins; that he taught a class she attended Saturdays in the spring of 1984. He produced his attendance record for the class. They showed, he said, that Joice had been present in his class for about six hours that day; that she had taken an exam that day, and scored 70 percent.

Wyatt was prepared for this. Joice had told him that sometimes the instructors had softball games scheduled on Saturdays, and canceled the class but marked everyone present anyway. That's what happened that day, she'd said. The instructor, on the stand, denied this.

"Your class was not in session between the hours of 5 P.M. and midnight, was it?" Wyatt asked.

"No," the instructor said.

The state called Larry Johnson, the deputy sheriff of Lincoln County, to shoot down one of Richard Kerner's scenarios: that among the possible suspects in the Haraway case were Don Wilson Hawkins and Dale Austin Shelton, the two men still being sought in the recent kidnapping in Oklahoma City. The sheriff, a record book open on his lap, said that Don Hawkins had been in his jail from December 19,

1982, to September 18, 1984—which covered the night of the Haraway disappearance.

On cross-examination, Wyatt asked if Dale Shelton was in his jail that night. The sheriff said no.

"How about Mr. Jason Lurch, was he in your jail?"

"I don't recall the name," the deputy said.

The state recalled Karen Wise to the stand, in an attempt to show that Jason Lurch and Ricky Brewer were not the ones she'd seen in J.P.'s the night Denice Haraway disappeared. Peterson showed her a photograph of Brewer, asked if she knew him. "I didn't know him by name. He was a regular customer of mine," Ms. Wise said.

He showed her a picture of Lurch, asked if he was in her store that night. "No, sir, I don't believe so," Ms. Wise said. "They were regular customers, but I don't believe so."

On cross-examination, she was asked, "If this is your old buddy you knew from the store, I'm wondering why he would make you nervous."

"He looked familiar to me, and he was staring at me," Ms. Wise said. "I do not like to be stared at."

Wise was excused. Wyatt hoped that Jason Lurch would be next.

Bill Peterson huddled with Ross and Rogers. He decided that Karen Wise had effectively shot down the Lurch-Brewer scenario, when she said they were regular customers. The district attorney stood. It was 10:22 A.M. "Your honor, the State of Oklahoma rests," he said.

Seven minutes passed while Wyatt, Butner, and Austin conferred about whether to call rebuttal witnesses of their own. Then Wyatt and Butner stood.

"The defense rests," Wyatt said.

"The defense rests," Butner echoed.

Despite all the backstage drama, the jurors would never see Jason Lurch, the "mystery man."

The judge sent the jury from the courtroom. Ward and Fontenot, in their respective chairs, watched silently. Butner asked that the judge issue a directed verdict of acquittal, for lack of evidence, and that the charges against Karl Fontenot be dismissed.

"Overruled," Judge Powers said.

Wyatt adopted the same motion on behalf of Tommy Ward.

"Overruled," the judge said.

He retired to his chambers, to consider his instructions to the jury. An hour later the jury was returned to the room. The judge told them that as of that moment they were under sequestration; they were in the custody of the bailiff, and could go nowhere without him. The bailiff was sworn in to sequester the jury.

It was time for lunch. The judge told the jurors they would be escorted by the bailiff to Mercy's sandwich shop.

17

VERDICT

With testimony completed, the ban on witnesses in the courtroom had ended. The personal tragedy of the case was ever more visible in the second and third rows. In the second row, Steve Haraway's father, mother, sister still sat; Steve would come tomorrow. Directly behind them, filling the entire third row, were the Wards— Tommy's mother, three of his sisters, all of his brothers. The rest of the courtroom was jammed as well—with seekers of justice or of vengeance; with students of legal procedure; with lovers of a mystery.

Bill Peterson, who had lived with this case as with a ghost in the bedroom since the day of the arrests, had gone to lunch, alone, at McCartney's Drug Store on Main Street; had eaten a sandwich at a formica table. Now he sat at the prosecution table, listening, as the judge read sixty-nine technical legal instructions to the jury. He would be first up when the judge was through.

Dennis Smith, who had lived with the case since Baskin's phone call awakened him that Saturday night, could sit in the courtroom for the first time since he testified; he squeezed into a space in the press row.

The defendants sat in their customary seats, the judge's instructions passing over their heads like clouds. The lawyers sat behind them, listening carefully. On such technical matters as the instructions to a jury many a conviction has been overturned on appeal.

Above the witness stand a microphone hung, useless, dead. It had hung there throughout the trial, without being used, like a mute symbol, signifying nothing. Whether it would have worked, had a switch been thrown, was a matter of speculation.

The judge's instructions took twenty minutes. When he was finished, at 3:04 P.M., Bill Peterson went to a blackboard on the wall. He wrote on it the critical dates of the case:

April 28, 1984
May 1, 1984
October 12, 1984
October 18, 1984
Others

Then he began his summation. In his customary, logical way, the only way he liked to work, he began at the beginning, and worked forward. He recalled for the jury every witness the state had presented, and what they had said under oath. He recited at length all the work the Ada police and the OSBI had put into solving the case.

In the press row, Dorothy Hogue whispered to a colleague: "Is he trying to convict them, or defend the investigation?"

He recalled what Jim Moyer had seen at McAnally's at 7:30 that night; what Karen Wise and Jack Paschall had seen at J.P.'s at 8. Then his voice grew rounder, filled the courtroom. "About 8:30 that evening," Peterson said, "death drove up to the front of McAnally's, in a gray primer pickup."

In lengthy detail, the D.A. reiterated the testimony of all those at the scene: the witnesses, the cops. As he talked, Barney Ward, the blind attorney, stood outside the courtroom, conversing with a man in a peaked cap. The attorney had sat in on the trial several times, guided by his secretary.

"Barney, I don't know how they're going to get a verdict," the man in the cap said.

"I don't know either," Barney Ward said, from behind his opaque black glasses.

"I don't know how they got a jury," the man said.

"Neither do I," Barney Ward said.

Then he added, "But I'll tell you this. They've got the best judge in the state."

In the courtroom, Peterson continued his review of the case. He spoke with derision of Jannette Roberts's hand-dated Easter pictures. They could have been taken any year, he said.

He reviewed the gruesome story on the confession tapes. "Was it a dream to Denice?" he asked, his voice rising again. "Or a living nightmare?"

He turned to the testimony of the defense's private investigator. "Richard Kerner, crime-fighter!" he said, his voice heavy with sarcasm. "Dick Tracy in disguise! . . . I for one am going to sleep a lot easier knowing that Mr. Kerner is out there, solving crimes by taking pictures of people and pickups that had absolutely nothing to do with the disappearance."

Recalling Kerner's testimony that Jason Lurch and Ricky Brewer resembled the composite drawings, Peterson pointed a finger at his own assistant D.A. "If Mr. Ross would lose about fifty pounds, *he* would resemble that composite," Peterson said.

"There's only two people in this courtroom who know where Denice is," the D.A. said. And he stared at the defendants.

The summation went on for hours. The key moment in the case, Peterson suggested, was when David Timmons saw a man and a woman leaving McAnally's, the man's arm around the woman's waist. "What was in that hand," Peterson asked the jury, "and why did she walk out of there?"

It was ten minutes after six in the evening when the district attorney concluded. The judge acknowledged to the jury that they had already put in a long day; but he wanted to finish the closing arguments this evening, he said. The jury would be taken during the supper hour to their place of sequestration, the Raintree Motor Inn, where they would be assigned rooms. He would like them back in court by 7:30 P.M., or as soon thereafter as possible.

"We certainly won't start till you get back," he said.

They were not back at 7:30. They were not back at 8:15. The courtroom was packed with spectators, waiting, wanting to be in on the climax. On the second floor, alone, Don Wyatt paced the dim corridor, his closing remarks running through his head. In the press row, the most experienced of the news reporters, Cheryl Fathree of the Tulsa *World*, offered a bit of gallows humor: "What's the difference," she asked, "between a dead skunk in the road and a dead lawyer in the road?"

No one knew.

"There are skid marks in front of the skunk."

Fed and registered at the motel, the jurors returned, accompanied by the bailiff, at 8:45 P.M. George Butner began his closing statement on behalf of Karl Fontenot.

Butner noted that while three people had placed Tommy Ward in the area, not one of these—or anyone else—had placed Fontenot there. He pointed out that the "other man" had been described as sandy-haired, and that Karl's hair is black.

There was not one shred of evidence, he said, to back up the taped statements. Where is the pickup? he wanted to know. Where is the knife? Where is the body? The prosecution did not even have a scene where it took place, he said. "Nothing. Not anything."

He recalled how Gordon Calhoun and Terry Holland had said Karl took pride in telling a good story. "Do you put more credibility in Wise and Moyer, or in Karl?" he asked. "Wise and Moyer said he wasn't there!"

He castigated the police actions in the case. "Two good confessions," Butner said, "can cure a lot of incompetent investigation."

He said he had a problem in his mind with the times before the videotapes were turned on. He recalled Karen Wise's fear of Jason Lurch at the hearings; her fear of the man in the alley outside her house, who fit Lurch's description. He recalled the threatening calls she had received, long after these defendants were in jail.

"You've heard all the evidence about Karl," he said. "It doesn't fly. No ifs, ands, buts, or ors. It doesn't fly."

He concluded by urging the jury to give each defendant "separate consideration."

As Butner moved toward his seat, Tommy Ward looked at him with what seemed like pained hatred. Either Ward did not understand the separate loyalties of the two attorneys, or he understood it, at that moment, all too well.

Butner concluded at 9:17. Don Wyatt rose and took his place.

He began by focusing on the Polaroid pictures of Ward and Fontenot with short hair. These, he said, were "the only hard physical evidence in the case."

Of the tapes, he said, "The statements are gruesome. They're gruesome! But they're also not true."

He said the ideas on the tapes had been planted during the October 12 questioning; that on October 18, Tommy Ward had already been programmed to elaborate his dream into the fantasy they had seen on the tape.

He defended Richard Kerner against the sarcasm Bill Peterson had displayed. The state, Wyatt said, had all the resources of the Ada police, the sheriff's office, the OSBI. "And we had one detective. And he was a good one. A darn good one."

He recounted for the jury his theory of two separate incidents. He said the truck that had belonged to Jason Lurch's nephew was "identical in every way" to the one seen at J.P.'s.

"I'm not saying he did it," Wyatt said. He was saying that Lurch and Brewer were the ones seen in J.P.'s that night—not Tommy Ward and Karl Fontenot.

"Confessions are highly suspect," Wyatt told the jury. That was why, under the law, a crime had to be proven before the jury could consider a confession.

He reviewed what he called the pressure tactics of the police in this case: the pressure put on Odell Titsworth, the bringing of the bones to the jail. "You have the opportunity," he said, "to stop the type of tactics the police are using—to coerce, to intimidate."

He recalled the testimony of the alibi witnesses, who had sworn under oath that Tommy Ward was somewhere else—was in his own home—at the time the alleged crime was taking place.

He asked why the state had not called Jannette Roberts to the stand, which it had every right to do. And he answered his own question: "Because they could not disprove those photos!"

He concluded by reading a newspaper quotation from Bill Peterson, which had appeared the previous November. In it, the D.A. had warned that it would be difficult to get a conviction in this case without a body.

And Wyatt asked for an acquittal.

It was 10 P.M. when he finished. The judge ordered a fifteen-minute break. Tommy Ward's family huddled around him, hugging him, showing their support, after the jurors had filed out.

Karl Fontenot sat alone.

There was weariness in the faces of the jurors when they filed back in, settled into their chairs; one juror, a gentleman, appeared to be well over seventy years old. Weariness was reflected in the visage of Judge Powers, in the rumpled suits of the attorneys on both sides, in the slumping shoulders of the defendants. A weary determination seemed to pervade both the Haraways and the Wards, and even the spectators with no personal stake in the trial.

Chris Ross walked to the center of the courtroom, his broad shoulders squared. And he launched eagerly into his closing statement, the last argumentative words the jury would hear before being sent to deliberate.

Ross tweaked the defense attorneys. "We don't attract clients if we win a big case," he said of the D.A.'s office. And he defended the police. "It is no great flaw in investigative technique that they couldn't find a truck or a knife six months later." He justified a conviction even though no body had been found: "We are not to reward criminals for their stealth."

Of Karl Fontenot, he said his hair had become darker during his long months in jail, out of the sunlight. Of Fontenot's confession, he said, "There's many a man who tells a good fish story. But how many of them tell it to the game ranger?"

He derided Odell Titsworth's testimony about intense pressure from the police. "He's a con!" Ross said. And he asked, "Who testified to the pressure on Ward and Fontenot who was there? Not a person!"

He held up for the jury the Polaroid pictures offered by Jannette Blood Roberts, showing both men with short hair. He recited with scorn her criminal record. "Her credibility stinks!" he shouted.

The pictures, he said, could have been taken in Easter of 1982 or

1983. But not 1984. The child in the picture, he said, was much too small to be seven years old.

He asked why, if Jason Lurch was a suspect, Don Wyatt had not put him in the witness chair, instead of just showing a snapshot with "his spanking new building in the background."

Of the private investigator, Ross said, "Mr. Kerner is a hired gun, who came in this courtroom loaded with blanks."

The assistant D.A. retold, in vivid, bloody detail, the story of rape and murder on the tapes, the rape of a corpse with her entrails showing. Cinda Haraway began to sob. She ran out of the courtroom, to hear no more of this tale of the murder of her brother's wife.

Ross said the defense had implied the police knew Ward and Fontenot were innocent. "Why show them the bones to get more evidence, if police knew they didn't know?"

"Who was playing mind games with who?" Ross asked.

Tommy Ward stared at him with hatred as he spoke; Fontenot, as always, looked impassive.

Conviction in this case, Ross said, would be "a very small step indeed, when you consider they've already told you they did it."

A frequent question in the case, Ross said, was why Denice did not seek help from Lenny Timmons when he passed her in the doorway of McAnally's. "How would she know he wasn't in on it too?" Ross asked.

Then he offered the jury his own interpretation of the confession tapes, as he had refined it in the bathtub the week before. He said "Odell" on Tommy's tape was Tommy himself. The proof, he said, was that everywhere on the tape, when Odell was doing something, Tommy was not present. And vice-versa. Because if Tommy had said "Odell and me" did this, it would have amounted to saying "me and me did this."

On the tape, Odell raped her first, Ross said. But that was really Tommy raping her first. And because he had already raped her as "Odell," Tommy himself could not get an erection. Tommy was not in the store, because "Odell" was, Ross said. But "Odell" was Tommy; they could not do anything together. When "Odell" was stabbing her to death, Ross noted, Tommy was back at his house. Because, Ross said, Tommy was Odell, and they could not both be in the same scene.

In truth, he said, it was Tommy who had stabbed her to death, Tommy who set fire to the body. Because we know Odell Titsworth wasn't there!

Denice Haraway's body was burned, Ross said, "maybe not in that house, but somewhere!"

"Surely," he said, "God did not intend for Denice Haraway to die that night. These two men made that decision.

"We ask for everything in the name of truth. All we want is the truth.

"The evidence proves beyond a reasonable doubt that these defendants are guilty of these crimes."

Ross stopped. Ross sat. A dark, total silence enveloped the courtroom, suggesting a black vacuum hole in outer space. The silence was thunderous, the inverse of a burst of theatrical applause. The assistant D.A. had brought the trial to its emotional height. The understudy had become, for this moment, the star.

The round-faced clock above the spectators showed 11:45. Fifteen minutes till the witching hour. Perhaps because of that, there was an eerie power to Ross's interpretation of Ward's tape; a power that few in the courtroom could escape, could deny. Or perhaps it was more than the hour. Perhaps it was the infusion of interior logic into a story, into a tape, into a case itself, where logic had been a stranger.

For some in the courtroom it would be several long midnight hours before the eeriness fell away, before other logical questions would begin to assert themselves. Such as: If "Odell" was an aberration, merely Tommy's alter ego, why did Odell Titsworth appear in Fontenot's tape as well? Such as: On Tommy's tape, Odell and Tommy *were* in the store together. Such as: This was an interesting theory Ross had, but it was only a theory; it was not evidence; the case still was supposed to be decided on evidence. Where had the body gone? And the truck? Why give a genuine confession made of lies?

What would hold sway in the minds of the jury, no one, at that late hour, could say.

The testimony and the arguments were done. The judge dismissed the two alternate jurors. And he submitted the case to the jury. He told them to retire to the jury room, to select a foreman. After that, he said, they could stay as long as they wanted to deliberate; or they could return to their motel till morning.

The jury was led out by the bailiff. George Butner crossed the courtroom and shook Chris Ross's hand. He congratulated him on a strong summation. Privately, Butner was in turmoil. He felt that Ross's theory made sense. The assistant D.A. smiled about his statement, winked to someone at the rear of the courtroom.

In the corridor, Jannette Roberts, who had sat through the summations, was crying quietly. Ross's shouted words—"Her credibility stinks!"—would not fade from her mind.

"I'm so sorry. I'm so sorry," she murmured, over and over.

"For what?" Bill Willett asked.

"For my past," she said.

It was six minutes after midnight when the jury returned to the courtroom. They would like to retire for the night, they told the judge, and begin their deliberations in the morning.

The judge asked if they had chosen a foreman.

They had.

They had chosen juror number one: a young man named Leslie Penn. He was the man, in his early thirties, perhaps, who had spent the past nine days, almost without interruption, staring at the defendants with a stern, unwavering look.

The judge recessed the trial till 9 A.M. The weary jury filed out. In the corridor, Jannette Roberts continued to cry.

"My daughter is small," she said, telling anyone who would listen. "I should have brought her down here."

DAY TWELVE

When the jurors returned in the morning after a night's rest at the Raintree, two to a room, men with men, women with women, they filed slowly into the jury room, behind the courtroom, to deliberate. The people who would decide the fate of the defendants, perhaps even whether they lived or died, were, in the position in which they sat in the jury box:

Front row—Leslie Penn, Claudia Mornhinweg, Larry Myers, Joanne Manning, Janet Williams, Nina Ambrose.

Second row—Darlene Berry, Virginia Rowe, Thomas Daniel, Diana Brotherton, Mary Floyd, Alfred Byers.

A handful of spectators sat in the quiet courtroom. Among them was Steve Haraway, making his first appearance since he testified two weeks earlier. Unable to watch the trial because he was a witness, he had also been unable to work, because his job selling pharmaceuticals involved travel. He had spent the time chopping wood, doing paperwork for his job. Each night his mother and father and sister would tell him how it was going. He said he had no doubts that the defendants were guilty.

Several of the Wards, too, sat in the courtroom, or stood in the corridors. One of them, Melvin, was still incensed about Chris Ross's closing argument the night before. "He wasn't only attacking Tommy," Melvin said, fighting back tears his shipmates on the *Coral Sea* had never seen, "he was calling my whole family liars."

At 10:15, the jury sent three oral requests to the judge. They would like to have all of the exhibits brought to the jury room, except for the skull and bones; they would like a magnifying glass; and they would like to review the tapes, with no one else present, so they could discuss them while they watched.

Judge Powers responded that a magnifying glass was not available, and that even if one was, he was not sure its use would be proper, since none had been used in the courtroom. He had a problem with letting them see the tapes again. "Giving them part of the testimony, but not all, magnifies one part out of proportion," he said.

The attorneys debated. Bill Peterson wanted the jury to see the tapes again. Butner argued that after eight and a half days of testimony, to allow them to review only two hours of it would be prejudicial. He and Leo Austin objected strenuously.

The judge denied the jury's request.

In a second-floor corridor, Jannette Roberts sat with her daughter, Jessica, the little girl in the picture with the Easter basket. Jessica had turned eight years old two weeks earlier. She appeared very small for her age—the point Mrs. Roberts wanted to make.

"I used to let them baby-sit my kids," she said of Tommy and Karl. "I've been in prison. I've talked to murderers. I know how they speak. I have a little bit of insight of how they would act and talk. I spent six years in there. It's an experience I had that helps me choose my friends, and the people I want around my children."

She recalled how she and her husband had urged Tommy to talk to the police, because they knew he had nothing to hide; they were devastated when he was arrested. "I still feel I threw him to the wolves over a dream," she said. "I can't believe they took that dream and twisted it. This whole thing seems like a dream."

Remembering Chris Ross's scathing attack on her credibility the night before, she turned away, to hide her eyes, to maintain her image of toughness. "I was planning to move back to Ada," she said, bitterly. "He blew it."

Jannette, too, once had a dream about Denice Haraway. It was a few nights after Tommy and Karl had been arrested. She dreamed that she and her husband were standing someplace, looking at Denice Haraway, who was alive. No one else was in the dream. In the morning she told the dream to her husband. "God," Mike said. "Don't say nothing about it."

At 12:40 P.M., the judge summoned the jury to the courtroom. He asked if they had reached any verdicts, on any of the six counts. The foreman said they had not.

The foreman reiterated the jury's desire to review the tapes. The judge again denied it. He sent them, in the care of the bailiff, to lunch, at Polo's Restaurant, on Main Street.

George Butner, always pessimistic about the outcome, saw a small ray of light for the defense. "The thing I'm encouraged about is that we've got someone—at least one person—in there holding out for acquittal. Even if he's a weak noodle, it's someone."

But he could not get too optimistic. Whenever he tried to, he thought again of Fontenot's tape, and how, despite the discrepancies, it told basically the same story as Ward's. The tapes, he feared, would "marry them together."

"It looks like there's light at the end of the tunnel," Butner said.

"And then every time you get there, it's not light, but a brick wall you run smack into."

The jury returned from lunch, resumed its deliberations. Bill Peterson remained in his office. The defense attorneys chatted in the office of the court clerk. Some of the Haraways and some of the Wards sat quietly in the courtroom. The defendants were across the lawn in the jail. Charlene, the young woman who said she wanted to marry Tommy, stood, stocky and tough-looking, alone on a stairway landing, waiting nervously, chain-smoking.

At 4:20, word spread—the jurors would be returning to the courtroom. It filled quickly, with the D.A., the defense attorneys, the spectators, the press. The defendants were brought in.

The bailiff said the jurors would like some Cokes in the jury room. For a moment, it seemed that was why everyone had hurried back.

The law says no refreshments in the jury room, Judge Powers said. But when both sides stipulated it would be okay, the judge agreed.

Judge Powers turned toward the spectators. He warned them to show no facial expressions or emotions toward the jurors, to let them do their job. Any outburst could be subject to contempt of court. "I know none of you would want to spend time in the county jail," the judge said.

The jurors entered and took their seats.

"Have you reached a verdict?" Judge Powers asked.

"Not yet," the foreman, Leslie Penn, said.

"Have you reached a verdict on one or more of the counts?" the judge asked.

"Yes," the foreman said.

"You are not at an impasse at this time?"

"No."

He sent them back to continue deliberating, with Cokes.

Outside the courthouse, from which the town now seemed to spread in concentric circles, people were following the case avidly. There were bulletins on the radio. The case led the local TV newscasts. Copies of the Ada *News*, which often languished unbought in the metal cages in which they were offered for sale, were grabbed up as soon as they hit the streets. People continued to go to work, of course, to do their jobs, to earn their pay; Bud Wolf, sometime "big brother" to Tommy, whose emotions were strung tight, was at the feed mill as usual that afternoon, preparing feed that would be shipped throughout the Midwest for the coming winter.

In mid-afternoon, one of Bud's co-workers approached him. "I just heard it on the radio," the man said. "They convicted Tommy."

"You're a lying scuzzball," Bud replied.

"No, I just heard it. They convicted him!"

"You're a lying scuzzball," Bud said again.

At five in the afternoon, with the jury still out, Don Wyatt received a phone call at the courthouse. His wife's father had been undergoing exploratory surgery that day, in Oklahoma City, for a problem the doctors couldn't define. They'd opened him up and found many of his vital organs rife with cancer. It was spread wide; it was inoperable. They'd sewn him up and given him three months to live, at most. He was still under the anesthetic; he might not come out of it. Jean needed to get up there right away; she wanted Don to come with her.

For a few moments the lawyer felt impaled. His wife needed him—her father was dying. His client needed him—his fate, his life, was in the balance.

He felt a sense of déjà vu. About five years earlier, in the middle of a trial, Jean's grandfather had died. Wyatt had decided then that the trial was too important to leave. He had stayed in court.

Neither had forgotten it. His decision had become one of those faint gray clouds that hang over even the best of marriages.

Wyatt decided he could not do that again.

His defense of Tommy Ward was completed, he reasoned; the testimony was done, the final arguments had been made. Now it was up to the jury.

Should they bring in a guilty verdict, and have to go into the second phase, the penalty phase—deciding on life imprisonment or death—Leo Austin could handle that.

Wyatt told Austin and Willett the situation. He hurried out of the courthouse, across to the parking lot, climbed into his Charger, drove home to get his wife. He drove her the ninety miles to the city, believing he had done the right thing.

From Baptist Memorial Hospital, where his father-in-law still lay under the anesthetic, he phoned Tricia at her home. He explained the situation, assured her that Tommy's case was still in good hands.

Tricia understood. She was grateful he had taken the trouble, personally, to call.

For a few minutes after 5 there was bustling in the courthouse as municipal workers, not involved in the trial, went home. Dennis Smith, Mike Baskin, Bill Peterson, Gary Rogers chatted in the D.A.'s office, waiting. Rogers had his jacket off; his pistol in its shoulder holster was exposed. When the workers had gone, the only sound in the first-floor hallway was the refrigerator-like shuddering of the Dr Pepper machine.

Half an hour passed. It was 5:55. The bailiffs summoned all sides to the courtroom. No one knew if this was for a supper break or a verdict. The jury was brought in. They did not have their coats with them.

"Have you reached a verdict in the case?" Judge Powers asked.

"No, sir," the foreman said.

There was a moment of wild hope in the minds of the defense attorneys. The longer it went, the better chance they had. A quick verdict, they knew, in this town, in this case, would have to be "guilty."

But their hope was short-lived. The judge asked if verdicts had been reached on any of the six counts—the three against Ward, the three against Fontenot.

They had agreed on four verdicts, the foreman said.

The judge suggested they take a dinner break, and then resume.

"We have a few people that's tired, and some that's hurting," the foreman said. "We'd like to retire for the night."

The judge honored the request. He sent them back to the Raintree. They were to resume at 8:30 in the morning.

When the jurors left, the corridors were abuzz with speculation. Four verdicts after eight hours of deliberation. It seemed to indicate a victory for the prosecution.

"Somebody ain't walkin'," Chris Ross said, happily.

The possible combinations of four verdicts seemed endless. Was one defendant guilty on all three charges, and the other, for now, on one? Or was it two and two? And had they dealt with the lesser charges first—robbery and kidnapping—or had they started with murder?

The prosecutors, hanging out in the D.A.'s office, were buoyant, almost in a party mood. The defense attorneys, Butner and Austin, seemed resigned now to a conviction, at least of Ward. Leo Austin began to ponder how to handle phase two of the hearing—the death penalty phase—should Ward be convicted.

Don Wyatt phoned Bill Willett from the hospital in Oklahoma City; Willett told him the news: Wyatt agreed that it sounded bad.

His father-in-law was still under the anesthetic. Wyatt would be staying there overnight.

Bill Cathy went to Bud and Tricia's home, to get some of the religious poems Tommy had been writing in the jail; perhaps they would help the jury show mercy. At the house the family was eating; a TV set brought from Tulsa by Joel, to keep the kids entertained, was on. A sense of weariness pervaded the household. They understood that the worst might be coming; that a quick verdict would mean conviction.

In the courthouse block, George Butner walked toward his car. Chris Ross pulled up in his own car, at a red light.

"What do you think?" Ross called out.

"I'd rather be sitting at your table," Butner replied.

"Come on over," Ross shouted back. "We'll still trade a life sentence for the body."

Butner did not respond. The light changed to green. The assistant D.A.'s car moved away.

DAY THIRTEEN

The morning was gloomy, rainy, dark. As the jurors moved in a slow motorcade from the Raintree Motor Inn to the courthouse, the headlights of their cars were on. At the courthouse they parked, walked silently up the stairs. It was 8:30 A.M. when they resumed their deliberations.

Jannette Roberts was waiting at the courthouse when Tricia, Kay, Joel, and Miz Ward arrived. She had something to tell them. Don't get your hopes up, she warned. But the night before, one of her daughters had gone to a Girl Scout meeting. A woman there told her that her best friend worked at Anthony's department store—and that three weeks ago, a check had cleared through the store, signed by Denice Haraway.

The Wards hurried up the stairs, found Bill Willett. They repeated what Jannette had said. It was a wild notion, Willett thought. The jury was already out; they had already reached four verdicts. But stranger things had already happened in this case; nothing could be taken for granted; nothing was as it seemed. It was worth checking out. Willett hurried to his car across the street, drove the four miles out on Mississippi, out on Arlington, in the dreary drizzle, to Anthony's.

Tricia and Miz Ward sat on a bench in the dim second-floor corridor, a floor below the jury room. They speculated about the check at Anthony's, clutching at this one last straw. Why would someone say that if it wasn't true?

But they knew there had been so many rumors, right from the beginning . . .

On the first floor, the prosecutors and the police were speculating again about the four decided verdicts. Mike Baskin was confidently expecting six-for-six convictions.

The jurors continued to debate.

Bill Willett returned from Anthony's, light drops clinging to his raincoat. He had talked to the manager there. There was no record of any recent check signed by Denice Haraway.

At 9:30, one hour after they entered the courthouse, the jurors got word to the bailiff: they had a verdict.

Word spread through the building as if by osmosis. The courtroom filled quickly. Two young girl reporters from KTEN set up a camera just outside the courtroom, with the permission of Judge Powers; until then he had barred cameras or recording equipment above the first floor.

Steve Haraway and his parents entered, took their customary places in the second row. The Wards sat in the fourth row. Dennis Smith entered, Mike Baskin, Gary Rogers. The OSBI agent, tight-visaged throughout the trial, was laughing, joking with the press, as if the pressure finally were off; as if the quick verdicts must surely be "guilty."

The judge summoned the attorneys for both sides into his chambers. The defendants were brought into the courtroom. Ward was wearing the three-piece rust corduroy suit from the Salvation Army that Fontenot had worn the first day of the trial, two and a half weeks ago; Fontenot was wearing the three-piece beige suit that Tommy had worn that day, which belonged to Bud Wolf. Ward looked around the courtroom, a worried expression on his face. Fontenot, impassive, gazed at the empty jury box and yawned.

The spectator section was full. Courthouse workers, deputies, others stood at the rear; standing, too, had been barred until now. The defendants had their hands clasped in their laps.

The D.A.s and the attorneys returned from chambers, sat at their respective tables. All rose as Judge Powers entered, then sat.

"The court will not tolerate any outburst or show of emotion," the judge told the spectators. "If you don't think you can handle it, leave now."

No one left.

The jurors filed in at 9:45. All had their eyes cast down as they found their seats. Then they looked at the judge—all except the foreman, Leslie Penn, who stared hard at the defendants, as he had done through most of the trial.

All seemed impassive except juror number six, Nina Ambrose, a middle-aged housewife, in the end seat, first row—the seat closest to the defendants. Nina Ambrose had tears in her eyes.

The judge asked the jury if it had reached a verdict.

"Yes," the foreman said.

He handed the bailiff six sheets of paper. A verdict was contained on each. The bailiff crossed the courtroom, handed the papers to the judge. In silence he looked at them, one after the other. The faces of the jurors were blank.

At 9:47 A.M., the court clerk began to read the verdicts aloud. She began with Tommy Ward.

On count number one, robbery with a dangerous weapon: "Guilty."

The jury's sentence: twenty years in prison.

Tommy Ward began to weep. He brought his hands up to cover his face.

On count number two, kidnapping: "Guilty."

The sentence: ten years in prison; the maximum.

Ward was crying quietly, uncontrollably; his entire body was shaking. In the fourth row, all of the Wards had tears on their cheeks. An occasional sniffle was the only sound.

On count number three, murder in the first degree: "Guilty."

Tommy Ward was shaking his head, his palms pressed to his face, the quiet tears flowing.

Karl Fontenot, beside him, showed no reaction.

The clerk read the verdicts on Fontenot.

Robbery with a dangerous weapon: "Guilty." Twenty years in prison.

Kidnapping: "Guilty." Ten years in prison.

Murder in the first degree: "Guilty."

Tommy Ward could not stop crying, could not stop shuddering.

Karl Fontenot showed no reaction.

The judge declared a fifteen-minute recess. He told the jurors to "go back and relax." Then they would return for the penalty phase, in which the jury would recommend the penalty on the murder convictions: life imprisonment or death.

The defendants were led out. Fontenot appeared as if nothing unusual had happened. Ward leaned heavily on a deputy.

The Ward family left the courtroom, all of them crying. Joel had to support his mother. Only Melvin stayed. And Charlene, who wanted to marry Tommy Ward.

Betty Haraway chatted with a friend in the courtroom, the slightest hint of a smile on her face. A girl approached Steve Haraway. "Congratulations," she said.

Dennis Smith, the detective captain, was elated; he could not put his emotions into words. He took Steve Haraway into a private office, to talk.

Downstairs, just outside the courthouse, a KTEN reporter asked Tricia for her reaction. "Just because the jury says he did it," Tricia said, "doesn't mean he did it. Only the Lord knows the truth. On Judgment Day, He will decide."

The reporter liked the statement. She asked if Tricia would be interviewed on camera. Tricia declined.

In the penalty phase, to get a death sentence, the state would have to prove one of three things: that the murder had been especially heinous or cruel; that it had been committed to prevent the victim from identifying the perpetrators of a felony; or that the defendants constituted a continuing threat to society. Both sides could present witnesses, who could be cross-examined. There would be closing arguments, deliberations by the jury. Like the verdicts, a death sentence would have to be unanimous.

When the defendants were brought back in, Fontenot still looked bland; Ward was crying quietly.

The jurors took their seats. Bill Peterson began his opening remarks. He said the state's first witness would be a woman named Joanne Price. Mrs. Price, he said, would tell the jury that on July 30, 1984, three months after Denice Haraway was murdered, Mrs. Price had been threatened, and her car attacked, by Tommy Ward and another man, who resembled Fontenot.

Juror number two, Claudia Mornhinweg, a dark-haired young woman, began to cry.

"You liar!" Karl Fontenot said, in a fierce whisper to the D.A., who was standing a few feet from him. "Son of a bitch!"

Ms. Mornhinweg began to cry louder, to sob beyond control. Leo Austin and George Butner leaped up and approached Judge Powers. The judge asked the juror if she would like a recess. Both the woman and the foreman said yes.

The jurors left the room.

The lawyers huddled with the defendants. Tommy told Leo Austin he'd been working in Norman at the time of this alleged attack. The lawyers scurried for a 1984 calendar, to make sure July 30 had not been on a weekend. It hadn't.

They placed a call to Mike Roberts, Jannette's husband, who had been Tommy's boss in the aluminum-siding business at the time; they told him to drive down from Norman as quickly as he could, so he could testify that Tommy had been working that day, and to bring any written proof he might have.

The jury returned, all of them again composed. Peterson called Joanne Price to the stand; she was a sturdy, blond young woman, wearing a red blouse with white ruffles. She testified that about 5 P.M. on July 30, she had been driving near the town of Allen, about twenty miles from Ada, with her baby, when a pickup drove up behind her. It was gray-primered, she said. She said several times the pickup came close to her rear bumper, then passed her, then slowed down in front of her. About ten miles east of Ada, she said, the passenger in the pickup threw a beer bottle that hit her driver-side window. Frightened, she pulled off the road. The driver, she said, got out and began pounding on her car and calling her names.

"I told him I had a gun and would shoot him," Mrs. Price said. "It seemed to enrage him. He started screaming and hollering. He ran back to the pickup and got a board." She said the man then began beating on her windshield with the board, breaking it.

The man, she said, she now knew was Tommy Ward. The passenger, who remained in the truck, resembled Karl Fontenot, she said, but she could not be certain it had been him.

Mrs. Price said she threw her baby into the backseat, put her car in gear, and sped away, knocking Ward down. "He got up, got in the truck, got in behind me again," she said.

When she came to a store, she said, she stopped and called the sheriff's office. She said she gave a description of the two men to the authorities. But she did not know who they were, she said, until October, after Ward and Fontenot were arrested in the Haraway case. At that time she was shown a photo lineup by Dennis Smith, she said, and she picked Ward's and Fontenot's pictures from the lineup.

It was Mrs. Price's testimony that Judge Powers had barred from the main phase of the trial, because the alleged incident happened after the Haraway case, and therefore was not related to the pending charges.

On cross-examination, Leo Austin brought out that no charges had ever been filed in the alleged attack. Butner emphasized that Mrs. Price had seen the passenger only in a passing glance, and was not sure it had been Fontenot. Neither attorney raised the question of how this mysterious gray-primered pickup was capable of disappearing and reappearing and disappearing again despite the constant efforts of the police to find it.

The witness was excused.

"The state rests," Bill Peterson said.

The judge ordered the noon recess. Betty Haraway hugged the district attorney. Jack Haraway shook his hand, a big smile on the dentist's face. "It feels better," he said.

The Ward family had not remained in the courtroom during this penalty phase; they stood outside the courthouse, under skies that had brightened, and waited, and talked, and tried not to cry. As they stood there and the noon recess was ordered and the jurors began to move down the stairs, a florist delivery van from Donaghey's Greenhouse pulled up and double-parked in front of the main entrance, near where the Wards were standing. A delivery man got out, moved to the rear of the van, opened the rear doors. From the van he took a large green wreath, about four feet across, and a metal stand. He carried them to the grass in front of the entrance. He set the stand up beside the walkway, and placed the wreath on it, facing the entrance. Then he walked back to the van to get another.

A large ribbon across the front of the wreath bore the words: IN MEMORY OF DONNA DENICE HARAWAY.

Tricia, Miz Ward, Kay, Joice, Joel, standing about fifteen feet away, were horrified. Tricia began to cry.

Dennis Smith, down from the courtroom, had entered the D.A.'s office. He looked out the window, saw what was going on. He became infuriated. He hurried outside, approached the delivery man, who was in the process of flanking the walkway with a second wreath, a duplicate of the first. The detective told the man to get the wreaths away from the courthouse. He could leave them inside the police station, a block away, if he wanted; but he should get them the hell away from here.

Upstairs, Leo Austin telephoned Don Wyatt at the hospital in Oklahoma City, and told him of the guilty verdicts. Wyatt, knowing the jury had reached four verdicts the night before, had been prepared for the worst; he was not surprised.

Tricia went home. She called Maxine, to tell her of the outcome. Maxine was crying when she answered the phone; she had already heard, on the radio.

Tricia told her of the incident of the wreaths. Maxine felt sudden warmth for Dennis Smith; but she was furious at the greenhouse; she was a regular customer, buying all her plants, her flowers there, for celebrations, for sick friends. She phoned the greenhouse, and spoke to a clerk.

"There are two families involved in this," Maxine said. "We may not have the money the Haraways have, but we have the feelings."

The woman was apologetic. "We should have had second thoughts about that," she said.

"You should have had first thoughts," Maxine said. "I feel sorry for the Haraways. They can send anything they want to their home. But not to the courthouse like that."

At the courthouse, one of the ladies of the press, hearing of the wreaths in memory of Denice Haraway, asked if the Wards had sent them.

Mike Roberts arrived during the recess. He told Austin that he and Tommy had been working in Norman the day Joanne Price said she had been attacked. He would gladly swear to it. They always worked, in the summer, till dark, he said. But he had no written records. They installed siding together, he said; they did not punch a time clock.

Austin decided it would be useless to put Mike on the stand. The D.A. would point out that he was a friend of Tommy's; that he was Jannette's husband; and that he had no proof. The lawyer decided to call only Miz Ward.

The afternoon session began. Tommy looked destroyed as he sat, pale, his whole body shaking. Karl looked unmoved.

Don Wyatt was still in Oklahoma City; his father-in-law had survived the operation, the anesthetic, but was still in critical condition;

he might die at any time. Leo Austin would make the opening re-marks for the defense, seeking a life sentence instead of death.

Austin pointed out what he said were mitigating circumstances in the case: that no body had been found; that no pickup had been found; that the defendants did not have previous criminal records; that Ward had a loving, supportive family; that he had a steady job when he was arrested. Over and over he repeated his theme: the state had introduced no physical evidence of the crime.

George Butner made the same points, adding that not a single wit-ness had even identified Karl.

The defense called its only witness: Susie Ward.

Gray-haired, shy, Miz Ward moved slowly to the witness chair. Austin asked if she had anything she would like to say to the jury.

"I know he didn't do it. That's all I know," Miz Ward said in a low voice.

"Are you asking this jury not to take the life of your son?" Austin said.

"Yes, I am," Miz Ward said.

As she stepped down, she began to cry.

Juror number ten, Diana Brotherton, a stylish young woman with close-cropped hair, was also crying. She wiped her eyes with her fingers.

Outside the courtroom, Miz Ward half-fell into Tricia's arms.

Bill Peterson made his closing remarks. "Denice has suffered one of the most grueling deaths that any of you has ever heard of," he said. She was killed so the defendants could avoid lawful arrest, he said. Joanne Price had shown, he said, that, if allowed to live, the defen-dants would constitute a continuing threat to society.

"I'm going to ask you to return a verdict sentencing them to death."

Leo Austin, the former judge, moved soberly to the center of the room. He was silent for a moment, then began.

"I'm afraid, he said. "I've never had to stand before a jury and plead for a man's life. It scares me that I am not up to the task to ask you to find mercy in your heart . . .

"You're asked to put on the black cloak of death, and to do it. It's no longer an abstract idea . . .

"By the length of time you deliberated, and by some of the looks I see, I think some of you have some doubts . . . It didn't raise to the level of reasonable doubt, but I'm sure some of you have some doubts."

He emphasized again that no body had been found, no pickup. You have been asked to believe, he told the jurors, that these two boys are either two of the most brilliant criminals who ever lived, to be able to rid themselves of all evidence of the crime—or two of the luckiest, since the police had found nothing.

"What they are," he said, "are a couple of stupid boys. But don't send them to the death penalty on stupidity . . .

"Ask yourself a question—ask it now—was there no doubt in your mind? . . . Has all doubt been removed from your mind that, somewhere in this land, Denice Haraway lives?

"In white slavery somewhere? Walking this land somewhere?

"If you harbor the hope that Denice Haraway walks the land—and God knows, I do, too—then you've got a doubt. I hope the Haraways harbor that hope as well."

If someone ever sees Denice Haraway alive, he said, "the ultimate mistake would be made. Tommy Ward would be dead."

He was not against the death penalty, Austin told the jurors; the death sentence should remain on the books.

"But this case is replete with doubts."

He repeated his hope that, somewhere, Denice Haraway walks this land.

When he was through, George Butner faced the jury.

"You stand as twelve as a decision-making body," he told them, but said that each of them also stood as one. "Nothing you do will change what happened yesterday. Your decision is what will happen tomorrow . . .

"You can say numerous things about the death penalty, but if it's implemented, there's no turning back . . .

"In this case we have question after question. I think you can see that . . .

"On a number of occasions, people who should not have died did, in fact, die . . . With the unanswered questions in this case, we're asking for the lives of Thomas Jesse Ward and Karl Allen Fontenot."

Butner sat. Because the burden of proof was on the state, the D.A.

would again get the last word. Bill Peterson told the jurors the defense attorneys had been trying to put a burden of guilt on the jury.

"The burden is not on you," he said. "Don't you forget what these two defendants did to Donna Denice Haraway, and almost did to Joanne Price!"

His voice rose as he said the last part. Both defense attorneys jumped up and objected. They spelled out their objections at the bench. Judge Powers ordered the jurors to disregard what the D.A. had said about what almost happened to Joanne Price; that had not been a proper statement, he said.

Peterson resumed. "Denice not only asked for her life, but she screamed for it," he said.

"Courage is being scared to death, but saddling up anyway. And I'm going to ask you to saddle up."

He asked them to bring in a sentence of death.

It was 2:40 P.M. when he finished. The jury retired to consider the penalty. The defendants were taken across the lawn to the jail. Throughout the trial they had been led across and back handcuffed side by side, wrist to wrist, with a single set of cuffs. This time, both arms were handcuffed behind their backs.

The lawyers retired to private offices. The spectators dispersed, to use the restrooms, to drink soft drinks, to wait. In the dim corridor of the second floor, one of them leaned against the wall, smoking, thinking. He was lean, intelligent-looking, wore glasses, was thirty-five years old. His name was Barry Andersen.

He had been born and raised in Ada. He went to East Central University, studied pre-law. But he married young, had three children quickly; he could not afford to go to law school. He went into construction work to support his family.

In August, Andersen was one of the 225 citizens of Pontotoc County notified to report for jury duty on September 9. He did not try to get out of it. Instead, he arranged his schedule so he would begin no construction jobs in September, so he could serve.

When he arrived in court that first Monday, the list of prospective jurors was in alphabetical order. Barry Andersen was number six. For two days he sat in the courtroom while the clerk pulled tags out of a box, with the numbers and names of prospective jurors attached. Panelists were dismissed; others replaced them. When the jury was sworn in, only about fifteen numbers, fifteen names, had not been called. One of them was his.

Andersen still harbored dreams of becoming a lawyer one day. Since his construction schedule was clear, he decided to sit in on the trial, to watch the attorneys at work, to see if that was really what he wanted.

Every day of the trial, he had shown up promptly at nine, and taken a seat at the rear of the courtroom. He never left till court was adjourned. He had heard every minute of the testimony of every witness, just as the jurors had. He had seen them render their verdicts in the case; now he was waiting to hear their sentence.

He had become a familiar face in the courtroom. Few knew who he was—the husband of a juror, perhaps. During recesses, he stood alone in the halls, smoking, rarely speaking with anyone.

Now, smoking, waiting, he offered his opinion. He said he could hardly believe the jurors had voted to convict. There were so many doubts raised, he said, so many reasonable doubts. If he was on the jury, he said, there was no way he would have voted to convict.

But he was not in the jury room. Suppose, he was asked, the vote had been ten to two for conviction. Or eleven to one.

"I have the courage of my beliefs," he said, softly. "I would have held out for acquittal. Even if it was eleven to one."

In the luck of the draw, his number had not been called.

What about the taped confessions, he was asked, how did he explain those?

"You can get anyone to confess to anything," Andersen said. He puffed on his cigarette. "I know. I was in Vietnam. Everyone has a different pressure point. But if you want, you can get anyone to say anything."

His questioner hesitated, then asked, "Were you a prisoner of war in Vietnam?"

"No," Andersen said. He crushed out the cigarette. "I interrogated prisoners of war."

George Butner, waiting, had no doubts. He had been practicing criminal law in this area for ten years; he was convinced the jury would impose the death penalty.

The Wards went home; they could not bear to sit and watch.

The Haraway family remained in the courtroom.

At 4:15, a bailiff approached Dennis Smith. He told the detective the latest gossip: Tommy Ward's girlfriend was in the county clerk's office, trying to get a marriage license.

At 5:30, the jury had a verdict. The courtroom filled quickly. Karl Fontenot strolled in casually, his hands in his pockets. Tommy Ward looked devastated.

A folded sheet of paper was handed from the foreman to the bailiff to the judge.

It sentenced Thomas Jesse Ward to death.

All three of the aggravating circumstances had been checked as existing.

The paper was signed: "Leslie Penn, foreman."

Tommy Ward's head was pressed to his knuckles as the judge read the verdict. He seemed too worn out to react anymore.

Leo Austin asked that the jurors be polled, to affirm that this was the verdict of each and every one. As their names were called, each juror responded.

Leslie Penn said yes.

Claudia Mornhinweg said yes.

Larry Myers said yes.

Joanne Manning said yes.

Janet Williams said yes.

Nina Ambrose said yes.

Darlene Berry said yes.

Virginia Rowe said yes.

Thomas Daniel said yes.

Diana Brotherton said yes.

Mary Floyd said yes.

Alfred Byers said yes.

Judge Powers read aloud the jury's verdict on Karl Allen Fontenot: death.

Again the jurors were polled. Again each of them said yes.

The judge thanked the jurors for their services, and discharged them. It was the end of the thirteenth day of the trial. In thirty years on the bench he had never had a criminal case last that long.

The jurors removed from their blouses and shirts round buttons that said JUROR, which they had worn since being sworn in. As they filed out they dropped the buttons into the pocket of a woman bailiff. The only sound in the courtroom was a faint clink . . . clink . . . clink . . . as one by one the buttons dropped.

The date was September 25. Under Oklahoma law, Judge Powers had to wait at least thirty days before formally imposing sentence. He set sentencing for 1:30 in the afternoon of Friday, October 25.

It was 5:54 P.M. The judge announced: "The court will be in recess."

The defendants were led away in handcuffs. In the corridor, Bud Wolf hugged Tommy. When Tricia, eight months pregnant, tried to do the same, a female deputy prevented her.

"But I've been doing it all week," Tricia protested.

"It's a whole new ballgame now," the deputy said.

They moved toward the exit in a convoy of deputies. Fontenot's face was blank. Ward appeared dazed. "I can't believe they're doing this to me!" he said. "I can't believe they're doing this!"

18

FALL PARTNERS

Donald Powers removed his black judicial robe. Beneath it he was wearing gray suit pants, a white shirt, a tie; the jacket of his suit hung on a hanger, on a coatrack. The judge was standing, after a long day of sitting at the bench. A clerk of the court came into the chambers, handed him a batch of legal papers to sign, to formally conclude the trial. The judge remained standing as he glanced through each paper, set it on a table, leaned over, and signed it. As he did, he discussed the trial with a visiting journalist.

It was, he said, the most unusual case he had ever encountered. "The state spent most of its time proving parts of the confessions weren't true. That was certainly unusual."

He was not, however, surprised by the jury's verdict.

He had once before, in 1967, imposed the death penalty on a defendant; that had later been commuted to life; the man was still in the state prison at McAlester. In this case, as always in Oklahoma, the judge would have the discretion of following the jury's recommendation, or of imposing a life sentence instead. Judge Powers indicated he had no inclination to overrule the jury.

The judge volunteered that on the most critical legal question of the case—whether the state had proved the corpus delicti prior to showing the confession tapes—his decision in favor of the state had been "a close call."

"I think I made the right decision," he said. "But I'm always glad for the appellate court to review my ruling. I certainly don't want anyone to die for the wrong reason."

If he imposed the death penalty, a review by the Court of Criminal Appeals would be practically automatic; all the attorneys would have to do was file a paper requesting one.

The judge completed his paperwork. He put on his jacket, crossed the courtroom, walked down the two flights of stairs. He would drive home to Chandler immediately. In the morning he hoped to get in some golf.

As the judge left, the courtroom was empty except for one person, sitting alone in the back, disconsolate. It was Mike Roberts, Tommy's friend and former boss.

"The guys who did it were here," Mike said. "In the courtroom. They heard the death penalty and got up and left."

"What makes you think that?" he was asked.

"Joice said so. She was downstairs. She said they got into a gray-primer pickup, and drove away. I believe it. The way this town is . . ."

His words trailed off, into silence.

Downstairs, in the first-floor lobby, Steve Haraway was standing in front of a camera and floodlights, being interviewed by the girls from KTEN. It was the first formal interview he had granted since the disappearance of his wife, seventeen months before. He said he wanted to thank the police and the district attorney's office for all the work they had done on the case.

"With these people at the helm," Steve said, "the people of Ada should feel good."

Most of the Ward family went to Tulsa that night, to stay at Joel's place; there would be no spiriting Tommy out of town, as they had hoped. They left Tricia and Bud alone in Ada with their children and their grief.

Tricia gathered the children around: Rhonda, Buddy, Laura Sue. She told them that whatever they might hear in school or in the streets the next few days, nothing had been decided about Tommy; that nothing would be decided for a long time.

She reasoned that this was not a lie; nothing would be decided until all the appeals ran out.

C.L. and Maxine came over. They brought white bread and bologna for sandwiches, and soda pop. While the grandparents baby-sat, Bud and Tricia went to see the principal of Rhonda's school. They were thinking of transferring Rhonda to a school out in the country, they told him, where her relationship to Tommy would not be known.

The principal advised against it. Word would spread. In a new school, anything could happen. Here he would take control of the situation. He guaranteed it.

The next day, Tricia kept the kids home from school. The principal addressed the students. He told them that anyone who said a word to Rhonda Wolf about her uncle Tommy would have to write a 500-word report, and would be kept inside during recess for a week.

The threat proved effective. When the kids returned to school the following day, no one said a word about the case.

The day after the trial, Bill Peterson went out of town. His district-attorney district included two neighboring counties, Seminole and Hughes; his work in those counties needed attention.

Chris Ross sat in his own office, his feet up on his desk, relaxing. Gary Rogers stopped by to chat, in obvious good spirits. He asked if the D.A.'s office would still trade a life sentence in return for Denice Haraway's body. Ross said that would be up to the Haraway family; that if such an offer were made by the defendants, he thought the family would agree.

The verdicts and the death penalty led the TV and radio newscasts. On Thursday afternoon the headline crossed the entire front page of the Ada *News*: "Jury issues sentence of death." Below it, for the first time in the case, there was a second, sidebar story. It detailed the testimony of Joanne Price: "Attack revealed in supplemental hearing."

The reaction of the town to the verdict was divided. Most of those who had believed from the beginning that the suspects were guilty were reaffirmed in their beliefs. But some of these, having followed the trial, felt the state had not produced enough physical evidence to warrant a conviction. Among the poorer classes, there remained a widespread perception of a "railroad job" by the authorities.

The police and the district attorney's office received congratulations. To Tricia, most people were kind; they told her they were shocked by the verdicts, and especially by the sentence, in a case where there was no body; where, some felt, Denice Haraway could still be alive. At the feed mill, Bud found a tense atmosphere; Joanne Price's husband worked there.

Saturday night, Winifred Harrell went to the Oak Hills Country Club. A man she knew approached her. "I like Don Wyatt," he said. "But I'm glad that he lost this one." Winifred replied, "If I were you, I wouldn't let your daughter out on the streets alone too soon."

One of those who continued to believe the suspects were probably innocent was Barney Ward, who had refused to take the case in the early days. "I don't think they did it," the attorney said a few days after the trial. "Or if they did, they weren't alone. I don't know these boys, but they're not what you'd call Rhodes scholars. I'm sure they've been offered a deal: turn in who did it or tell where the body is, and we'll go easy. But they haven't done that. I don't think they're that loyal. Or that smart. I don't think they know where the body is. Of course, the terrible thing is, if they didn't do it, whoever did is still out there."

The jurors had returned to their homes, in Ada and the surrounding county—to their jobs, to their private lives. Some had been emotionally shaken by the ordeal; they preferred not to discuss it with anyone, even with friends. But there was one prominent exception—the jury foreman, Leslie Penn.

An employee of the Ideal Cement plant, Penn had told the other jurors when they began deliberations late that Tuesday night that he had served on a jury before, in a civil case. Because of that, and his take-charge attitude, he was elected foreman.

Early in the deliberations, several of the jurors were not convinced the state had proved its case; they had reasonable doubt. Leslie Penn believed the defendants were guilty. "They looked guilty," he would tell someone later. He proceeded to act as "prosecutor" within the jury room. He saw it as his job to knock down any argument raised by other jurors in favor of the defense.

The most critical issue in the jury room was the Polaroid pictures showing the suspects with short hair. It was to examine these more closely that they requested a magnifying glass. Leslie Penn convinced the doubting jurors that the pictures were not honestly dated. His "proof" was that Jannette Roberts's little girl was taller in some of the pictures than she was in others; and that therefore the pictures had not been taken the same year.

All of this Penn freely recounted to Don Wyatt's aide, Bill Willett, a few days after the trial.

"The pictures were taken from different angles, different perspectives!" Wyatt said when he heard. But by then it was—in a phrase Wyatt fancied—"blood under the bridge."

Nearly a year after the trial, most of the jurors still would be reluctant to discuss the case. One who did requested anonymity. According to this juror, when the jurors began deliberations they went around the table, each person stating his feelings, before any vote was taken. Most believed the suspects were guilty, but a few—"one or two or three"— had more of a problem than the others in saying so. This was also the case in the penalty phase. "It's like when you have to hit someone," the juror said. "It's easier for some people to do than for others."

The most convincing evidence for the state was the confession tapes, the juror said. Some jurors had "a little trouble" with the lack of identifications of Fontenot, but the tapes were so similar that they felt that both men were guilty. Of Jannette Roberts's Polaroid pictures showing the suspects with short hair, the juror said: "The person's background who put the dates, you know—I don't know, it kind of looked fishy. There was different colors of ink. You know, it didn't look right. Anybody can find pictures and write dates on 'em."

The Sunday after the trial, as always, Tricia went to church. Throughout the service, she dreaded what was to follow; she dreaded going to see Tommy at the jail; it would be the first time since they led him from the courtroom, convicted of murder.

When she got there, she was amazed to find him in good spirits, joking, apparently recovered from the total devastation of the verdicts. She had not been sure if she would be able to take the strain. But Tommy was in such a good mood, it made Tricia feel better.

Outside the jail, Tricia had encountered Charlene, also waiting to see Tommy. They had gone in together. Charlene told Tommy she wanted to marry him, that she had already made plans. Tommy apparently had not been aware of this. He shook his head.

"It's just not right," he said. "Not until after I get out of this mess. I want a wife I can come home to. I believe we should know each other better than we do. I'm old-fashioned that way."

Charlene, upset, left the visiting room. When she was gone, Tommy told Tricia, "She used to run with some bikers. She's into drugs pretty bad. I told her that if she changed, perhaps we could get together. But she hasn't changed enough."

For a few days afterward, Charlene continued to write to Tommy every day. Tommy stopped answering. So Charlene stopped writing.

Soon after, Tricia heard rumors, in two different places, that Charlene had been a plant by the district attorney's office; that she had been promised a clean criminal record if she could get Tommy to confess, if she could find out where the body was.

Tricia did not know what to believe. The whole time the jury was out, Charlene had stood alone in the courthouse, crying.

That first Sunday, C.L. and Maxine also found Tommy in a joking mood.

"It's been a long time," Tommy said to C.L., who had not been to visit for a while.

"How you been?" C.L. asked.

"I've been hiding out," Tommy said, grinning.

They, too, were amazed at his sense of humor, his good spirits.

He told them as well that he had no plans to marry. "You have to know you have a life ahead of you before you do that," he said.

He told them he was feeling calm. "If God wants to take me now," he said, "I must be at peace with that. There must be a reason."

At the conclusion of the preliminary hearing, back in February, Judge John Miller had dismissed one of the four charges against the defendants—the charge of rape—for lack of evidence. The district attorney had appealed the dismissal. Now, weeks after the trial ended, the Oklahoma Court of Criminal Appeals reinstated the charge.

Bill Peterson, having won convictions and death sentences on the murder charge, said he would not try the suspects for rape.

The ruling of the appeals court did not state that sufficient evidence existed to hold a trial for rape. It said, in a nonbinding opinion, that the decision of whether the state had proved the corpus delicti on any or all of the counts should have been made by the trial judge, in a pretrial hearing—before any evidence was presented to a jury.

Attorneys on both sides declined to speculate on what effect this opinion might have when the appeals in the case were heard.

The appeals could not be filed until the defense attorneys had transcripts of the trial. Under the law, court reporter Dawn DeVoe had until six months after the date of sentencing—until April 25, 1986—to complete the transcripts. She indicated that because of the length of the trial, it would take at least that long.

On October 7, in California, police arrested Don "Bubba" Hawkins and Dale Austin Shelton, both of Seminole, Oklahoma. They were the men wanted in the August 19 kidnapping of Linda Thompson from Oklahoma City. Because they came from nearby Seminole, had long criminal records, and were being sought for kidnapping, Richard Kerner had mentioned them at the trial as possible suspects in the Haraway case. The state had introduced testimony that Hawkins had been in jail the night Denice Haraway disappeared; it had not introduced such testimony about Shelton.

After a night in jail on the west coast, Don Hawkins confessed that he and Shelton had kidnapped Mrs. Thompson. He said they had raped her, had taken her to Seminole, and that he had drowned her in a lake there. And he told police where they could find her body—in a wooded area near the lake.

On October 11, following Hawkins's directions, police in Seminole found the remains of a woman. This was reported in the Ada News. Reading of it, Tommy Ward's family experienced a day of hope. If the body somehow turned out to be that of Denice Haraway, then Hawkins and Shelton had killed her.

The next day the remains in Seminole were positively identified as those of Linda Thompson. Hawkins and Shelton were charged with kidnapping and murder. They were brought back to Oklahoma to stand trial. They would later be convicted.

In the county jail, awaiting formal sentencing, Ward and Fontenot continued to insist on their innocence. Most of the other inmates believed them and had been surprised when they were convicted.

Karl read romance magazines, brought by the woman who had befriended him. Tommy and Karl read the Bible aloud to each other.

Fontenot had been afraid, after the conviction, that someone might come into the jail who was out to get them. But he and Ward were now locked in a cell together. That made Karl feel safe.

October 25 was exceptionally warm for autumn; the air conditioning in the courthouse was straining as Judge Powers arrived from Chandler and put on his black robe, as Jack and Betty Haraway took seats in the courtroom, as Tricia, Miz Ward, and others of the Wards arrived.

The defendants were led across from the jail, beneath the shade of the pecan tree, into the courthouse, and up in the elevator. They were wearing the same suits they had shared at the trial. In the courtroom, the defense attorneys and Bill Peterson were waiting.

The attorneys began by presenting motions for a new trial. One reason they cited was that testimony about rape in the confessions should not have been seen by the jury, because the men were not being tried for rape. Judge Powers overruled the motion; he said the rape references were so integrated into the confessions that they could not have been removed.

Another motion sought a new trial because a woman had been excluded from the jury solely because she was opposed to the death penalty. A federal district court had ruled recently that such disqualifications unfairly tainted juries in favor of the prosecution; the issue would soon go before the U.S. Supreme Court. Judge Powers overruled the motion.

The time had come for sentencing. It was one year and one week after the suspects were arrested. Judge Powers called Tommy Ward before the bench. He asked if Ward had anything he would like to say before being sentenced.

Tommy spoke four words, the only words he had spoken for the record during the long court proceedings: "I didn't do it."

The judge then followed all of the jury's recommendations. He sentenced Tommy Ward to death.

He set the date of execution as January 21, 1986.

Tommy returned to his seat. He didn't break down this time. Tricia, Miz Ward were crying. The Haraways showed no emotion.

Karl Fontenot was called before the bench. The judge asked if he would like to say anything before being sentenced.

"I would like the court to let me know when they find the people who committed these crimes," Fontenot said.

Judge Powers was momentarily startled by the request. Then he replied, "It is the court's opinion that they have found those who committed these crimes."

He gave Fontenot the same sentences as Ward, the same date of execution: January 21, 1986.

The judge pointed out that there was an automatic appeals process in regard to the death penalty; that the sentence would not be carried out until the appeals were exhausted.

The men were entitled to spend ten more days in the Pontotoc County jail, the judge told them, if they so desired. Then they would be taken to the State Evaluation and Assessment Center at Lexington; and from there to Death Row at the Oklahoma State Penitentiary at McAlester. Fontenot waived the ten days, said he would rather go straight to Lexington. Tommy Ward chose to remain in Ada as long as possible.

The judge asked Fontenot if he had any money to hire a lawyer. "No, I never will," Karl said.

Because Fontenot already had a court-appointed attorney, the judge said the appeals in his case would be handled by the Appellate Public Defender's Office in Norman.

Tommy Ward was put on the witness stand by Don Wyatt. Asked if he had any money, Ward said no; he said that his family had hired Wyatt; that he himself had paid no part of the fee; he had no assets and no income, he said. Wyatt told the judge his own contract had been only through the trial. The judge assigned Ward's appeals to the Appellate Public Defender's Office as well. Upon filing the notices of appeal, the judge said, the attorneys would be relieved of their responsibility in the case, and the executions would be officially stayed.

Soon after, the defendants, handcuffed, were led across the lawn to the jail.

The Ada *News* did not publish on Saturdays. An account of the sentencing appeared on the front page of Sunday's paper. On page two of the same edition was a paid advertisement, two columns wide and five inches high. It read:

THANK YOU
GOD BLESS YOU

We would like to thank the law enforcement officers, the fraternities, the Boy Scouts, all the friends and citizens of Ada who helped search for my daughter Donna Denice Haraway.

We appreciate so much the giving of your time and effort to find her.

A special thanks goes to District Attorney Peterson and Assistant District Attorney Ross, Detective Baskins [sic], Detective Smith, O.S.B.I. Agent Gary Rogers and all the police officers that worked on the case. Our family feels they did a splendid job together and we cannot praise them enough. We are so proud to know all the men that worked on the case. The caring and concern for my family will always be remembered.

I know I can never repay you men or thank you enough for all the help and the long hours you spent, but again I thank you from the bottom of my heart for everything.

I know that God will bless each and every one of you for everything you did.

Thank You All,
Pat Virgin, Mother
and the Family of
Donna Denice Haraway

Now, pending the outcome of the long appeals process, the town of Ada would try to put the Haraway case behind it.

Don Wyatt, for one, would not be sorry to see it go.

Of his fee of $25,000 for taking the case, Wyatt had received $6,000 in cash from the Ward family, most of it from Joel. The old Ward house on Ashland Avenue, deeded to him, turned out to be unfinished and a partial wreck inside; he sold the house and the land for $7,000. Of this $13,000 in income, he had spent about $8,500 for the preliminary hearing transcript, for Richard Kerner's fees, and for the psychiatrist who examined Ward but did not testify. His net fee was thus about $4,500 for a year's work by himself and his staff. It was more than George Butner would be paid as a court-appointed attorney—but not a lot more.

Wyatt also didn't like to lose, even if he was well paid.

"I've figured out over the years," he said a few days after the sentencing, "that you have to close the door and move on to the next one. If you spend your time second-guessing 'em, you just drive yourself crazy. This one's been tried, and it's been lost. I hope somebody on appeal can overturn it. I think it's a good possibility. But it will be a long, drawn-out process."

Wyatt could not know, then, that he wasn't really free of the case yet.

On Thursday, November 7, at 6 A.M., Tricia entered Valley View Hospital. She was several days past her expected delivery date; her doctor had decided to induce labor.

At forty-nine minutes past noon, the baby was born. It was delivered by a nurse; the doctor arrived too late.

The nurse put the child on Tricia's chest. Tricia counted the fingers and the toes. They were all there. It was a healthy baby girl.

Tricia had been afraid the stress about Tommy during her pregnancy might have affected the child's formation.

They named her Yuvonda Maxine. The unusual first name Bud and Tricia had invented; the middle name was for Bud's mother.

Little Buddy noted the date of birth and said Yuvonda would be a lucky little girl. "She was born on seven-eleven," he said.

On Sunday, Tricia and the child went home from the hospital. Tommy, though more than ten days had passed since his sentencing, was still in the county jail. Bud sent cigars over with Miz Ward. Later he went himself, and pressed against the glass a Polaroid picture of the four kids.

"Awright!" Tommy said.

In the aftermath of the formal sentencing, Judge Powers signed the legal documents to be filed within the judicial system, to be part of the record of the case. Among the papers he signed was the formal notice of appeal on behalf of Karl Fontenot, filed by Fontenot's attorney, George Butner. The paper would lead to an automatic stay of execution for Fontenot, and would transfer his representation from Butner to the appellate public defender's office.

No notice of appeal and transfer was filed for Tommy Ward.

Don Wyatt apparently believed the state would take care of that, either through the D.A.'s office or the public defender's office. The D.A. routinely assumed the defense attorney would do so, as was the common practice; it was not the D.A.'s task to look out for Tommy Ward.

Judge Powers did not notice that an appeal document for Ward, and a transfer of the case to the public defender's office, were not among the papers he signed.

On Cherry Street, near Main, it was the hour of the pecan cracker. The nuts on the trees of Ada were a rich, ripe brown. They were falling by gravity's pull, or in the November breeze, or being knocked down with poles. The old box springs, the veneer furniture, the glass objects that were sold there in the off-season were gone from in front of the small white building. The space was needed for parking, for stacking up the bags of pecans being ground inside. The iron gears meshed, day after day, week after week.

Tricia, feeding her newborn child, remembered sometimes the pecans they used to gather under the tree planted by her father, the day he married her mother, on the lawn of the house on Ashland Avenue. And a sadness, never far away, would enter the moment. This year, for the first time in her life, the house belonged to a stranger, and the tree and the pecans.

The town of McAlester is sixty miles northeast of Ada. Oklahoma's maximum-security state prison was opened there in 1911. More cell blocks were added later. In the fall of 1985 it held just over 600 prisoners.

In mid-November, among the new files opened at the prison were ones marked 148909—Karl Fontenot, and 148915—Tommy Ward.

Death Row at the prison had been housed for years in E-block, an isolated section of the sprawling facility. Warden Gary Maynard was in the process of constructing a new Death Row in a more accessible area of F-block, which had been built in 1935 and renovated in 1981. The cell block was being converted from manual to electronic control. There would be forty-eight cells in the Death Row "run." The admission of Ward and Fontenot brought the number of Death Row inmates to fifty-four. Some would have to room together.

Until the new section was completed, Ward and Fontenot were placed with the other inmates in the old Death Row in E-block. They were in separate cells, a few cells apart. Each cell was walled with concrete, about eight feet across and ten feet long. They had metal doors with narrow Plexiglas windows in them. At the rear of the cell, barred windows looked into the prison yard. Bunks and toilets were the only amenities.

Prisoners could receive mail, and one package a year, which could contain only sweat suits. Everything they needed had to be purchased at the prison canteen. This included soap and toothpaste. Money could be sent to them in the form of bank checks. These they could deposit at the canteen and draw against. Radios and TV sets were permitted in the cells. They had to be purchased at the canteen. The going rate for a small black-and-white television set was $92; the same set sold in stores outside the prison for about $69. Inmates who had no money, even for soap and toothpaste, had to do without.

The high cost of items at the canteen was one of many grievances among the inmates that were leading to an explosive atmosphere in the prison at the time that Ward and Fontenot were brought in.

The inmates could mail letters if they had the money for stamps. A plug-in telephone was available for them to make collect calls to the outside, when it was not in use by someone else. They could receive books, magazines, newspapers—but only if these were sent directly by the publishers. Such reading matter could not be sent by relatives or friends, for fear the pages might be pre-dipped in drugs, and the paper then chewed by the inmate.

Visiting was permitted Thursday through Sunday. The visitor and the inmate sat separated by a glass partition and spoke to each other through telephones. Each inmate was allowed a visitor list with ten names on it; the lists were completed only after slow paperwork, and the visitors were issued clearances. Each visitor could come twice a month.

The only exceptions were spouses and parents; in the cases of Tommy and Karl, that applied only to Miz Ward; she could visit twice a week, and the lengthy paperwork was waived.

The Death Row inmates were allowed to exercise twice a day, five inmates at a time, in narrow pens in the yard that reminded Tommy Ward of dog runs at a kennel. At the beginning, Tommy and Karl were in the same exercise group, along with three others. Of the others, one boasted he had killed thirteen people; one boasted he had killed five people; one said he had killed a cop. Tommy and Karl told their fellow inmates that they were innocent.

They told how their case had evolved, how no body had been found. They had given confessions to get "the laws" out of their faces, they said; but they hadn't done it.

The other prisoners believed them, said they could take one look at Ward and Fontenot and know they hadn't killed anyone; the other prisoners called them idiots for confessing to something they hadn't done.

In the prison argot, because they had been convicted together, for the same crime, they were known as "fall partners."

On his way to the prison from a brief stay at the Lexington evaluation center, Tommy Ward, reading his Bible, had thought he might like to become a preacher in the prison. Now he took one look at his fellow inmates—at how tough they were—and decided he'd better think about that for a while.

There was something about their eyes, he thought. You could look at their eyes and know that they had killed.

A few days after they arrived at McAlester, Tommy heard strange noises outside the window of his cell. His impulse was to look out the window into the prison yard. He took a few steps in that direction. Then he stopped. A voice inside him told him not to look out the window. He didn't. He lay down on his bunk instead.

That night, for a short time, the guards thought there had been an escape. A prisoner was missing from his cell. The next morning, they found the missing inmate. He was dead, his body stuffed into a garbage can.

The noises Tommy heard had been the killing.

Tommy told of the incident to another inmate. He was assured he had done the right thing. If he had looked out the window, and been a witness to the killing, he was told, he would have been the next victim.

Every few days or weeks a tour of visiting dignitaries was escorted through the prison. As they moved through the corridor between the cells holding the Death Row inmates, a guard would tell what each man was in for. The first week, outside Tommy Ward's cell, the guard said he'd been convicted of robbery, kidnapping, and murder. "Of course, they never found a body," the guard said.

"No body?" a man in the tour said. "How did they ever prove murder? What was the corpus delicti?"

"They got all her relatives up there to say they hadn't heard from her," Tommy said.

"That doesn't prove she's dead," the man said.

In Ada, the Haraway case faded slowly from conversation, except among those involved in the trial. The participants would be asked at social gatherings—more often now than before the trial—if they thought the defendants were guilty or innocent.

The harvesting of the pecans went on, and the cracking. Thanksgiving arrived. For the second year in a row, Bud and Tricia Wolf "won" the free-turkey lottery from their loan company.

Tommy called them frequently from McAlester. The calls had to be collect. They could not afford such calls, with maternity bills to pay off—but neither could they say no to a call from Death Row.

On December 2, they got a phone bill for about $150. They did not have the money, were about to lose their phone; a sympathetic friend helped them out. This allowed the calls to continue.

They could not yet visit Tommy; the paperwork had not been completed.

In California, collect calls from Karl Fontenot came to the homes of his brother, his sisters. They were not accepted.

Letters came to these same homes, from Karl Fontenot, No. 148909, P. O. Box 97, McAlester, Oklahoma 74502. They were not answered.

An inmate called Hank (name changed), who had killed several people, owned two decks of cards. One sunny day, in the exercise yard, he asked the others if they wanted to play poker. Karl declined, said he would watch. Tommy accepted, thinking it would help to pass the time.

Tommy and three others stood around a table in the yard. They played poker with a deck of blue cards. A deck of red cards was used for chips. After an hour or more, Tommy had a large pile of the "chip" cards in front of him. He was ahead about $1,800, but he was getting bored; he said he did not want to play anymore.

"You can't quit when you're ahead like that," Hank said.

"Why not?" Tommy asked. "It ain't real money."

"Whattaya mean? Of course it's real money. We owe you eighteen hundred bucks."

"No, you don't," Tommy said. "It's just a game. It ain't for real."

The others looked at one another, as if Tommy were insane. They insisted the stakes were real.

"I don't want your money," Tommy said. "Let's just forget about it."

According to the Bible, he felt, gambling was sinful.

The others told him they couldn't forget about it; it would mess up their game; he had to keep playing.

"Okay," Tommy said. "But I don't want your money. I'm gonna start losing on purpose. You just tell me when we're even, and then I'm gonna quit."

The card game resumed. Tommy began to lose on purpose. He would raise on every card—and then fold his hand just before the last card was dealt. He did that hand after hand; the "money" in front of him dwindled.

The exercise period ended. They totaled up the cards. Hank told Tommy he owed $1,200.

"What are you talking about?" Tommy said. "You were supposed to tell me when I got down to even."

"You owe me twelve hundred," Hank said. "We'll play more later."

When the game resumed, Tommy began to win again. He cut his losses to $700. Then the game was over.

"I don't got seven hundred dollars," Tommy told Hank. "I don't got nothin'."

"Well, you better get it," Hank said.

There was menace in his voice.

The next time Miz Ward came to visit, Tommy told her about the poker game, about the money he owed. She didn't know where she could get that kind of money; no one in the family had that kind of money.

Tommy told Hank what his mother had said.

"Well, you better get it somewhere," Hank warned.

Every day, Karl cleaned his cell thoroughly, to pass time. He still wrote letters to his family, even though they didn't answer. He wrote letters to the young woman in Ada who had come to visit him during the trial, and to her mother. Both were sympathetic. They answered his letters, accepted phone calls. They sent small checks to both Tommy and Karl, to help with their canteen money for soap, for cigarettes.

In one letter he sent from his cell, Karl wrote: "We go out in the yard during the morning and evening. I don't talk to the other guys. They are guilty of what they done. Me and Tommy are the only two who look like we came from a church somewhere and look innocent. All the other guys brag about killing people. I never speak over 10 words a day out there on the yard. The only way I figure I will make it here is be myself and stay with the Lord and His word. My feelings toward all this is I pray every night for these people who lied on me to get me in here on death row and the death penalty, to save themselves from sin. I wouldn't ever want anyone to go to the burning pits of hell. I want to see them all in heaven some day."

Solitary by nature, Karl began to brood a lot. The more he brooded, the more he focused on one thought. It had to do with Tommy. If Tommy hadn't mentioned Karl's name to the police, he thought, he, Karl, wouldn't be in this jam. Sure, he had given the police a statement himself. But only after they picked him up. And they picked him up because Tommy had mentioned his name.

More and more the same thought entered Karl's mind. If it weren't for Tommy, he wouldn't be in this jam; he wouldn't be on Death Row; he wouldn't even be in prison.

The more the thought came, the less he wanted to talk to Tommy. Sometimes he would chat with him in the yard. But more and more, he wanted nothing to do with him.

Early one evening, a week before Christmas, Tommy called Tricia. As always, she accepted the call. They talked for a time, and then Tricia looked at the clock. It was 6:25. Bud, who normally got off work at the feed mill at four, was working overtime, to help pay all the bills. She had to hang up, she told Tommy; she had to pick up Bud at 6:30.

They said goodbye. Tommy began to place another call with the operator, to his mother, in Tulsa. Before the call went through, the phone went dead.

Tommy went to the door of his cell, peered out the narrow window. A guard was double-locking the cell block.

That was the first he knew that anything was wrong.

There were noises outside. He went to the window, looked out. Helicopters were hovering overhead. Guards were crawling through the prison yard, carrying shotguns. Soon after, National Guardsmen were in the yard. There was a riot going on at McAlester.

For eighteen hours the prison was locked down. Inmates in two cell blocks had rioted, had stabbed three guards, had taken seven as hostages. The cell block housing the Death Row inmates was not involved: except for the extra locks, the canceling of exercise, of the telephone, of all privileges.

After a day and a half, the warden met with a committee of the inmates. The hostages were released unharmed. The warden told the press that many of the grievances of the inmates were justified.

The major grievance had been jobs; there were 612 inmates in the prison and 151 prison jobs.

One of the inmate negotiators, Jerry Kinney, told the press the uprising had not been planned, but that there had been idle talk of it for some time. "It's been kind of a joke for a while," he said. "People were walking around saying, 'When's it going to go? When's it going to go?'"

On the morning of Friday, December 20, a guard came to Tommy Ward's cell, and unlocked the door. He told Tommy he had to go to the warden's office. Tommy asked, "What for?"

The guard said there was something wrong with Tommy's papers; he didn't have a lawyer. His stay of execution had not come through.

They walked through the corridors of the cell block. Tommy had been waiting day after day for some new lawyer to come see him; he'd been wondering why one hadn't.

There were seven or eight people in the warden's office, one of them a preacher. Warden Gary Maynard sat at one end of a long table. The others, some kind of prison officials, Tommy figured, sat along both sides. Tommy was told to sit at the other end, facing the warden. The guard remained in the room, standing near Tommy.

The warden had a sheaf of papers in front of him. He began to read aloud from them. He said that Tommy had been sentenced to be executed at 12:30 A.M. on Tuesday, January 21, 1986. No stay of execution had been received, he said. Therefore, the prison was required to proceed with plans for the execution.

Tommy began to shake.

A form had been mailed out to Tommy's mother, the warden said, asking her what they wanted done with Tommy's body following the execution. If they received no reply, then the body would be sent to her.

The shaking was hard to stop. Tommy didn't understand how this could be happening.

Thirty days before execution, the warden continued, prisoners are transferred from Death Row to a thirty-day holding area near the execution chamber. The last five days prior to execution, the warden said, the prisoner could be visited only by immediate family, with a limit of five people. Tommy would have to give them, tomorrow, a list of the five people he wanted.

There was supposed to be a stay of execution in such cases, the warden said. But no such stay had been received. Until one was, plans for the execution would have to proceed.

"What about Fontenot?" the guard asked.

Fontenot has a lawyer, the warden replied. His notice of appeal had been filed. A stay of execution had been granted Fontenot by the Court of Criminal Appeals. But none of that had been done for Ward.

Tommy felt weak, sick. He asked if he could have the phone in his cell, to make some calls. The warden suggested that he call his mother, to warn her of the papers that would be arriving in the mail.

Tommy gathered his strength to stand. The warden gave him copies of the papers he'd been reading from. The guard led Tommy back through the corridors to his cell.

He sat on his bunk, shaking. He did not understand what had happened, what had gone wrong. All he knew was that they were planning to kill him in thirty days.

It was late afternoon before he could reach anyone on the phone. Finally he talked to his mother. Miz Ward began to cry. She did not understand, did not know what to do.

He called the woman in Ada who had become sympathetic to both boys, who accepted phone calls. The woman called Don Wyatt's office. She told Winifred Harrell what Tommy had said. Winifred looked at the clock. It was a quarter to five, on the Friday before Christmas. Winifred said she would straighten it out.

Tommy called Tricia. By the time he reached her, it was early evening. Tricia called Don Wyatt at home; he was out to dinner; he would be back later. Tricia called a friend. There was disbelief in her voice, and fear. She had never thought the case would go to trial, without a body; but it had. She had never thought the boys would be convicted, without a body; but they had. She'd been sure they would not get a death sentence; but they had. Now, she felt, she could be assured a hundred times that they wouldn't execute Tommy before his appeals were heard, and she wouldn't believe a word of it. Now she believed that anything was possible.

At the law office, Winifred explained the situation to Don Wyatt; the lawyer said it had been his impression that the judge had instructed the district attorney to file the papers turning the case over to the public defender's office. Winifred called George Butner in Wewoka. According to Winifred, that had been Butner's impression as well; but since he happened to have one of the forms in his office, Butner had given it to the judge himself. Winifred called Bill Peterson; he was already gone for the day. She called the Appellate Public Defender's Office in Norman. They had never received notification that they were to represent Tommy Ward in the appeals process. And now they could not do so. They were already representing Karl Fontenot, because that appointment had come through. And in death penalty cases, they said, they could not represent co-defendants, because at some point there might be a conflict of interest.

Frustrated, Winifred called Judge Powers at his home in Chandler, and explained the situation. The judge chose not to assess blame. He took the blame upon himself; he should have noticed the Ward paper was missing from those he signed.

The judge would try to work it out on the phone, he said. If he could not, then he and Winifred would meet somewhere on Monday, and he would sign the necessary forms.

To keep the record in order, the judge said, he would have to formally assign the case to the public defender's office. They would have to formally decline it. Then he would appoint a private attorney to handle Ward's appeals.

Winifred thanked the judge. She called the warden at McAlester, and told him what was being done, that the paperwork would be forthcoming, that a stay of execution was in the works.

The next night, Saturday, the first day of winter, Tommy had a dream. He dreamed he was in the death chamber: not strapped in a chair, but lying down. He was allowed two witnesses in the chamber with him. They were his mother and his brother Joel. Two clergymen were also present. As a tube was hooked up to his arm, and a doctor was about to administer the fatal injection, Tommy said, "Stop!" The others paused. Then, in his dream, Tommy said, "My momma brought me into this world. I want her to take me out of it."

He woke up before she did.

An unexpected delivery was made two days before Christmas to Bud and Tricia's house. It was a gift of enormous cans of baked beans, pork and beans, pie fillings, and other basic foods. It had been sent by the Ada Kiwanis Club.

Money was tight, and the gifts were gratefully accepted. Bud and Tricia did not know why they'd been sent. They felt that perhaps, at some deep but informal level, the town was beginning to have a guilty conscience.

Late the next afternoon, Christmas Eve, Barney Ward came to their house. He, too, brought with him gifts of food: a hundred-pound sack of potatoes, a fifty-pound sack of yellow onions, a turkey, and other foodstuffs. The blind attorney shook Bud's hand and wished him a Merry Christmas.

The attorney, wanting to help out a deserving family in the holiday spirit, had called a woman who worked at a loan company to ask who needed help. The woman had suggested that, what with their raising foster kids and other good works, the Bud Wolf family was the most deserving in town.

For the families of Denice Haraway—her own and her husband's—Christmas was, of course, subdued. The year before, there had been rage: the terrible tale of the October confession tapes was still fresh; ahead lay the ordeal of the trial. Now there was continued mourning for Denice, and unavoidable recollections of happy Christmases past. But there was also, perhaps, a measure of grim satisfaction. The trial was done. The suspects had been convicted and sentenced to die. Denice could not be brought back to life, but if religion meant anything at all, then she was at peace, in the fields of the Lord. And here on Earth the gears of justice had meshed; justice was being done. And, one day, perhaps, retribution.

In his cell at McAlester, Tommy Ward was shaking more than ever. His body had erupted in a nervous rash. They were going to kill him on January 21, unless a stay of execution came through. By Christmas Day it had not come through.

His mother came to visit, bringing along Jimmy's two boys, Jesse and Jack. As they talked, Jesse began to cry. Tommy began to joke around, to cheer him up, to get the boy laughing.

Afterward, in his cell, Tommy cried, because he could not be with them.

A few cells away, Karl Fontenot wrote a letter, on a yellow legal pad. He, too, had his family on his mind. "While I was in the city jail on Christmas of 1984," he wrote, "my real family didn't even come see me, write me or sent me no Christmas gifts. I wrote them continuously trying to get them to write me some letters but they never wrote me. I wrote them one letter which said if you love me at all family like I love you all you will write me or come visit me. That was like proof to me that they don't love me."

In the afternoon, Tommy called Tricia and Bud, to say Merry Christmas; they'd all been over at C.L. and Maxine's in the morning, exchanging gifts; now they were at home, serving a turkey dinner to Tricia's side of the family.

Tommy planned to spend Christmas night reading his Bible, and praying. But about eight o'clock, for unexplained reasons, the lights in the cell block went out. They stayed out till eleven the next morning. Reading was impossible. Tommy just prayed.

When he fell asleep, he dreamed again of the Haraway case. He dreamed that Denice Haraway was alive, was being held prisoner by some guys; and that he, Tommy Ward, was the head of the investigating team trying to find her. He was in a truck with a bunch of men, who were armed with rifles and automatic weapons. They jumped out of the truck, surrounded a house in which Denice Haraway was being held against her will.

He woke up before the rescue.

The paperwork on Ward's and Fontenot's visitor lists was completed. On the last weekend of the year, Tricia and Bud were able to see Tommy for the first time at McAlester. They brought along Rhonda and Yuvonda; they held the infant up to the glass, for Tommy to get a good look. It was a cheerful visit.

The sight of the baby summoned up yearnings in Tommy. He wrote them down that night: "Today was the first time I seen Yuvonda. She is a doll. I about started to cry when I saw her. I love baby's. I always wanted one of my own. I always like looking at magazines with pictures of baby's in them. And cry for hours wanting one of my own. I also think about this mess and how those people are trying not to let me have a chance of a famaly of my own.

"I wish I could only had been able to take my heart out and show those people in Ada how it beets and let them hold it and they'd see that there is no way I did it."

New Year's Eve came and went. And New Year's Day.

It was 1986.

Tommy Ward still believed he was scheduled to die on January 21. No one had told him differently.

And he was right.

The judge, the lawyers, all thought the problem about the stay of execution had been taken care of. But in the bureaucratic labyrinth of the criminal justice system of the state of Oklahoma, there existed no stay of execution for him. Tommy Ward, though he had not been moved to the thirty-day holding area, was scheduled to be executed in twenty-one days.

The week ended. Another weekend passed. On Monday, January 6, Miz Ward received a call from the warden's office. They still had received no stay of execution, she was told. She'd better find out what was going on.

The current of fear and uncertainty on which Miz Susie Ward's life had floated helplessly since her son was arrested seemed to have no end to its twists, its turns, its rocky shoals. She called Winifred Harrell at Don Wyatt's office; Tommy had not yet been assigned another lawyer.

Winifred, too, thought the matter had been taken care of. She telephoned Patti Palmer, the deputy appellate public defender, in Norman. Ms. Palmer told Winifred she had been at the Court of Criminal Appeals the previous Friday, January 3, that a stay had been granted, that the paperwork was on the way.

Winifred reassured Miz Ward.

No one reassured Tommy. He could make phone calls out, but no one could phone in.

At his home in Chandler, Judge Powers was pondering the case. He needed to appoint a private attorney to represent Tommy Ward, because the public defender was representing Fontenot. But he knew how unpopular the case was among the attorneys of Ada.

Finally he hit upon what seemed like the perfect solution. Who else could better represent Tommy Ward's interests? Who understood the complex case better?

He looked up the Ada number and dialed. Judy Wood answered. She buzzed her boss's office. She told him Judge Powers was calling.

At his large desk, beneath the shelf of Philip Roths and Stephen Kings, Don Wyatt picked up the phone.

Judge Powers told him his decision. He, Don Wyatt, would be Tommy Ward's court-appointed attorney for the appeals.

Wyatt groaned. His chest sank. He did not want the assignment. He had had his fill of this case.

The judge told him the assignment was his anyway. The official document appointing him was on the way.

Wyatt hung up. He called in Winifred. As his legal assistant, much of the work load in handling the appeals would fall on her. He told her the news.

Winifred's mind flashed to the Ward file she had maintained from the day she joined the firm. It had been in perfect order, until the trial. But after the trial everything had been shoved in any which way; it would not be needed for a long time, if ever, she'd thought; the case would be someone else's.

"I quit," she said. "I'd rather go on welfare."

Winifred knew she was joking, but barely.

That same day was moving day at McAlester. The new Death Row had been completed, and fifty-six inmates, their cases in various states of appeal, would be relocated there. Because there were so many—the last execution in Oklahoma had been twenty years before—sixteen would have to double up, two to a cell; there were only forty-eight cells on Death Row.

From the beginning, Ward and Fontenot had talked about rooming together. But in recent weeks, with Karl increasingly blaming Tommy for his predicament, they had hardly been talking, had just had some desultory conversations in the yard. Now Karl told Tommy he wouldn't share a cell with him.

Moved to Death Row, they were placed in cells across the corridor from one another. Karl was in a cell alone. Tommy's cell had two bunks, and an inmate called Luke (name changed) was asked if he would share Tommy's cell. Luke, who had murdered several people, said he would; he liked Tommy okay.

The inmates settled in, those who had them plugging in television sets, radios, arranging their toilet articles, their writing pads, spare prison outfits of dark blue shirts, blue jeans, blue boxer shorts, T-shirts. After a few hours, Luke turned to Ward. "Come over here and I'll masturbate you," he said.

Tommy was horrified.

"The hell you will!" he said.

"Look, I never done it before with a guy either," Luke said. "But I'm here for life. I'm not getting out of here except in a box. I might as well get used to it. You'll do it, after a while."

Tommy knew that a lot of the men in the prison had turned gay. He made it clear to Luke that the idea revolted him.

The men kept apart. Afternoon became evening. Evening became night. In their new cells, the inmates were keyed up, restless. Long into the night, TV sets remained on, and radios. The inmates stayed awake, talking, shouting conversations from cell to cell. That was easier here than where they'd been; the doors here were made of bars instead of solid metal.

It was past 3 A.M. Most of the inmates were still awake. The sound of radios, TVs, tuned to different stations, cluttered the corridor. Karl Fontenot stood behind the barred door of his cell, looking out. An inmate in another cell started a conversation. They had to half-shout over the din.

"How come you ain't rooming with your fall partner?" the man asked.

Karl replied, "Tommy? I don't want to room with him. Tommy's a snitch!"

Suddenly it was as if some implosion of sound had occurred on Death Row. The word "snitch" was the catalyst. As soon as it was spoken, loudly over the noise, conversation stopped. In the sudden, comparative quiet, radios were turned off, and TV sets. Quiet moved down the corridor like a snake, until there was total silence.

Fontenot had never spent a minute in jail, anywhere, until his arrest in the Haraway case. He was, perhaps, unaware that the deadliest word in any prison in America is the word "snitch."

"Say that again?" the inmate said.

"Tommy's a snitch," Karl said. "If it wasn't for Tommy, I wouldn't be in here. If Tommy hadn't given the cops my name, they never would of come to question me, for me to make that tape."

There was silence again on Death Row. Then the other inmates started talking. They didn't want snitches around. They started talking about killing Tommy.

They started planning aloud how to do it.

Tommy, listening, began to shake.

We could do it, one of them said, when they open the cell door to let Luke out for exercise. We could rush in and beat Tommy to death.

But then the guards would know who done it, another said. We should kill Tommy when no one is around.

Tommy became afraid, terrified. He began to shout for a guard.

A guard came down the corridor. He asked what was wrong. Tommy said, "You just get me out of here!"

The guard asked why.

"I'll tell you after you get me out of here!"

"I have to get a sergeant for that," the guard said.

The guard walked away. Minute after minute passed. The other inmates continued to talk about killing Tommy. The sergeant did not appear.

Luke looked at Tommy slyly. "I guess they're waiting to see if I'm the one who's going to get you," he said.

Tommy was petrified. He knew Luke had killed before.

The guard returned. A few minutes later a sergeant arrived. They took Tommy out of the cell, led him down the corridor, to another section of Death Row. They put him in a cell, alone; it was larger than the other one.

"Now, tell me what's wrong," the guard said.

"They were threatening to kill me," Tommy said.

He did not give details about who, or why. He did not want to get a reputation as a snitch.

He could tell the word had beat him to this unofficial protective custody area: word that "a snitch was coming down." He told an inmate in a nearby cell that it wasn't true; that Karl was telling lies.

"Your fall partner?" the inmate said. "That don't make you a snitch. It happens all the time. Fall partners turnin' on each other."

In the morning, the news was brought to Tommy in his new cell in protective isolation: his stay of execution by the courts had been received. The stay would be in effect pending the outcome of his appeals. The state of Oklahoma no longer was planning to kill him on January 21.

In the afternoon, a guard told Ward he could go out and exercise if he wanted—not with the Death Row inmates who had threatened him, but with the Christians with whom he went to church. Tommy said he would wait a while. He wanted to make sure they were really Christians.

19

GERTY

Allan Tatum had lived in Gerty, Oklahoma, for twenty-seven years. When asked the population of the small community, he liked to reply, "About thirty-seven." A more accurate count would be 125 to 150, depending on how many of the children scampering through the countryside stood still long enough to be counted.

Gerty is in Hughes County, about twenty-seven miles east, and slightly north, of Ada; about eight miles east of the Pontotoc County line. It consists of a single grocery store and a scattering of houses. There is no post office, no school. State maps of Oklahoma show no roads leading to Gerty; in fact, there are two or three, all of them dirt. One leads down from Allen, just inside Pontotoc about nine miles to the northwest; another leads down from Atwood, farther to the north. It is an area of rugged hillsides choked with thick underbrush. The coons and the possums far outnumber the people.

Tatum, sixty-one, and his wife, Linda, lived in a house a quarter mile south of the Gerty store. He was a carpenter by trade. Linda worked at Toot's Barbecue, out on Highway 75 to the east. Most winters, when the weather turned cold and snow covered the countryside, carpentry work was slow; Tatum would spend his time hunting and trapping in the woods. It was mostly for sport; depending on what he caught, he might barbecue the meat and sell the pelts.

The winter of 1985–86 was unusually warm in Oklahoma, as it was in most of the Southwest. Afternoon temperatures were often in the sixties. The weather stayed so good that Tatum was kept busy with his carpentry, repairing fences, building barns or cabins. By the middle of January he had not gone hunting once.

Then a project on which he was working was delayed; some hardware was late in arriving. Tatum woke up on the morning of Monday, January 20, with no work to do. He decided to go out and lay some traps. He was hoping he would get a bobcat.

His wife fixed him lunch before she went off to her job at Toot's. Tatum ate, loaded his pickup with his traps and bait. He tossed his .22-caliber single-shot rifle into the truck and climbed in. For January, the seat of the pickup parked in the sun felt extra warm against his Levis.

He drove west three miles over rutted dirt roads to open land that abutted his property. He parked the truck and carried the traps and the liquid bait into the underbrush, away from the road, where hunting would be best, making mental note of the locations; he'd be required by law to run the traps every day, to see if any animals had gotten caught, were injured but alive.

The carpenter spent the whole long afternoon out in the brush. Then, with the winter sun dying early, he headed slowly back toward the pickup. He was pushing his way through the leafless brambles of huckleberry bushes, on a sloping hillside, when a rounded white object caught his notice, lying under a bush. In the fading light he thought it was a Styrofoam head, the kind sold in five-and-dime stores, for women to keep their hats on, or their wigs.

Tatum reached down and rolled the object over with his finger. A skull was staring up at him.

He did not touch it again.

He noted the location, and continued on to his truck.

As he drove home, his thought was to keep his mouth shut about what he had found. He had no idea who it might be, how long it had been there, where things might lead if he mentioned it to anyone. He parked the pickup, went into the house, sat. Linda was still at work, would be gone till after the supper hour. He looked at the telephone, silent. Tatum had a hard time with telephones. He was hard of hearing, could not understand what people were saying on a phone.

He waited. On toward seven o'clock, his brother-in-law, Leonard

Muck, came over. Leonard lived just down the road, and came by most every night to pass the time. They often hunted together.

Tatum told Leonard, and asked him to telephone Orville Rose. They both knew Orville Rose. He was the sheriff of Hughes County, had been the sheriff for eleven years.

Leonard Muck told the sheriff what Allan Tatum had found. It was already dark outside. The sheriff asked questions, and Muck repeated them loudly to Tatum. The carpenter told his brother-in-law the answers, and Muck spoke them into the phone. It was agreed that the sheriff would come out to Tatum's place at eleven o'clock the next morning, and Tatum would take him to the place where the skull was.

None of them speculated on what the skull was doing there, or on who it might be. The sheriff especially didn't speculate. In his eleven years he'd gotten many calls like this. Most of the time it turned out to be a dog.

Orville Rose's office was in Holdenville, the Hughes County seat; the birthplace, twenty-five years earlier, of Donna Denice Haraway. He left there Tuesday morning with his undersheriff, Floyd Trivitt, in Trivitt's squad car. With Floyd behind the wheel, they drove in the morning sun down Highway 48, across the South Canadian River, past Atwood, down the unnumbered dirt road into Gerty. The sheriff had considered calling the OSBI, but first he wanted to make sure the skull was human. They picked up Allan Tatum at his house. Tatum directed them the three and a half miles to where he had seen the skull.

It was still there, on the ground under leafless brush, on a bed of autumn-colored leaves, about 200 yards up a slope from the dirt road. The sheriff knelt beside it. The lower jaw was missing. In the teeth of the human upper jaw he could see a lot of silver fillings.

He could not tell if it was male or female.

They looked about in the immediate area. They saw bits of fabric on the ground, and snagged in the bushes: little more than frayed remnants; they appeared to be from blue jeans. They came upon other bones, scattered. There was no hint of flesh; that would have been devoured by dogs or buzzards, the sheriff figured, in no time. They came upon the soles of a pair of tennis shoes; the upper, cloth part was gone. Tatum saw what he thought was bits of some kind of blouse or top. It was a "streakedy, stripedy blue." Sheriff Rose would not recall seeing any part of a blouse or top.

The sheriff decided not to disturb the scene. They drove back to Tatum's house. The sheriff called the OSBI office in McAlester. The agent there said he was too busy to come down, but that he would notify the crime lab in Oklahoma City; they would send someone.

Two OSBI lab technicians arrived at Holdenville in early afternoon. The dispatcher sent them out to Gerty. They met up at the grocery store with Sheriff Rose and Undersheriff Trivitt; Allan Tatum stayed home. The sheriff led the technicians to the site.

They took photographs. They placed the skull in a paper sack, along with what other bones they could find: rib bones, finger bones. They took the soles of the tennis shoes, the frayed pieces of cloth. The largest piece was the waistband of blue jeans. It was marked "Size 9."

Sheriff Rose produced a rake, began to rake the leaves around where they had found the skull. He came upon something bright and shiny: an earring, white-gold in appearance, with a bit of red in it.

Between the earring and the size 9 waistband, they were fairly sure the remains were of a woman.

Not far from the shoe soles, they found two white socks, about half-knee-length. Inside the socks were toe bones. In another spot they found the zipper of the jeans.

The sun, still warm for January, caught the light color of some of the bones; others were uncovered as the men continued to rake the leaves in an area about forty feet across. They found leg bones, arm bones, a pelvis. Perhaps eight or ten ribs. One of the lab men, wearing gloves, placed each find carefully in a paper sack.

Before they placed the skull in the sack, the men studied it. Near the back were two holes, one on each side. They looked to Sheriff Rose like bullet holes, as if a bullet had been fired into the back of the head on one side, and had come out the other side. The hole was too big for a .22-caliber, he guessed; it must have been at least a .38.

It was nearly four in the afternoon when they left the scene. Rose and Trivitt drove back to Holdenville. The lab men—with the bones, the bits of fabric, the single earring—drove back to Oklahoma City, where the medical examiner found a tiny bullet fragment in the skull they brought.

By chance, District Attorney Bill Peterson was working in Holdenville that day; it was part of his three-county jurisdiction. Sheriff Rose found Peterson in the office of his assistant. He told the D.A. they had found a body out near Gerty.

"Did that Haraway girl have a lot of fillings in her upper teeth?" Rose asked.

Bill Peterson said yes; her father-in-law was a dentist; she had a lot of fillings.

"How was she dressed?" the sheriff asked.

Tennis shoes and blue jeans, Bill Peterson said.

"Then I'm pretty sure this will be her," the sheriff said. "That's what we found out there."

Hearing of the fillings, the blue jeans, the tennis shoes, the size 9 waistband, Bill Peterson was fairly certain, too, that they had found Donna Denice Haraway at last.

The date was January 21, 1986—the day on which, prior to their stays, Tommy Ward and Karl Fontenot had been scheduled to be executed.

The fact of the discovery of a skeleton near Gerty was kept secret that night. Even Dennis Smith, the detective captain, did not learn of it until Chris Ross mentioned it at police headquarters the following day. Ross said they suspected it might be Denice Haraway; he was on his way to Dr. Haraway's office, to get her dental charts, her dental X-rays.

The detective captain met the assistant D.A. at the dentist's office. They stood outside and discussed the possible new evidence, beneath the windows of the apartment in which Steve and Denice had lived. Ross went inside and talked with Dr. Haraway, who had already been told of the find. He came out with Denice's dental impressions. Smith took them and drove, with Mike Baskin, ninety miles to the state medical examiner's office in Oklahoma City, to deliver them personally.

It was about 6 P.M. when they got there. The office was already closed. The detectives left the impressions with a night attendant, and returned to Ada. Positive identification would have to wait till morning.

Smith was excited during the drive up and back. From what Ross had told him, there were strong indications it was Denice: proof positive of what he'd assumed from the very first night, that she was dead. The thoughts that ran through his mind he put into spoken words a few days later: "Someone had already looked at the teeth that had been found, and had unofficially said it looked like her. I was pretty excited at her being found. I knew there was a bullet hole in the head. [But] nothing was going to surprise me in this case. The location wasn't really going to surprise me because of the different areas that we had searched."

Hughes County had not been searched during the investigation. "Ward and Fontenot's statement said it was out west of town. Initially the people at the scene said the vehicle went east, and in the initial search they searched out east and south and that area. There are so many possibilities. They could have gone west first. In Tommy's statement he said that after he got through raping her, he said they were cuttin' on her and he decided he didn't want anything more to do with it and he went home. He said after he got home he was washing up or something and he got to thinking about them leaving her body up there, and the police might find her close to his house. I don't know, it's hard to really say what actually did happen. Only they really know. From him saying that, you can kind of—he's thinking about the police finding that body, so he goes back. That's what he says. He goes back. It's conceivable that the body may have been there and he may have loaded the body back up, in whatever kind of vehicle. He could have gone around the loop. There are so many ways of getting to where the body was found. There are so many likelihoods, possibilities. With him being out there so close to his house. He knew all that area. But, on the other hand, it's always conceivable that he could have gone east from the store, and gone straight out there. We had wondered ourselves [why they would go through the center of town on a Saturday night]."

About the evidence that a gun had been used, and had not been mentioned on the tapes, Smith said, "Well, I don't know. It really didn't surprise me. I'm open for game on anything anymore. Anything's conceivable. I can see 'em just making damn sure she's dead before they left her. That would be the final act, a gunshot to the head."

When the detectives arrived back in Ada from the medical examiner's office that night, Mike Baskin telephoned Pat Virgin, Denice's mother, in Purcell, to tell her they had found a body, that while it had not yet been definitely confirmed, it probably was Denice.

"It was good news for us that the body was found," Smith said. "The family acted as if they were relieved to know that her body had been found. Where she was at and everything."

The next morning, in Oklahoma City, the state medical examiner compared the dental impression of Denice Haraway's teeth, delivered by the detectives, with the upper jaw in the skull found at Gerty. It was a perfect match. The identification was now positive. The skeleton found at Gerty was that of Donna Denice Haraway.

The identification was given out to the media. Tommy Ward heard it on a borrowed TV set in his cell.

Ward was frightened by the report. He asked for the telephone, called his mother's house in Tulsa, spoke to his brother Melvin. He told Melvin he'd been hoping Denice Haraway would turn up alive; that way everyone would know for sure that he didn't do it. Now there was no chance of that.

Melvin calmed Tommy down. He told him that now perhaps the police would find evidence that proved someone else did it.

Tommy called a friend. "I was hoping and praying she was still alive," he said. "I'm gritting my teeth and hoping they'll find evidence that proves I didn't do it."

"I never even heard of Gerty," Tommy said. "I heard of Atwood, because you pass it on the way to McAlester. But I never heard of Gerty."

Karl Fontenot also saw the report in his cell. It made him feel good, he said, for two reasons. One was that the woman had been shot, and his tape said nothing about shooting. The other was that she'd been found a long way from where it said on the tape she'd been put. "Maybe now they'll see the tape was all lies," he said.

In Ada, District Attorney Peterson was answering questions from the press about the finding of the body, about whether it would affect the convictions of Ward and Fontenot.

"Why would it?" Peterson said. "We convicted them without a body, and now we have one."

He said the finding of the body simply confirmed the justness of the convictions. "They sent us out looking north, south, and west," he said. "Every direction but the right one. I should have known to look east. They said they put her in a bunker. Everything stands up except what they did with the body."

Peterson told the press Ms. Haraway had been stabbed in the chest and shot once in the head, "according to the medical examiner." This statement would be reported in the media in Ada and throughout the state—that Denice had been stabbed and shot. "Nothing found so far proves their innocence," Peterson said.

Across town, in his office on Arlington, Don Wyatt had a different reaction. "If the body suffered a gunshot wound," he said, "this cuts against what they were trying to prove. They said the instrument of death was a lock-blade knife. If the body was clothed, this cuts against what they were trying to prove. If there was a blouse on it, I'd like to know a description of the blouse, if it was different. The people their witnesses saw on Richardson Loop must have been someone else. I heard OSBI chemists have had the body. We need to see what they found. Is there any physical evidence out there that ties the body to the defendants? We don't know. Or to anyone else? I don't know how hard they're going to look out there. They feel they have their convictions."

In late fall, Bud Wolf had bought a small black-and-white TV set to replace the color one that had been burned out by lightning before the trial. Bud and Tricia were watching it Wednesday night when the first unofficial announcement about the finding of a body was made. Tricia was watching it in the living room Thursday morning when the identification of Denice Haraway was made official. Her first reaction was a sick feeling. She felt that Tommy and Karl were now doomed. She had been hoping that Denice Haraway was alive. She had known Denice was dead, but had been hoping she was alive—both for Tommy's sake and for the sake of the Haraways.

In the afternoon she read the Ada *News*, as most of the town was doing. The headline "Haraway's remains are found" crossed the top of the front page, beside the old yearbook picture of Denice. The story in the newspaper contained more details than had been mentioned on television. It told of the blue jeans, the tennis shoes, the earring being found. It did not mention a blouse. And it contained Bill Peterson's comment that the finding of the body would not affect the case.

After her first feeling of doom, Tricia grew hopeful again. Perhaps they could trace the bullet fragment to a gun that would lead to the killer, she thought. Maybe they would find the gun itself, or something else that the killer dropped.

And she grew suspicious. If they had found blue jeans and tennis shoes, she wondered, why hadn't they found a blouse? She knew the blouse was the key. If they had found a blouse, she figured, and it was different from the one on the tapes, that would prove the police had fed Tommy and Karl the story on the tapes. Because how else would Tommy and Karl know about Denice having a blouse with little blue flowers, if she hadn't been wearing it?

The hopes and the suspicions and the fears all ran together in her mind. Like Don Wyatt, she wondered how hard the authorities would look for evidence that might clear Tommy and Karl.

Richard Kerner was out of town that day. He did not hear of the discovery of the body until the TV news that night.

His first thought was "She was shot!" That, he felt, cast further doubt on the confession tapes.

His second thought was of Jason Lurch's grandmother. The investigator had visited the grandmother when he was first trying to locate Lurch. He'd learned that Lurch had lived with her for a time, had once shoved his grandmother so hard she fell down and broke an arm or a hip. The place she lived—where Lurch had once lived—was called Centrahoma. It was in an open area of trees and scrub and hills. If you drove north from Centrahoma on Highway 75, the first community you could turn off to, about twenty miles to the north, was Gerty.

Kerner's next thought was of Larry Jett, standing among the plaster birds and Bambis in the yard ornaments shop, lying to him about having lived in Kansas at the time Denice Haraway disappeared. Larry Jett, the investigator recalled, looked a lot like Tommy Ward. And he came from Allen, the closest village to Gerty. The place the body had been found was a no-man's-land about one-third down from Allen and two-thirds up from Centrahoma. Both Lurch and Jett could be familiar with the area, Kerner figured.

The investigator had never relinquished his suspicion of Lurch for having attended every scattered day of the preliminary hearing, and then for not attending the trial; and for Karen Wise and Jim Moyer thinking they might have seen him that night. A combined scenario formed in the investigator's mind: the real killers might have been Lurch and Jett, in Lurch's nephew's truck.

And yet all of his suspicions, Kerner knew, proved nothing.

The officers who had been working on the case from the beginning—Dennis Smith, Gary Rogers, Mike Baskin—wanted to see the spot where Denice Haraway had been found. They also wanted to search for more evidence there. A weapon, perhaps. More bones. More clothing. The story in the Ada *News* had quoted Bill Peterson as saying a complete rib cage had been found. That was not the case. Some rib bones were missing, and it was on the rib bones that evidence of stabbing was most likely to appear. So they wanted to find more rib bones, with stab marks.

None of the published accounts had mentioned anything about a blouse or top being found. Dennis Smith had heard that when the lab technicians removed the skeleton, under it, on the leaves, they had found evidence of a blouse. It was so decayed, so fragile, that if they had tried to touch it, it would have disintegrated. But the lab men had photographed it, Smith had been told. It was pale lavender, with little blue flowers on it.

If this was true, it had not been made public.

The three officers decided to meet at police headquarters Friday morning and go out to Gerty to conduct their own search. They would be joined by Bruce Johnson, a new investigator for the district attorney's office; by another detective; and by Sheriff Rose of Hughes County, who could show them the place.

Detective Smith arose early, as always, to distribute the *Oklahoman* through the town before going to work. A story about the finding of Denice Haraway's body appeared on the lower part of the front page, and continued inside. He paused to read it—and his blood pressure rose as he read the last part of the story. It consisted of comments the reporter had obtained from Don Wyatt, who had not been quoted in the Ada *News*.

Wyatt was quoted as saying the finding of the body would help the defendants in their appeals. The story continued:

"The description of that blouse was fed to them by the police" during their interrogation, the lawyer said.

"That's how the police got those confessions. They kept going over and over on them until they gave them those stories to get them off their backs," Wyatt said.

"They thought the police would eventually disprove their stories and [they would] be released.

"But that wasn't the case. The police chose to believe those cock and bull stories," Wyatt said.

The detective was incensed by Wyatt's statements. He was furious as he met the others at headquarters, as they climbed into a black unmarked car, Smith at the wheel, and drove east on Arlington toward Gerty. As they passed Don Wyatt's expensive law building, which happened to be on the route, Smith suddenly swung the car to the right, up the short, steep driveway, and into the parking lot behind the red brick building. It was 8:30 in the morning. The lot was empty, the building not yet open.

Frustrated, the detective captain turned the car around and started back toward the driveway. As he did, a van swung off the road into the driveway. The van was wide; there was not enough space for the car and the van to pass in the drive. Smith backed up his car. The van came up the drive, then paused beside the car. The driver of the van was Winifred Harrell; she was often the first of Don Wyatt's employees to arrive at work.

Winifred did not recognize the black car. But she saw Dennis Smith behind the wheel. She rolled down her window to talk. She liked Dennis, thought he was a fine person. Way back ten years ago, she and her first husband, and Dennis and Sandi, sometimes took vacations together. Their contact since had always been friendly. He had chatted with her amiably during the trial. Just a few weeks before, doing Christmas shopping in Oklahoma City, she had run into Dennis and Sandi and one of their boys, and they'd had a nice chat.

The detective rolled down the window of the car. Winifred smiled.

"What are you doing?" she asked, wondering why the police would be at Wyatt's office so early in the morning.

"When you see Don Wyatt," Smith said, "you tell him I said, 'Bullshit.' "

"What?" Winifred said. She was taken aback. Smith had not even said good morning.

"When you see Don Wyatt," the detective repeated, "you tell him I said, 'Bullshit.' "

"He's in Muskogee today," Winifred said. "But what's going on, Dennis? What's the problem?"

"Read the *Daily Oklahoman*," Smith said, "and tell him I said, 'Bullshit.' "

"Well, you don't have to take it out on me," Winifred said. "I just work here."

Another officer was seated beside Smith. Mike Baskin was in the backseat. He rolled the back window down. "Birds of a feather flock together," he said.

Angry, Winifred drove off, into the parking lot. She expected that kind of attitude from Baskin, but not from Dennis. She felt they had an honest disagreement about the case. She felt the detective captain truly believed that Ward and Fontenot were guilty. He was not the kind of person to knowingly frame someone. But she had observed Tommy Ward, had spoken to him. If Tommy was guilty, she thought, he was the best dad-gum con artist she had ever run into.

The finding of the body in Gerty had only confirmed her belief in his innocence. She felt it made no sense for the boys to give a true confession, and then not tell where the body was, even after they had been convicted and sentenced to death. Smith had maintained before that if they burned the body, they had nothing to trade for a life sentence; or if they had thrown her in the river, they would have had no idea where she was by the time they were arrested. But now they had found the body, not burned, not thrown in the river: just left under some bushes. If Ward and Fontenot had put it there, Winifred felt, it made no sense for them not to have told the police where it was.

Dennis Smith swung the car east again on Arlington and drove out to Gerty. Sheriff Rose met them there, showed them the place where the body had been. The men walked about, searching. Then they got down on their hands and knees to search. Two autumns of leaves had fallen since the night of the disappearance. They poked about in the mulch, using their hands, using a metal detector in hopes of finding a knife, or a gun, or both.

They spent all of the morning there, and part of the afternoon. The metal detector unearthed the second earring, white-gold with red in it. But no weapon. They found more bones—the lower jaw with all the teeth intact, a few small bones. But no additional ribs. The winter-bare branches of huckleberry bushes tried to scratch at their faces as they crawled underneath. Dennis Smith felt that with the dirt road running only 200 yards away, the place was fairly accessible, a lot less rugged than he had been led to believe.

The next day, Saturday, Don Wyatt and Bill Willett decided to go bird hunting. Not exactly by chance, they decided to hunt in the wooded area near Gerty. As they prowled with their shotguns, up the sloping terrain, Wyatt was reminded of the hill country of Tennessee. A person would have to know his way around, to come in here at night, he thought; it was rugged country.

One juror in the case, hearing of the finding of the body, felt relief for Denice Haraway's family. Only after you bury a loved one, she felt, can you put the death behind you and get on with your life. The fact that Denice had been shot did not lead her to question the verdict, she said.

Another juror echoed that feeling. "It doesn't really matter how you do it," he said. "She's still dead. Just because you say you killed her one way, and you did it another way, doesn't make you any less guilty."

Fontenot's trial attorney, George Butner, was conducting another murder trial, in Duncan, Oklahoma, in the south-central part of the state, when he heard that Denice Haraway's body may have been found. The initial report did not include the cause of death, and Butner's first thought was about the clothing—the blouse. If they found her blouse out there, and it was different from the one described on both tapes, then that would be monumental, he felt; then the boys would be home free. He assumed that the cause of death would be stabbing. "In my wildest dreams," he said later, "I never thought that they would find the body and they would discover she had been killed with some other kind of weapon, that she had been shot."

With the fact of Denice Haraway's death now established beyond all doubt, Butner did not think an appeals court would free the defendants on any grounds without ordering a new trial. But he felt that this new evidence—the cause of death being a bullet wound—was extremely exculpatory. Since the state's case rested so heavily on the confession tapes, and those made no mention of shooting, he believed the Court of Criminal Appeals—or some other court along the way—would order a new trial, and let a jury decide whether the confessions stood up.

In a profession where he was frequently called upon to defend murderers who were probably—or admittedly—guilty, Butner had never been sure about Karl Fontenot, one way or the other. The discovery of the body with a bullet in the skull raised new doubts in his mind, increased the likelihood that Karl was innocent.

About Tommy Ward he had more of a problem, because Ward had placed himself at the scene twice—not only in the confession tape, but again more than two months later, when he told his Marty Ashley story. If Ward had not been there that night, Butner felt, then he had real psychological problems.

The responsibility of getting Fontenot's conviction overturned was no longer Butner's. The case was now in the hands of Terry Hull, a female attorney in the Appellate Public Defender's Office.

Terry Hull knew of the case, had been following it in the newspapers. She called George Butner to get more details. She felt that the case, with all its twists and turns, was the most incredible, the most difficult to believe, that she had ever encountered or heard of. The finding of the body in Gerty, with a bullet wound in the skull, was yet one more incredible twist.

Her early reaction was that there would be many promising grounds for appeal in the case: not because of the actions of Judge Powers, whom she felt was an excellent judge, but because of the nature of the case. But she could not determine what lines of appeal to follow until she read the voluminous transcript of the trial, and that would not be ready until April 25—six months after the date of sentencing.

Like all appeals, these would be decided one day in the calm, orderly atmosphere of the Court of Criminal Appeals in Oklahoma City. That, Ms. Hull felt, was one hundred percent to the good of her client—to get the decision making away from the roiled emotions and passions of a small town like Ada.

Her first action after the discovery of the body was to petition Judge Powers to hold a disclosure hearing: to compel the district attorney to turn over to the appeals attorneys all exculpatory evidence that may have been found along with the body, as well as the official medical examiner's reports.

In the medical examiner's office, meanwhile, opinions had changed. The first examination of the rib cage had been made for the office by Dr. Richard McWilliams, a consulting forensic anthropologist. He had reported "a scalloped cut wound" on one of the ribs. On the basis of that finding, Bill Peterson and the press had been informed that Denice Haraway had been stabbed as well as shot. During the next eight days, however, Dr. Larry E. Balding, a forensic pathologist in the medical examiner's office, had made further studies. He had also called in for consultation Dr. Clyde Snow, a nationally known physical anthropologist on the staff of the University of Oklahoma. (In

June of 1985, Dr. Snow had been one of six U.S. experts sent to Brazil to study and verify the remains of Nazi torturer Josef Mengele.) Together, Drs. Balding and Snow came to a new conclusion: that the marks on Denice Haraway's rib cage had not been made by a knife, but had been made by animal teeth, "to a 98 percent degree of certainty."

On January 31, Dr. Balding telephoned Bill Peterson and told him of this finding. He made a memo of the phone conversation for his files.

Peterson did not notify the defense attorneys of this new finding. Nor did he tell the press or the public, who were left to believe there was evidence that Denice Haraway had been stabbed as well as shot.

Inside the prison, Tommy and Karl were still not speaking. Tommy remained in protective isolation; Karl hung out increasingly with the man who was threatening to kill Tommy because of his unpaid poker debt; with the men who were threatening to kill Tommy because Karl had said he was a snitch. Tommy read his Bible, took a Bible correspondence course, went to chapel regularly. Karl dropped all pretense of religious faith. He was in with, in Tommy's view, "a bad bunch."

In the Pontotoc County Jail, Ward's weight had dropped forty pounds, from 165 to 125. He had not liked the food; he'd been too nervous to eat much, and lack of exercise had decreased his appetite. At McAlester, though he was still nervous, there was exercise and better food: real milk instead of powdered milk; even a steak sometimes. He built up rapidly to his normal weight, grew muscular from doing pushups in his cell, joked about developing a small belly.

One day he was handed a note by a trustee. It was from the inmate in the cell across the corridor. The inmate wrote Tommy that he was falling in love with him.

Tommy was repelled. One day he'd seen that same inmate performing oral sex on a trustee through the bars of his cell. Tommy kept away from the door, out of sight, as much as possible after that.

His cell was a few feet from the shower room. In protective isolation he was allowed to shower alone. Karl usually was brought to shower with two or three of his new buddies. One day Tommy could hear them talking by the shower room. One of the inmates was urging Karl to tell the authorities that Tommy had killed Denice Haraway. Then, the inmate said, they could kill Tommy in the prison, and no one would care—and Karl would go free.

Tommy was afraid Karl might do that, might believe he could get freed that way.

A month after the body was found, Ada authorities decided to conduct one more search of the fateful hillside near Gerty. They scheduled it for Saturday, February 22. Members of Denice Haraway's family learned of the planned search, and asked if they could go along and help. The district attorney's office felt it could not refuse the request.

The weather had turned warm again after a brief period of snow. The peach trees in Dennis Smith's yard were already in early bloom; he was hoping a frost would not destroy them.

The day of the search was sunny and blue, the temperature near sixty degrees. The detective captain was apprehensive as he headed to Gerty. Another search might prove useful in turning up more bones, more clothing, perhaps even the murder weapon. But with members of Denice's family along, it could become an emotional scene. A professional police officer looking for pieces of a skeleton was one thing; a family looking for pieces of a daughter, a wife, a sister they had loved, was something else.

About forty people had gathered at Gerty when the search began at 9 A.M.: officers and family both. They lined up a few hundred feet from where the skull had been found. Shoulder to shoulder, they got down on their hands and knees, and began to rake through the fallen leaves with their fingers, their hands. Among them were Steve Haraway; Dr. Jack Haraway; Jimmy Lyon, Denice's father; Ron Lyon, her brother; and other relatives, including several women. Side by side with the law officers, they crawled across the hillside, turning up the dead leaves, brushing past thickets beginning to show green buds of new life. They reached the spot where the skull had been, searched there; continued past it for many more yards. The searching went on for hours. There were no outbursts, no tears. Smith's fear of an emotional scene wasn't realized. The searchers were stoic, methodical.

When they had crossed the hillside, they did another search, walking this time. It was late afternoon by the time they quit. They had found more bits of blue-jean fabric, a few small bones. Nothing more.

Some time later, when the lab people had finished photographing and cataloguing the bones, X-raying the skull, testing the remnants with chemicals—recording the evidence of the homicide, in case a new trial were ever ordered—the remains of Donna Denice Haraway would be turned over to her family for interment.

The service would be private. Not even the police would be invited. No public announcement would be made.

On Monday, March 3, the principals—judge, attorneys, D.A.—were back in the courtroom where the trial had taken place, this time for the evidentiary hearing. It was mostly routine. Terry Hull, joined by Don Wyatt, requested that all exculpatory evidence obtained by the D.A. since the trial—including the medical examiner's report—be turned over to the defense. Bill Peterson said he had not yet received the official report, that he would make it available when he did. Judge Powers ordered that all new evidence in the case, already obtained or that might be obtained in the future, be turned over to the appeals attorneys within five days of discovery.

As the hearing neared its end, Don Wyatt approached the bench. His ailing father-in-law, he told the judge, had died in December. And his own father had died, unexpectedly, of a heart attack just eight days before, on February 23. Because of this, it was an extremely difficult time, Wyatt told the judge. He requested, for personal reasons, to be relieved of his duties as Tommy Ward's court-appointed attorney for the appeals process.

Judge Powers denied the oral motion. But he told Wyatt to submit the request again in writing.

In the ensuing days, the judge contacted other Ada attorneys. None of them wanted to work on behalf of Tommy Ward. The judge could have appointed them against their will, but he did not like to do that; he did not think it made for good justice.

About a week later, the judge found an attorney in Seminole, thirty miles north of Ada, who agreed to take the case. His name was Joe Wrigley. The judge then granted Don Wyatt's motion to withdraw, and he appointed Wrigley to be Ward's new lawyer.

For the second time, Winifred Harrell closed her file on the Tommy Ward case. "In one way, it's a relief," she said. "In another way, I hate to get out of it."

Miz Ward drove down from Tulsa to visit Tommy, a two-hour drive, on Saturday, March 8. It was one of their better visits; they spent most of it reminiscing about Tommy's childhood, about his dad.

Tommy remembered a game they used to play, where his dad would look like he was asleep in a chair. The kids would go over to him and stick their finger in his hand, and he would grab their finger and hold it tight and not let go, all the time pretending that he was asleep. The kids would start yelling, "Let me go, let me go." But he would not let go.

They reminisced about times Tommy got whipped with a switch his dad kept in the back of his 1949 pickup. Usually he got whipped for going to another kid's house after school without getting permission; he'd always be sure to be home by dark, by suppertime, but he'd still get whipped if he hadn't gotten permission first. He remembered one time when he left a note at home that he was going to a friend's house to help with a yard sale. When he got home, he got whipped in spite of the note. "You're supposed to be here," his dad said. "The note ain't you."

These personal visits were the only times Tommy could hear his family's voices now; Bud and Tricia had lost their telephone in January, because they could not pay for the collect calls, and could not say no to them; Miz Ward, living at Joel's house, had lost the phone there for the same reason.

Miz Ward remembered times when Tommy's dad would be upset because someone had done something wrong and none of the kids would own up to it. He would get angry, trying to get somebody to admit doing it. Tommy would sit at the table, twitching his fingers, twitching and twitching, and finally he would say, "I did it, Daddy!" He would take the blame, and get the whipping, when a lot of the time he hadn't done it. He just couldn't stand to see his father angry like that.

When Miz Ward recollected that, Tommy said, "Just like now."

One day as Tommy was led from the visiting area, an inmate on his way there began to talk to him. He said he had been amazed that Tommy and Karl were convicted, and said that he knew they didn't do it. Tommy did not recognize him at first; then he realized who it was. It was Billy Charley, from Ada: the fellow whose name had been called in to the police about thirty times, the same number as Tommy's, as looking like one of the composite drawings. Now Billy Charley was in McAlester himself, doing time for burglary.

Billy Charley asked Tommy Ward how he was doing. They wished each other luck.

On April 25, 1986, six months to the day after Ward and Fontenot were sentenced to death, their petitions in error—the formal name for their notices of appeal—were filed with the Oklahoma Court of Criminal Appeals. On the same day—the deadline—the twelve-volume transcript of the trial was filed with the court, and was sent to the two appeals attorneys. That set a new calendar in motion. The attorneys, Terry Hull for Fontenot and Joe Wrigley for Ward, would have 120 days to file written briefs supporting their motions to overturn the convictions on various grounds. The state of Oklahoma would then have 60 days to file answering briefs. These would be prepared not by District Attorney Peterson, but by the State Attorney General's office. The appeals attorneys could request time to reply to the answer briefs; it was normally granted by the court if sought.

When all of the briefs had been filed, the Court of Criminal Appeals would schedule oral arguments. Only after these were heard would the court issue its rulings. The appeals on behalf of Ward and Fontenot would be handled separately throughout, as independent cases.

This initial appeals process normally would take up to a year, or more. The court, on the various motions, could overturn the convictions, could order a new trial for one or both defendants, or could turn down the motions and let the convictions and the death sentences stand. If that happened, the attorneys could find other avenues of appeal. There were inmates at McAlester who had been sentenced to death in 1977 and whose appeals had not run out nine years later.

One hope of Death Row inmates throughout the country was the case pending before the U.S. Supreme Court concerning the exclusion from juries of persons opposed to the death penalty. If the court ruled that such exclusions in capital cases were unconstitutional, hundreds of death sentences might well be commuted to life. The attorneys for Ward and Fontenot had that possibility in mind, because of the single gray-haired lady in the Ada courtroom who had been dismissed for that reason. But on May 5, 1986, the Supreme Court ruled, by a 6–3 vote, that such exclusions were permissible. The convictions, the sentences, would stand.

In the spring, the attorneys finally received their copies of the medical examiner's report on Denice Haraway. The probable cause of death was listed as a gunshot wound to the head. It described "an entry gunshot wound to the left occiput and an exit gunshot wound to the right temporal region." There was no reference anywhere in the report to stab wounds. There was also no reference to the expert finding, "to a 98 percent degree of certainty," that there were no stab wounds evident. The attorneys remained uninformed of that finding.

Asked why the D.A.'s office had told the press Denice Haraway had been stabbed and shot, Chris Ross said the rib bones found had scratches on them "that would be consistent with being stabbed—that could have been stab wounds." He conceded that the marks could also have been made by the teeth of dogs, coons, or other animals. He, too, did not mention the "98 percent" finding that they were animal marks.

The absence of any reference to stabbing in the official document was not reported in the media.

If there was any photographic evidence of the lavender blouse—as Dennis Smith had heard, but not seen—it was not included in the medical report.

In late spring, Karl Fontenot voluntarily roomed with Hank—one of the men who wanted to kill Tommy Ward. Those few people on the outside who had befriended Karl, including his new attorney, became concerned. They began to wonder, should he ever be cleared and released, what kind of life he would lead on the outside, after his time in McAlester.

Tommy Ward remained alone in his isolation cell, reading his Bible, writing letters and poems. One poem he called "Loneliness."

In a letter, Tommy wrote:

> I've seen with my owne eyes 3 deaths. One my dad and I seen a boy named Earney Horner at school get hit by a cemi truck. And seen a guy wreck on a motorcycle . . . That is the most frightning moments of my life, when I seen those 3 deaths.

In another letter, he wrote about his father:

> After dad retired from the glass plant in Ada we picked up beer cans and sold them. We use to go out every pretty day and pick up beer cans on the side of the highways. There propely isn't a highway in Oklahoma that we didn't pick up cans on.
>
> After we colected the cans for a wile we would smash them and put them in toe sacks and take them to the beer company in Shawnee. Back then the cans was 10 cents a pound. When we would take the cans and sell them we would get quiet a bit of money for them because we had so many pounds of cans. We didn't half to pick up the cans because we needed the money. We picked them up so dad would get walking exercise. Since dad enjoyed walking he decided to pick up cans wile he did it. At first we would walk around near our house in Ada. Then as time went by we started going out on the highways all over the place.
>
> At that time I believe all of us kids were home besides Jimmy. Dad went into the hospitle of a heart atac. After that when he got out we quit picking up cans. I went out a few times around the house picking up cans for a wile. The summer of 83 I picked up cans because I didn't have a job. I also

picked pecans and sold them at the place they bie them in
Ada. But getting back to the story. After dad had the heart atac
we quit picking up cans. We didn't go fishing as much eather.
Then dad went into the hospitle again with gaulstones. After
dad got out a cuple of years later he went back in the hospitle
because the tube they put in him grew back wrong or was
pinched some way. But they took tests on him and figgered
that was what was wrong with him. When they operated on
him they found surosis of the liver. The doctors sowed him
back up and told the famaly. We all were at the hospitle when
the doctor called mom and Joel (I believe) into the office. We
all knew that something had must be wrong. Then mom and
Joel came back to the waiting room crying and they told us
about dad. The doctor told mom that he had only 6 months
or so to live. Dad only lived 3 months.

Dad stayed in the hospitle a couple of weeks then came
home. Dad was a pretty good size man. In the 3 months time
he lived he lost a lot of weight. The first month he was home
he got around pretty well on his own. The second month he
got to were he stayed in bed the most of the time. He slep a lot
also. He would be siting in his chair and fall to sleep with a lit
cigarett in his hand and birn holes in his chair. We kept pretty
well watch on him wile we were home from school and wile
we were at school mom kept pretty well watch on him. Then
in the third month he lived dad got real bad. Me or Melvin or
Joel would half to help him up and down. The time was drawing nearer and nearer to his death and we knew it. I cry every
time I think about how bad he got. I would half to hold him
up wile he used the bathroom. And hold him so he wouldn't
pee all over the place. I had to help him to the bathroom the
most of the time because Melvin would start crying and run
outside. Joel was working at Don Hays Osmobeal and Caddlac
and would come home around 5 or 6 oclock in the afternoon.

It was a hurrafying experance seeing dad get weeker and
weeker. Then one day the teacher came in the classroom and
told me that my sister was on her way to pick us kids up that
our dad was about to die. I left the classroom crying and went

outside. Me and Kay was the only ones in school at that time. Mom came picked us up at school and took us home. It was on a Friday that she picked us up from school. Dad was in bed bearly breathing with his eyes closed. We stayed in his bedroom for 3 days watching his breaths get smaller and smaller. That Saturday night dad stoped breathing. My sister Trisha screamed No Daddy and grabed him he all of the sudden started breathing again. We all cryed for a long time after he started breathing again. Then the next morning (Sunday) about 9:00 dad took his last breath and died. I ran out of his room to the living room and cryed. I could hear Trisha crying and screaming no daddy no. I got up and went outside. Thadd Sellers was outside and I told him about dad and he came over. We didn't have a phone so Thadd called the fuenarl home and they came after him.

When the people came to take dad away my famaly was crying and telling thim no that they cant take him away. Trisha cept screaming wake up daddy wake up. Joel and Melvin was screaming no daddy wake up. I went around to the back of the house and sit down crying. I couldn't watch them people take my dad away.

One night, on his bunk in McAlester, Tommy Ward had a dream. He dreamed he had gotten out of prison, and was asleep at the house on Ashland Avenue; the house in which his father had lived, and had shaded with a pecan tree, and had died; the house the lawyers had sold. In the dream it was still his home. In the dream he was asleep in his bed when a drill came poking through the wall. The man who killed Denice Haraway was drilling through the wall into his room. The guy knew that the police would be after him, now that Tommy had been cleared and freed. Tommy saw the drill coming through the wall. He saw a hand coming through the hole. He tried to get out of bed, but he couldn't move. The hole kept getting larger; the hand of Denice Haraway's killer was pushing through it, coming after him. He tried to scream, but he couldn't make a sound. He heard voices in another room. He tried to get up and run to them, but his feet wouldn't move. The hand was coming closer.

He woke before the hand could get him. He had not seen the face of the man who killed Denice Haraway, only the hand.

His whole body was sweating. He got up from his bunk and took a drink of water. Then he sat on the edge of the bunk, trying to calm himself. His heart was going ninety-to-nothin'.

20

SECOND CHANCES

In June of 1986, after only a few weeks together, Karl Fontenot and his cellmate grew tired of each other. Karl apologized to Tommy Ward, said he was sorry he had called Tommy a snitch, and asked if Tommy would share a cell with him. Tommy accepted the apology. Friends again, they roomed together on Death Row while their attorneys worked on their appeals.

In mid-July, Fontenot's attorney, Terry Hull, learned for the first time, from the medical examiner's office, of the January finding that the marks on Denice Haraway's rib cage had not been stab wounds, "to a 98 percent degree of certainty." On August 8 she filed a motion for a new trial on the basis of newly discovered evidence—the finding of the body, and the withholding of this expert opinion by the district attorney.

Ms. Hull and Ward's attorney, Joe Wrigley, worked independently, but conferred occasionally, on the separate briefs they would file seeking to have the convictions overturned. The briefs were filed in late summer and early autumn. They cited many legal grounds on which they asked the Court of Criminal Appeals to overturn the convictions. Among the principal ones were the following: that the denial of a change of venue had denied the suspects their right to a fair and impartial jury; that the two men should have been tried separately; that they had been denied due process of law by "official police misconduct"; that the confessions should not have been admitted, because they were not knowing and intelligent confessions; and that there was a lack of sufficient evidence to support a verdict of guilt.

After the filing of the briefs, Terry Hull asked the warden at McAlester to place Karl in a separate cell from Tommy. She felt that, should one or both be granted new trials, it would be better if they were not celling together. This was done immediately, in early September. In separate cells they continued to wait for the courts to decide their fates.

The Oklahoma State Attorney General's office filed answer briefs to the appeals in the fall. The brief answering Ward's appeal said that the state stood by its contention that Denice Haraway had been stabbed to death by the defendants; it maintained that the stab wounds did not show up on the skeletal remains. The brief said that since the body was found by a hunter, the bullet wound in the skull had been caused by a hunter's stray bullet. No evidence was included to support this theory.

The defense filed their replies in December. The judges on the backlogged Court of Appeals would have to read all the materials, then set a date for oral arguments. Rulings on the appeal of the convictions of Tommy Ward and Karl Fontenot were not expected until late in 1987.

Terry Hull made repeated requests to see a copy of the OSBI report on the finding of Denice Haraway's body. Her requests were denied, despite the fact that she worked for the Appellate Public Defender's Office, another state agency. Her curiosity increased when she learned that Allan Tatum, the hunter who found the remains, claimed he had seen a piece of a blouse—and that it was not pale lavender with little blue flowers. The Ada authorities were still maintaining that no evidence of a blouse had been found.

In late February, Ms. Hull asked Richard Kerner if he would go to Gerty and interview Tatum about the matter. Kerner said he would. The hunter agreed to meet with Kerner; he took him to the spot where he had found the remains; they spent about two hours together. Tatum told Kerner he had clearly seen a piece of blouse, about three inches by one inch, right beside the rib cage. He said the blouse was a sort of multicolored gingham, like a plaid, and could not have been blue flowers that faded. He agreed to sign a sworn affidavit to that effect.

On April 1, in the presence of a notary public, Tatum signed an affidavit recounting his February 20 visit with Kerner and describing the piece of blouse he had seen when he found the skeleton. "I can only describe this blouse material," the affidavit said, "as a gingham cloth, multi-colored, as in a calico cat. The blouse material was not just blue flowers on a lighter-colored material, as it contained other colors, not just blue."

Kerner forwarded the affidavit to Terry Hull, who added it to her massive brief on behalf of Karl Fontenot's appeal. A few days later, a researcher for a national television news program came to Ada. Learning of the affidavit, she asked the authorities about it. She was told that the fabric Tatum had seen was merely part of a "hunter's shirt." This was the first time they had acknowledged finding any part of a shirt or blouse at the scene.

Kerner made one further inquiry on behalf of the defendants. He went to the Court of Criminal Appeals, where the evidence introduced in the trial was on file; he obtained the full serial numbers of the two rolls of Polaroid film showing Tommy Ward and Karl Fontenot with short hair, which were hand-dated around Easter, 1984 a week before the Haraway disappearance. One shot showed an unopened Easter basket; the state had claimed in closing arguments that the pictures could have been taken on Easter of 1983, or even 1982. Kerner called the Polaroid Corporation. One of the rolls, he was told, had been manufactured in October of 1983; the other roll in February of 1984. This supported the defense contention that the pictures had been taken at Easter of 1984; it could prove pivotal if new trials were granted by the court.

On April 21, 1987, the U.S. Supreme Court issued a ruling in an unrelated case that directly affected the futures of Karl Fontenot and Tommy Ward. In the case *Cruz* vs. *New York*, the court overturned the conviction of a man whose co-defendant's confession had been introduced at their joint trial. Until that time, when "interlocking" confessions were used at a joint trial, the judge routinely instructed the jury not to consider the confession of one defendant in considering the guilt or innocence of the other. The reason for this was that if the co-defendant did not take the witness stand, the defendant could not cross-examine his accuser, as allowed by the Sixth Amendment. But in *Cruz*, the Supreme Court held that the confession of a nontestifying co-defendant could be so devastating that a jury could not humanly disregard it, even if instructed to do so by the judge; and that in such instances it violated the defendant's constitutional right to confront his accuser.

This opinion was clearly relevant to the joint trial of Ward and Fontenot. The Oklahoma Court of Criminal Appeals immediately requested both sides in the Ward and Fontenot cases to file briefs on how the Cruz case applied to these appeals.

Oral arguments on the two appeals were held, separately, on June 16. At 3 o'clock in the afternoon, Tuesday, August 11, the Oklahoma Court of Criminal Appeals, in a unanimous decision, reversed Karl Fontenot's conviction. It remanded the case to Pontotoc County for a new trial.

The three judges said that the trial court had erred in admitting Ward's accusatory statement at the joint trial, and that this error was harmful enough to have violated Karl Fontenot's rights. It cited the Cruz case as the underpinning for the ruling. "Other than the statements given by Ward and Fontenot," the court wrote, "there was no evidence linking appellant to the crimes."

The reversal of Fontenot's conviction put the Haraway case on the front page again in Ada. Assistant D.A. Chris Ross told the Ada *News* he was not surprised by the decision, in light of the Cruz ruling. He said he expected that Ward's conviction would soon be reversed on the same grounds. "It is just a procedural error," he said. And he compared the case to a boxing match: "You have to get up and go for the next round even though you won the last one."

Tommy Ward and his family hoped that a similar ruling would soon be forthcoming in Tommy's case. But one attorney close to the case noted privately that the court did not have to rule the same way in the Ward appeal. Error had definitely been committed in Ward's case as well, this attorney said, but the court would have to find with Ward, as it had with Fontenot, that it was not "harmless error."

For five more weeks, Ward and Fontenot remained in their adjacent cells at the state prison. On the morning of Thursday, September 17, Karl Fontenot was returned to the Pontotoc County jail, to await a new trial. George Butner, his court-appointed trial attorney, agreed to represent him again.

Tommy Ward remained in the state prison. The court had not yet ruled on his appeal.

Week after week passed, and still no ruling came. No one outside the court knew why. The briefs filed by Terry Hull on behalf of Karl Fontenot had been much more voluminous and complete than those filed by Joe Wrigley on behalf of Ward. Whether this fact was delaying the Ward ruling, no one could say.

As the new year, 1988, began, the court still hadn't ruled on the appeal. Tommy Ward remained on Death Row.

In the spring and summer of 1987, a string of burglaries was committed in Ada in which more than $55,000 worth of property was stolen or destroyed. Police cracked the case in August and came up with twelve suspects, many of whom confessed. District Attorney Bill Peterson declined to file any charges—stating that the suspects were good boys from good homes, whose lives should not be destroyed by a criminal record. When this became public knowledge, a group of outraged citizens began circulating petitions calling for an investigation of Peterson's handling of the D.A.'s office in this and other cases. In January of 1988, they filed enough signatures to force the empaneling of a grand jury to conduct an investigation. Among the cases the jury would be asked to look into were those against Tommy Ward and Karl Fontenot.

The grand jury's proceedings, as always, were secret; whether the handling of the Ward-Fontenot matter was discussed was not made public. In any case, the grand jury issued no charges of wrongdoing against the district attorney. Bill Peterson remained in office.

As more months passed, life went on outside the courtroom: Dennis Smith retired from the Ada police department; Steve Haraway was remarried, to a legal secretary from Oklahoma City. On Death Row, Tommy Ward waited.

Finally, on May 20, 1988, the Oklahoma Court of Criminal Appeals ruled on the Ward case. In a unanimous decision, the three-member court reversed Ward's convictions and ordered him remanded to Pontotoc County for a new trial. The grounds were the same as in the Fontenot reversal. The court held that under the Cruz ruling, the introduction of Fontenot's confession in Ward's trial had been prejudicial. No reason was given for the long delay in issuing this opinion.

Tommy called Tricia when he learned of the ruling. "He's at least getting his hopes up again," Tricia said. "He's really excited. I just hope he can prove his innocence. Last time, everybody was really angry and upset. I just hope that this time people will listen to his side . . . We just keep praying, and everything is looking good once again—better than it has in a long time."

The second trial of Karl Fontenot began on June 6, less than three weeks after the Ward conviction was overturned. It was not held in Ada. Both the prosecutor and the defense attorney had asked for a change of venue; they maintained that an impartial jury could not be empaneled in Ada because of publicity surrounding the case. Judge Donald E. Powers, the same judge who presided at the first trial, was presiding again. He ordered the new trial be moved to Holdenville, the county seat of adjacent Hughes County, in which Denice Haraway's body had been found. It also happened to be the town in which Denice Haraway had been born.

From the prosecution point of view, the major difference in the second trial was that there would be no doubt that Denice Haraway was dead.

According to expert witnesses who testified early in the trial, dental records had established that the skeleton found by hunter Allan Tatum in Gerty was that of Denice Haraway. The medical examiner testified that she had been shot in the head, but he could not say for certain whether the shot had been fired before or after she was dead. He said there was no evidence on the skeleton that she had been stabbed repeatedly, as Fontenot had said in his taped statement. But he said it was possible that she could have been stabbed without this being evident on the skeleton. He said there was no evidence the body had been burned.

Most of the pretrial motions made by the defense attorney, George Butner, were turned down by the judge. But he did permit Butner to examine all the evidence found along with the body. In examining this evidence, Butner found a small portion of a red and white shirt. This had been listed as irrelevant by the prosecutors, because it had not been mentioned in the confessions. Butner spoke with appeals attorney Terry Hull. They reread what Tommy Ward had written to his attorney shortly after his arrest; he had said the police had given him a choice of two blouses that Denice Haraway might have been wearing: either little blue flowers, or red and white stripes. Here, the attorneys thought, was part of the blouse with red and white stripes! How could Tommy Ward have known about two of Haraway's blouses, they asked themselves, unless he had been fed this information by the police.

Butner could not enter Ward's statement into this trial, because that would bring Ward right back into Fontenot's case. Instead, he tried to link the piece of red and white fabric with the red and gold earrings found with the body; he suggested to the jury that a young woman would more likely wear red earrings with a red and white shirt than with a lavender and blue shirt.

The prosecution argued that the red and white material was less decomposed than the other cloth found at the scene, and thus had not belonged to Denice Haraway; they suggested it was part of a boy's T-shirt.

For the most part, the prosecution case was the same as at the first trial. There was no solid evidence at all against Karl Fontenot—until the devastating confession tape was shown. The prosecutors conceded that many of the details in the confession were false. But they maintained that the essence was true: that Karl Fontenot had been one of those who kidnapped and raped and murdered Denice Haraway.

For Fontenot's defense, attorney Butner relied primarily on the testimony of an Oklahoma psychiatrist, Dr. Joel Dreyer, who had examined Fontenot for several hours. The doctor testified that Karl Fontenot suffers from "post-traumatic stress disorder." He said Fontenot did not kill Denice Haraway. Dreyer described to the jury how Fontenot's mother had been killed in front of his eyes while their car was stalled on the highway after a minor traffic accident. He said Fontenot blames himself for his mother's death, and had been "willing to take the place of Haraway's murderer and confess to a killing he didn't do." Dreyer said Fontenot felt "worthless, and believed he should be punished for his mother's death."

The psychiatrist said Fontenot's confession had been supplied to him by police officers. He said Fontenot has "abnormally low intelligence" and "is not bright enough to distinguish between right and wrong." He said Fontenot had told lies to police officers to get attention.

Dr. Sandra Petrick, director of psychiatry at Eastern State Hospital, who had examined Fontenot before his first trial, testified that she believed Fontenot did not understand his Miranda rights when he talked to the police. She said Fontenot had told her he would not have talked with the police if he had understood the meaning of a "confession."

OSBI agent Gary Rogers conceded that Fontenot had not been charged with the murder until seventeen days after his arrest. But he denied that police had planted information for his confession during that time. "If we wanted to frame him," Rogers said, "we could have provided other evidence."

In his closing argument, Assistant District Attorney Chris Ross belittled the testimony of Dreyer, who had formerly practiced in Michigan. He referred to the psychiatrist as "Dr. Detroit" and "The Detroit Flash," and said the doctor was merely parroting back what Fontenot had told him. The sneering nicknames played to two prejudices prevalent in that part of Oklahoma—a mistrust of outsiders, and a mistrust of psychiatrists.

The case went to the jury on Tuesday, June 14. The jurors deliberated for about an hour. Then they returned their verdicts. They found Karl Fontenot guilty of robbery, of kidnapping, and of first degree murder.

Once again the confession tape, though provably false in many respects, had been impossible for the defense to overcome.

Next came the penalty phase. Bill Peterson read to the jury the testimony of Joanne Price from the first trial, in which Price said she had been run off the road by a gray-primered pickup with two men in it.

This was permitted because Price allegedly had moved from Ada and could not be located to testify in person.

The jury deliberated the penalty for about three hours. Then it recommended that Karl Fontenot be put to death.

The sentence was formally imposed by Judge Powers on July 8. He set an execution date of October 5, 1988. The execution would be automatically stayed pending appeal. Fontenot was returned to Death Row in McAlester.

At the office of the appellate public defender in Oklahoma City, Terry Hull and others were appalled that Fontenot had been convicted again with virtually no evidence against him beyond the questionable taped confession. "I can't believe it happened twice," Hull said. She volunteered to handle Fontenot's appeal again. Months later, when she was able to read the transcript of the second trial, she found a brutal irony in it. She felt that without the Ward tape, which the prosecution had been forced by the courts to omit, the case against Fontenot seemed more consistent—because the jury was not aware of all the contradictions between the two "confessions."

The conviction of Fontenot brought new gloom to Tommy Ward and his family. Tommy had won a reprieve from the appeals court only a few weeks earlier; now it seemed unlikely that Tommy's second trial would turn out different than Karl's. They could only pray for a miracle.

The road to Ward's new trial was fraught with delays. Judge Powers appointed attorney Bill Cathey to represent him. It seemed like a sensible move; Cathey was a member of the Wyatt law firm that had represented Ward at his first trial; he did not have a lot of criminal court experience, but he was familiar with the case, and he believed in Tommy's innocence. But Cathey had to withdraw from the case because of illness. A new attorney had to be appointed, and had to familiarize himself with the complex case. This led to delays in the start of the trial, from October of 1988 to February of 1989, and finally to May of 1989.

Powers ordered that this trial, too, be moved from Ada. It would be held in Shawnee, in Pottawatomie County, about forty-five miles north of Ada. Ward's new court-appointed attorney was a Shawnee lawyer named Truman Simpson.

Jury selection began on May 31. Six men and six women were chosen. The prosecution case was virtually the same as at the Fontenot trial—Jack Paschall, Karen Wise, Jim Moyer, Dennis Smith—all of it building up, this time, to the showing of the Ward confession tape. Then the prosecution rested.

Defense attorney Simpson, aware that Karl Fontenot had been convicted by virtually the same testimony, decided to take a major risk. He put Tommy Ward on the witness stand in his own defense—leaving him open to cross-examination in front of the jury.

Ward told the jury what he had been telling his family and others for years: that he was innocent; that he had told the police he was innocent; that only after they kept badgering him did he tell them a dream he'd had. The police told him this dream was about the Haraway case, Ward testified, and they pressured him until he made up lies for his taped statement. When they found out these were lies, he said, he hoped he would be freed. He admitted he had told a series of lies while being held in jail. He swore he was telling the truth now.

His attorney asked him if he knew who had committed the crime. "I wish to God I did," he answered, "because I wouldn't be here."

Several new witnesses came forward to aid Ward before this second trial, and Simpson called them to testify:

One was a woman named Edna Harris. She said she had seen a blond man in a blue and gray van at McAnally's the night Denice Haraway was abducted. She said the man made her nervous because he kept staring at her. She said she told investigators about the man, but that she was never called to testify.

A man named Joe McCarty told jurors his 1973 pickup was stolen from his nearby farm the weekend Denice Haraway disappeared. He said a farm employee, Jim Raines, had stolen the truck along with cash, credit cards, and several guns. He said the truck was green but had been painted with gray primer. When he reported the pickup stolen, McCarty said Raines was thirty-six years old and about six feet tall. He said he had told investigators Raines resembled the composite drawing of a suspect in the Haraway case.

McCarty testified that Raines was later arrested in Galveston, Texas, and that the truck had been impounded by police there. He said he had not been able to get the truck back because he did not have a title to it.

On cross-examination by Ross, McCarty said he could not be certain which day of the weekend the truck had been stolen. And he said it was a GMC truck, not a Chevrolet. The prosecutors later recalled several witnesses, including Jack Paschall and Jim Moyer, and showed them a picture of the stolen pickup. They said it was not the pickup they had seen on the night five years earlier that Denice Haraway had disappeared. And they said Jim Raines was not the man they had seen.

Another new defense witness was Dr. Edith King, an Oklahoma County psychologist. King testified that she had administered four psychological tests to Ward while he was awaiting this second trial. She said the results showed Tommy Ward to be passive, nonassertive, and sensitive to others. She said the tests did not show him to be a violent or antisocial person. She said he seemed religious, had positive family values, and that his general attitude was "mainstream."

King also said she had watched the two videotapes of Ward's statements. She said that in the October 12 tape, when he insisted on his innocence, he appeared normal; but that in the second, "confession" tape, he was "too rehearsed and automatic," and seemed to be reciting his lines.

Under cross-examination by Chris Ross, the psychologist conceded that the results might have been different if the tests had been administered five years earlier. She also conceded that behavior is affected by drugs and alcohol, and that she could not predict how patients would act under the influence of those substances.

After closing arguments, the case went to the jury, which had been listening to testimony for twelve days. The jurors deliberated for several hours on Thursday night, June 15, and for several more hours on Friday morning. Then it handed down its verdict. Tommy Ward once again was found guilty on all counts.

When the verdict was announced, Ward began to sob uncontrollably. "You're all liars," he shouted. He stood and looked toward the prosecutors. "I hope you're satisfied," he said. "I'm getting punished for something I didn't do."

After a recess, the penalty phase on the murder charge was held: life in prison, or death? The testimony of Joanne Price was once more read into the record. But this time the defense had a rebuttal. Attorney Simpson showed the jury a radio log from the Pontotoc County sheriff's office, which had received the call about the attack on Price. The typewritten log stated that the vehicle that forced Price off the road was a "silver and black Plymouth"—not a gray-primered pickup, as Price had testified at the first trial.

In response, the prosecutors called to the stand a former county jailer, Paul Harbin. He testified that the log was in error. He said Price had described a gray-colored pickup, but that the person who typed the log must have mistaken his notes and typed the wrong description.

The jury deliberated for two hours. At 11:20 Friday night, it handed down its verdict: life in prison.

Unlike Fontenot, Tommy Ward had escaped a death sentence.

The death penalty was averted by a lone female juror. She told the others that no matter how long they sat in the jury room, she would not vote for the death penalty in this case.

After the trial, this juror spoke with Tommy Ward's family. According to Tricia, the juror told them she believed that Tommy was innocent. But she had voted "guilty" for the following reason: if she voted "not guilty," and the trial ended in a hung jury, a new trial would be held, Ward would be found guilty again, and would be given the death penalty again. By finding him guilty, the juror told the family, she had been able to spare Tommy the death penalty.

In early July, 1989, Judge Powers made the sentences official. He ordered that they be served consecutively, not concurrently: ten years for robbery, twenty years for kidnapping, and life in prison for murder. According to the district attorney's office, this meant that Tommy Ward would be eligible for parole in about twenty-one years.

A year had passed since Karl Fontenot's second conviction; he remained on Death Row in McAlester. Tommy Ward, no longer under sentence of death, was incarcerated at the Lexington Correctional Center, a medium security prison in Lexington, Oklahoma.

Another year passed. Now it was June of 1990. The two men had been imprisoned for nearly six years. Backed up with other cases, Terry Hull was only now able to plunge into the task of fashioning an appeal of Karl Fontenot's second conviction. She remained convinced that both Fontenot and Ward were innocent.

In prison, Fontenot watched television, sat in front of a small fan in his cell, made picture frames out of toothpicks and glue—when he had enough toothpicks and enough glue. He and Tommy were not corresponding. Karl could not help feeling a certain bitterness that he had been dealt with more harshly than Tommy had.

The appellate process eventually rewarded Fontenot with a victory—of sorts. The court found that in the penalty phase of his trial, the jurors had been given only two choices—life in prison or death. They should have been offered a third choice, life in prison without parole. Because of that judicial error, the court commuted his sentence from death to the omitted choice. Karl Fontenot would be permitted to live out all of his natural days—behind bars, with no hope of ever getting out. He was transferred from Death Row to a prison in a town called Hominy.

Tommy found life at Lexington infinitely preferable to life on Death Row. He could receive visits from his family in a visiting room, where hugs were permitted. He could walk the grounds, the softball field. Most of all, he was no longer under sentence of death. His voice no longer trembled the way it had at McAlester. He began to plan for a future, however distant it might be. He took a course in Rational Behavior Training, and he began to work toward a GED—a high school equivalency degree. Beyond that he envisioned taking vocational classes in heating and air-conditioning maintenance.

Some days he was grateful that he was no longer in McAlester; other days were not as bright, and he referred to what he had been through as "pure hell." Even at Lexington there were inmates who might stick a knife in his back at any time. He felt lucky to survive each day.

"It's been over five years since I've been out," he said one evening, a year after his second conviction. "To me the outside is like a dream, a remembrance. At night, when I have dreams now, I'm always locked up. Sometimes people I know are in the dreams, people from the town—but the town always has a fence around it."

Kafka in Oklahoma

"As a rule all our cases are foregone conclusions."
—Franz Kafka, *The Trial*

The summer of 2006 dawned hot and dry in Ada. A severe drought was suffocating the entire region. Straw-colored patches were beginning to appear in the broad green lawns. Pecans on the trees were turning brown before they got ripe. Creeks were evaporating, exposing the sandy beds. People complained about the heat and the drought, and waited for promised rain.

Few were thinking about two local boys, now grown men, once in the headlines, now long gone from view. Tommy Ward in Lexington and Karl Fontenot in Hominy were each serving the twenty-first year of their life sentences for a murder they still insisted they did not commit.

It had been a long time since their names had been on the lips of Ada's citizens. But that was soon to change.

Bill Peterson, the man who had prosecuted Ward and Fontenot, was still ensconced as district attorney. Gary Rogers, formerly of the Oklahoma State Bureau of Investigation, was now an investigator for Peterson's office. Both were secure in their jobs—but they had reason to be apprehensive about their images. For more than a year, one of the best-selling novelists in the world and an experienced trial lawyer, John Grisham, had been visiting Ada intermittently, researching his first nonfiction book. What he was writing was no secret: a book about two Ada men who had been convicted of the brutal murder of an attractive young woman and who had been sentenced respectively to life in prison and to death—two men who were later proven innocent. Grisham's book—certain to be a bestseller, like his novels—was likely to give the police and the prosecutors of Ada, and perhaps the whole town, a black eye all across America.

Grisham was not writing about Tommy Ward and Karl Fontenot; his book was about two other men whose trials and convictions closely paralleled theirs. Grisham's research convinced him, however, that Ward and Fontenot had nothing to do with the murder of Denice Haraway, that they were innocent men spending their lives in prison cells. He would state this conclusion in his book *The Innocent Man*, and the town most likely would be talking again about Tommy Ward and Karl Fontenot—and pondering again who really killed Denice Haraway.

The case that had caught Grisham's attention (described early in this book) was the rape and murder of a young woman named Debbie Carter on December 8, 1982—sixteen months before Denice Haraway disappeared. The police soon believed they knew who had killed her—a man named Ron Williamson. Their belief was based primarily on two facts: that he was known to suffer from mental problems and that he lived not far from Debbie Carter. There was no real evidence. And Williamson's mother, who was well respected in the town, gave him an alibi. She said he had been at home that night. The police made no official move against Williamson until after his mother died three years later, until after Tommy Ward and Karl Fontenot had been tried and convicted of killing Denice Haraway. The police then arrested Williamson and an acquaintance, Dennis Fritz, charged them with the killing, and obtained murder convictions on both. Fritz was sentenced to life in prison. Williamson was sentenced to die.

Their convictions were Kafkaesque—ludicrous but tragic—and shed further light on the cases of Tommy Ward and Karl Fontenot.

"Make your confession at the first chance you get. Until you do that, there's no possibility of getting out of their clutches, none at all."

—Franz Kafka, *The Trial*

The only real evidence against Ward and Fontenot was their taped confessions—which turned out to be filled with false information, as the police themselves proved. Ward insisted his was based on a dream. At their trials, the tapes were bolstered by other "confessions" they allegedly made in the presence of jailhouse snitches. In the Debbie Carter murder, the police had no more evidence against Williamson and Fritz than they had in the Haraway case against Ward and Fontenot. Yet they also obtained convictions—and a death sentence—in the Carter case. So how did they do it? They restaged virtually the same trial to convict two more men.

The Ward and Fontenot convictions had proven how powerful a confession, even a dubious one, could be to a jury. The prosecutors introduced a confession allegedly made by Ron Williamson—supposedly emanating from a dream he'd had! It was not on videotape. It was not on audiotape. It was not in Williamson's handwriting. OSBI agent Gary Rogers merely testified that it had been made by Williamson. He did not read it to the suspect. Williamson did not sign it. But at the trial, in one of the less salutary moments in the history of jurisprudence, this "confession" was allowed as evidence.

Since additional damaging testimony in the Ward-Fontenot case was given by prison snitches, the prosecutors apparently decided that tactic was worth trying again. A woman testified that she had heard Williamson confess while in the county jail. But this was not just any prison snitch. This was Terry Holland—the same woman who had testified in the Ward-Fontenot trial. Now she swore that while she had been in the county jail, in addition to hearing Fontenot confess, she had also heard Ron Williamson confess. She had not reported this at the time it allegedly happened, two years earlier, but no matter.

The case against Williamson and Fritz was clinched by the testimony of a so-called hair expert at the OSBI lab. He said his analysis had shown that hair found at the scene of Debbie Carter's murder *could* have come from the defendants. Not that it *did*—hair is not like fingerprints or DNA; there is no such thing as a definitive match. But the jury bought it, and convicted both men.

The suspects were tried in 1988. Dennis Fritz spent eleven years of a life sentence in prison. Ron Williamson spent most of that time on Death Row while Oklahoma appellate courts upheld the convictions. Williamson was five days from being put to death when federal judge

Frank Seay delayed the execution so he and his staff could study the case. In September 1995, he issued a lengthy opinion critical of the district attorney, the judge, and a court-appointed defense counsel. He overturned the conviction of Williamson and ordered a new trial.

Responding to the judge's actions, Bill Peterson told the Ada *Evening News*: "I'm flabbergasted, bumfuzzled, angry, confused and a lot of other things. . . . It simply doesn't make any sense."

In a footnote to his opinion, Judge Seay cited an earlier edition of this book and questioned the multiple dream confessions leading to convictions in Ada. Peterson told the press, "It is simply not true that any of these three men—Williamson, Fontenot, or Ward—were convicted based on dream confessions."

During the intervening years, DNA had come into use as a foolproof tool in the search for justice. With a new trial in the offing, semen and pubic hair found on Debbie Carter's body was sent to several different labs for testing. The results proved that neither the semen nor the hairs came from either Williamson or Fritz. Both men were innocent. In April 1999 they were freed.

Williamson and Fritz sued the authorities, asking $100 million for false imprisonment. The suit never went to trial. It was settled for an undisclosed amount, reliably reported as $6.5 million. Local property taxes were increased twice to help pay for the settlement.

In a curious sidelight, the DNA in the case matched that of a fellow named Glen Gore, who had been the last person seen with Debbie Carter the night she was murdered—and who had never been investigated by the police. Years later, Gore, already in prison on other charges, was convicted of the killing on the basis of the DNA evidence. But his conviction was also overturned, on the ground that the fact that two other men had previously been convicted of the murder should have been allowed into evidence for Gore's jury to hear.

Gore's second trial took place in June 2006. He was convicted again. Because one juror held out against the death penalty, he was sentenced to life in prison without parole—a lesser sentence than the innocent Ron Williamson had received.

The lead detective in both the Carter and Haraway cases, Dennis Smith, though long gone from the Ada police force, was a witness at the Gore trial. He testified about the bloody scene he had found in Debbie Carter's apartment. Less than three weeks after his testimony, on June 30, Smith died of a heart attack, at age 63. He was the first lawman to take to the grave the intimate truth about the Ward and Fontenot confessions.

The exoneration of Williamson and Fritz cast further doubt on the guilt of Tommy Ward and Karl Fontenot; it called into question the judgment, techniques, and veracity of certain Ada law-enforcement officials. Some citizens who had recognized the absurdity of the confessions of Ward and Fontenot still had trouble believing that those confessions had been choreographed by the police, and that the district attorney had put innocent men in prison. But the Carter case showed that they had marshaled a false case against two innocent men. Who could say that they had not done the same thing to Tommy Ward and Karl Fontenot?

Another case in Ada, with Dennis Smith investigating and Bill Peterson's office prosecuting, raises similar questions. In 1983, a man named Calvin Lee Scott was tried for rape, convicted, and sentenced to twenty-five years in prison. He proclaimed his innocence. He served twenty years before being released. After he was out of prison, DNA testing showed that he could not have been the perpetrator.

In the Denice Haraway case, only skeletal remains of her body were found, so there was no DNA material that might clear Ward and Fontenot. In the summer of 2006 they remained in prison, serving their life terms. Fontenot had no possibility of parole. Ward could come up for parole in the next few years, but Bill Peterson, still the D.A., liked to attend parole board hearings and demand that those he convicted remain in prison. For whatever reason, Bill Peterson usually got what he wanted.

One long shot existed. The attorney who had represented Ron Williamson during the DNA testing, Mark Barrett of Norman, had come to believe strongly in the innocence of Ward and Fontenot. He decided to represent them, and was seeking evidence that would clear them; with evidence of actual innocence, he could appeal to the courts or go to the governor and the parole board on their behalf. To aid in this search, he was preparing a Web site to bring further attention to the frustrating case. The site registered was www.wardandfontenot.com.

Karl Fontenot was now forty-one years old. Tommy Ward was forty-five. All they could do for themselves, from behind prison walls, was to claim again to unheeding ears that they are innocent.

"In the first years he curses his evil fate aloud; later, as he grows old, he only mutters to himself."

—Franz Kafka, *The Trial*

Robert Mayer was born and raised in New York City. As a journalist and columnist for *Newsday*, he twice won the Mike Berger Award for the year's best writing about New York City, as well as a National Headliner Award as best feature columnist in the country. Mayer has written seven novels and two works of nonfiction. He currently lives in New Mexico.